The Manual of Horsemanship

The Pony Club
Stoneleigh Park
Kenilworth
Warwickshire
CV8 2RW

Website: www.pcuk.org

The Manual of Horsemanship
is published by The Pony Club

First published 1950
Fourteenth edition 2011
Updated and reprinted 2013
Reprinted 2018, 2019, 2021

British Library Cataloguing in Publication Data.
A catalogue record for this book is available from the British Library.

ISBN 978-1-907279-13-3

Director of Publications and General Editor: Nikki Herbert BHSI
Design and Production: Paul G. Harding (www.hardingbooks.com)

Cover Photograph: Thorowgood Saddles (www.thorowgood.com)

Printed in the Czech Republic

Distribution by Kenilworth Press
An imprint of Quiller Publishing Ltd.
Wykey House, Wykey, Shrewsbury, SY4 1JA
Tel: 01939 261616
E-mail: info@quillerbooks.com
Website: www.quillerpublishing.com

The Manual of Horsemanship

The Official Manual of The Pony Club

Introduction

Riding is one of the very few sports which can be enjoyed from early childhood to old age and at many different levels. At its simplest it provides a means of travelling from one place to another. At its most developed it is one of the supreme partnerships between man and animal. No matter how simple or how developed, even greater enjoyment can be achieved by the continuous process of learning. The purpose of *The Manual of Horsemanship* is to assist in this process.

The first part of the book covers all important aspects of horsemastership: bearing in mind that the performance of a horse for his rider is inextricably linked with his well-being and comfort. The later chapters are devoted to the art of horsemanship: encouraging riders to improve their skills and in so doing produce better horses.

We hope that the *Manual* will prove useful to riders of all ages, and that it will be particularly beneficial to young people who are acquiring a horse or pony for the first time—especially those from families with no equestrian tradition or where there is no experienced older relation to advise in times of need.

In dealing with horses there is a right way and a wrong way of doing everything. Sometimes there are several right ways of doing the same thing. The Pony Club's aim is to teach a right way which is safe for the horse and safe for the rider or handler.

Few people would deny the beauty and grace of the horse. Most riders come to realise his generosity and gentleness. Those who learn to be true horsemen discover with gratitude his willingness to please and serve. A bad or ungenerous horse is invariably the result of human lack of knowledge, understanding or ability.

For all readers of this book, whether Pony Club members or other like-minded people, there is a lifetime of discovery and pleasure ahead. Every horse or pony that you ride and look after is an individual, who will teach you something new. As your confidence and knowledge increase, your standard will improve. You will discover the satisfaction of producing a fit and healthy horse. Above all, you will discover the joy of skilful riding.

Contents

Part One: The Horse

Part Two: The Rider and Riding

Part Three: Saddlery and Lorinery

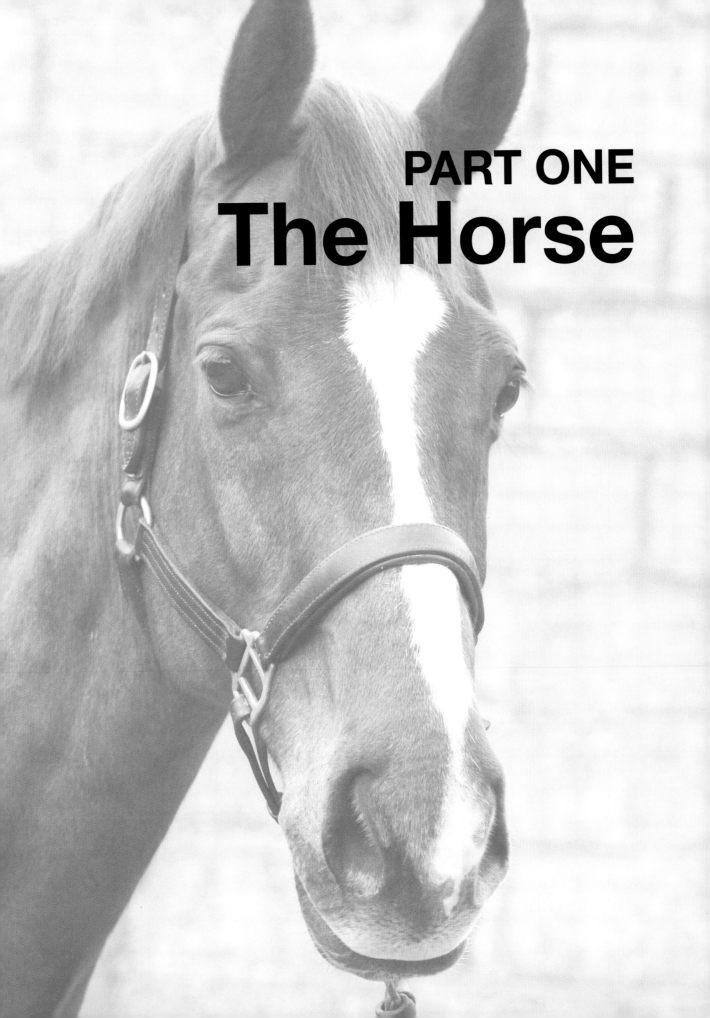

PART ONE
The Horse

1. Classification and Identification

BREEDS

To be accepted officially as belonging to a specific breed, a horse must be recorded in the stud register of that breed, or must have the necessary qualifications to be so registered. If these qualifications are not met, the animal may be referred to as 'of the type': for example, 'New Forest type'.

Some of the recognised British breeds of light horses and ponies are: Hackney, Arab, Anglo-Arab, Cleveland Bay, Irish Draught, Thoroughbred (horses); and Shetland, New Forest, Dartmoor, Exmoor, Dales, Fell, Highland, Welsh, Connemara (ponies). Stud Registers exist for all of these horse and pony breeds. (A Thoroughbred is an animal registered in the *General Stud Book).*

Terms Related to Breeds

Half-bred	One parent is a Thoroughbred.
Anglo-Arab	A cross between a pure Arabian and a Thoroughbred.
Part-bred	A cross between one pure-bred parent and one which is not pure-bred.
Warm-blood	Of European origin; heavier than a Thoroughbred, but lighter than a heavy horse. Not a pure breed, but stud registers exist, mostly in Continental Europe but also in the UK (the British Sports Horse Register and British Warm Blood Society), the Americas, Australia, New Zealand and South Africa. Their purpose is to encourage the selective breeding of competition horses, particularly for dressage, showjumping and driving.
Light Horse	A general term usually used to refer to horses bred for riding.
Heavy Horse	Large, strong horses bred for agricultural purposes to pull hay carts, ploughs, etc.
Mule	A cross between a donkey stallion and a pony mare. (A jennet or hinny is the product of a pony stallion out of a female donkey.)

TYPES

Hunters, hacks, polo ponies and cobs are types of horse, not breeds. This is because they lack fixed character. For example. the hunter is a horse used for hunting, and neither conformation, size, character nor colour bear any importance on this type.

COLOURS

The colour of a horse or pony is assessed by considering the colour of his coat and the colour of the *points.* The points are the muzzle, the tips of the ears, the mane, the tail and the extremities of the four legs.

Black	A black horse is black in colour with black points.
Brown	A brown horse is dark brown or nearly black in colour with brown points.
Bay	A bay is brown-coloured with black points. *Light, bright* and *dark* are variations of the colour.

Bay-brown	Bay-brown is a term used for a horse that appears to conform partly but not exactly to bay or brown.
Chestnut	A chestnut is a ginger or reddish colour, usually with a similar mane and tail. *Flaxen* manes and tails should be described as such. *Light*, *dark* and *liver* chestnuts are variations of chestnut.
Grey	A grey has black and white hairs occurring throughout his coat. An *iron grey* horse is one on whom the black hairs are predominant. A *dappled* grey horse has light grey circular patches on a darker background. A *flea-bitten* grey is one on whom the dark hairs occur in tufts over most of his body, giving a speckled appearance. A *light* grey is one on whom white hairs predominate. A horse is never correctly described as a *white* horse. White is not a colour but a lack of pigmentation.
Dun	A dun varies from mouse-colour (*blue* dun) to golden (*yellow* dun). He generally has black points and may show either *zebra* marks on the limbs and/or a *list* or *eel stripe*, which is a dark line along the back.
Roan	A roan has white hairs throughout his coat. Variations are *strawberry* roan (chestnut coat), *red* roan (bay coat), *blue* roan (very dark bay, brown or black coat).
Piebald	A piebald has large irregular patches of black and white: i.e. like a magpie.
Skewbald	A skewbald has large irregular patches of white and any other colour except black.
Spotted Horses	Three different types of marking are recognised: *Leopard*—spots of any colour on a light or white coloured background. *Blanket*—animals having a white rump on which are spots of any colour. *Snowflake*—white spots on a foundation of any colour. (Piebald or skewbald markings with any of the above are not acceptable to The Spotted Horse and Pony Society.)
Palomino	Palomino is a colour, not a breed. The body colour is golden, but (limited) variations of shade are allowed. The mane and tail are very light—almost white.
Odd-Coloured	A term used to describe a horse who does not conform to a standard colour.

MARKINGS

Head *(Fig. 1a, b and c)*

Any white markings on the head should be clearly defined for a description to be accurate. The following terms are traditionally used:

Star	A white mark on the forehead.
Stripe	A narrow white mark down the face.
Blaze	A broad white mark down the face which extends over the bones of the nose.
White Face	Includes the forehead, eyes, nose and part of the muzzle. (Also flecked, and with white hairs above eyes.)
Snip	A white mark between the nostrils. In some cases it extends into the nostrils.
Wall Eye	An eye which shows white or blue-white colouring in place of the normal coloration.

Legs *(Fig. 1d, e and f)*

For an accurate description, any white markings on the limbs should be defined with reference to the anatomy and the upper limit of the marking: e.g. *white pastern; white to fetlock,* or *white to half-cannon,* etc. Traditionally, a *stocking* extends as far as the knee or hock; a *sock* extends no further than the fetlock.

'*Ermine*' refers to black spots on white markings—usually on the coronet *(fig. 1d)*.

Whorls

Whorls are changes in the hair pattern at a certain point—usually on the crest of the neck, forehead and chest. These marks are used for accurate identification on a passport, registration papers or veterinary certificate. Whorls on the head and neck must be noted. For a horse with no other distinctive markings, all whorls should be included.

BRANDS

Pure-bred native ponies are often branded with the personal brand mark of the breeder, as are horses from parts of the Americas and Australia where brands are needed for identification. Pure-bred European horses are branded according to their breed and grade. Brands are often placed on the flat of the shoulder, the saddle region or the quarters.

Freeze-Branding

In Britain, for identification purposes and to help facilitate the recovery of stolen animals, some horses are freeze-branded with a serial number. Various freeze-branding agencies exist, so seek expert advice before you go ahead.

PASSPORTS AND MICROCHIPPING

All equines must have a passport with an identification chart (*see fig. 5*) and vaccination record. All horses, ponies, mules and donkeys being issued with a passport for the first time must also be microchipped.

AGE

A horse's age is usually determined by examining his front teeth (*see* page 16). Some indication of age can be given by the horse's general appearance and physiology, especially if the animal is young or very old.

Foals

Easily recognised: the body is small, the limbs excessively long with large joints. The head appears soft and ill-defined with large eyes and ears and a small, soft muzzle. The mane and tail are very short and fluffy. Movement is erratic. Greys are often born black, the coat becoming lighter over the years.

Yearlings

Very obviously young, ungainly and unfurnished, changing all the time. The limbs are still rather long in proportion to the body. The head lacks definition. The mane and tail are very untidy, short and somewhat fluffy. Movement is still erratic.

Two-year-olds

Still young-looking, but with limbs in proportion. The head is defined much as it will be as an adult. The body lacks maturity and has very limited muscle. The mane and tail have grown longer from the previous year but are still fairly short and untidy.

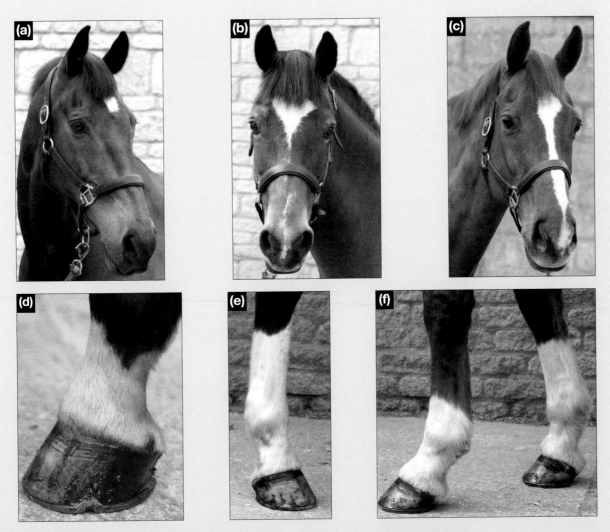

1 Some head-markings: **(a)** Star; **(b)** Broad triangular star; **(c)** Stripe and snip.
Some limb-markings: **(d)** A sock—white pastern with ermine mark; **(e)** A stocking—white to lower hock;
(f) Two socks—white to mid-cannon (left-fore), white to lower knee (right-fore).

Three-year-olds

They look very much as they will as adults, but are not so strong. They still have a young expression.

Very Old Horses

They show signs of their age in general lack of body tone. The head shows sunken hollows over the eyes, and pronounced bone structure. Often the lower lip is loose and floppy. The neck loses strength. The withers are more pronounced and the back often hollow. Along the back and the quarters, muscle is reduced, even poor. The limbs and joints may well show signs of wear (bony or soft enlargements). The horse's movement is usually slower, more careful and may well be stiff.

Ageing by the Teeth

Age up to about eight years can be more accurately assessed by reference to the front (incisor) teeth *(fig. 2)*. There are six of these teeth in each jaw. During his lifetime a horse has two complete sets: namely, the milk (or temporary) teeth, and the permanent (adult) teeth. A milk tooth is small and white, with a distinct neck and a short fang. A permanent tooth is more of a creamy, yellowish colour, much larger and has no distinct neck to it.

The changeover from milk to permanent teeth occurs at certain definite ages and the ageing of a horse is based mainly upon this fact. *(See also* Teeth *on page 121.)*

1 year	The horse has a full set of incisor milk teeth (six) on both upper and lower jaws.
2 years	The horse still has six incisor milk teeth on each jaw, but they are slightly worn.
2½ years	The central incisors (two per jaw) come out, and permanent teeth start to erupt.

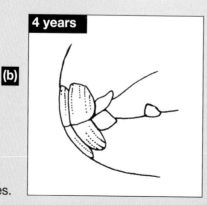

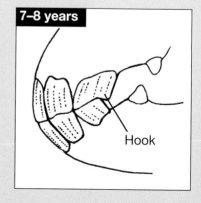

2 Ageing by teeth:
(a) Section of an incisor from the lower jaw, showing the effect of wear on the 'tables';
(b) The incisors at various ages.

3 years	Central incisors now fully grown.
3½ years	The two lateral milk teeth on each jaw come away.
4 years	The lateral permanent teeth are fully grown.
4½ years	The two corner milk teeth on each jaw come away.
4–5 years	In male horses, and very occasionally female, tushes appear behind the corners.
5 years	The corner permanent teeth are fully grown.
6 years	The horse has a *full* mouth of permanent teeth, which are said to be *in use*.
7 years	A hook appears on the corner teeth of the upper jaw which may remain for a year or so. A similar hook may show at about thirteen years of age, and this may lead to confusion.
8 years	From this age on, there is variation, and assessments—even by experts—are not reliable. The shapes and markings of the *tables* (the biting surfaces of the incisors) provide a very rough guide. *(See fig. 2a.)*
9 years	From nine onwards the horse is said to be aged.
10 years	*Galvayne's Groove* appears on the upper corner incisors.
15 years	*Galvayne's Groove* reaches approximately half way down the tooth.
20 years	*Galvayne's Groove reaches all* the way down. It then begins to disappear from the top.
25 years	Galvayne's Groove will have disappeared from the top half.

Official Birthday

The age of horses and ponies is taken from January 1st. 'Rising' means that the horse is approaching his next birthday: for example, 'rising five' (after January 1st, but before his actual birthday).

MEASUREMENT

Height

The traditional standard measurement of height for a horse is the hand, which is equivalent to approximately 10cm (4in). For example, a height given as 15.1hh indicates that the horse measures fifteen hands and one inch. Shetland ponies are measured in inches. Standard measurements are given in centimetres as well as in hands.

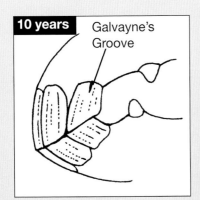

10 years — Galvayne's Groove

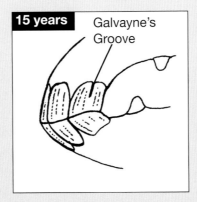

15 years — Galvayne's Groove

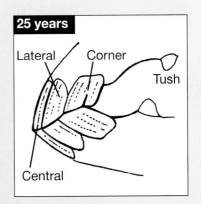

25 years — Lateral, Corner, Tush, Central

hh	cm
10.0	101.60
10.2	106.68
11.0	111.76
11.2	116.84
12.0	121.92
12.2	127.0
13.0	134.62
13.2	137.16
14.0	142.24
14.2	147.32
14.3	149.86
15.0	152.40
15.2	157.48
16.0	162.56
16.2	167.64
17.0	172.72
17.2	177.80
18.0	182.88

3 Converting hands into centimetres

Since there are slight differences in the traditional measurements and their metric equivalents (for example, 14.2hh is slightly shorter than its official metric equivalent of 148cm), it is important if you wish to compete and your pony is near to the height limit of his class, to check which scale is being used under the rules for that class.

Measurement is made from ground level to the highest point of the withers. For accuracy, the following conditions must be met:
♦ Choose a smooth and level place.
♦ Use a special measuring stick provided with spirit levels on the cross and upright bars.
♦ The horse must stand squarely on all four feet with his front feet together and his head lowered so that the poll comes in line with the withers.
♦ To obtain a Joint Measurement Scheme certificate, a horse must be measured without shoes, but for Pony Club competitions it is permissible to allow 12mm (½in) off the recorded height for the shoes, if they are normal: i.e. not racing plates.

Life measurement certificates are granted subject to two conditions: firstly, that the horse is six years of age or over, and secondly, that the measurement is taken by one of the officially appointed measurers on the panel of the Joint Measurement Scheme, with the horse standing unshod.

Height measurement has many uses. It forms part of the correct description of the horse. It provides for subdivision of horses into classes for show purposes. It is an indication of the size of a horse offered in a sale catalogue, or for an intending purchaser. It serves as an approximate indication for the size of clothing, saddlery or harness required.

Bone
This term is used to refer to the measurement taken around the foreleg immediately below the knee. A hunter of about 155cm (15.2hh) with good bone would measure 21.75cm (8½in) or more at this point. Where the measurement falls short of requirements, the horse is said to be *light of bone*, indicating that his limbs are not up to the weight that his body should carry.

TERMS APPLIED TO HORSES AND PONIES

Horse or Pony?

The difference between a horse and pony is difficult to define because as well as height, it depends on whether the animal is of a *horse* or *pony* type. Generally, horses measure over 148cm (14.2hh).

These terms apply to all horses and ponies:

Foal From birth up to first day of January following birth.

Colt A young male up to three years (at birth, colt foal).

Filly A young female up to three years (at birth, filly foal).

Yearling In the year after birth.

Two-year-old In second year after birth.

Gelding A castrated male (any age).

Entire/ stallion An uncastrated male of over three years.

Mare A female over three years of age.

HOW TO DESCRIBE A HORSE OR PONY

An Informal Description *(Fig. 4)*

'MURRAY HALL MAYTIME (Maggie May), a pure-bred Welsh section D bay mare born in 1993. 148cm (14.2hh) with a broad star and narrow stripe. Short socks on both hind legs. An excellent jumping pony. Very experienced in all Pony Club competitions. Not a novice ride.'

A Formal Description

The identification chart on Maggie May's influenza vaccination certificate is shown overleaf in *fig. 5*. Even without her freeze brand the formal description would contain enough information to identify her beyond reasonable doubt in normal circumstances.

4 'Maggie May'.

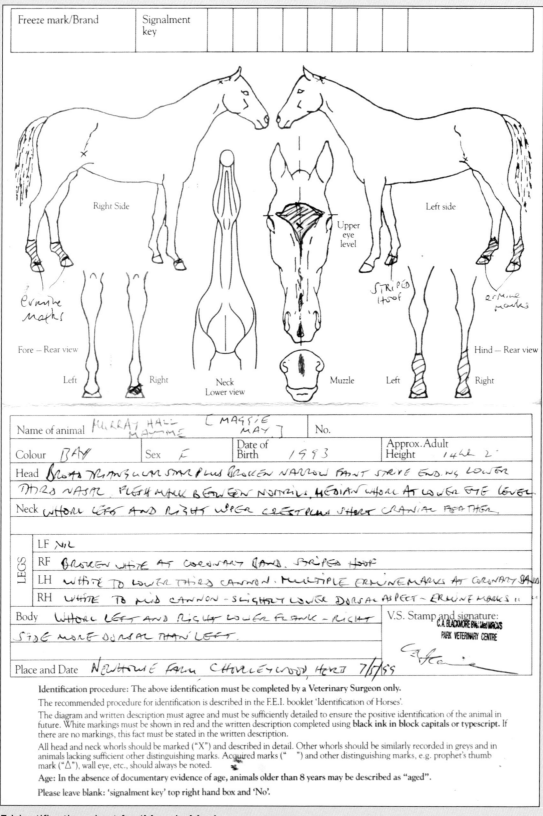

Freeze mark/Brand	Signalment key							

Right Side

Left side

Upper eye level

Ermine marks

STRIPED HOOF

ermine marks

Fore – Rear view

Hind – Rear view

Left   Right   Neck   Muzzle   Left   Right
                    Lower view

Name of animal	MURRAY HALL MADAME [MAGGIE MAY]		No.	
Colour BAY	Sex F	Date of Birth 1993		Approx. Adult Height 14hh 2

Head: BROAD TRIANGULAR STAR PLUS BROKEN NARROW FAINT STRIPE ENDING LOWER
THIRD NASAL. FLESH MARK BETWEEN NOSTRILS. MEDIAN WHORL AT LOWER EYE LEVEL.

Neck: WHORL LEFT AND RIGHT UPPER CREST PLUS SHORT CRANIAL FEATHER.

LEGS
LF: NIL
RF: BROKEN WHITE AT CORONARY BAND. STRIPED HOOF
LH: WHITE TO LOWER THIRD CANNON. MULTIPLE ERMINE MARKS AT CORONARY BAND
RH: WHITE TO MID CANNON – SLIGHTLY LOWER DORSAL ASPECT – ERMINE MARKS "

Body: WHORL LEFT AND RIGHT LOWER FLANK – RIGHT
SIDE MORE DORSAL THAN LEFT.

V.S. Stamp and signature:
C.A. BLACKMORE BVet.Med MRCVS
PARK VETERINARY CENTRE

Place and Date: NEWHOUSE FARM CHORLEYWOOD, HERTS 7/5/55

Identification procedure: The above identification must be completed by a Veterinary Surgeon only.

The recommended procedure for identification is described in the F.E.I. booklet 'Identification of Horses'.

The diagram and written description must agree and must be sufficiently detailed to ensure the positive identification of the animal in future. White markings must be shown in red and the written description completed using **black ink in block capitals or typescript**. If there are no markings, this fact must be stated in the written description.

All head and neck whorls should be marked ("X") and described in detail. Other whorls should be similarly recorded in greys and in animals lacking sufficient other distinguishing marks. Acquired marks ("   ") and other distinguishing marks, e.g. prophet's thumb mark ("Δ"), wall eye, etc., should always be noted.

Age: In the absence of documentary evidence of age, animals older than 8 years may be described as "aged".

Please leave blank: 'signalment key' top right hand box and 'No'.

5 Identification chart for 'Maggie May'.

2. Conformation

Conformation is the term used to refer to the physical characteristics of a horse. It is often known as *'The Make and Shape'*. The ideal varies slightly according to the work for which the horse is required. Information given in this chapter applies to riding horses.

GENERAL IMPRESSION

It is said that there is no perfect horse, but one with good conformation will have many favourable points and no seriously bad ones. Experience will help you to evaluate the suitability of a horse for the work that he is expected to do. Your first impression is most important. Stand well back from the horse and take your time to observe him from both sides, from the front, and from behind.

* Does he have a bold, kind and generous outlook?
* Does he look intelligent and alert?
* Are the parts of his body generally in proportion?

Take note of any enlargements or blemishes which could affect the performance or value of the horse. You will assess his action later.

POINTS TO CONSIDER

If your first impression is favourable, look carefully at the basic characteristics, as described below under the various headings. Then consider the more detailed points.

Eyes

The eyes should be large, clear and set well out at the side of the head, with width between them to give a broad range of vision and a bold, kind look. Bad-tempered, nervous or frightened horses often show the white of the eye, while those with small, deeply-set eyes (pig eyes) may well be wilful and obstinate.

Feet

The front feet and the hind feet should each be a pair and should point straight forwards *(fig. 6)*.

* A horse's front feet are rounder than his hind feet and should slope at an angle of approx 45° to 50° depending on the breed of horse. Warm-bloods tend to have feet which are more upright than those of thoroughbreds. The angle of slope of the hind feet is slightly wider. The angle of slope of each pair of feet should be the same. Regard any difference with suspicion.
* The heels should be wide; the frog should be large and full, to absorb concussion; the sole should be slightly concave.
* The wall of the foot should be smooth and free from rings and grooves—though grass rings, which indicate changes

6 A useful type of horse.

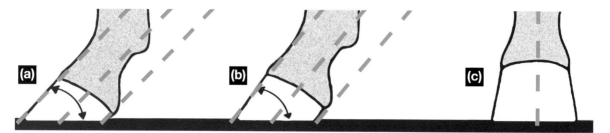

7 Normal feet: **(a)** Forefoot (45–50°) and **(b)** Hind foot (50–55°) from the side. **(c)** Front view.

in the diet, are acceptable. *(See also* LAMINITIS, *pages 162 and 167).*

♦ Avoid narrow, donkey-like feet which, if contracted, do not provide enough bearing-surface for the horse, and seldom stand up to hard work.

♦ Flat feet (feet with flat soles) are generally weak. They are often larger than normal, very sloping and with low heels which do not provide any protection to the foot. Such feet are prone to corns and bruising.

♦ The feet should not turn outwards as this is likely to cause brushing. Toes turning inwards (pin or pigeon-toed) though unsightly, are serious only if excessive. Outwards or inwards could result in uneven wear on the joints of the legs.

The Forehand

The Head

♦ The head should be light, well set on, and in proportion to the size of the horse. It should not be long and heavy, as this tends to put the horse on his forehand.

♦ It should have a general appearance of leanness, with width between the eyes and the branches of the jaw—the latter to allow ample room for the tongue and the top of the windpipe.

♦ The angle at which the head meets the neck is most important. If it is too acute it may compress the larynx. If the angle is not acute enough, the horse will have difficulty flexing at the poll.

♦ The line of the lower jaw (jowl) should be clearly defined at the throat, where the head and neck meet.

♦ In profile, the line of the face should

8 Three types of head: **(a)** Straight profile; **(b)** Roman nose; **(c)** Dish face.

be straight. A convex (*Roman*) nose is sometimes found in horses who have heavy-horse blood. Roman-nosed horses are often generous and genuine, but a horse with a bump between the eyes is often wilful and stubborn. A concave profile (*dish face*) indicates Arabian blood.

* The ears should be of medium size, finely pointed, alert and generally carried forward (pricked). *Lop* ears, which flop (either forward or out to each side) are not so correct but are very often signs of a kind, generous and easy-going horse. Ears frequently laid back indicate bad temper.

The Neck

The neck should be muscular, long enough to be in proportion, and slightly arched from poll to withers. There should be no clear demarcation between neck and shoulders. Examples of poorly-shaped necks include:

Bull neck	Short and thick—it is difficult to obtain any flexion with this type.
Ewe neck	Concave topline—with a weak crest and a bulky underside. Such horses often poke the nose or star gaze, making the rider's control more difficult. A ewe neck can sometimes be improved by building up the muscles of the neck through correct training (*see* CONTACT, *page 192)* and correct feeding.
Cock-throttled	Neck shaped like a cock's, which causes the head to be carried very high.
Low-set	This causes the horse to be on his forehand.

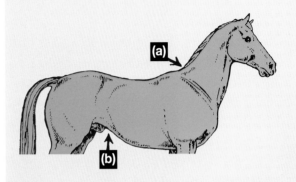

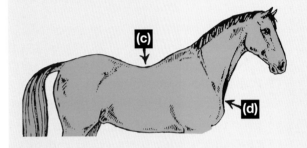

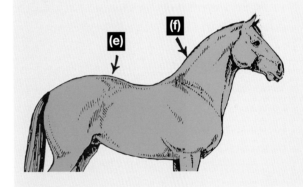

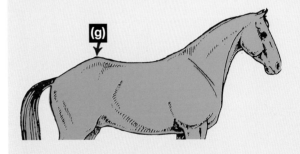

9 Conformation faults: **(a)** Ewe neck; **(b)** Herring gut; **(c)** Hollow back; **(d)** Straight shoulder; **(e)** Roach back; **(f)** Bull neck; **(g)** Goose rump.

The Shoulders

The shoulders should be deep and should slope well back from the point of shoulder up to the withers in order to give a good reach of stride. The slope of the shoulder should be roughly the same as the angle of the pastern.

A very straight shoulder gives a short stride and jarring action and, when jumping, difficulty in recovering in an emergency.

The Withers

The withers should be well-defined and of reasonable height. Withers which are too high may cause problems when fitting a saddle and are often associated with a narrow chest. Low, thick withers (*loaded shoulders*) are undesirable because they limit the freedom of the shoulders and cause difficulties in keeping a saddle in place.

The Forelegs

Seen from the front the forelegs should appear to drop straight from the forearm to the foot *(fig. 10a)* with plenty of bone immediately below the knee—that is, the circumference around the bone should be generous *(see page 18)*. The bone should be clean and flat and the tendons should be well-defined.

- *The forearm* should be well-muscled and long.
- *The elbows* should be clear of the body, so that there is no interference with the correct action of the horse, which might cause strain and increase the chances of the horse injuring himself by brushing, speedicutting etc. *Out at the elbow* is also a fault.
- *The knees* should be broad, flat and deep from front to back, allowing enough room for the muscles which are attached to them, and for the tendons which run over them.

Indentations at the front of the knee (*open knees*), are a sign of weakness, as are *calf knees* (*back at the knee*), presenting a concave, rather than a convex profile when viewed from the side. These are often tied in below the knee: the measurement around the cannon bone, directly below the knee, being smaller than that lower down.

Any *lateral deviation* of the knee,

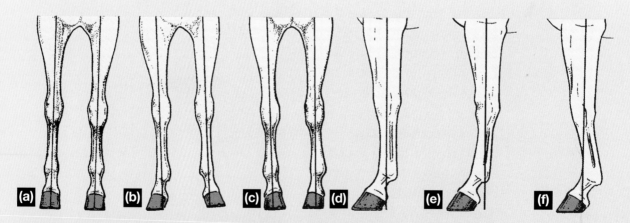

10 Forelegs. *From front:* **(a)** Correct; **(b)** Turned-out; **(c)** Turned-in.
From side: **(d)** Correct; **(e)** Back at the knee (and open knee); **(f)** Over at the knee.

visible from the front, is a serious fault, as the displacement causes strain.

    Over at the knee or *standing over* is the opposite to *back at the knee*. A mild degree of this is not a fault, but if exaggerated it may cause stumbling.

- *The cannon bones* should have plenty of bone, and should be short and straight. The tendons and ligaments should stand out in clear, hard lines and should show no signs of bowing.
- *The fetlocks* should look *clean* and *flat* rather than having a rounded appearance.
- *The pasterns* should be of medium length, and should slope. Longer pasterns give a springy, comfortable action, but are prone to strain. Upright pasterns absorb less concussion so that more jar is transmitted to the joints higher up the leg, and to the rider.

The Body

The ribcage protects the major organs of the body and should allow ample room for the heart, lungs, bowels, kidneys, etc. The ribs should extend well back so that the loins are comparatively short.

- When viewed from the side the horse should be *deep through the girth*: that is, with a generous depth of the body from immediately behind the withers to the lower line (or *girth line*), just behind the elbows. The lower line of the body, from the end of the sternum, should slope slightly upwards towards the stifle.
- The horse should have *well-sprung* ribs which arch a generous distance away from the backbone on either side, before sloping down and inwards. This allows room for maximum expansion of the lungs.

- The chest should be substantial enough to allow room for the heart.
- If his chest is *too wide* the horse will have a short, rolling, gait and be an uncomfortable ride.
- In a *narrow-chested, flat-sided* horse, if the forelegs are too close together, the horse will be liable to *brush (see page 159)*.
- *Herring-gutted.* The lower line of the body runs up like a greyhound's *(fig. 9)*. Traditionally this has been thought to indicate a possible lack of stamina.

The Back

A horse required for fast work should have some length of back, but the loins should be short, muscular, broad and deep, to provide a good foundation for muscles used in galloping and jumping. Mares are sometimes longer in the back than stallions or geldings.

- A horse with a *long, narrow, weak back* will not carry weight efficiently. On the other hand, an over-short back can make for an uncomfortable ride, especially if the horse also has a straight shoulder or short pasterns
- A *hollow back*—i.e. a back which is unduly dipped—may be a sign of considerable age, damage to the vertebrae *(fig. 9c)* or an unsuitable saddle.
- A *roach back* is one which shows a curve upwards *(fig. 9e)*.
- *Cold-backed horses* (those who dip their backs when first mounted) should be viewed with suspicion. There might be a reason, such as spinal or muscular damage, which could be a source of trouble; or it might indicate the possibility of a behavioural problem, caused by an ill-fitting saddle.

The Hind Quarters

The hind quarters should be strong and muscular, as they provide most of the power to move the horse. Wide, well-muscled, flat quarters are found in fast horses. Rounded quarters are typical of cobs and ponies.

When viewed from the side, the quarters must have depth and, in particular, a generous distance from the point of hip to the point of buttock. Quarters that slope sharply from croup to dock are known as goose-rumped *(fig. 9g)*. Horses with goose rumps may show good jumping ability.

When seen from behind, as the eye travels downwards, the quarters should look rounded at the hip, showing a gradual swell of muscle on either side, and they should be well closed-up under the tail. The points of the hips should be symmetrical, level, and not too prominent. The old adage of 'a head like a duchess and a bottom like a cook' is well worth remembering!

The Hind Legs *(Fig. 11)*

The hind legs propel the body forward and upward. They must therefore be strong and well-made. When they are viewed from the side there should be plenty of length from stifle to hock *(well let-down)*, and the muscle (second thigh or gaskin) must be well-developed. The point of the hock should be directly below the point of the buttock, with the line down the back of the cannon bone dropping straight towards the ground.

When viewed from behind, the limbs should be upright and parallel.

- *The hocks* are very important joints, as they are the hardest worked. They should be large, with a prominent point, wider when viewed from the side than the front, and deep—with a clean, well-defined look.
- *The cannon bone*, below the hock, should be short and strong.
- *Bent or sickle hocks* may be liable to strains.
- *Cow hocks* (toes turned out, hocks turned in) cause the limbs to move outward instead of forward in a straight line. This can also result in strain.
- *Bowed hocks* (toes turned in, hocks turned out) cause the horse to twist the hock outward as the foot touches the ground, and can cause strain.

ACTION

It is important for you to see the horse run up in hand, so that you can watch his movement in walk and trot—from behind, in front, and from the side.

From Behind and in Front

In walk and trot the horse should move freely and straight, with the hind feet following the line of the forefeet. There should be no indication that the horse might strike his own legs by moving incorrectly. (See SELF-INFLICTED WOUNDS, page 159.)

From the Side

You will see how the horse uses himself. He should walk out relaxed and free; the hind feet should overstride the imprint of the forefeet (*over-tracking*). A good length of stride at walk often indicates the ability to gallop. In trot the following faults in movements are sometimes seen:

- *Dishing* is faulty action either in one or

both front legs, which are thrown in a circular movement outwards as the legs come forward. Young horses who are weak and unbalanced may dish slightly. This should improve as the muscles develop with work and maturity, and can be helped by good shoeing.

• *Plaiting* is also faulty action. As the horse puts his feet to the ground he swings them inwards, so that his steps are almost on a single line. This is also sometimes remedied as the muscles develop, and can be helped by correct shoeing. *(See The Newly-Shod Foot, page 114.)*

VETERINARY CERTIFICATE

You are strongly advised to obtain a certificate from an independent veterinary surgeon when buying a horse. *(See Routine Visits: Assessment of a Horse Before Purchase, page 143.)*

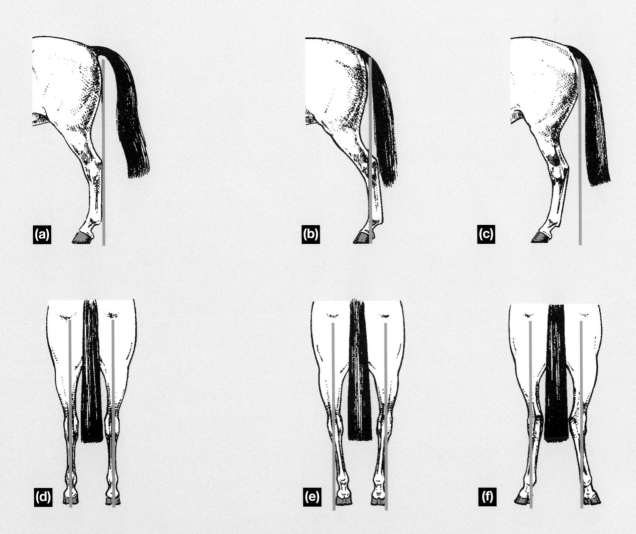

11 Hind legs. *From side:* **(a)** Correct; **(b)** Out behind (often hocks too straight);
(c) Too far forward (often hocks too bent). *From rear:* **(d)** Correct; **(e)** Bowed hocks; **(f)** Cow hocks

3. The Internal Systems of the Horse

This chapter is for readers who wish to make a more scientific study of the horse. All the systems are interrelated, but their functions are easier to understand if they are studied separately. Theoretical knowledge will never be a substitute for practical experience in the day-to-day care of horses and ponies, but it will help to explain the reasons for the practical ideas contained in the previous chapters.

MUSCULOSKELETAL SYSTEM
(The System of Movement and Support)

The skeleton is the framework of a horse's body. It is made up of bone and cartilage. It provides support and protection for the vital organs contained within it. Movement and locomotion are created and controlled by means of joints, ligaments and muscles which hold the parts of the skeleton together.

The Skeleton
There are two distinct parts:
• The axial skeleton *(see fig. 12)*.
• The appendicular skeleton *(see fig. 13)*.

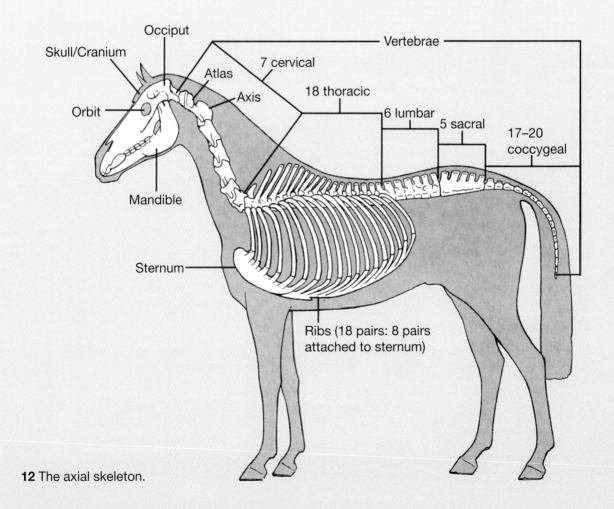

12 The axial skeleton.

The axial skeleton gives the body its shape and protects vital parts. It consists of:
* The skull, which protects the brain.
* The backbone, which runs from the skull to the tail and which carries and protects the spinal cord.
* The ribcage (sternum and ribs), which protect the heart, lungs and other important parts of the circulatory and digestive systems.

It is supported in a sling of muscles and ligaments between the shoulders, and at the hind quarters by the pelvic girdle, which is attached to the spine. The forelegs support the larger portion of the horse's weight, so the structure from the shoulder blade down is designed to alleviate as much concussion as possible. The hind quarters are the horse's engine and are constructed to produce quick and controlled power.

The appendicular skeleton supports the body, and consists of:
* The shoulders and forelegs.
* The pelvic girdle and hind legs.

Unlike the human skeleton there is no bony joint connecting the axial and appendicular skeletons. They are attached by muscle and ligaments. (See *Stablemates* book 2, *Body Basics* for more details.)

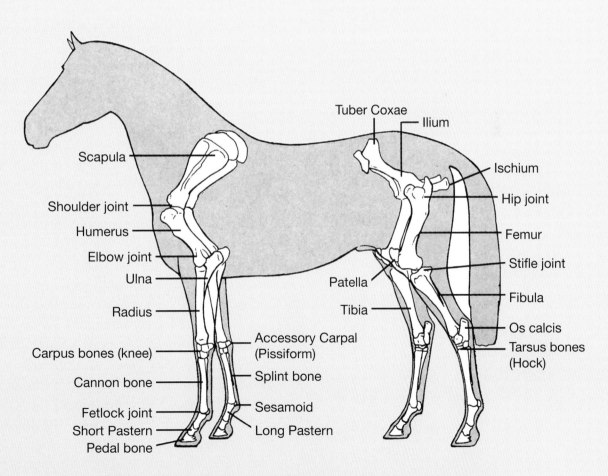

13 The appendicular skeleton. (*See* fig. 78 for a detailed illustration of the lower leg and foot.)

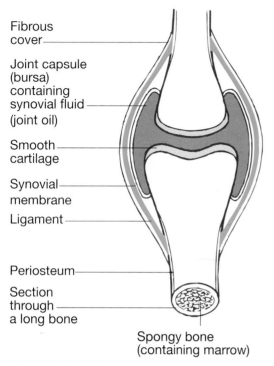

Fibrous cover

Joint capsule (bursa) containing synovial fluid (joint oil)

Smooth cartilage

Synovial membrane

Ligament

Periosteum

Section through a long bone

Spongy bone (containing marrow)

14 A simple joint.

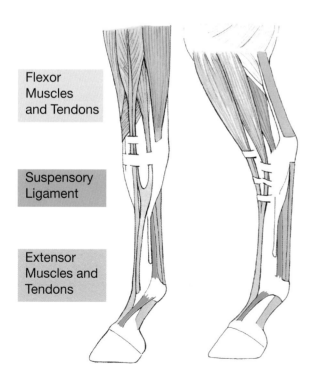

Flexor Muscles and Tendons

Suspensory Ligament

Extensor Muscles and Tendons

15 Muscles and tendons of the front and hind legs.

Bones

Bones consist mainly of collagen, calcium and phosphorus. Collagen is fibrous tissue made up of protein. Calcium and phosphorus are minerals. Bones are covered with a thin but tough membrane—the periosteum—to which tendons and ligaments are attached.

As well as providing support and protection, bones act as a store for minerals, and the marrow contained within larger bones produces red blood cells.

Joints

Where two or more bones meet, there is a joint *(fig. 14)*. Joints enable the skeleton to move, although in some cases—notably in the cranium (the front of the skull) and the sacrum (part of the spine)—there is little or no movement between the bones.

The ends of bones are covered with cartilage: a smooth but tough substance which prevents friction in the joint. Movement in joints such as knees, hocks and fetlocks is eased by joint oil (synovial fluid) contained in sacs (bursae) which encase the joints. The bursae are lined with synovial membranes which produce and secrete synovial fluid. *(See also* BURSAL ENLARGEMENTS, *page 172.)*

Ligaments

Ligaments are rigid bands of fibrous tissue. They attach bones to bones, and they support and regulate the movement of joints. In the lower limbs there are many ligaments. The one most clearly seen is the suspensory ligament which lies directly behind the cannon bone; it helps to support the fetlock joint and, to a lesser extent, the tendons. The check ligament helps to support the knee, and it regulates the movement, acting as a safeguard against overextension.

Muscles

Muscles are made up of thousands of fibres which flex and extend to provide movement. They are arranged in overlapping layers of bands and are controlled by nerves. *(See* THE NERVOUS SYSTEM, *page 33.)* The major superficial muscles are shown in *fig. 16.* Each muscle originates from a stable part of the skeleton to which it is attached, the other end being attached, sometimes by means of a tendon, to the part of the body or leg which it is responsible for moving. Most muscles work in pairs or groups. To enable the horse to move, one muscle must shorten (contract) while its opposing muscle lengthens (relaxes) and vice versa. When muscles work in this way they are known as *antagonistic pairs.*

When the horse is resting, the muscles maintain the correct position of the skeletal frame and keep the horse in balance. The antagonistic pairs act simultaneously to keep the joints still by preventing flexion or extension.

Tendons

Tendons are cords which extend from the muscles and attach them to the bones. They consist of collagen, a fibrous tissue. They have a relatively poor blood supply,

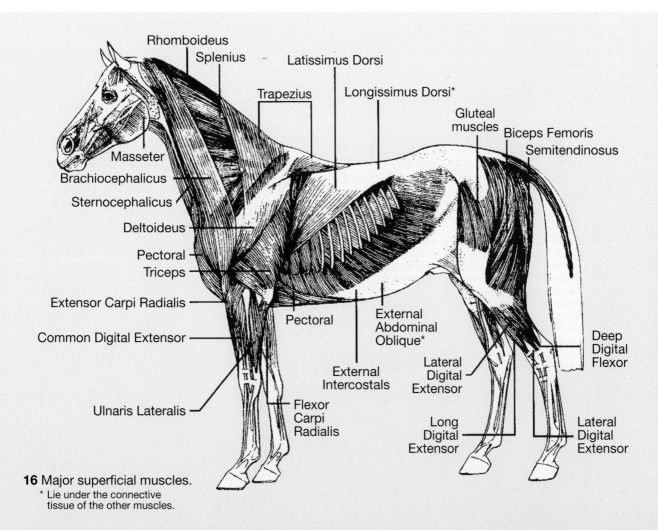

16 Major superficial muscles.
* Lie under the connective tissue of the other muscles.

Rhomboideus
Splenius
Latissimus Dorsi
Trapezius
Longissimus Dorsi*
Gluteal muscles
Biceps Femoris
Semitendinosus
Masseter
Brachiocephalicus
Sternocephalicus
Deltoideus
Pectoral
Triceps
Extensor Carpi Radialis
Common Digital Extensor
Ulnaris Lateralis
Pectoral
External Abdominal Oblique*
External Intercostals
Flexor Carpi Radialis
Lateral Digital Extensor
Long Digital Extensor
Deep Digital Flexor
Lateral Digital Extensor

so if damaged they heal slowly and with difficulty. Their structure is such that they can stretch up to 4% of their actual length, but muscles are more elastic than this, so when strains occur it is usually the tendon or the supportive ligaments which are damaged rather than the muscle to which the tendon is attached.

The tendons most clearly seen are those which lie behind the cannon bone and the suspensory ligament on the foreleg. These important tendons are attached to the muscles of the forearm. The muscles and tendons at the front of the leg are responsible for extending the leg, while those at the back flex the leg: hence flexor and extensor tendons *(fig. 15)*.

THE SKIN

The skin consists of an outer layer, the *epidermis*, and an inner layer, the dermis *(fig. 17)*. It is tough and elastic, and varies in thickness in different areas of the body according to the need for protection. It should feel supple and should move freely over the structures below the surface.

The outer layer of skin is constantly dying and being replaced by new cells. The dead cells are shed in the form of scurf, and it is this process which requires the stabled horse to be groomed regularly.

Principal Functions

1 To protect the tissues beneath from the weather, infection and minor injuries or damage caused by friction (as in the case of badly fitted rugs or saddlery).
2 To inform the brain of outside conditions. The skin is a sensory organ *(see* THE NERVOUS SYSTEM, *page 33)*. The many nerve endings in the skin enable the horse to feel pain, touch, pressure, heat and cold.
3 To stabilise body heat by warming and cooling.
4 To absorb ultraviolet rays from sunlight. By synthesis the body is able to make Vitamin D from the sun's rays, via the skin and from thence the blood. Stable-kept horses and many horses in the winter may require a Vitamin D supplement to compensate for the lack of sunlight. *(See also* VITAMINS, *page 87.)*
5 To act as camouflage. The colour of the horse's/pony's coat may blend into the background in the wild.

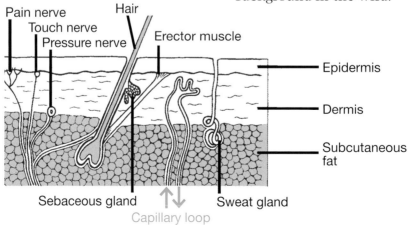

17 A cross-section of the skin.

Warmth

The coat is naturally short in summer and long and thick in winter to keep the horse warm. Oil from the sebaceous glands at the base of the hairs waterproofs the coat and keeps the skin supple. In cold conditions, minute erector muscles raise the hair to trap the air close to the body, thus creating a warming effect. This is seen as a staring coat.

In cold conditions the tiny capillaries which bring blood to the surface of the skin contract so that heat from the blood does not escape through the skin, but is retained in the body.

The layer of fat which lies under the skin (subcutaneous fat) also helps to keep the horse warm by acting as insulation.

Cooling Methods

The process of sweat evaporating on the skin helps to cool the horse. Heat is also expelled through the thin walls of the capillaries which are close to the surface of the skin.

THE NERVOUS SYSTEM

The nervous system is highly complex and controls all the actions of the horse and the functions of his body. The system is interconnected like a telephone network—with the brain acting as the central exchange.

The combination of the brain and the spinal cord which runs through the centre and length of the spine, is known as the *central nervous system*. Branches of nerve fibres run from this to all parts of the body,

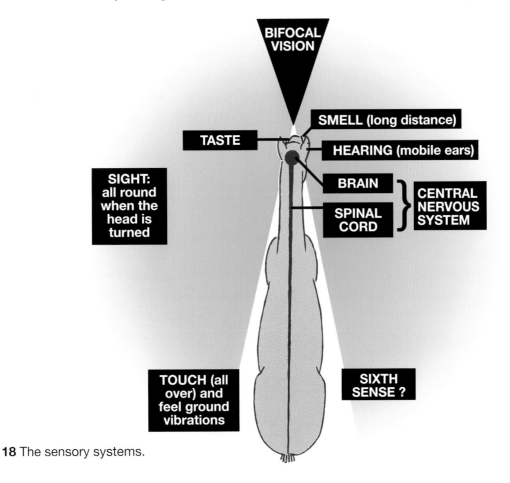

BIFOCAL VISION

SMELL (long distance)

TASTE

HEARING (mobile ears)

SIGHT: all round when the head is turned

BRAIN

SPINAL CORD

CENTRAL NERVOUS SYSTEM

TOUCH (all over) and feel ground vibrations

SIXTH SENSE ?

18 The sensory systems.

terminating in *sensory nerve cells* which record sensation, or *motor nerve cells* which regulate movement.

The sensory nerves pass information to the brain which stores and/or assesses it in relation to instinct and experience. The necessary command is then passed back, by way of the motor nerves, to the muscles for appropriate action. For example, if a horse loose in his field is confronted by rain, the sensory nerves register discomfort, the brain decides that the hind quarters should be turned to the wind, and the motor nerves tell the appropriate muscles to act. This is voluntary action: i.e. controlled by the animal.

Reflex action is an immediate action (e.g. coughing or flicking away a fly), when the message passes directly via a sensory nerve—to spinal cord—to motor nerve—to muscle without going through the brain.

Automatic action is beyond the will of the animal to control: for example, the heart beats constantly night and day and the pupils of the eyes dilate and contract in response to the light.

The Sensory Systems *(Fig. 18)*

The five senses are *seeing*, *hearing*, *smelling*, *tasting* and *feeling*.

A horse's eyes, as they are set on the side of his head, give him a wide angle of vision which enables him to see behind as well as in front. Horses with big bold eyes set at the sides of a broad forehead do this most effectively, but all horses prefer to turn their heads and focus both eyes on any object which they need to assess accurately (bifocal vision).

The horse has a well-developed sense of hearing. By turning his ears, he can pinpoint the direction from which the sound is coming.

His sense of smell is also well-developed. He selects his food by smelling it, but will taste and identify its texture before swallowing it. His sense of feel is highly developed. Internally it indicates his bodily needs, such as a sensation of thirst when water is required. Externally he is sensitive to cold, heat, touch, pressure and pain. He can also feel what his body is doing and how his limbs are working. He can feel vibrations from the ground, and has almost a sixth sense, being ultra-sensitive to the conditions around him—such as approaching weather, radio activity—and to the mood of his rider! However, Nature's defence is to allow sensitive areas to become numb through abuse, so his sides can become dulled with constant kicking from the rider's heels, and the bars of the mouth can become insensitive due to hard hands and the resulting succession of severe bits.

THE ENDOCRINE SYSTEM

The nervous system supplies the horse with information and the means to react, but the endocrine system also influences his behaviour through the release of hormones. These are secreted into the blood and lymph systems from the ductless glands which are known as endocrine glands. (The word *hormone* comes from the Greek *hormon* which means '*to arouse activity*' or '*to stir up*'.)

Hormones influence growth, ageing, metabolism (the chemical activity in the body), natural immunity and the activity of involuntary muscles such as the heart. They also play a vital part in the reproductive systems of both mares and stallions.

The position of the endocrine glands, and what is generally accepted to be their main functions, are shown in *fig. 19*. The horse has no voluntary control over the release of hormones into his systems.

THE CIRCULATORY SYSTEM

All the living cells which make up the horse's body need oxygen, water and nutrients. These are supplied in the blood and are distributed via the circulatory system. In addition, the functions of the circulatory system are:

- To maintain a constant body temperature, distributing heat evenly around the body.
- To carry hormones from the endocrine glands around the body.
- To clear waste products from the body by taking carbon dioxide to the lungs, urea to the kidneys, and—to a lesser extent—water to the lungs, which is expelled when the horse breathes out.
- To circulate and distribute white blood cells, which fight disease and infection, to wherever they are needed in the body.
- To promote healing and to restrict the loss of blood from injured parts by clotting. The blood travels through veins and arteries (blood vessels) and is circulated by the pumping action of the heart.

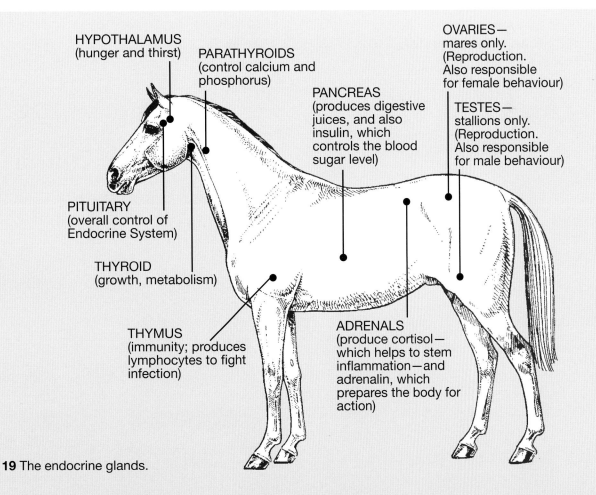

19 The endocrine glands.

The Heart

The heart is situated in the chest *(fig. 21)*. It is made up of cardiac muscles which work constantly and are not under voluntary control of the horse. It has its own individual blood supply. The contractions of the heart muscles pump the blood around the circulatory system. The pumping action (heartbeat) can be heard if you listen behind the left elbow.

When the horse is resting, the heartbeat should be between 35 and 45 beats per minute. During fast or strenuous work it may increase to 200 beats per minute.

Circulation

Arteries carry blood away from the heart and have thicker walls than veins to withstand the pressure as the blood is pumped through. If an artery is cut, blood will gush out in the rhythm of the heartbeat (pulse).

Veins carry blood back to the heart. If a vein is cut, blood escapes in a regular flow. Generally, arteries carry oxygenated blood, and veins carry deoxygenated blood; but in the pulmonary system, this rule is not followed.

Blood is made up plasma, cells and platelets *(fig. 20)*.

The circulation is divided into two parts *(fig. 23)*: the *pulmonary system* which circulates blood between the heart and lungs and the *systemic system* which circulates blood to the rest of the body.

The Pulmonary System

- Deoxygenated blood—blood which does not contain oxygen—enters the right atrium of the heart through the vena cava, the main vein of the body.
- It then passes through a one-way valve—the tricuspid valve—into the right ventricle.
- From the right ventricle, blood is pumped out of the heart through the pulmonary artery to the lungs, where carbon dioxide is expelled and oxygen is picked up. This

```
                    BLOOD
                      |
        ┌─────────────┼─────────────┐
     PLASMA       PLATELETS        CELLS
                  Help to clot
                  blood
        |                            |
   ┌────┴────┐              ┌────────┴────────┐
 SERUM    FIBRIN-         WHITE            RED
Supplies   OGEN           BLOOD           BLOOD
nutrients Helps to clot   CELLS           CELLS
and removes  blood      (Leucocytes)   (Erythrocytes)
 waste                    —some          originate in
                        components       bone marrow
                        originate in     and contain
                         lymphatic       haemoglobin
                          system
```

20 The composition of the blood.

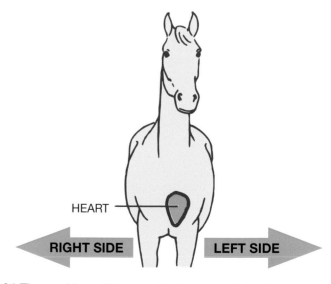

21 The position of the heart in the horse's body.

HEART

RIGHT SIDE   LEFT SIDE

process is known as the gaseous exchange. *(See THE RESPIRATORY SYSTEM, page 40.)*

- The oxygenated blood then leaves the lungs via the pulmonary vein, which carries it into the left atrium of the heart.
- In the heart, the blood passes through another one-way valve—the bicuspid valve—into the left ventricle. From here the oxygenated blood is pumped around the body via the systemic system.

The Systemic System

- From the left ventricle, the oxygenated blood is pumped out of the heart via the aorta—the main artery of the body.
- From the aorta, arteries branch out and then continue to branch further into smaller arteries (arterioles) eventually ending in a network of tiny capillaries which reach every living cell in the body *(fig. 23)*.

- Nutrients and water are collected (absorbed into the blood) through the walls of the intestines.
- Through the capillaries, water, nutrients and oxygen are supplied to the cells. Waste products are absorbed into the bloodstream from the cells and are carried away for disposal.
- Blood passes through the liver. The liver is large, complicated and important. It has two main functions: the first is to filter and purify blood from the intestines before it is circulated around the body. Waste is extracted and disposed of via the kidneys. *(See THE URINARY SYSTEM, page 44.)* The second main function is to act as a store, retaining extra nutrients which would otherwise be expelled. It is able to release these when they are required.

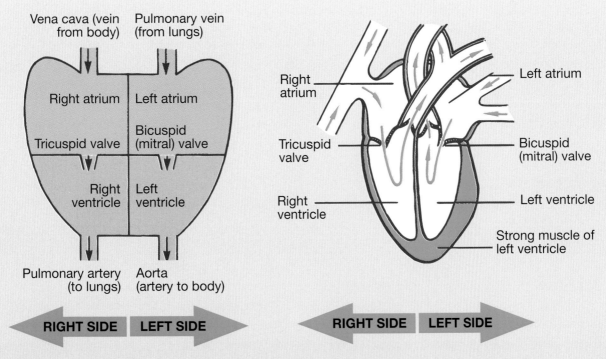

22 (a) A simplified diagram of the horse's heart; **(b)** with more detail.

- Deoxygenated blood travels back to the heart through a network of venules (small veins) then larger veins and ultimately the main vein—vena cava—through which it returns to the heart. The whole process then begins again...

THE LYMPHATIC SYSTEM

This system acts as an auxiliary to the circulatory system (fig. 23).

Lymph is an almost colourless, watery fluid containing chiefly white blood cells, serum and fats. It comes from the blood and has to be returned to it.

Lymphatics are thin-walled vessels which carry lymph, following almost the same routes as the blood vessels. However, whereas arteries eventually become veins through which blood is returned to the heart, the lymphatic system comes to a dead end, when branches of its vessels—having become increasingly small—end in tiny capillaries. Lymph, carrying vital substances, is transmitted to the cells through the capillaries and the walls of the lymphatics. Waste is removed in the same way.

Unlike the circulatory system, through which blood is pumped by the heart, lymph is pushed through the lymphatic system only through pressure, caused by tendons and muscles when the horse moves. This is why the lower limbs and joints of a stabled horse are sometimes slightly swollen in the morning before exercise (a condition known as 'filled legs'). Unlike swelling caused by an injury, the swelling will *pit* when pressure is applied with the fingers.

One-way valves, set at intervals along the system, ensure that the lymph drains away towards the heart. Lymph nodes (*glands*) filter and monitor the content of the lymph.

Main Functions

- *To prevent an accumulation of fluid,* especially in the lower parts of the legs where the pressure of fluids in the blood vessels is greatest because of gravity. Surplus fluid is absorbed from the blood through the capillaries into the lymphatics. This happens by osmosis—the drawing of a weak liquid into a stronger (denser) one. The fluid is carried away and deposited back into the bloodstream (the vena cava) near to the heart.

- *To help to fight infection,* and to repair injuries. The lymph nodes (glands) react to infection by producing lymphocytes and antibodies which are carried via the circulatory and lymphatic systems to the site of infection, and by filtering off toxic substances and bacteria. The lymphocytes and antibodies fight the infection. Damaged cells are dispersed through the lymphatic system. When the lymph nodes are fighting infection they become enlarged and can be felt and sometimes seen. For example, if the horse has influenza, the nodes at the junction of the neck and jaws can be seen to be swollen.

- *To transport, and to supply the cells with, nutrients*—the fat content being particularly important because the tiny capillaries of the circulatory system are too small to allow fat to be transported effectively by blood.

- *To remove waste*—particularly dead or damaged tissue.

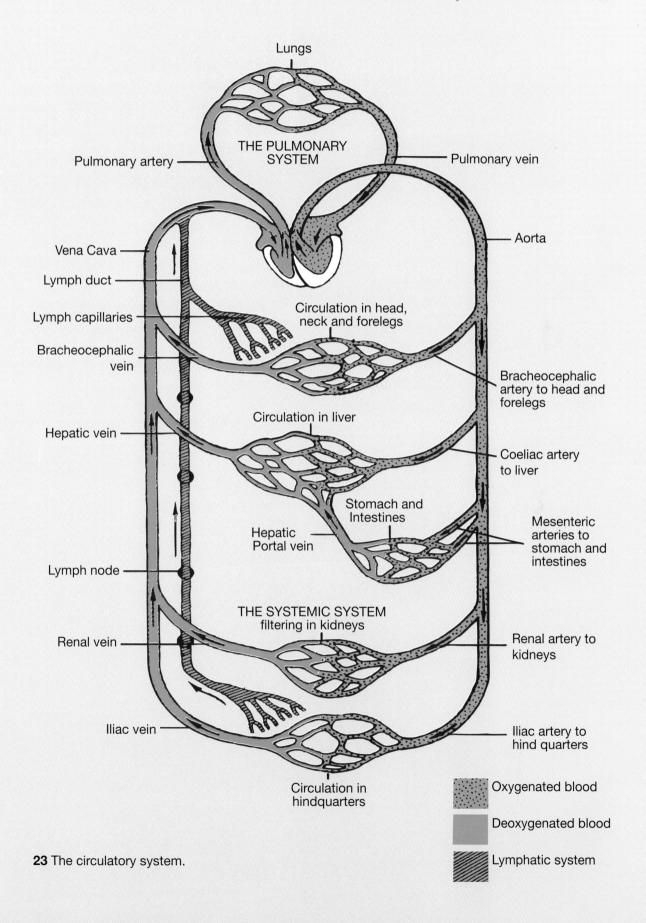

23 The circulatory system.

THE RESPIRATORY SYSTEM

The principal function of the respiratory system is to carry oxygen breathed in by the horse to the blood. A horse starved of oxygen will be dead within minutes.

Main Tasks

- To provide the body with oxygen via the blood.
- To remove carbon dioxide from the blood.
- To help to control the body's temperature. The horse breathes in cold air and breathes out warmer air.
- To expel excess water as the horse breathes out.
- To enable the horse to smell.
- To provide a means of communication (snorting, squealing or neighing).

In the Head and Neck

Air is drawn in to the respiratory system as the horse breathes in through his nostrils; he cannot breathe through his mouth. The air goes up through the nasal cavities. On the way, it is warmed and filtered (dust is trapped) by the microscopic hairs (cilia) and the mucous membrane which line the nasal cavities. This process is aided by the tiny turbinate bones which are also covered with mucous membrane and are found in the nasal cavities.

The air passes through the pharynx, the larynx (*voice box*), and down through the trachea (*windpipe*). The trachea is lined with cilia and a mucus membrane. Dust particles are trapped in the mucus and expelled, as phlegm, back through the nostrils, particularly when the horse coughs.

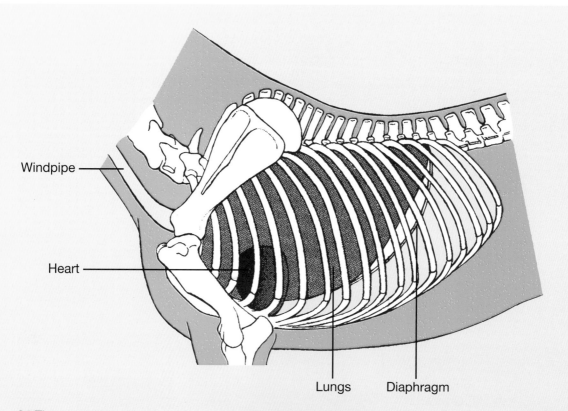

Windpipe

Heart

Lungs   Diaphragm

24 The protective role of the ribcage in the respiratory system.

At the Chest

The trachea divides into two tubes called bronchi, one going to each lung.

The Lungs

The lungs are two large elastic organs. They are covered with a smooth and slippery membrane (*the pleura*) which prevents friction and damage while they expand and contract as the horse breathes.

Within the lungs the bronchi divide and become bronchioles. The bronchioles continue to subdivide until they are very small, ending ultimately in millions of single air sacs (*alveoli*). When the oxygen breathed in by the horse reaches the alveoli, it passes through the very thin walls (*semi-permeable membranes*) of the alveoli into the blood, to be distributed around the body. From the blood, waste products, such as carbon dioxide and excess water, pass out through the semi-permeable membranes into the alveoli, to be expelled back through the respiratory system when the horse breathes out. This process of exchange between alveoli and blood is known as the gaseous exchange. *(See also THE CIRCULATORY SYSTEM, page 35).*

The Ribcage

The heart and the lungs are protected by the sternum in front and the ribs at the sides *(fig. 24)*. Behind the lungs is the diaphragm, a muscular partition which separates the heart and lungs from the stomach and the intestines (the chest from the abdomen).

Air is drawn in through the nostrils and down to the lungs by the muscular expansion of the ribcage and diaphragm— the horse breathes in. When the diaphragm and ribcage contract, air is expelled—the horse breathes out.

The diaphragm can adapt its shape to increase the size of the lung cavity when the lungs need extra room to expand and take in more air. They need to do this if the horse is to perform efficiently at faster speeds. *(See The RULES OF GOOD FEEDING [5], page 71.)*

THE DIGESTIVE SYSTEM

The function of the digestive system is to take in food and to extract the nutrients required by the horse for utilization *(figs. 25 and 26)*. Waste and superfluous matter are passed out in the form of droppings.

The horse needs to use the nutrients for the following purposes:

* To maintain good condition.
* To keep warm.
* For energy to move.
* To grow and to develop muscle.
* To replace damaged tissue—in the healing of wounds, etc.

The Mouth, Throat and Gullet

The system starts with the lips and muzzle, which together select the food. The incisor teeth bite off the herbage and the tongue pushes it back to the molar teeth, where it is ground up and mixed with saliva. The saliva is secreted by three pairs of salivary glands: the *parotid*, which are found at the base of the ear; the *sublingual*, which lie under the tongue; and the *mandibular*, which are at the back of the jawbone (or mandible). The purpose of saliva is to warm and dampen the food, but it also has a low enzyme content, which starts to break down the ingested matter into a more digestible form.

The chewed-up food is then formed

into a bolus (*ball*) by the tongue, ready for swallowing. As the horse starts to swallow, the soft palate, which separates the nasal cavity from the back of the mouth, lifts and triggers off a process which closes the windpipe (*trachea*) in the throat, and allows the bolus to pass through, into the gullet (*oesophagus*).

The bolus can be seen and felt going down the oesophagus. It is forced along by wave-like muscular contractions called *peristalsis*. The process of peristalsis continues throughout the digestive tract. The oesophagus goes through the chest, between the lungs and through the diaphragm.

The Stomach

The food then enters the stomach through the cardiac sphincter, which is a ring-shaped muscle. Under normal circumstances, this muscle will let food pass into the stomach, but not back out of it. This is why a horse cannot normally vomit.

The stomach can comfortably hold up to roughly 2.27kg (5lb) of hard food at a time depending on the type of food and its absorbency. It is important not to offer more than this in one feed, because the food would be forced through the system too quickly for efficient digestion.

There are three main enzymes present in the stomach: pepsin, which begins to break down proteins into a more digestible form; renin, the enzyme which coagulates milk drunk by foals; and lipase, which begins to break down fats. Some of the food may stay in the stomach for several hours. A little at a time is passed out through the pyloric sphincter, into the first of the three parts of the small intestine—the duodenum.

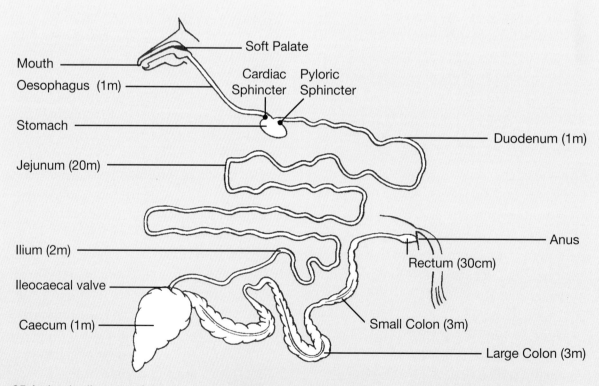

25 A simple diagram of the digestive system.

The Small Intestine

The horse does not have a gall bladder so bile flows from the liver, via the bile duct, direct to the duodenum. Its purpose is to emulsify fats and oils and to neutralise the effect of the acids from the stomach (to make the environment more alkaline). Insulin and other digestive juices from the pancreas are also found in the duodenum, where they aid the digestive process.

The jejunum, which follows the duodenum, is the largest part of the small intestine, and here the main digestion of protein and soluble carbohydrates, including sugars, takes place. Fats are also absorbed in the jejunum.

The final part of the small intestine is the ileum. Here the process of digestion is continued and, in particular, calcium and other minerals are absorbed.

The Large Intestine

The food passes through the ileo-caecal valve into the large intestine which is considered in three parts. The first is the caecum. The caecum acts as a holding chamber for the next part of the large intestine. Water absorption which takes place throughout most of the system continues here.

The large colon follows the caecum. The breakdown of food in the large colon may take several days, during which time more food will arrive. This is why the large colon is so bulky and why the horse living out on good pasture has a big belly.

The final part of the large intestine is the small colon. Water, minerals and any remaining nutrients will be absorbed here.

Throughout the three parts of the large intestine, hay, grass and other fibrous

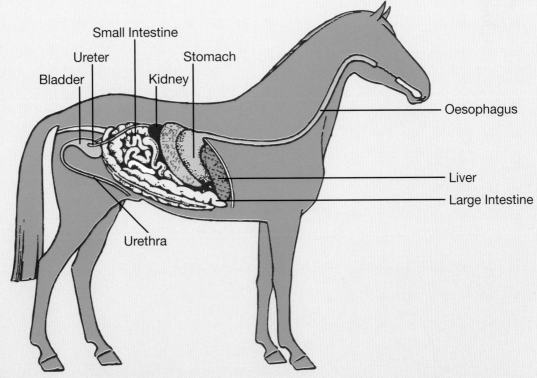

26 The digestive and urinary system.

matter, which has not already been digested, are broken down by bacteria. There are many types—each being specific to a certain foodstuff. The bacteria, or flora, as they are also called, will adjust to the type of food consumed. It is important to make major changes in the diet gradually so that the bacteria have time to adjust. For example, changes of hay should be made over a period of seven to ten days.

The Rectum and Anus

What remains is mainly fibrous waste which is formed into boluses in the rectum, and expelled as droppings through the final sphincter muscle, the anus.

During the digestive process, nutrients are absorbed through the walls of the small and large intestines into the blood to be distributed around the body by the circulatory system for utilization.

THE URINARY SYSTEM

The urinary system is the means by which liquid waste is expelled from the body. Water is essential to life: approximately 65% of a horse's body consists of water. It acts as a solvent in which substances can be dissolved and transported round the body. None of the systems can function correctly if the horse is short of water. The urinary system consists of:

- Two kidneys, each with its own tube called a ureter which runs into the bladder.
- The bladder.
- Another tube (the urethra) by which urine is passed out from the bladder and expelled.

The two kidneys act as filters and regulators to extract urea, other waste products and surplus water from the blood. From each kidney the waste liquid runs through the ureter into the bladder which acts as a holding chamber until the horse stales. Urine is then passed out of the bladder via the urethra and is expelled through the penis of male horses and through the vulva of mares. The urinary system of a male horse is shown in *fig. 26*.

4. Handling and Leading

To understand and to be in sympathy with a horse's mentality is essential to success. A horse is very much a creature of habit, and favours the same thing happening at the same time every day. Picking out feet, for example, is much more easily accomplished if they are picked out in the same order each time. Likewise, a horse brought into the stable at night is more easily dealt with if the same timetable is followed each evening. It is a good plan, therefore, to adopt—and adhere to, as far as possible—a fixed daily stable routine.

The gregarious instinct in horses is highly developed. In their natural state they live in herds, and they love the company of their own kind. Much that might otherwise prove difficult can often be easily accomplished by keeping stable companions within sight or hearing of one another.

When handling a horse always be aware of the look in his eye. This will help you to know his thoughts and to anticipate his movements. You can tell from his eye and his actions whether he is calm or excited.

For the rest, the golden rules are:

- *Speak quietly.*
- *Handle gently but firmly.*
- *Avoid sudden movements.*

There is simply no place in the stable for anyone rough or loud-voiced.

Speaking

Always speak to the horse before approaching. Speak before handling. Speak before moving. This is a simple but most important lesson to learn.

A word frequently repeated soon becomes familiar. A horse learns much from the inflection of the voice and from the tone and manner in which it is used. He soon comes to recognise the voice of the person who feeds him, or from whom some kindness is to be expected. For safety's sake, speak before you do anything else.

The Approach

The approach should always be to the shoulder, taking deliberate steps and never rushing. Speak as you advance; and when you are near enough, pat or stroke the horse's lower neck or shoulder.

27 Tying a quick-release knot.

FITTING THE HALTER OR HEADCOLLAR

The Headcollar *(Fig. 28)*

This is made of leather or synthetic fabric, with a buckle on the nearside cheekpiece. The noseband and throatlash are connected by a short strap. They may or may not be adjustable. Some headcollars also have a browband. The lead rope is normally attached to a ring in the centre of the back of the noseband.

Before fitting the headcollar, unfasten the buckle on the nearside cheekpiece. Having approached the horse, pass the lead rope over his neck, place the noseband over the muzzle and the headpiece over the poll behind the ears. Then fasten the cheekpiece.

28 Headcollar.

29 Halter.

The Halter *(Fig. 29)*

This is usually made of webbing or rope. To fit the halter, loosen the noseband and pass the free end of the rope over the neck. Manoeuvre the noseband over the muzzle, and the headpiece over the ears. Then tie a knot on the left (leading) side to prevent the noseband from becoming either too loose or too tight.

TYING UP A HORSE

Securing a Horse to a Ring (Racking Up)

The best way to secure a horse is by a headcollar and leadrope, the latter being attached to the back O-ring of the noseband. It is most important to use some recognised form of quick-release knot *(fig. 27)*.

The lead rope should be passed through a small loop of string (of a strength that would break in an emergency) attached to the securing ring, rather than through the ring itself. This will secure the horse for normal purposes but will give way should he panic and struggle hard to free himself.

- Unless a horse is reliable it is advisable to tie him up only in a stable or other enclosed place.
- Beware of tying up to an unsafe wall or rail which might give way before the string.
- Haynets should always be tied up separately. Never tie a horse to a haynet.
- If a horse is inclined to chew the lead rope, a rack chain should be used. In this case the string, which would break in an emergency, should be used to secure the chain to the headcollar and not to the ring.

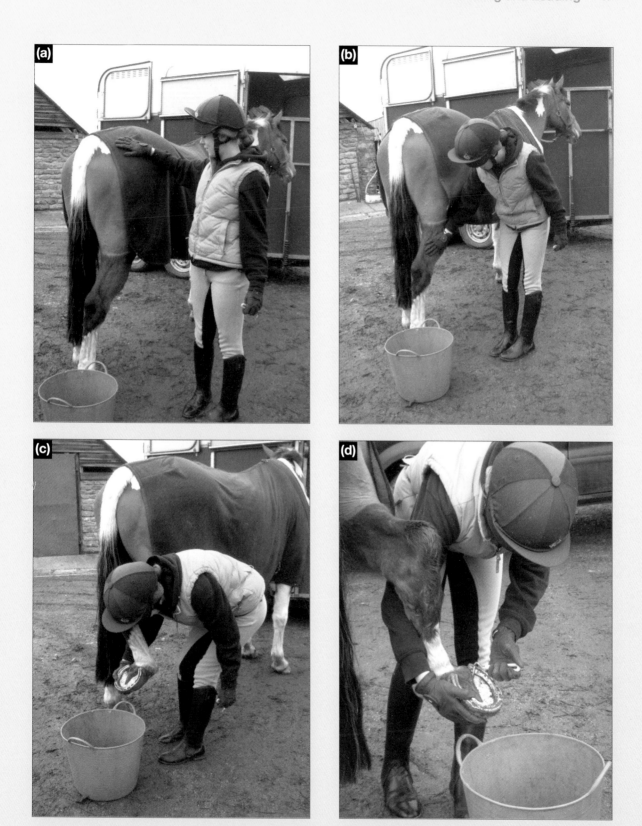

30 Four stages in lifting a hind leg. **(a)** Putting a hand on the horse's quarters; **(b)** Moving the hand to the front of the hock; **(c)** Saying 'Up'; **(d)** The foot can now be held in one hand and picked out with the other.

Cross-Tying
(Placing a Horse on Pillar Reins)

This is a way of securing a horse by means of two lead ropes or chains rather than one. The horse is positioned between two walls or stout posts roughly 2 metres (6 ½ft) apart with the ropes or chains fastened to the Ds on each side of his headcollar. In barns or yards where cross-tying is a normal practice, chains are permanent fixtures on appropriate posts or walls. Cross-tying is also used when transporting a single horse in a double trailer without a partition.

HANDLING THE LEGS

Lifting a Foreleg

First speak to the horse. Then place a hand on his neck and turn to face his tail. Run your hand down over his shoulder, elbow, back of his knees and tendons. On reaching the fetlock, say 'Up' and squeeze the joint. With your free hand, catch the toe and hold it with your fingers; less weight falls on the arm when you hold the foot at the toe rather than at the pastern. If the horse will not lift his foot when spoken to, he may be encouraged to do so if you lean against his shoulder and push his weight on to the other leg.

Lifting a Hind Leg *(Fig. 30)*

Speak to the horse. Then stand abreast of his hip and face his tail, placing the hand nearest to the horse on his quarters. Run this hand down the back of his leg as far as the point of the hock. Then move your hand to the front of the hock and run it down on the inside front of the cannon bone. On reaching the fetlock, say 'Up'. When the horse raises his foot, move the joint slightly backwards and then slide your hand down to encircle the hoof from the inside. Do not lift it high or carry it far back. Either of these actions would probably be resisted, as they would upset the horse's balance.

LEADING AND SHOWING IN HAND

Leading in Hand

Leading in hand is when a person on the ground leads a horse without a rider, by the reins or lead rope. The horse should be accustomed to being led from either side, but as most horses will expect to be led from the left (near) side, you should at first lead a strange horse from that side.

In Britain, when leading on the highway the horse must travel in the same direction as the traffic and the person leading him always be on the right (off) side, so as to be between the horse and overtaking traffic. For further information, see *The Highway Code.*

Occasionally it is advisable to lead a horse in a well-fitting snaffle bridle. If the area has any access to the public highway a bridle must be worn for control and for insurance purposes.

Horse Wearing a Bridle

Pass the reins over the horse's head and hold them with one hand a short distance from the bit and with one finger dividing them. Hold the buckle end in the other hand.

If being used with a running martingale the buckle on the reins must be undone and the martingale knotted back to the neck strap in order to lead, or for a short distance only, you may hold the reins close to the bit leaving them in place.

Horse Wearing a Headcollar or a Halter

Hold the rope with one hand a short distance from the headcollar or halter, keeping the free end of the rope in the other hand. Never put your fingers through the D-ring of the headcollar, or wrap the rope round your hand. Both can be dangerous.

To Move the Horse

Ask him to 'walk on', and move forward. A trained horse will readily walk forward alongside you. Most horses will refuse to move if you stare them in the face.

If the horse hangs back, do not pull at his head. Either carry a whip in the outside hand and, moving it behind your back, tap his flank—or, preferably, ask a helper to move behind him.

When Turning

Steady and balance the horse and then turn him away from you, keeping yourself on the outside of the turn. He will then be more likely to keep his hocks under him, remaining balanced and under control.

Showing a Horse and Running Up in Hand

The object is to show off the horse without a rider either at the halt (standing up in hand) or while moving as freely as possible at the walk and trot (running up in hand). The general principles are the same as for leading in hand. This procedure is used during veterinary inspections.

Standing Up in Hand

Make sure that the horse is looking alert, standing still, and showing his conformation to the best advantage. Stand directly in front of and facing him, holding one rein in each hand near to the bit, to keep control and his attention. Raise your elbows so that the horse cannot nibble your wrists.

Running Up in Hand

It is usual to lead from the left side. Run or walk as requested, looking straight ahead and not at the horse. The horse should be moved directly away from the person inspecting him, then turned as described above, and led straight back. The person inspecting him will step to one side if he wishes you to carry on past him.

It is most important for the rein or rope to be slack enough to allow the horse to carry his head naturally. He should be encouraged to move confidently and well. The pace should be active, but not hurried or unbalanced.

RIDE-AND-LEAD

Ride-and-lead is the method by which a mounted rider leads by the reins another horse who has no rider. A horse should be trained to be led on both sides.

Take the reins of the horse you are leading in the hand nearest to him. With one finger dividing the reins hold them midway down, keeping your hand close to your knee and as still as possible.

Do not allow the led horse to get his head in front of the horse you are riding—and do not allow him to hang back.

When leading on the public highway you must always keep to the left-hand side of the road with the led horse on your left, so that he is sheltered from the traffic.

If either horse is fresh or liable to get upset, keep the led horse on a short rein—about 30cm (1ft) from head to hand—with his head about level with your knee. If the led horse tries to break away, give in at first and gradually get him under control; otherwise he may well pull the reins out of your hand, or you out of the saddle.

Led Horse in Snaffle Bridle and Saddle

There are many ways of leading a horse: the following are two most frequently adopted:

• Using the snaffle with the reins straight to the hand.
• With the far rein passed through the ring on the side of the snaffle nearest to you. This prevents a jointed snaffle turning backwards in the horse's mouth if he hangs back.

The stirrup irons should be run up to prevent them flapping about. Fasten them by the method shown in *fig. 31*, or knot the leathers securely around the irons.

It is advisable to fit a surcingle over the saddle in order to secure the saddle flaps.

If the leathers fit loosely on the bars you should turn up the safety catches to prevent the leathers slipping off. Make sure that the catches are turned down again before the horse is ridden. Running martingales should be detached from the reins and secured to the neckstrap.

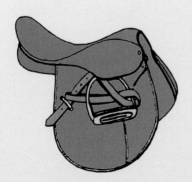

31 Stirrup irons run up and secured.

Led Horse in Double Bridle

The horse should be led from the bridoon (snaffle) rein, used as above. The curb rein should be secured by either of the following methods:

• By crossing the two halves (if they can be unbuckled at the centre) under the neck of the led horse, passing them over and round the neck, and refastening them under it.
• By winding them round each other under the throat, then threading the throat lash through one of them and securing it. The curb rein should be at the correct length—long enough for there to be no curb action, but short enough to prevent the horse chewing the reins.

5. The Stable Yard and Managing the Stabled Horse

It should be the ambition of every good horseman to strive for the highest attainable standard in the turnout of his horse, in the management of the stable, in the care of tack, and in the general hygiene of the premises. Hygienic conditions are particularly important: germs, disease and infection thrive in dirty conditions.

THE STABLE YARD

Building a new yard is a project which requires professional advice. In all circumstances you should consider and work towards the following:

Pure Air—but sheltered from severe prevailing winds.

Good Light—making the best of natural light, but employing a safe electrical circuit to provide light at night and in winter in the stables, tack room and across the extent of the yard.

Dry Foundations—adequate for the type of soil.

Good Drainage—especially from stables, under taps and in any area where horses or vehicles may be hosed.

Good Water Supply—fresh water should be available very near to the stables. It should be protected from frost.

Security—the yard should be enclosed, gates should be substantial and with easy but secure latches.

Hay and Straw Storage

Ideally, barns should be detached from the stable block to alleviate the risk of fire and dust. Floors should be dry and impervious to seeping damp.

The Muck Heap

This should be away from, but with easy access to, the stables, in the opposite direction to that of the prevailing wind. If it is to be removed regularly, it can be kept in a pit or bunker on hard standing. It should not be too near to the hay barn, nor in a position where it is offensive to neighbours or people on a public thoroughfare (*see DISPOSAL OF MANURE, page 57).*

The Saddle Room

This should be dry, and should be large enough to accommodate all necessary saddlery, trunks for horse clothing, and cupboards for veterinary items, leaving room for tack cleaning and the airing of equipment. There should be some form of heating for winter use. Hot and cold running water are useful. Attention to security is imperative. Doors and windows should be soundly constructed and fitted with locks.

Firefighting Equipment

Extinguishers should be readily accessible from all areas of the yard, but in particular from the stables and hay barn. The numbers and sizes required will depend on the size of the yard. Your local fire officer will advise you.

Stable for Clipping

An extra stable, with particularly good lighting and an accessible electric point, is useful for clipping and for treating injured horses in winter. If the drainage is good and the electrical circuit safe, the same stable can be used for cold-hosing, etc.

Isolation Stables

Larger yards should have one or two stables away from the main yard, so that a contagious horse may be isolated.

CONSTRUCTION AND EQUIPMENT OF STABLES

Loose Boxes

These provide the most satisfactory stable accommodation. The horse has more freedom of movement, is encouraged to lie down and rest, and is therefore more comfortable than in a stall. To accommodate a horse, a loose box should measure at least 3.7m square (12ft square); to accommodate a pony, about 3.7m (12ft) by 3m (10ft).

Access to a loose box should be either by

way of a stable door direct from the yard, or by a stable door and passageway within the stable (American Barn-type stabling). If access is from a passageway, evacuation in the case of fire must be considered. Access from both ends is essential. Stable doors which open directly on to the yard should be in two parts, so that the upper portion can be hooked back and left open, allowing the horse to look out over the lower portion. Horses greatly appreciate the chance to see what is taking place in their immediate vicinity. If you have a horse who habitually bites at passers-by, or who attempts to jump out, grilles are available which can be fastened across the top, open half of the door. There are also special anti-weaving grilles *(fig. 32). (See WEAVING, page 176.)*

The door should be at least 1.1m (roughly 3ft 7in) wide. Narrow doorways are dangerous. The height of the doorway should be 2.1m (7ft) and the height of the lower door 1.25m (roughly 4ft). These dimensions are approximate and should depend on the size of the animal to be accommodated.

The sides of the top door frame and the top of the lower door should be fitted with galvanised framing (anti-chew strip).

It is advisable to have the doors of loose boxes opening outwards so that you can enter the box without interference from bedding. This is also important if an animal should become cast (unable to get up) in his box near to the door.

Latches should be of a special non-projecting type, so that there is no risk of the horse being injured by them when passing through the doorway. Two are needed: one at the top of the door and another at the bottom. The lower one keeps the door shut should the top one fail. It also prevents damage caused by kicking. The foot-operated type is preferable. An overhang or verandah outside a row of boxes is useful, as it gives protection from the weather.

Stalls

Stalls have the advantage of providing accommodation for a greater number of animals in a given area and of saving labour and bedding material.

Disadvantages are that the horses are unable to move around and may become

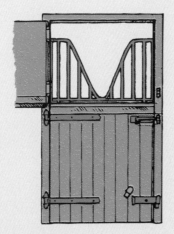

32 Stable door with anti-weaving grille and two latches.

33 Swinging-bail stall.

bored because they cannot look out; nor do they have direct access to fresh air. A shy or nervous animal may be deprived of rest as a result of bullying by his neighbour in the adjoining stall.

Access to stalls is normally by way of a passage within the stable. Securing a horse in a stall is described on page 54.

Swinging-Bail Stalls *(Fig. 33)*

These are sometimes used at Pony Club camps, and by riding schools, for the temporary accommodation of horses caught up from grass. They are easily cleaned, allow free circulation of air, and facilitate drying-off of the standings. The bail should be approximately the length of the stall. It must be hung high enough to prevent a horse from getting a leg over it, and must be slightly higher off the ground at the front end than at the back. The front rope must be short enough to prevent swinging. It should be suspended by a stout cord tied with a quick-release knot. If, by any mischance, a horse should get a leg over the bail, he can then be released quickly. Chains or wire should not be used. One of the great disadvantages of the swinging bail is that it provides no protection against bullying and neck-biting.

NOTE: Horses kept in stalls overnight should always be secured as described on page 54.

Floors

It is essential for surfaces to be non-slippery, impervious to moisture, and durable. A variety of materials is available. Concrete is often used, as it has proved to be practical and is easily installed. It must have a roughened facing. On sandy or chalky soil which drain well it may not be necessary to have a man-made floor. A natural base is conducive to quiet, and is also restful for tired legs and joints; but it is not so easy to disinfect.

Stable floors must slope slightly to allow for drainage, but no more than the minimum amount for the purpose; a fall of 1:48 is recommended. Drains should be either in the corner of the box away from the manger, haynet and door, or outside the box or stall. Gullies leading towards them should be shallow and open. If shavings, peat or paper are used for bedding, care should be taken to see that drains are kept clear, or that the opening is covered up.

Ventilation

This is an important matter. Horses are likely to be healthier and less prone to coughs, colds and allergies in an environment which has a circulation of fresh air but is draught-free. Circulation is best achieved by the entry of fresh air through the top of the stable door and the window; and the exit of foul air (which rises, having been warmed by the heat of the horse's body) through a vent at the highest point of the stable. The vent

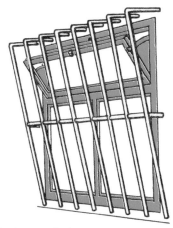

34 Sheringham window.

must be designed so that it will expel air but will not admit rain. The top of the stable door should be kept open day and night, summer and winter; this is almost always possible as long as the stable faces south and the top of the bottom portion is high enough to exclude draughts. A stable with a south-facing aspect is therefore recommended.

To prevent draughts, the window should be on the same wall as the door, but positioned so that its light is not blocked by the open door. It should be glazed with reinforced glass, or the glass should be protected by iron bars. Sheringham windows, which are hinged so that they open inwards from the top, allow the incoming air to circulate upwards and over, and not on to the back of the horse *(fig. 34)*. If the stable is in a sheltered area, these windows may be positioned on any outside wall. Draughts under doors should be excluded.

If necessary, extra warmth should be provided by means of clothing, rather than by restricting fresh air.

35 Horse secured by a 'log' (inset) and rope.

Electricity
All electrical fittings must be of the tough, outdoor variety, and must be out of reach of the horse. Bulb or fluorescent strips should be positioned to give maximum light and minimum shadow. They should be well guarded. Switches should be outside the stable and of a special type designed to prevent electrocution if a horse should seize hold of one with his teeth.

FIXTURES AND FITTINGS
These should be kept to the minimum so that the stable is clear of encumbrances.

Securing Rings
All rings must be firmly fixed.
- *In a stable,* there should be one ring at approximately 1.5m (5ft) to which the horse can be tied up (racked up). The haynet may either be tied to the same ring or to a second ring. The second ring is a convenience rather than a necessity and should be set at the highest level that you can reach.
- *In a stall,* the horse is tied up all the time and must be able to lie down without getting his legs entangled in the lead rope, so an additional ring beside, or fixed to, the manger, is essential. The horse is secured by a rope which runs through this ring. A log is attached to the free end, so that the rope is never slack, but the horse may take the extra length when necessary *(fig. 35)*. Another ring at 1.5m (5ft) is used for short racking and for the haynet as described previously.

Mangers
A manger, if fitted, should be positioned in

the front corner, away from the door, and preferably boxed in underneath to prevent injury. It should be approximately the same height as the horse's chest. A manger must be shallow enough to prevent the horse getting his jaw caught in it, but deep enough to prevent him throwing his feed out. If it is removable from its frame, it will be easier to keep clean. Alternatively, plastic mangers which either hook over the door or are fixed to brackets on the wall are convenient and easy to keep clean. Removable feed bowls on the floor are sometimes used. Some fitted mangers extend to include a separate compartment for hay. Improvised mangers are rarely a success.

Hay Racks

Hay racks above eye-level are now generally disapproved of, because they make the horse feed at an unnatural height, with the risk of dust and hayseeds falling into his eyes.

Hay racks fitted at about the same height as a haynet can be satisfactory.

Salt/Mineral Lick Holders

Blocks of these licks and their holders are obtainable from feed merchants and provide a constant source of salt for the stabled horse.

Water Bowls

Gravity-fed or lever-operated bowls fixed to the wall, each with a separate stopcock, are favoured by some people. They should not be sited near the manger or haynet in case they become blocked with food (*see* WATERING, *page 69*).

Bucket Fittings

In some stables, large, hinged rings are fixed to the wall about 1.2m (4ft) off the ground to hold the feed or water bucket so that it cannot be knocked over. When not in use, the rings can be folded down against the wall.

Stables Without Fittings

A stable without fitted mangers, hayracks and water bowls is easier to clean. Feeding and watering can be carried out at ground level—a much more natural position—using water buckets and a removable plastic or heavy rubber feed bowl. Hay is either fed from a haynet secured to the short-rack ring or from the ground, which can be rather wasteful.

UTENSILS

Feeding and Watering

All mangers, feed bowls and water buckets must be kept scrupulously clean.

- Water buckets (if no automatic water bowl).
- A plastic or heavy rubber feed bowl (if there is no manger).
- If there is a manger, a plastic bowl or bucket to mix the feed in and take to the horse.
- A haynet, if used.

Mucking Out

- Wheelbarrow
- Stable shovel
- Broom
- Pitchfork, with blunted prongs
- Four-pronged fork, with blunted prongs
- Skip (for droppings)
- Hosepipe
- Muck sheet (for carrying straw)
- Rake or pronged shovel (for peat, paper or shavings)

BEDDING

Some form of bedding material is necessary for the stabled horse, to allow him to lie down and rest, to encourage him to stale, to provide insulation, and to prevent his feet from being jarred during long hours spent standing on a hard surface. Rubber matting is widely used on stable floors nowadays. It provides a shock-absorbing, level surface to stand on but should be used with some form of moisture-absorbing bedding and cleaned regularly.

Straw

Straw must have been baled dry and should be clean and dust-free. It should be as long as possible and free of grass and weeds. Wheat straw is the hardest. Barley and oat straw are more absorbent, but horses are more inclined to eat them.

Management of Straw Bedding (Mucking Out)

Each day the droppings and the wettest of the bedding should be removed. Replace bedding and add fresh straw as necessary. Each week the floor should be swept clean, disinfected, and allowed to dry.

When bedding down, the used straw should be put down first, and fresh, clean straw added: or, if the horse tends to eat his bedding, it is better to mix the old and new straw together. Baled straw should be well tossed when making the bed. As an extra precaution against injury or draughts it is usual to bed more thickly around the walls of a loose box or the sides of a stall. A good, deep bed makes for comfort and is more economical in the long run.

If a horse eats an excessive amount of his straw bedding, you must decide whether he is greedy or whether he is not receiving sufficient suitable bulk feed. (Or perhaps his hay is unpalatable.) If he is greedy and overweight, shavings, peat or paper should be used for bedding. Alternatively, some horses can be dissuaded from eating their straw beds by covering fresh with older bedding.

Straw should not be used for horses with respiratory problems.

Droppings should be removed each time you visit the stable. This is done by lifting the straw from underneath and tipping the droppings into a basket or tin, called a dung skip. A plastic laundry basket, a muck sack or a manure collector are satisfactory substitutes.

Shavings, Paper and Hemp

- *Baled shavings* make a good, relatively dust-free, comfortable bed. With other shavings, care must be taken to check that there are no sharp splinters of wood in amongst them.
- *Diced-paper bedding* is warm and dust-free. The disadvantages are that some horses are allergic to the ink, and the paper becomes very heavy when damp.
- *Chopped hemp, dust-extracted chopped straw* or *corrugated cardboard* provide sound, dust-free bedding.

Management of Shavings, Paper and Hemp (Mucking Out)

Before shavings, paper or hemp are used, drains must be cleaned and, if necessary, sealed up, so that they do not become blocked and unfit for use with straw bedding in the future. Wet and soiled patches must be changed frequently and the bed forked and raked over daily; this keeps the bedding soft and prevents it from becoming packed and soggy. As with straw, droppings should be removed each time you visit the stable. The disposal of soiled peat is not a problem, as it is in great demand from gardeners, especially where there is clay soil.

Deep Litter

The method of bedding known as the deep litter system is suitable for horses who are turned out all day. Under this system—which can use either straw, shavings, paper or hemp—droppings must be removed at every opportunity, and fresh bedding added to an existing deep bed when necessary. The advantages of this method are: less bedding is needed; it is more labour-saving (except when periodically the entire bed is cleared out); and it provides a deep, warm bed which does not need to be shaken up each day.

Shavings, 15 to 20cm (6 to 8in) deep, under a top layer of straw, make a good weekly deep litter bed, but if the stable walls are of wood, damp shavings can cause rotting.

With adequate ventilation, enough fresh bedding, and the frequent removal of droppings, there should be no nasty smell.

Carefully tended, and depending on the height of the box, a deep litter bed can last through a whole winter season, but bear in mind that cleaning out the box will be very heavy work, and farm machinery may be needed to remove it in the spring.

With all deep bedding, care must be taken to see that the horse's feet are kept clean, dry and healthy. Deep litter is inclined to be warm, so if the feet are not picked out regularly, infection (thrush) will occur.

When hemp or shavings are used, the damp patches should be removed periodically, and the bed well raked over to keep it at a constant depth.

Disposal Of Manure

If the manure is kept in a pit, arrangements should be made for the pit to be emptied frequently. If the manure is to be stacked, choose a place further away from the stables and store it in three heaps: the oldest pile consisting of well-rotted manure ready for use on the garden; a second pile to which manure is no longer added, being in the process of rotting; and a third pile in current use as a dump for fresh manure. Burning is an effective method of disposal, but may not be environmentally permissible in certain areas.

A PROGRAMME OF STABLE ROUTINE

The next page shows an ideal daily routine for a horse in work. In most stables this will be adapted to suit your own requirements. The routine shown is for a horse being ridden once a day. The priorities are:

- Regular feed times.
- Sufficient exercise for the work expected.
- Adequate grooming.
- Access to grazing if possible.

7.00am

- Look for the signs of good health in your horse *(see page 118)*.
- Put on headcollar, and tie up.
- Look round the horse to see that he has suffered no injury during the night.
- Adjust rugs if necessary.
- Tie up a small net of hay.
- Muck out, pick out the feet and put down the bed. Some people prefer to put down a thin day bed after mucking out and a thicker bed for the night.
- Clean water buckets and refill.
- Remove headcollar.*
- Feed. (NOTE: The horse must not be exercised within one and a half hours of feeding.)
- Remove haynet in preparation for exercise.

9.00am

- Put on headcollar and tie up.
- Remove droppings (skip out).
- Quarter—short groom to tidy up.
- Saddle up.
- Exercise.

On Return

- Tie up. Remove tack. Brush off saddle, girth and bridle areas with a body brush, or sponge off if necessary.
- Pick out feet.
- Rug up according to circumstances.
- Give a net of hay, or allow horse access to grass if possible.
- Remove headcollar.

12.00 noon

- Clean tack. Give second feed.

2.00pm

- Tie up. Groom thoroughly.
- Replace rugs
- Check water. Set fair the bed.
- Remove headcollar.*
- Tidy yard.

4.30pm

- Tie up. If the horse has been in the paddock, remove any mud and pick out feet. In any case, re-rug for the night.
- Skip out and set fair. Check water.
- Refill haynet. (If the horse is greedy, half the night's hay may be put in a second net and fed later.)
- Remove headcollar.*
- Third feed.

9.00pm

- Tie up.
- Skip out.
- Check rugs.
- Top up water.
- If necessary, refill or put in second haynet.
- Remove headcollar.*
- Fourth feed.

* If the horse is inclined to kick or misbehave at feed time, you should position the feed and then untie him and remove the headcollar.

36 A programme of stable routine.

6. The Horse at Grass and his Paddock

Advantages

Under this natural system the horse or pony is more able to look after himself. If it is properly managed, many horses thrive on it and there are considerable savings in time and money.

In the growing seasons of spring and early summer, if the acreage is sufficient to provide the amount of feed required, the total diet of the horse will be supplied naturally by the grass. In this case, a salt lick and fresh water will be the only additions needed. (See WATERING: IN THE PADDOCK, page 69.)

The grass-kept horse exercises himself enough to keep healthy, and because he is not restricted he is less likely to be over-fresh when ridden. As long as he is getting the exercise appropriate to the work required, he is less likely to suffer injury to wind and limb than a stabled horse, since his legs, and to some extent his lungs, are being constantly exercised.

Disadvantages

Horses are not always near to hand when you need them, and may be very dirty and wet. The field may be some distance from the house, or the horse may refuse to be caught.

If you leave a well-fitted headcollar on, make sure it is made of leather as it is more likely to break than a synthetic type should it catch on anything.

It is difficult to regulate the diet. The horse may become overweight in early summer, with a belly which is too grass fat for fast and strenuous work. On the other hand, additional feed will be needed during the winter months, and in the summer, too, if the grass is inadequate or if the horse is working. Whether he is stabled, at grass, or kept on the combined system, the horse will need regular exercise if he is to be fit enough for hard work.

GENERAL MANAGEMENT

A horse turned out to grass should be visited at least twice a day. He should be looked over for injuries, condition of feet and/or shoes, and general indications of health (see THE SIGNS OF GOOD HEALTH, page 118).

The coat should be lying smoothly, and in warm weather it should be glossy. If it is dull and standing up (staring) this indicates poor condition or cold, or sometimes both. If the former, seek expert advice; if the latter, the horse will need a turnout rug, or more adequate shelter. While checking the horse you should also check the gate, the fence, and the water supply, and make sure that everything is as it should be.

Whether the horse is being ridden or not, it is advisable to catch him every day, as this will ensure that he will be caught easily when he is required for work. Always take some titbits—such as pony cubes or slices of carrot or apple—in a bowl, bucket or scoop. This will encourage the horse to move towards you. In order to catch him approach him quietly towards the shoulder, or let him come to you, and avoid jerky or sudden movements that might frighten him off.

Before work, pick out the feet and brush the horse lightly, making sure that the areas where the saddlery will lie are free from mud or dried sweat. In warm weather, sponge the eyes, lips, nose and dock.

On return from exercise, if the weather is warm, sponge off the sweat marks.

Avoid excessive grooming, which removes the grease from the coat, nature's protection against wet and cold. *(See also* GROOMING PONIES WHO LIVE OUT, *page 104.)*

An unclipped horse is unlikely to have dried off completely on return from work, but will probably roll and is less likely to catch a chill if turned out straightaway than if left to stand in the stable to dry off.

Rolling

The grass-kept horse has a great advantage over his stabled counterpart in that he is able to indulge in a hearty roll in unrestricted conditions whenever he feels like it.

Why horses roll is by no means clear. In springtime it undoubtedly helps to shift the winter coat. After work it is probably because those parts of the skin subjected to pressure under the saddlery need a rub. Rolling helps a horse to cover any wet parts of his coat with dust, thus speeding up the drying-off process. Horses at grass frequently have a layer of mud on their backs from rolling; this helps to keep out the cold and wind, and to retain warmth. Quite clearly, rolling is also an act of sheer enjoyment, and is to be encouraged as natural, healthy, and relaxing.

The Horse Living Out in a Turnout Rug

The horse should be brought in from exercise dry. Waterproof clothing allows little evaporation and the horse should not be left in a damp state overnight. If for some unavoidable reason he is wet on his body, rub him down until he is warm and comfortable, making sure that his ears are dry. He can then go out in his turnout rug. After a few hours, check that he is comfortable, and change the rug if it is damp on the inside. *(For fitting and management, see* TURNOUT RUGS, *page 88.)*

The Combined System

This is a routine whereby the stabled horse is turned out to grass for a portion of each day. It is a compromise between stabling and keeping a horse at grass, and by making the best of both methods has much to recommend it.

It is a system well suited to an animal required frequently for showing, hacking or other purposes, where peak fitness is not necessary, labour is scarce, and time for regular daily exercise not available. However, horses on this system can become extremely fit, as long as they are exercised and managed appropriately.

On the combined system the horse is turned out to grass by day and stabled at night, except during the heat of the summer, and when flies are particularly troublesome. Then the procedure can be reversed—that is, the horses are out during the night and stabled by day. In winter the horse can be turned out after his morning feed (if he needs one) with part of his hay ration. The rest of the hay and the balance of his concentrates should be given when he comes in. This arrangement, as well as ensuring that the horse is in the stable when required, provides suitable facilities for grooming and feeding. When several horses are turned out together, it ensures that each receives his correct amount of hay and concentrates.

It is under this system that the turnout rug comes into its own, as it overcomes the problem of turning out a clipped-out, trace-clipped or thin-skinned horse in winter or in inclement weather.

THE SEASONS

Early Summer

Some horses and many ponies, particularly small ponies, tend to grow too fat during the summer months. Excess weight can be dangerous because of the extra effort that the horse must make to move and to carry his rider. A fat horse or pony is never a pleasant ride. Laminitis, which can be very serious, is often a result of the greedy characteristics of ponies *(see LAMINITIS, pages 162 and 167).* Any pony who shows a tendency to put on too much weight should be moved to a field which offers only bare keep, so that he finds less to eat and has to move further in search of it.

Hay fields, or portions of the paddock on which hay is to be made, should be closed off and the grass allowed to grow. Ideally the hay should be made at the height of the growing season before the grass goes to seed.

Flies are a great trial in summer, so if possible the horse should be provided with a shelter shed. Failing that, make sure that he has ample shade and the companionship of another horse with whom he can stand head to tail, so that each can flick away the flies from the other's face. Though various insect repellents are available and may ease the problem, it should be remembered that flies may well be nature's way of keeping a horse at grass active and on the move, rather than just standing about and gorging himself.

Late Summer

An abnormally dry summer may result in grassland becoming barer than at any other time of year. In extreme cases, the grass may become so brown or burnt up that no keep for the horse remains. When this happens, the horse must either be moved to better pasture, or fed hay as a temporary measure. On sandy soil in these conditions horses have been known to suffer from sand colic—the result of taking in sand along with the poor herbage available.

It must not be forgotten that in a dry summer the normal water supply may also fail, in which case you must find another way of providing water.

Flies may continue to be troublesome at this time of year.

Late Autumn

At this time, when the food value in the grass is deteriorating, the horse might scavenge from hedgerows and trees. Blackberries are seldom a problem. Crab apples (wild apples) have been known to cause colic if eaten to excess. Beech and oak leaves are slightly toxic. Acorns and beech nuts, especially when unripe, can be dangerous, and horses who develop a liking for them should not be allowed access to oak or beech trees at this time of year. *(See fig. 39.)*

Midwinter

In the winter months the time arrives when the feeding of hay, as a supplement to grass, becomes necessary. Do not put this off for too long or the good condition carried by the horse from the summer will be lost. A thin horse is also a cold horse.

Cold, wet, windy weather causes maximum loss of heat and is more debilitating than cold, dry weather. In cold weather horses tend to spend their time sheltering rather than grazing. Hardy native ponies are better suited to living out at night in winter than horses. Keeping lightweight horses out all through the winter is not as a rule satisfactory. However, if it must be done, extra concentrates and bulk feed should be supplied so that the horses can produce the calories needed to keep warm. *(For what and how to feed, see Feeding, page 71.)*

Depending on the weather and the state of the grass, hay should be fed at night, or night and morning. It is more economical and easier to weigh if fed in a net, but this method is not always practical. If a number of horses or ponies share a field, hay should be shaken out in heaps, spaced well apart on a circle, allowing more heaps than there are animals. All should be fed at the same time. Feed should be provided in the part of the field where the animals shelter.

Snow does not cause acute discomfort but puts a stop to grazing, so while the snow lasts, the quantity of hay should be increased by feeding at an extra time or two each day.

If the grass keep is very poor, the horse or pony will become dependent on his hay ration to survive. In this case, hay should be available for most of the day and at night.

During the early months of the year, when the horses' coats are at their longest, lice infestation may occur. Any signs of rubbing should be investigated and action taken if appropriate. *(See Lice, page 173).*

Early Spring

Hay and concentrates should be continued as supplements until there is real feed value in the grass. This is often not until late May.

GRAZING LAND

Acreages

It is impossible to lay down any hard-and-fast rule about the acreage needed to support a horse, as so much depends upon the quality of the grass, the drainage of the land and the nature of the soil. If a number of horses are at grass together, one acre (0.4 ha) per horse is adequate, as there will be room for grassland management. One acre for one horse on its own is insufficient, especially if the paddock is in use all year round and

GOOD	POOR

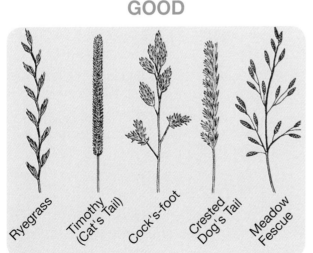

Ryegrass Timothy (Cat's Tail) Cock's-foot Crested Dog's Tail Meadow Fescue

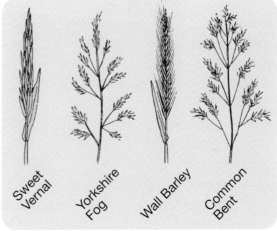

Sweet Vernal Yorkshire Fog Wall Barley Common Bent

37 Good and poor grasses.

a horse, rather than a pony, is to live in it. In this case, alternative grazing must be found, so that the paddock can be rested and treated for a few weeks, at least once a year, in order to keep it in good condition.

The Pasture

The food value of the pasture depends on the time of year—whether the herbage is growing actively, flowering, gone to seed or dying back—and on the type, variety and quality of the grass. Rye grass, timothy, cock's-foot, crested dog's-tail, white clover and meadow fescue are good. Yorkshire fog, sweet vernal, wall barley and common bent grass are poor *(fig. 37)*. The sward should contain a variety of good grasses and a bottom rich in low-growing herbs such as chicory, ribwort, yarrow and burnet. Old, well-established pastures provide the best grazing for horses because their mixture of weeds, herbs, seeds, grasses and hedges normally supply all the ingredients of a healthy diet.

Minerals present in the ground and absorbed by the herbage vary according to the area and the amount and type of fertilizer used. New pasture, or pasture which has been fertilized for dairy herds and other farm stock, is sometimes too lush and too high in nitrogen for horses. It may also lack the variety of plants on which a horse depends for his vitamin and mineral requirements. To counteract any deficiencies, especially when old pasture is not available, extra bulk feed, with a vitamin/mineral supplement, may be required.

Conservation

The keeping of a horse at grass requires careful and intelligent use of land. Horses are among the most wasteful of grazing animals; in their search for the most palatable grasses, they trample down and destroy potentially valuable food. Furthermore, portions of the field eventually become so tainted with droppings that the grass turns coarse and sour and is no longer acceptable as food. During wet winters some fields become badly poached, especially if the horses are shod, and mud is not a satisfactory environment for horses.

It may be possible to fence off the muddy places, or to feed and water the horses in a fresh part of the paddock. Otherwise they should be brought in or moved to a well drained area. This will also conserve the grazing in the wet area for future use. On badly-draining soil such as clay, a drainage scheme might be beneficial. Your local farmer/contractor will advise you.

If the land is to be used economically, it is essential to adopt a long-term plan. The following are some of the ways in which waste may be avoided and pastures kept as clean as possible:

Dividing the Field

On limited acreages, even in the best growing periods, the grass will be eaten right down and will not have a chance to recover and regrow, unless the field is rested. It is sensible to subdivide the field, preferably into three or four sections, and rotate them, so that each receives a period of grazing followed by a period of rest and/or treatment.

Grazing Periods

While horses are present, the daily removal of droppings by shovel and barrow is recommended. It conserves the pasture and limits the parasites (redworms, etc.). In large paddocks the removal of droppings may not be practical.

Harrowing is an alternative. Worms thrive in damp conditions, so if the droppings are scattered by harrowing in dry and sunny weather, they will dry out and the worm infestation of the paddock will be reduced.

Treatment Periods

Fertilizing

Seek the advice of a local farmer or, having explained that the pasture is for horses, ask a representative from a fertilizer company to assess the nutrients in the soil. An expert will be able to advise on the correct levels of nitrogen, potassium, phosphorous, etc., and will suggest an appropriate fertilizer. The paddock may need to be dressed once a year. This should be carried out in early spring.

Liming

It is also sensible to have the acidity (pH) level of your soil checked every three to four years to see if it requires lime.

Weed Control

General weed spraying is not satisfactory, as horses benefit from all manner of herbage often considered to be weeds. Ragwort is poisonous. It should be pulled or dug up with its roots and burned. Docks, thistles and bracken can be spot-sprayed, using a knapsack sprayer. Buttercups, if a problem, may have to be treated generally.

NOTE: Before spraying or fertilizing, the horses must be removed from the field, and not returned until at least three weeks have elapsed and after it has rained hard enough to wash the chemicals well into the soil.

Mixed Grazing

Grazing by sheep or cattle will clean the paddock. They will eat off the grass rejected by horses, and in doing so will ingest the parasites detrimental to the horse. Redworms and most other parasites cannot survive the digestive systems of cattle or sheep, so the life cycle of the worms will be broken. As the droppings of farm stock help to fertilize, it may not be necessary to dress the field so often.

Topping

Alternatively, top the fields (mow the tops off the sward) to stunt the weeds, to keep long grass from growing coarse and rank, and to encourage more even grazing.

Rest Periods

Having treated the field, allow the grass three to eight weeks to grow, depending on the state of the sward, the climate, and the time of year.

SAMPLE PADDOCK MAINTENANCE PLAN

The suggested plan opposite (fig. 38) is for a three-acre paddock on which two ponies of approximately 14hh (142cm) are kept all the year round. The paddock is divided into three one-acre plots. Plot A should be the driest area and preferably on a slope.

The rotation should always depend on the weather and the subsequent condition of the grass. Expert advice should be sought in choosing the correct fertilizer and, every five years or so, in determining the acidity level of the soil. The ponies must not be taken back on to a plot which has been fertilized or treated with weedkiller until after at least three weeks and it has rained well. Ragwort (fig. 39) and other poisonous plants should be dug or pulled up with their roots, and burned.

Month	Plot A	Plot B	Plot C
December* **January*** **February***	PONIES *Feed supplementary hay if and when necessary. (Pick up droppings.)*	RESTING	RESTING
March	RESTING	PONIES *(Pick up droppings.)*	RESTING *Harrow and fertilize. Roll if necessary.*
April	RESTING *Harrow and fertilize. Roll if necessary.*	RESTING *Harrow and fertilize. Roll if necessary.*	PONIES *(Pick up droppings.) Roll if necessary.*
May	PONIES *(Pick up droppings.)*	RESTING *Spot-spray large weeds, using knapsack weedkiller.*	RESTING *Spot-spray (as Plot B).*
June	RESTING *Spot-spray large weeds, using knapsack weedkiller.*	RESTING FOR HAY *Look out for ragwort. Pull up and burn.*	PONIES *(Pick up droppings.)*
July	PONIES *(Pick up droppings.)*	MAKE HAY *(June or early July.)*	PONIES
August	RESTING *Pull up any ragwort. Mow to top weeds.*	PONIES *(Pick up droppings.)*	RESTING *Pull up any ragwort. Mow to top weeds.*
September	RESTING *Fertilize if necessary.*	RESTING *Fertilize if necessary.*	PONIES *(Pick up droppings.)*
October	RESTING	PONIES *(Pick up droppings.)*	RESTING *Fertilize if necessary.*
November	RESTING	PONIES *(Pick up droppings.)*	PONIES

* For the welfare of the paddock, arrangements should be made for the ponies to live elsewhere during the winter—but this might not be practical.

38 Sample paddock maintenance plan

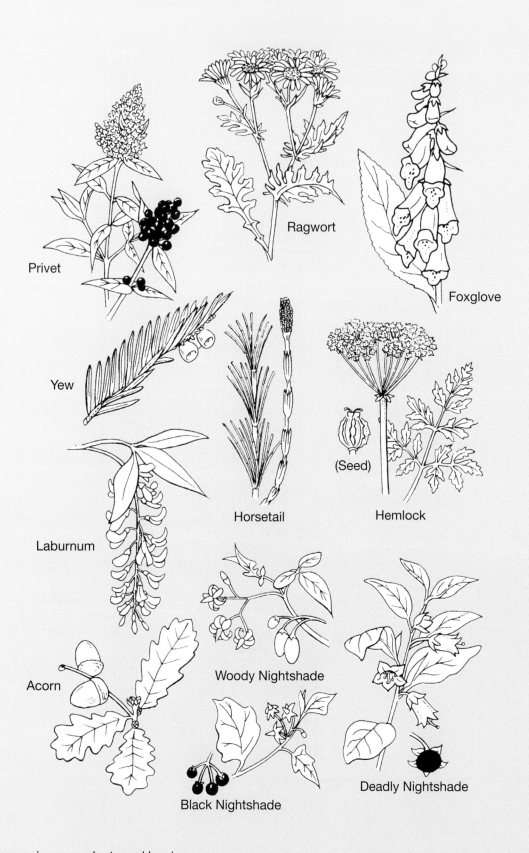

Privet

Ragwort

Foxglove

Yew

Horsetail

Hemlock

(Seed)

Laburnum

Acorn

Woody Nightshade

Black Nightshade

Deadly Nightshade

39 Some poisonous plants and berries.

FENCING *(Fig. 40)*

The fencing of land for use by horses differs from that needed by other stock in two essentials. Firstly the risk of injury to a horse is greater, and secondly, there is the possibility that a horse will jump the fence.

Hedges

If tough, strong and well-maintained, hedges are the first choice and have the additional advantage of providing windbreaks and shelter in all weathers. Country hedges are usually safe from poisonous plants, but they should be checked, particularly for yew and deadly nightshade *(fig. 39)*.

Hedges in urban areas sometimes contain ornamental trees and plants, such as laburnum, rhododendron and laurel, which are poisonous. These must be fenced out of reach. Privet and beech can also be toxic and have been known to cause problems. If you are in any doubt about plants in your hedges, seek expert advice.

Post and Rails

These are the second choice, even though the cost of erecting and maintaining them is high. A modern substitute is heavy duty plastic fencing, which is not as expensive to maintain. Post and rail fences should always be constructed from timber which has been pressure-treated with preservative to prevent rotting. Creosote is the best preservative, as horses will not chew timber treated with it.

Electric Fencing

Electrified fencing—preferably in the form of wide, coloured or white tape—has

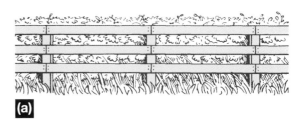

(a)

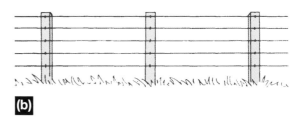

(b)

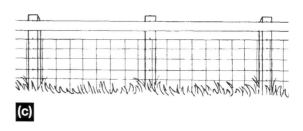

(c)

(d)

40 Types of fencing: **(a)** Post and rails with shelter hedge; **(b)** Plain wire; **(c)** Heavy-duty plastic with pig netting; **(d)** Makeshift.
(a) Hedge and/or post is recommended; (b) is acceptable; (c) is sometimes unavoidable; (d) is dangerous for horses.

the advantage of being easily erected and dismantled for use elsewhere, as well as being easily seen. It is undoubtedly an efficient type of fencing, and horses learn to respect it. If you use a length of wire, you should tie eye-catching strips of plastic or material round it at regular intervals.

Plain Wire Fencing

All wire fencing is potentially hazardous, and therefore must always be stretched taut between the posts. Use five or six strands of plain wire, or three strands of barbed wire. The lowest strand should be not less than 50cm (1ft 8in) from the ground to reduce the risk of injury. Where wire is used it is very unwise to graze horses in adjacent fields. They will inevitably bicker amongst themselves over the fence, and kicking and striking can result in very serious injury.

Pig Netting

Sometimes pig netting has to be used in a field to fence against sheep. Unfortunately it is dangerous for horses, who might put a foot through one of the holes. Shod horses have even been known to get the wire caught between hoof and shoe.

SHELTERS

Windbreaks

Horses need shelter from the wind, especially when it is accompanied by rain. Windbreaks or wind-screens formed by thick coppices—or even a high hedge along the north side of a field or along the side from which the prevailing wind blows—offer excellent protection, and horses generally prefer them to a shelter shed in winter.

Shelter Sheds *(Fig. 41)*

Though these offer all-year-round shelter from the elements, horses seldom resort to them in winter. However, in summer they are invaluable, as they provide much-needed protection against flies.

Ideally, a shelter shed should be built in the corner of a field, back to the prevailing wind and easily accessible for feeding. It should be positioned so that a horse cannot get trapped between it and the boundary fence. A circular shed, or one which is open-fronted or has a double doorway, will lessen the possibility of one horse being cornered and injured by another.

Cobwebs should not be removed from a shelter shed, as they act as a useful trap for flies.

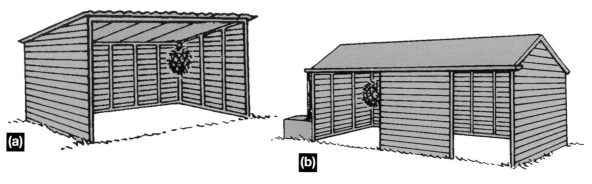

41 Shelter-sheds: **(a)** Single; **(b)** Double.

7. Watering

The importance of a clean and constant supply of water cannot be too strongly emphasised. A horse's health deteriorates rapidly if he is deprived of water or if he becomes dehydrated for any reason. When he knows that water is always available while in his stable or field, he will drink when necessary.

IN THE STABLE

Buckets or an automatic drinking bowl are the most satisfactory ways to provide drinking water in a stable.

Buckets

Rubber, plastic or polythene buckets are best because they are lightweight, noiseless and will not cause injury to the horse. Two buckets may be necessary to ensure a constant supply of water. They must be kept clean and the water frequently changed.

Stabled horses—particularly those in hard work—will not drink their fill if the water is stale or tainted by feed or bedding. Water fresh out of the tap is much more acceptable than water a few hours old. Place buckets (preferably, but not necessarily) in the corner of the box, either on the floor or suspended from a special ring-fitting, and away from the manger and the hay (where they may become soiled) and from the door (where they may be knocked over). If possible they should be within sight of the door so that their contents can be checked more easily.

Automatic Drinking Bowls

Though not all horses take readily to these bowls, they have their advantages.

To install them, special plumbing is necessary: for example, each bowl must have its own stopcock. They must be inspected and cleaned out each day. In winter they may freeze up and the pipes may burst; also, it is difficult to tell how much water each horse is drinking. But if they are working efficiently and the horses will use them confidently, it means that fresh, clean water is always available, and the carrying of heavy buckets is avoided.

IN THE PADDOCK

Field Troughs *(Fig. 42)*

The best way to water a horse kept at grass is to use field troughs filled from a piped water supply. Galvanised iron troughs are excellent. They should be approximately 1–2m (3–6ft) long, about 38cm (15in) deep and placed so that the top is about 60cm (2ft) from the ground. An outlet at the base is helpful for emptying. Troughs should be placed clear of trees so that leaves do not accumulate in them. The ground should be well drained, otherwise the earth surrounding the trough will become muddy in winter. The nearer the trough is to the house, gate or road, the better the chance that it will be regularly inspected. The water must be clear, and leaves and other matter floating on the surface scooped out daily.

Empty the trough occasionally and scrub it out with fresh water. If possible, leave it empty for a few hours to allow the air to sweeten it, but if a horse has no alternative water supply, it must not remain empty for long. In summer, when algae grows actively, the trough must be cleaned frequently.

During periods of frost and snow, attend to troughs at least twice a day. The horse will suffer no ill-effects if the ice is broken up and a large piece removed so that he can reach and drink the water.

The best way to fill a trough is a ballcock apparatus enclosed in a covered compartment at one end of it. The trough will automatically top itself up whenever the horse takes a drink. If a tap is used, it should be placed at ground level and the pipework fitted in such a way that it hugs the side of the trough with no projections on which the horse may injure himself.

Rivers, Streams and Ponds

Rivers or streams with a good approach and with water running over a gravel bottom are ideal, but streams with steep, unstable banks or a muddy or poached approach may prove to be inaccessible. A shallow stream with a sandy bottom may result in the horse taking up a small quantity of sand every time he drinks. If sand accumulates inside him it can cause an attack of sand colic.

Ponds of stagnant water, and streams which may have been polluted by industry or agriculture, should not be used and must be fenced off. An alternative source of clean, fresh water must be provided.

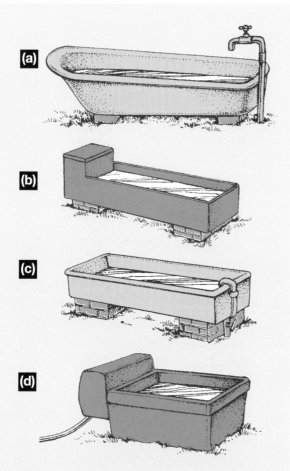

42 Field troughs connected to piped water:
(a) Unsuitable (sharp-edged and tap protruding); **(b)** Suitable (self-filling);
(c) Suitable (with concealed tap);
(d) Suitable (heavy duty plastic with concealed tap).

AWAY FROM HOME

On long rides the horse should be watered whenever the opportunity occurs, making use of any suitable stream or other source. This is important, especially when the weather is hot and humid.

At rallies and competitions or other long days away from home, arrangements must be made for the horse to have access to clean water from time to time during rest periods. To avoid the risk of possible cross-infection from troughs used by other horses it is advisable to take a water container and a bucket with you.

AFTER HARD WORK

A horse who has been galloping (for example in a cross-country event) should not be offered water until his breathing has returned to normal. Then it is advisable to limit it to half a bucketful. After about twenty minutes a further half-bucket may be offered; and twenty minutes later, under normal circumstances, he should be allowed as much as he likes.

After hunting or a long day, if possible a drink should be offered before the journey home. On returning to his stable, the horse will be keen to drink. If his water has been slightly warmed (to approximately 21°C (70°F)) he may drink a bucketful and come to no harm. Otherwise, treat him as described above for a horse who has been galloping. In normal circumstances, twenty minutes later he may drink as much as he wishes from his usual supply. *(See also On Return from a Hard Day, page 131.)*

8. Feeding

GENERAL PRINCIPLES

Grazing is the natural method of feeding, and grass is the natural food. In nature the horse eats little and often, grazing over extensive areas, occasionally resting, but never being too full of food to escape rapidly from danger. The way in which he uses the food that he eats—his digestive system—has gradually adapted itself to cope with his way of life. An awareness of his natural habitat and of the way nature has intended him to live, will guide you towards feeding him sensibly.

A stabled horse can be helped to thrive in his unnatural environment by, for example, having a daily routine to look forward to, and by receiving the basis of his diet (hay rather than grass) at regular intervals. In this way, for much of the day and night he will be able to pick at his hay whenever he feels the inclination to eat.

Obeying the *Rules of Good Feeding* (below) will help you to keep your horse healthy, contented and well able to do the work required of him.

Be observant and constantly aware of your horse's state of health so that you can make any necessary adjustments to his diet before things go wrong. Remember the traditional quotation: '*The eye of the Master keepeth the horse fat*'.

RULES OF GOOD FEEDING

1 Keep clean, fresh waterw available.
2 Feed little and often.
3 Feed according to work, temperament and condition.
4 Feed at the same times each day
5 Do not work hard immediately after feeding.
6 Feed adequate roughage.
7 Introduce changes of food gradually.
8 Feed clean, good quality forage.
9 Feed something succulent every day.
10 Keep feed bowls and water buckets clean.

1. Keep clean, fresh water available.

The body of an adult horse is 60 to 70% water, and although a horse can lose almost all his body fat and half the body protein, and survive, a 20% loss of water can prove fatal. As a rough guide, horses drink 27–54 litres (6–12 gallons) a day, but may need more in hot weather.

Generally speaking, a horse should have access to clean, fresh water at all times and particularly before feeding. In winter, break ice on field troughs at least twice a day (morning and evening). In summer, keep troughs clear of leaves and algae. *(See also Watering, page 69.)*

2. Feed little and often.

Concentrates should be given in several small feeds daily, rather than in one or two large ones. Horses' and ponies' stomachs—from 8–14 litres (1–3 gallons) in capacity—are relatively small for such large animals: roughly the size of a football. By the time that the food reaches the stomach, the volume will have doubled, due to the addition of digestive juices. Digestion is most efficient when the stomach is about two-thirds full, so large feeds will not be properly digested and much of the food value will be wasted.

Food passes through the digestive system by rhythmical muscular contractions (peristalsis). This requires a reasonably constant supply of food.

At most, a horse must never be left for more than eight hours without food, so adequate hay or hay substitute must be fed to the stabled horse at night.

3. Feed according to work, temperament and condition.

Work: feed according to the work done and the size of horse or pony. As exercise and work are increased, the diet must be adjusted to produce more energy and to build up muscle. If work is decreased, or if the horse is laid up through injury or illness, the concentrates must be reduced and the roughage in the diet increased to compensate.

Temperament: all horses are individuals and must be treated as such. Some become excitable on oats and require an alternative form of concentrate. Sluggish horses sometimes benefit from more energy-giving foods to encourage them to be active.

Condition: whether a horse is stabled and working hard, or resting out at grass, he should be in good condition. If he is not, it

may be that he is not receiving the correct amount or type of food, and his diet must be adjusted accordingly. For example, if he is too thin he may need more food or a more nutritious diet: and if he is too fat, he may need less. *(See also* Condition, *page 119.)*

His well-being may also be influenced by:

* *Age:* both old and young horses need specialised feeding. Old horses may lose condition easily because they can no longer make such good use of their food. They may need an increase of cooked or processed concentrates which are easier to digest.

   Young horses who are growing may also need extra concentrates in a correctly balanced ration. They need more vitamins and minerals than a mature animal.

* *Brood mares:* pregnant mares, or those feeding a foal at foot (lactating) need extra concentrates. Specially formulated stud cubes contain the extra feed value, vitamins and minerals.

* *Type:* horses and ponies of the same height and weight do not necessarily thrive on the same diet. For example, ponies with Thoroughbred or Arab blood may require careful feeding—perhaps a more palatable diet—to maintain condition, whereas native ponies are more accommodating, thrive on bulk feeds (hay or grass), and may easily get laminitis if the diet is too rich.

* *Climate:* a large part of a horse's food is used to maintain body temperature. A horse or pony living out in cold, wet weather will need extra food to maintain condition and keep warm.

* *Company:* loss of condition could be due to constant bullying by companions, which may impede eating and resting. However, an animal who is used to

company may pine and lose condition if suddenly isolated.

- *Illness*: this may require a special diet. Your vet will advise you.
- *Worms:* these are one of the most likely cause of poor condition *(see WORM CONTROL, page 154).*
- *Teeth*: these may need attention *(see TEETH, page 121).*
- *Stable vices:* wind sucking and crib biting can interfere with digestion. Weaving and box walking waste energy.

4. Feed at the same times each day.

The horse is a creature of habit. His routine, once established, will help him to settle down and thrive. Plan to feed him at times which fit in with your other commitments so that you can keep to a regular timetable.

5. Do not work hard immediately after feeding.

Allow time for digestion: how much will depend on the severity of the work and the size of the feed. As a rough guide, the horse may take twenty minutes to eat his feed, one-and-a-half hours to digest it, and then be ready for normal work.

Never work a horse fast after a full feed or when his stomach is full of hay or grass, because:

- He cannot digest his food while galloping.
- A full stomach will take up too much room, which will prevent the diaphragm working effectively and the lungs from expanding. This will affect the horse's breathing.

6. Feed adequate roughage.

Feed plenty of roughage (hay or grass); it is the basis of any diet and keeps the digestive system working and healthy. The bulk of the hay ration is best given after work and at night, when the horse has time to eat it and to digest it quietly.

Adding some roughage in the form of chaff or bran to concentrate feeds helps the horse to masticate properly, so that the digestive juices can act more effectively.

Hay or grass should normally make up at least two-thirds of the diet.

7. Introduce any changes of food gradually.

In order to safeguard against indigestion, any changes of food should be made gradually. This will allow the digestive system to adjust effectively to the new food. The digestion of bulk feeds, hay, grass, etc., takes place in the large intestines, where bacteria (microbes) break down the food.

If sudden changes are made, there will not be enough of the appropriate bacteria to break down the new type of food which, being undigested, will be of no use to the horse and might even give him colic. Any changes should be made gradually over a period of days to give the horse's digestive system time to adjust to the new food.

8. Feed clean, good quality forage.

Feed clean and good quality forage only. The horse is a fussy feeder and will relish only the best. Musty and dusty food not only adversely affects condition, but is harmful, as is food contaminated by vermin.

9. Feed something succulent every day.

The stabled horse needs succulent feed, such as green food or carrots, to compensate for the lack of grass. If practicable, the horse should also be grazed in hand for ten minutes or so, or turned out for a short period.

10. Keep feed bowls and water buckets clean.

Dried-on food will taste sour and dirty buckets will put the horse off eating or drinking.

FORAGE

Concentrated Food

The horse should receive a balanced diet and enjoy his feeds. Traditional feeds based on oats, maize and barley should be fed with a vitamin and mineral supplement, particularly for providing calcium. Proprietary brands of mixes and cubes have minerals and vitamins added and need no extra supplements.

Cubes (Nuts)

Cubes are a carefully formulated mixture of ingredients, including added vitamins and minerals. There are many brands and varieties designed for different purposes (*Horse and Pony*, *Racehorse*, *Stud*, etc.). The well-known proprietary brands are reliable and their food value is always consistent. Each sack is stamped with an expiry date and should be used before then.

Cubes may be used as a substitute for all or part of the concentrates. Before buying them, read the instructions on the sack and choose the right type according to the needs of your horse. This is important because of the possible danger in feeding too much high-protein food to certain types of horse and pony.

Cubes are best fed with chaff, as this stops the horse eating too quickly and ensures that the cubes are moistened with saliva before being swallowed, which prevents choking. It is usual to dampen this dry type of food with a little water when it is being mixed, directly before feeding.

Mixes

These are made of the same balanced content as cubes. They also have a date-stamp, which should be carefully noted, but have not been processed into cube form. The well-known proprietary brands are recommended. The disadvantage is that when stored they may deteriorate more quickly than cubes.

Advantages of Mixes and Cubes

- They save storing several different kinds of grain.
- They save the mixing of feeds.
- They ensure that the horse has a standardized, balanced diet, with the necessary vitamins and minerals.
- With *Horse and Pony* cubes or *Pasture Mix*, the animals are less likely to hot up than when only oats are fed.

Disadvantages of Mixes and Cubes

- It is difficult to detect the quality of the ingredients.
- Fed in excess, they can become boring.
- They tend to deteriorate when stored.
- When the feed consists only of one type of mix or cube, adjustment of the diet is not possible as it is with traditional feeding.

Oats

Experience has shown that oats are the best all-round food for horses, but they must be fed sparingly to ponies, who respond rapidly to concentrated food and may become excitable (hot up) and therefore difficult to manage and to ride.

The grains should be large, hard and clean. They may be fed whole, but will be easier to digest if bruised, rolled or crushed. Having once been treated in this way, oats should not be stored for more than about three weeks, since they will go stale and lose their nutritional value. This will also happen if they are rolled or crushed too severely. Oats are best fed with chaff (of hay or straw), or a little bran, or with a mixture of both and some form of calcium-rich feed or supplement.

Barley

Rolled or crushed barley can be used to replace part of the oat ration. The grains should be bright, clean and plump. Barley should never be fed whole unless it is well cooked (boiled).

Micronised flaked barley is more easily digested and may be used as a substitute for oats if a horse hots up, or to provide variety. As with oats, it should be fed with bran or chaff and some form of calcium-rich feed or supplement.

Boiled barley is mixed in with a feed or fed warm as part of a bran mash. Because it is easily digestible, boiled barley is a useful food, especially after hard exercise such as hunting. Before cooking, the barley should be soaked for a few hours, then brought to the boil and simmered until the husks split and the grains are soft (two to three hours).

Flaked Maize

Flaked maize is a traditional feed used in small amounts to add variety to the diet, flaked maize is fattening, as it has a high carbohydrate content. It can cause overheating by increasing the sugar content of the blood and should be used sparingly.

Wheat

Wheat is not suitable for horses, except in the form of bran.

Bran

A by-product of the milling of wheat, bran may be added to the feed to encourage mastication, to add bulk and to assist digestion. It can be fed dry if the horse's droppings are loose, as it has a constipating effect. If it is very fine, it has little feed value. When fed damp it is a mild laxative. Fed in excess it can affect growth and health, because it inhibits calcium absorption, so should be fed with a calcium-rich feed such as soaked sugar beet or limestone flour.

Bran mash is a palatable warm feed which can be easily digested by a sick horse. It may also be fed as a mild laxative, and in this way may be of use if the horse is laid off work. To make it, put 1–1.5kg (about 2–3lb) of bran, depending on the size of the horse, into a bucket. Pour boiling water over it until it becomes damp throughout. Stir very thoroughly, adding up to one tablespoon of salt or Epsom salts. Then cover with a sack and leave until it has become cool enough to eat. A little linseed jelly mixed into it adds to the taste and is beneficial to the horse.

Linseed

This is provided either as jelly or as a gruel or tea. It is generally fed to horses during the winter only, to improve condition and to give a gloss to the coat. The main advantage of linseed is its palatability.

Linseed jelly: allow 57g (2oz) of seed, weighed before cooking. Put it in a large pan and cover with 1.7 litres (approximately 3 pints) of water. Soak for twenty-four hours to soften. Bring to the boil and simmer until all the seed has split. It is essential to cook it thoroughly, as when partially cooked, or uncooked, it is poisonous.

Beware of the thick jelly bubbling over the side of the pan, as it has an unusual property of pulling all the contents out over the stove! Mix it with the evening feed while still warm. Feed once—or at the most twice—a week, normally after hard work.

Linseed tea: prepare as for linseed jelly, but use more water. Linseed tea can be used as a gruel (warm drink) or instead of boiling water to make a bran mash.
NOTE: Any linseed tea or jelly which is left over must be fed within twenty-four hours.

Boiled Barley and Linseed
Soak 0.5kg (approximately 1lb) barley with 57g (2oz) linseed for twenty-four hours. Cook until the linseed is in jelly form and the barley has swollen and split. Mix in with the evening feed while still warm.

Chaff or Chop
Chaff or chop is either hay by itself or hay mixed with a small proportion of oat straw which has been passed through a chaff cutter. It is then fed with the corn feed. It adds roughage to the diet; aids mastication; prevents the horse from bolting his food; and helps digestion by breaking up the mass of cereal feed, allowing efficient use of the digestive juices.

If you have a chaff cutter (with appropriate guards) you can ensure that good quality forage is used to produce your chaff, and it can also be used for cutting suitable fresh green food to add variety to the diet. This should be fed immediately after it has been cut. (*See* Green Foods *on the next page.*)

Certain proprietary brands of chaff made from top-quality hay (sometimes lucerne/ alfalfa) are specially processed and packed to ensure that the nutritional value is retained and that the chaff is dust free.

Molassed Chaff
This is chaff treated with molasses to make it slightly damp and palatable. Various proprietary brands of this chaff or chop, some with additives such as oil or limestone flour, are available.

For ponies prone to problems due to sugars in their diet, unmolassed chaff is available.

Dried Sugar Beet Pulp
This is a useful source of digestible fibre with a high calcium content. It is palatable and energy-producing; however, soaked sugar beet contains so much water that a horse would have to eat a great deal before it made any difference to his way of going.

Sugar beet pulp must always be soaked in cold water for twelve hours before being fed to a horse. In its dry state it can cause choking and will swell in the stomach— probably resulting in colic. It should be prepared in a ratio of about three parts cold water to one part pulp. No more than 0.5kg (about 1lb) weighed dry or 1.5kg (about 3lb) weighed after soaking, should be fed per day. Once prepared it should be fed within twenty-four hours, as the fermentation process, which begins soon after it is mixed with water, will be harmful. Sugar beet should not be soaked in hot water, which increases the speed of fermentation.

The pulp can be purchased in cube form

which, being densely compressed, should be soaked for longer, a minimum of twenty-fourhours, and in a greater quantity of water, until the cubes are completely dissolved.

Both forms of sugar beet should be stored in a cool, dry place, as once the bag is opened, mould quickly forms.

Take care to differentiate between cubes of sugar beet and the other types of cube.

For ponies prone to problems due to sugars in their diet, unmolassed sugar beet pulp is available.

Succulent Foods

A conscientious horsemaster will be constantly on the lookout for good grass in a location where it is safe to graze a stabled horse. You should also seek succulent foods to add to the horse's diet. The latter makes the feed more appetising, and both provide bulk and variety and help to satisfy the natural craving for grass, as well as providing valuable vitamins

Grazing

All horses benefit from a certain amount of grass every day. For stabled horses even ten minutes' grazing in hand helps to keep a natural balance in the diet. It also ensures that they maintain an interest in their feed. Many a stale horse has been helped by 'Doctor Green'.

Green Foods

For the horse confined to his stable, every effort should be made to provide fresh-cut grass every day. It should be fed immediately after picking and not allowed to wilt.

NEVER feed lawn mowings and plants from roadside verges *(see Food, page 148)*.

Carrots

Carrots are particularly acceptable during winter months, when there is little goodness in grass. They are highly nutritious. Some horses also relish swedes, mangels, turnips, beetroots or parsnips.

To prepare any of these root vegetables, first scrub them well under a running tap. Large finger-shaped slices or whole roots are best. Square or round pieces of root must not be fed, as they are liable to become lodged in the throat and so choke the horse.

Begin by feeding 0.5kg (approximately 1lb) a day, and increase the amount to 1kg (approximately 2lb) or even more when the horse is accustomed to them.

Apples

These are always especially appreciated, but too many can cause colic. Small apples must be cut in pieces, to ensure that they are not swallowed whole.

Hydroponic Food

This is a fresh feed of green barley grown in water with nutrients, under artificial conditions, in a special cabinet. It has the advantage of containing the same nutrients as grass, and it freshens the palate.

Additives and Food Supplements

Salt

This is an essential part of a horse's diet. It is best made available as a salt lick in a special container fixed to the stable wall. A lump of rock salt should be provided in the field for horses at grass. In each case the horse is able to have a lick whenever he feels that he needs salt. Alternatively, up to a dessert-spoon of cooking salt per day can be split between the feeds. The amount will depend on the size of the animal and on the type of work being done. More will be needed if the horse is working hard and/or sweating for any other reason. *(See also* ELECTROLYTES, *pages 86 and 131.)*

Epsom Salts

These have a cleansing effect on the system. They are a useful addition to the weekly bran mash given before the horse's rest day. Feed up to one tablespoon depending on the size of the horse.

Proprietary Supplements

Proprietary brands of complete feed will have a correct balance of minerals and vitamins, and will not need extra supplements. Traditional feeds of cereals such as oats, bran, barley, etc., may need additional vitamins and minerals, particularly calcium. The mineral content of cereals varies according to the soil in which they are grown.

A good variety of supplements are on the market but get expert advice before choosing one and do not mix different brands without consulting your vet, as the ingredients may react against one another. If supplements are overfed, serious disorders may result.

Molasses

A by-product of the manufacture of sugar, molasses is of high nutritional value. As this feed is tasty, it is useful in persuading shy feeders to eat other foods, but on no account must it be used to persuade horses to eat inferior food. Do not feed it at the same time as sugar beet (which is also a sugar by-product) but molassed sugar beet pulp is acceptable.

Dilute (with a small amount of warm water) up to two tablespoonfuls of molasses—which in its liquid form resembles black treacle—and sprinkle it over, or mix it with, the feed. Alternatively, buy it in meal form (molassed meal), in which case a handful per feed is sufficient.

Bulk Foods (Roughage)

Hay

Hay provides all the bulk needed as a substitute for grass. Plenty of good quality hay should always be available for the stabled horse and for a horse living out during the winter.

A good sample of hay will be sweet-smelling, a light greenish-brown colour throughout, crisp and free from dust.

Good hay is made in dry, sunny weather, when the grass is coming into flower and before it has gone to seed. It should not be used before November of the year in which it is made. It will then be mature enough to be fed without causing digestive problems. The new hay should be introduced gradually by mixing it with that of the previous year.

The nutritional value of hay is only assessed by analysis, and appearances can be misleading. A dark yellow or brown colour indicates deterioration. Slices that smell musty, or that do not shake free immediately, will have been baled when the hay was damp. Both are bad for horses.

Meadow hay comes from pasture permanently laid down to grass. It is fairly soft and contains a good variety of grasses—rye grass, cock's-foot, timothy, etc., with a bottom of low-growing grasses, clovers and herbs. Well-made meadow hay is enjoyed by horses, but it must not contain harmful and poisonous plants such as ragwort.

Seed hay is made from a specially grown crop, usually rye grass. When grown with other seeds, such as clover or timothy, it is known as mixture hay. Seed hay is higher in nutritional value than meadow hay. It is lighter in colour and harder to the touch. Seed heads of the crop concerned can usually be seen. It is a quality crop and excellent feed for horses.

Lucerne/Alfalfa is a clover-type plant grown and processed in the same way as hay. It has a very concentrated nutritional value with a high proportion of essential amino acids in the protein that it contains. It also has a high calcium content and contains very little phosphorous. If used as part of a horse's diet, the concentrates fed must be reduced.

Soaked hay: horses with allergies to the spores in hay, or those with coughs or colds, will often benefit from having their hay soaked. This is best achieved by immersing a full hay net in clean water or by dousing it thoroughly with a hose. In both cases allow it to drain for a few minutes and then feed it to the horse.

Haylage, vacuum-packed, semi-wilted grass: this bulk feed is particularly useful for horses who are allergic to hay or straw dust. There are various proprietary brands, all of which are baled in waterproof airtight bags. Once a bag has been opened, or the seal broken, the contents must be used straight away, as they will become mouldy in a matter of days. If a bag has been badly damaged, the contents should be disposed of, because there is a danger of fatal botulism.

Semi-wilted grass is usually higher in protein than hay and should be fed in similar or smaller quantities, according to the manufacturer's instructions. Protein in the remainder of the diet may need to be reduced.

Silage

Cattle silage is not a suitable feed for horses as there is a high risk of contamination by harmful bacteria, which can be fatal. It may also be too rich in protein. A special form of silage for horses is sometimes available. Its properties are similar to vacuum-packed, semi-wilted grass, but it may well be richer and should be introduced very gradually over a period of two or three weeks.

Oat Straw

This sometimes makes up a proportion of the bulk food, used either on its own or in conjunction with hay when making chaff. It can provide up to one-third of the roughage fed and is better than very poor hay, but its nutritional value is low. The concentrate ration should be adjusted to allow for this. Barley and wheat straws are not suitable.

FEEDING SCALES

How Much Food Does a Horse or Pony Need?

As a rough guide, the (dry) weight of total food for a day will be 2.5% of body weight. If the animal is too fat, he should have less than this; if he is too thin, he will need more until his weight is normal. You should take into account the fact that every horse and pony is an individual. They differ in type according to their breeding and they differ in their ability to utilise the nutrients in the food that they are given.

A good horsemaster should feed according to what they see and feel and adjust the feeding to suit the individual.

A *good doer* will readily eat up and will thrive. He may even be greedy and gain too much weight.

A *bad doer* is difficult to keep in condition despite every care and attention. He may need a diet which is easier to digest, or one of a higher nutritional value. With the help of your vet the problem may be quickly identified, but dealing with it will always take patience and time. *(See* Causes of Bad Condition, *page 120.)*

A *shy* or *dainty feeder* may have to be tempted with succulents. Shy feeders sometimes eat up best at night when all is quiet. For them, feeding little and often is vital. A late-night feed can therefore be beneficial.

The total amount of food that a horse will eat daily can be worked out fairly accurately if you know his weight when he is in good condition. There are various formulae for estimating a horse's weight in relation to his girth and length other than by weighing him on a weighbridge or in a farm weight-crate.

Variations in weight can be a useful monitor of growth, health and training programme, and a comparison can be made simply by measuring his girth circumference behind the elbows and noting variations week by week.

Calculating the Total Amount of Food Per Day

Use the formula: $\dfrac{\text{weight} \times 2.5}{100}$

Examples
A 12hh (121.8cm) pony weighing 300kg would have an approximate food capacity of: 300 x 2.5/100 = 7.5kg (16½lb).

A 14hh (142.2cm) pony weighing 375kg would have an approximate food capacity of 375 x 2.5/100 = 9.375kg (20½ lb).

A 15.2hh (157cm) horse weighing 475kg would have an approximate food capacity of 475 x 2.5/100 = 11.875kg (26lb).

A 16.2hh (167.2cm) horse weighing 600kg would have an approximate food capacity of 600 x 2.5/100 = 15kg (33lb).

These quantities are guidelines only, and the amount of feed may have to be adjusted according to the needs of the horse, and to the demands made of him.

Adjusting the Diet According to the Work Required *(Figs. 43 and 44)*

As work is increased or decreased, the diet should be adjusted. The total daily weight of the food will remain the same, but as work is gradually increased, so some of the bulk feed (grass and hay) should be gradually reduced. Concentrates (corn and nuts, etc.) should be increased to supply the extra nutrients needed to build up muscle, to replace worn cells and to supply extra energy. The type of concentrate will depend on the temperament and needs of the individual horse. In general terms, the harder the work a horse is asked to do, the greater should be the percentage of concentrates. In the same way, when work is decreased, the amount of bulk feed should be increased and the concentrates reduced. The following *Levels of Work* are a guide to assessing the needs of the horse.

Maintenance

The horse is able to remain healthy and maintain all bodily functions, such as eating, breathing, keeping warm, growing a summer or winter coat, or repairing any injuries. Any working horse or pony who is put out to grass for a break from routine work will be living at maintenance level.

Light Work

Maintenance plus up to one hour's hacking daily, mostly walking and trotting. Very little cantering.

Medium Work

Maintenance plus an average of one-and-a-half hour's hacking daily, with active work which might include cantering, jumping, Pony Club rallies and competing at shows.

Hard Work

Maintenance plus final fitness programme for participating in:
- *Pony Club camp*
- *Polo*
- *Hunting*
- *Regular mounted games*
- *Team Training*
- *One-day horse trials*
- *Long distance training*

Very Hard Work

Maintenance plus preparations for Point-to-Points, Three-Day Eventing, and Long Distance Competitions.

FEEDING ARRANGEMENTS

Keeping to a Routine

Having decided on a suitable diet for your horse, plan your feeding arrangements according to the *Rules of Good Feeding*, page 71. Work out a routine that takes your horse's needs and your other commitments into account so that you can feed at the same times each day.

The horse should be given sufficient bulk feed at appropriate times in the daily routine. *(See A Programme of Stable Routine, page 57.)*

If the horse lives outdoors, the same principles apply, unless the diet consists of only bulk feed and the grazing is sufficient, in which case the horse can feed himself *(see The Horse at Grass and his Paddock, page 59, and, in particular, Midwinter, page 61).*

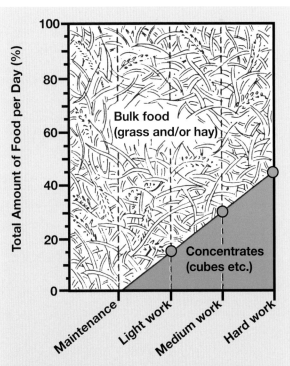

43 Chart showing diet related to work for a pony of approximately 14.2hh (148cms). Note the importance of bulk feed.

	Work Level	Guidelines
For a 12hh Pony Capacity = 7.5kg (16½ lb) per day.	Maintenance	The pony requires only good grass and/or hay (bulk feed)
	Light Work	The pony requires only good grass and/or hay.
	Medium Work	15% of the bulk feed may be replaced by concentrates (horse and pony cubes—beware of oats): i.e. 1kg (approx. 2¼ lb), divided into one or two feeds a day.
	Hard Work	Up to 30% of the bulk feed may be replaced by concentrates: i.e. approx. 2kg (4½lb), divided into two or three feeds per day.
For a 14hh Pony Capacity = 9.3kg (20½lb) per day. Depending on the temperament, behaviour and fitness of the pony, the amount and type of concentrates may need adjusting.	Maintenance	The pony requires only good grass and/or hay.
	Light Work	10% to 15% of the bulk feed may be replaced with concentrates: i.e. 1 to 1.5kg (2 to 3¼lb) divided into one or two feeds per day.
	Medium Work	Up to 25% concentrates in the diet: that is, up to 2.25kg (5lb) divided into two or three feeds per day.
	Hard Work	Up to 33.3% concentrates in the diet: i.e. up to 3kg (6½lb) in three or four feeds per day.
For a 15.2hh Horse Capacity = 11.8kg (26lb) per day. Horses of 15.2hh and over need feeding according to their individual requirements. The small horse with Thoroughbred blood will not be as hardy as a pony type, and may not make such good use of the natural food—good grass or hay.	Maintenance	The small horse should need only good grass and/or hay in good weather. Up to 10% of the roughage may be replaced with concentrates, depending on condition: that is, up to 1.2kg (approximately 2½lb) in one or two feeds per day.
	Light Work	20% of the bulk feed may be replaced by concentrates: i.e., 2.5kg (5½lb) in two or three feeds per day.
	Medium Work	33.3% of the bulk feed may be replaced by concentrates: i.e., 4kg (approximately 9lb) in three feeds per day.
	Hard Work	40% of the bulk feed may be replaced by concentrates: i.e., 4.7kg (10½lb) in three or four feeds per day.

44 Guidelines for adjusting a horse's diet according to the work required. The tables above and on the next page give amounts which are rounded up or down to the nearest sensible figure according to circumstances. NOTE: If the horse is being given a high-protein diet, the balance between work and feed becomes vital. If there is a sudden need to lay the horse off work, the proportion of concentrates must be lowered immediately, or protein poisoning will result. *(Continues on facing page.)*

	Work Level	Guidelines
For a 16.2hh Horse Capacity = 15kg (33lb) per day. Horses of this size must be fed according to their individual requirements. Their type and the kind of work they are expected to do can vary enormously. If they are asked to work hard or very hard in competitions or races they will need careful feeding to produce the energy required.	Maintenance	Good quality grass or hay may have to be supplemented to maintain good condition, with up to 15% in concentrates replacing bulk: i.e., 2.25kg (5lb) in two feeds per day.
	Light Work	25% of the diet as concentrates: 3.75kg (approximately 8lb) in three feeds per day.
	Medium Work	33.3% of the diet as concentrates: 5kg (11lb) in three or four feeds per day.
	Hard Work	40% of the diet as concentrates: 6kg (approximately 13lb) in three or four feeds per day.
	Very Hard Work	All horses in very hard work will need expert care. It may be necessary to feed up to 45% of the diet in the form of concentrates, split up into four feeds per day.

Making Up and Giving Feeds

Feeds should be made up and mixed in a container before being taken to the horse. It is important to know the exact quantities that you are feeding. Weigh your scoop, then weigh each ingredient separately to find the weight of a scoopful of each. Dry feeds, especially those containing bran, should be dampened.

Stabled Horses

Stabled horses are most conveniently fed from a manger, but if you do not have one, use a plastic or heavy rubber feed bowl, which will not tip over easily, on the floor. This should be removed from the box after the horse has finished his feed. Whether you use a manger or a feed bowl, it must be kept clean and should be washed out each day. Wasteful feeders (horses who throw their feed out of the manger) can be defeated by keeping a brick or large round stone in the manger or by fitting bars on the sides of the manger.

Horses at Grass

Horses at grass should be fed either from a bowl on the ground, or from a manger hung over the fence or gate *(fig. 45)*. There should be one feed bowl for each horse in the field. Bowls should be well apart (out of kicking range) and must be kept clean. If necessary, tie up all the horses for twenty minutes or so while they eat their feeds. This will ensure that they eat their own feeds and that all receive a fair share; but they should not be left unattended during this time.

Feeding Hay

Feeding from a haynet is probably the most economical method, both in the stable and in the field. It also has the advantage of being easily weighed. It must always be tied up high enough, so that when it is empty, a horse will not catch his foot in it. Tie up as in *fig. 46*, using a quick-release knot *(fig. 27).*

In the Stable

Hay is best fed from a haynet hung at about eye level. The natural feeding position is from ground level, but this is wasteful, as some of the hay will get trampled and soiled.

Out of Doors

When a haynet is used for feeding, it should be attached (well clear of the ground) to a fence or tree, and tied as illustrated.

Storing Forage

If possible, store forage away from the stable. It should be kept in vermin-proof bins, free from damp. The bins should have either secure catches or lids that are heavy enough to prevent a horse from raising them. Concentrates in particular must be safeguarded. Horses have been known to die of colic through overeating after having broken loose and strayed into the feed room.

Hay and straw should be stacked on wooden slats which allow the air to circulate underneath and prevent damp from rising into the bottom bales.

ESSENTIAL NUTRIENTS IN THE DIET

The food and water that a horse eats and drinks provide him with the nutrients of life. The basic nutrients are: water, carbohydrates, fats, proteins, minerals and vitamins.

45 Feed containers: **(a)** Portable manger; **(b)** Rubber feed bowl; **(c)** Metal feed bowl; **(d)** Plastic feed box.

Water

Water is vital. It is present in every cell in the body, and is involved in every chemical and physical process needed to maintain life: i.e. metabolism. Water carries all the nutrients around the body, regulates body temperature, acts as a lubricant, and helps in the removal of waste and toxins. A horse drinks up to 55 litres (12 gallons) a day.

Carbohydrates

These provide the energy for all body functions: the fuel for growth and body development, activity and warmth.

They are found in cellulose (grass and other forage) which makes up the larger part of the diet, and in starch (cereals) and sugar (molasses). Providing a constant supply of hay is a safe way of ensuring that the horse has all the carbohydrates that he requires to sustain him.

Extra energy food can be given in the form of concentrates (cereal feeds).
- Lack of carbohydrate results in thinness, loss of energy and a cold horse.
- Too much carbohydrate will result in a fat horse.

Fats

Carbohydrates can be stored in the form of fat. Fat and oil provide a concentrated source of slow-acting energy, producing a subcutaneous (under the skin) layer which helps to regulate body temperature and keeps the skin and coat in good condition.

A small but adequate amount of oil is present in proprietary brands of feeds and oats. Richer amounts are found in milk-based feeds and linseed. Additional oil is not normally needed, but cod liver oil may be used for vitamin value in winter.

Proteins

Proteins are for body building and tissue repair. They are made up of a number of amino acids, about half of which can be formed within the body. The other half, essential amino acids, must be provided in the diet.

Proteins are found in all foodstuffs to varying degrees, but the essential amino acids in cereals—particularly oats—are sufficient for the horse in normal work.

Lack of protein results in poor growth, poor performance, lack of appetite and condition, and a poor supply of milk in a brood mare. Excess protein is dangerous. It causes bodily and mental stress; overworks the kidneys; and can poison the whole system.

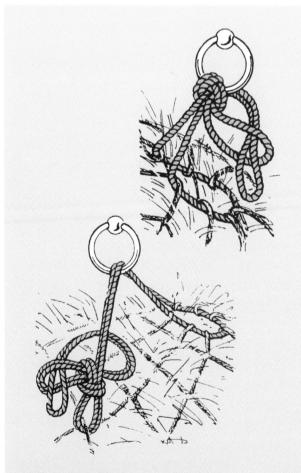

46 Two ways of tying up a haynet.

Peas, beans, lucerne and soya meal all contain a high proportion of the essential amino acids, but should be fed with caution and only to horses doing very hard work. Proprietary mixes and cubes contain appropriate amounts. As the workload increases, so do protein requirements—whether for the demands of high performance or for pregnancy and lactation. Energy food must also be increased so that the balance of protein and energy food is maintained.

Minerals

Minerals are necessary for all the functions of the body. The formation and upkeep of the skeletal frame (bone structure) makes the biggest demand for them. They are present in the fluid contents of cells and are involved in enzyme action, the nervous system, hormone system, and blood formation too.

Minerals are found in varying quantities in top-quality hay, grass and cereals and in low-growing herbs in good pasture *(see THE PASTURE, page 63).* They are divided into two groups—major minerals and trace elements.

Major Minerals

Calcium and *phosphorus* combine with vitamin D for bone development and maintenance. (Bones are partially made of calcium and phosphorus.)

The balance between these two minerals is very important and should be from 1.3% to 2% calcium to 1% phosphorus. A balanced diet will contain a mixture of feeds, so that this ratio is likely to be maintained.

If physical or reproductive demands on the body are increased, the need for both these minerals can increase by up to double the normal maintenance level, and must

be supplied. The extra concentrates that the horse is given will obviously supply some minerals, but it may be necessary to give supplementary calcium. Phosphorus is generously provided in cereal foodstuff.

• Oats, barley, bran, peas, beans and maize have too much phosphorus in relation to calcium.

• Sugar beet pulp, cane molasses and lucerne have a high proportion of calcium in relation to phosphorus.

• Limestone flour and bonemeal supply extra calcium.

• To ensure the necessary increase and balance of minerals in the diet, change to the appropriate type of good quality cube or mix as the workload increases.

• Calcium is also vitally important in the blood, though in small quantities. It aids blood clotting and is an essential factor in muscle contraction and nerve impulses.

Magnesium is needed for bone structure and as an enzyme activator.

Electrolytes (sodium, chlorine and potassium) are also major elements, referred to as tissue salts, and are essential for the regulation of body fluids.

• Sodium and chlorine can be supplied as common salt (sodium chloride). *(See also SALT, page 77.)*

• Potassium is found in low herbal growth, tree bark and wood. It can be supplemented in the form of cider vinegar.

Sulphur is needed for the production of enzymes, hormones and amino acids.

Trace Elements

These minerals are required in very small amounts, but they are essential for the correct functioning of the bodily processes.

Iron and copper are particularly important because they are involved in the formation of blood, whilst selenium is important because it interacts with vitamin E for muscle integrity. You should probably increase these three if demands on the body are extreme.

NOTE: Most of the essential minerals are present in the normal diet, but in some areas the land may be deficient in one or more of the following: potassium, iron, zinc, sulphur, copper and selenium. (See THE PASTURE, page 63.)

Vitamins

Vitamins are required for normal growth and basic well-being. High quality pasture and sunshine supply some of them, and bacterial action in the large intestine manufacture others.

There are two groups:

1. Fat-soluble, which can be stored in the body fat—vitamins A, D, E and K.

2. Water-soluble, which are required daily—vitamin B group and vitamin C. These are produced by bacteria in the intestines and can be reduced by sudden changes in the diet or by a course of antibiotics.

	Vitamin	Used for	Provided by
1. Fat-soluble	A	Vision, growth, reproduction, formation of tissue	Natural herbage and carrots
	D	Bone structure	Sunlight on the coat. Cod liver oil* Soya oil
	E	Quality of muscle structure, fertility	Green forage and hay
	K	Blood clotting	Green forage and hay
2. Water-soluble	B Group	Utilisation of food, correct functioning of the nervous system	Bacterial action on green food and forage in the gut
	C	Correct functions of the blood and blood vessels (interacting with iron and copper); Defence mechanism	Bacterial action in the gut

The excessive use of cod liver oil as a winter source of Vitamin D can be dangerous, as it will unbalance the vitamin/mineral content of the diet. Minerals and vitamins interact and must not be unbalanced by erratic supplementation.

47 The two groups of vitamins, and their uses and sources.

9. Clothing

RUGS AND BLANKETS

In normal circumstances, the horse's own coat will keep him comfortably warm, but if he has been clipped, or if his coat is very fine and he is groomed regularly, he will need further protection from the cold.

Rugs may be of either natural or synthetic fabric. The latter are light and easy to wash, but some are non-absorbent and do not allow the passage of air: that is, they do not breathe. These are not recommended, because when wearing them a horse is more likely to break out into a sweat in mild weather or after exercise. Though clothing made of natural fibres is heavier and more difficult to launder, it is more absorbent and will breathe.

Rugs are secured by a fastening at the chest and either by attached crossover surcingles or a detached roller with an extra pad to protect the spine. Rugs with crossover surcingles are preferable because they do not put extra pressure on the spine, but blankets used under them are inclined to slip back, so for extra warmth use an under rug rather than a blanket. Hind-leg straps are fitted on some rugs to keep the rug straight.

48 A stable-rug which fits the horse comfortably.

Stable Rugs (Night Rugs)

Traditional night rugs *(fig. 48)* made of jute lined with wool are excellent for warmth and comfort, and they have a long life. The disadvantages are that wool and jute are heavy and may shrink when laundered, so more-popular synthetic rugs are now produced with a wide variety of interlinings—polyester, Flectalon, etc.—used between the nylon surface and the cotton lining. They are light to handle, and the less bulky ones are machine-washable, but in time they all flatten out and lose their warmth.

Night rugs are likely to become soiled when the horse lies down, so it is useful to have a second set.

Under-rugs are made of thermal fabrics, lightweight wool or cotton. These can be used to provide extra warmth under the night rug.

Blankets are rectangular in shape and are used under night rugs to give extra warmth.. The best ones are made of wool, traditionally with stripes which should run parallel to the ground when the blanket is on the horse.

Day Rugs

Those made of woollen material bound with braid of another colour give the best appearance and are used for special occasions.

Turnout Rugs

These are designed for outdoor use in cold weather and are particularly useful for clipped or trace-clipped horses. Their special merit is that they provide protection against wind and rain, but they are not intended to be worn in the stable. Canvas turnout rugs are partially lined with wool and can be satisfactory for horses living out. Those made of synthetic fabrics are lighter, and some are excellent and hard wearing and will dry out more quickly than the old canvas type.

Turnout rugs have a variety of fittings and leg straps to keep them in place without causing pressure on the spine. Single, sewn-on surcingles are not recommended. Fastenings must be strong and easy to manipulate.

As the horse will be more active in his paddock than in the confines of his stable, his turnout rug must fit him particularly well. It must stay in place to keep him warm and dry without rubbing him. (*For fitting and putting on, see page 90 and fig. 50.*)

When using turnout rugs, remember:

- Before the horse is turned out he must become accustomed to the feel of the rug and its fastenings, particularly if he is unfamiliar with leg straps.
- Horses living outside in turnout rugs must be checked at least twice daily and the rugs readjusted as necessary.
- A spare rug must be available for the horse living out, in case the one he is wearing becomes too wet or damaged.

Anti-Sweat Rugs / Cooler Rugs

Made of cotton mesh, synthetic materials or towelling, these are used on a sweating horse while cooling, to prevent chills, or on a horse who tends to break out on return from work or whilst travelling. Mesh rugs are for use under a light rug.

Exercise Sheets

These short, square-fronted rugs are used in cold weather to keep the back, loins and quarter muscles warm. They are fitted under the saddle. Some have a slit on each side for the girth; others stay in place by being folded over the front of the saddle panel and secured

under the girth straps. All types should have a fillet string which passes behind the quarters to prevent the sheet from blowing forward (*fig. 49*). It is now possible to buy fluorescent quarter sheets which make the horse far more visible to drivers when you are out riding on a gloomy day.

Summer Sheets

Made of cotton or synthetic fabric, these are used to protect the groomed horse against dust and flies. They should also be provided with a fillet string to prevent them from blowing about in the wind.

ROLLERS, ROLLER PADS AND BREAST GIRTHS

Rollers are made of leather or webbing and are sometimes used to keep rugs in place. They must be fitted so that the pads rest on either side of the spine.

Roller pads provide additional padding and are necessary to prevent pressure on the spine. The pad must be thick, and wider than the roller.

Breast girths are used to prevent the roller slipping back. They should be attached to the Ds on the front of the roller.

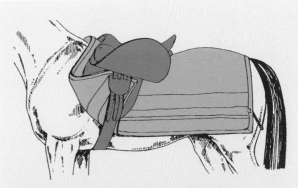

49 Exercise sheet fitted securely.

MEASUREMENT AND FIT

Choosing the Correct Size

A horse is measured for a rug by taking the distance between the centre of the chest and the furthest point of the hind quarters. The depth of the rug is usually standard, although some manufacturers give a choice of extra depth.

Some good quality rugs follow the curves of the top line of the horse from withers to croup. To fit satisfactorily they must be shaped around the neck and hind quarters.

Checking that the Rug fits the Horse

All types of rug must cover the horse's back from the front of his withers to his croup. They must be comfortably snug around the chest and deep enough to keep the horse's body warm.

Turnout rugs, in particular, must be capacious enough to protect the underside of the belly from wind and rain.

All rugs must be shaped to stay in position without relying on any straps or fittings which are too tight. Hind-leg straps should be long enough not to pull or rub the horse when he walks, but not so loose that his hind legs could be caught up in them when he lies down *(fig. 50a)*.

The projecting parts of a horse, such as withers and points of shoulders, must be checked regularly for signs of chafing. It may be necessary to sew sheepskin pads into the rug's lining to protect these parts; but unless the rug fits well the pads will not prevent rubbing.

PUTTING ON A RUG

1 Tie up the horse.
2 First gather up the rug and place it well forward over the horse's back.
3 Sort out the front part, and fasten the buckle.
4 Correct the position of the rug. If the horse is absolutely trustworthy you can do it from immediately behind. This is one of the few occasions when it is permissible to stand close behind a horse. If you are not certain that the horse is reliable, adjust the rug from the side.

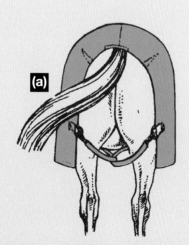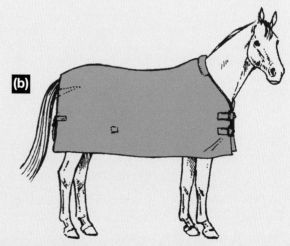

50 A well-fitting turnout rug: **(a)** Leg-straps crossed over; **(b)** Full enough to protect the whole belly.

When a Roller is Used

1 Put it and the roller pad in position, with the straps on the left side of the horse and the length of the roller on the right.
2 Move round to the right side and see that the roller hangs on the girth line and is not twisted. If it is too far back, it will slip forward and become loose later.
3 Buckle up the roller on the left side.
4 Smooth down the rug underneath the roller on both sides by running your fingers between roller and rug, at the same time giving the rug a slight pull to ease it forward in front of each elbow, thus preventing drag on the points of the shoulders.
5 Fasten the breast girth (if used), which should lie loosely above the points of the shoulders.
6 If you are using a plain blanket under a rug kept in place by a roller, put it on first and in the same way as the rug. An ample portion should lie on the neck so that the back of the blanket does not extend beyond the root of the tail. Put on the rug—then, having fastened the roller, as described above, fold back the surplus portion of the blanket lying on the horse's neck, as an extra precaution against slipping.

If the rug has crossed surcingles:

• Before the rug is thrown over the horse these should be loosely knotted. Then un-knot them and check that they are not twisted. Move to the left of the horse and secure them at a comfortable length around the horse's belly (but not as tight as a roller). Check that the rugs and surcingles are lying flat.

If the rug is fitted with hind-leg straps

(e.g. a New Zealand type of turnout rug):

• When the rug is thrown over the horse, the straps should not be left hanging down but should be fastened to prevent them from hitting you or the horse. To avoid chafing, the straps should be crossed through each other (fig. 50a). Mind that the horse does not kick you while you are fastening the straps around his thighs.
• Finally, check the pressure of the rug around the neck and shoulders and ensure that the mane is lying flat.

TAKING OFF A RUG

1 Tie up the horse.
2 Unbuckle and remove the roller, pad, and the breast girth if used.
3 If the rug has crossed surcingles, they should be unfastened and loosely knotted. If it has hind-leg straps, they should each be unfastened and fastened again on the outside, to prevent the straps and fastenings knocking against you or the horse.
4 Lastly, unfasten the breast buckle of the rug and, using both hands, fold back the front portion of the rug (and blanket, if used) over the top of the back portion.
5 With your left hand on the centre-front and your right hand on the centre-back, remove the clothing in one gentle backward sweep, following the lay of the horse's coat.
• Alternatively, rugs may be taken off one at a time in the above manner and either folded up immediately or placed temporarily over the door.

On dry, sunny days, while the horse is out on exercise his rugs can be hung outside to air and freshen up. Once a day the blanket or rug worn nearest to the body should be shaken vigorously outside the stable.

CARE OF RUGS

Light rugs should be washed at regular intervals. Winter clothing should also be washed before you store it away for the summer. Jute and canvas should be laid out on a clean part of the yard, scrubbed with a broom, hosed off and hung out to dry. Some rugs can be dry cleaned. Any repairs should be carried out, and waterproof clothing should be re-proofed according to the manufacturer's instructions. Leather fittings should be oiled with leather dressing and the rugs stored away, with mothballs, in a dry place free from vermin.

BANDAGES

Before use, bandages must be correctly rolled, with the tapes or velcro in the centre. If you use tapes, fold them neatly across the width of the bandage, then roll it with the sewn side of the tape inwards.

When applying or removing bandages, it is dangerous to kneel in the vicinity of the horse's legs. You should adopt a bending or crouching position at the side of the horse.

Stable Bandages

Stable bandages are made of wool or woollen-type material 10cm (4in) wide, 2.5 to 3.7m (8 to 12ft) long, and are supplied in sets of four. They improve circulation, provide protection, and are particularly useful for warming and drying cold, wet legs. In skilful hands they are very beneficial, but if they are wrongly or carelessly applied, they become a danger. A suitable padding such as Gamgee, Fibregee or softened straw should be used under the bandage to help equalise pressure, and to add warmth and protection. Bandages put on too tightly cause ringed marks on the legs or, more seriously, they damage the tendons. Stable bandages may be used for veterinary purposes. In this case crêpe is often used. (See VETERINARY BANDAGING, page 149.) If for any reason stable bandages are used constantly, they must be removed and replaced at least once a day.

Applying a Stable Bandage

Wrap the padding around the leg, making sure that it lies flat. Then, starting just below the knee or hock, pass the rolled-up bandage around the leg with even tension. Once the coronet is reached, the bandage takes a natural turn upwards. The crossover should then occur at the front just above the coronet. Continue unrolling in an upward direction, and finish off at the place where you started. Many stable bandages are too short. In this case, start just above the fetlock joint, bandaging down to the pastern and then up to just below the knee or hock. The tapes must be kept flat and tied so that the knot or bow lies to the outside or the inside of the leg—and not in front where it will press on the bone, or at the back where it will press on the tendons. Tuck in the spare ends, or alternatively, secure the velcro. (See fig. 51.)

Removing a Bandage from a Leg

Unfasten the tapes or velcro and unwind the bandage quickly, passing the unwound parts from hand to hand. Do not try to roll up the bandage while you are taking it off. Once it has been removed, run your hand down the tendons to check for any irregularities. Then hang the bandage up to dry and air.

Travelling Bandages

These are used to protect the legs from treads and other harm, either self-inflicted or from a companion. Put on as described above, but the padding and bandage should be continued lower down to protect the coronet band.

Exercise Bandages

As a rule, these should be used only by experienced people. Their primary purpose is to protect the legs while the horse is at exercise or at work. Approximately 7cm (3in) wide, they are made of crêpe or various synthetic materials, which should give slightly but not be too elastic. They should be used over Gamgee or a substitute and must be skilfully applied to ensure even tension. They must be removed promptly after work.

Applying an Exercise Bandage (Fig. 52)

Wrap the Gamgee (or equivalent) around the leg, making sure that it lies flat. Start just below the knee or hock, at the side of the leg, and bandage in the same direction as the overlap of the padding, going down and up again between the knee and the fetlock joint. Make the crossover (change of direction) just above the fetlock joint, in the centre at the front. Each turn around the leg should cover about two-thirds of the width of the bandage. The pressure should be even and just enough to ensure that the bandage does not slip, but not so tight as to affect the circulation or to impede movement of the tendons.

Finish off by folding over the beginning of the bandage and covering it as the top is reached. This fold should not lie across the back of the leg. The tapes should lie flat and be of the same tightness as the bandage. For extra security, plastic insulating tape can be laid over the fastening and around the leg; it must be no tighter than the bandage. (NOTE: The tape is dangerous to grazing animals and must never be left on the ground.)

For special occasions, or fast work, the end of the bandages should be sewn securely. Protruding Gamgee may be trimmed with scissors.

Tail Bandages

These should be 7 to 10cm (3 to 4in) wide and made of crêpe or synthetic material. They are used to improve appearance by keeping the hairs of the tail straight and to prevent rubbing when travelling. An over-elasticated bandage, if put on too tightly, will cause ridges round the tail and discomfort to the horse.

Tail bandages should not be used to excess and should never be left on all night or on long journeys.

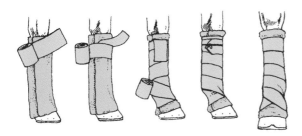

51 Applying a stable-bandage.

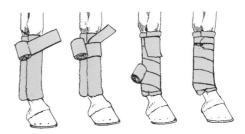

52 Applying an exercise bandage.

Applying a Tail Bandage (Fig. 53)
Lightly dampen the tail hair with a water brush. Wetting the bandage is wrong as it may shrink the material and injure the tail by cutting off the circulation.

Put your right hand at the top of the tail. Unroll about 20cm (8in) of bandage and place this spare piece over the top of the tail. Hold the end of the bandage in your left hand and the bandage roll in your right with the roll on the outside. Keep your left hand at the top of the tail until the bandage is secured. (The first turn is often difficult to keep in place, but you can overcome this by making the next turn above the first.) Then wind in the spare end of the bandage.

Unroll the bandage evenly around and downwards, stopping just above or below the last tailbone. Tie the tapes neatly—no tighter than the tension of the bandage. Tuck in the spare ends, then bend the tail back into a comfortable position.

Removing a Bandage from the Tail
Untie the tapes, grasp the bandage with both hands round the dock near the top of the tail, and slide off in a downwards direction.

TAIL GUARDS
These protect the horse's tail when travelling. Sometimes used over tail bandages, they may also be used on their own. There are several types: some are fastened around the tail with tapes or velcro and are attached to a ring at the back of the rug, or to the roller. Others zip up and stay in place independently.

POLL GUARDS
Poll guards are made of felt, leather and Neoprene, and are used to protect the top of the head while travelling. There are various designs, all of which fit on to the headcollar.

BOOTS
There are numerous types of boot designed to prevent a horse injuring himself or being injured *(figs. 54 and 55)*. The injuries involved are described on page 159. The principal types, each produced in a variety of materials and designs *(fig. 55)* are:

Brushing Boots
These include fetlock boots, and rubber rings.

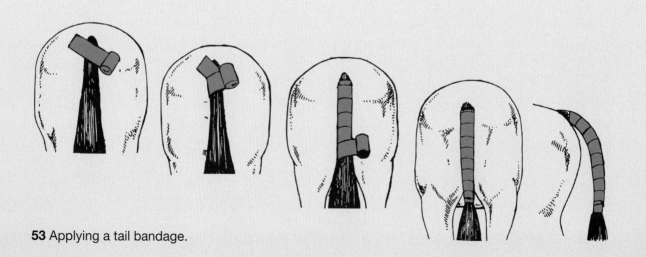

53 Applying a tail bandage.

Tendon Boots

These are designed to give extra protection to the tendons at the back of the leg. Some designs also act as brushing boots.

Open-Fronted Boots

These provide protection to the tendons against a high overreach. They are similar to brushing boots, with a shaped pad protecting the tendon and fetlocks. They are open at the front of the cannon bone and are mainly used for showjumping.

Sport Boots

A protective boot allowing flexibility and movement while supporting the fetlocks, tendons and ligaments.

Overreach Boots

Bell-shaped and made of rubber, these fit around the lower pastern, encompassing the hoof. They protect the heels and the coronet. Some are fitted with straps. If they are not, they are put on by turning them inside out and pulling them on over the hoof.

Travelling Boots

These are used to prevent injury while on a journey. Usually made of synthetic fibre, they encase the legs from above or just below the knee or hock, down to the coronet, which they overlap. They are usually fastened with velcro. The size must be correct for the horse or pony. They should only be used for short journeys as they have a tendency to slip down.

Knee Boots

Normally made of thick felt and leather or synthetic material, these are used for travelling but may also be worn when exercising on the road. The top strap must be fitted firmly enough to prevent the boot slipping down. The lower strap is there only to prevent the boot flapping about, and must be loose enough to avoid any restriction of leg movement.

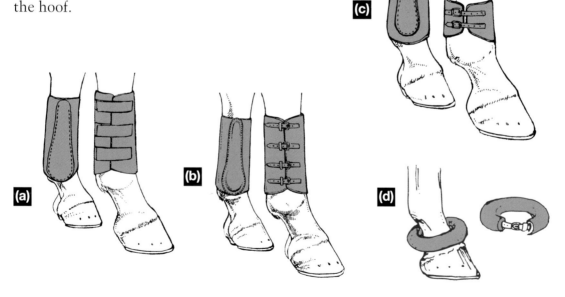

54 Brushing boots: **(a)** Neoprene with velcro fastening; **(b)** Leather; **(c)** Fetlock; **(d)** Anti-brushing ring

Hock Boots

These are used to protect the hocks while travelling. The horse must accept them in the stable before being loaded. The top and lower straps are fitted in the same way as those of knee boots.

Polo Boots

These are made in a variety of shapes but are too heavy for general use. They are usually larger than the normal boot and designed to provide protection against blows from polo balls or sticks, brushing, speedicut, treads, etc.

Sausage Boots

These ring-shaped, padded boots are fitted round the pastern to prevent the heel of the shoe damaging the elbow when the horse is lying down. They are required only when an injury has been sustained, or when the shoes, for a specific reason, are unusually long. They are not for day-to-day protection.

Equiboots

Designed to fit around and under the hoof, these are used for protecting the foot in the absence of a shoe. They are useful in an emergency but should not be considered as a long-term substitute for shoes.

The Use and Fitting of Brushing and Tendon Boots

All working boots are designed for protection over a short period. If worn for a long period, they are likely to cause soreness, especially in muddy or wet conditions. Well-made boots are shaped to fit the contours of the leg. Badly-shaped boots may develop ridges which can cause pressure on the tendons and result in permanent damage.

Keep boots in pairs or sets. Sometimes the front and hind-leg boots of a set are different in shape. In a set of four, the front boots generally have one less strap than the hind.

When fitted, the fastenings should be on the outside of the leg with the strap ends pointing to the rear.

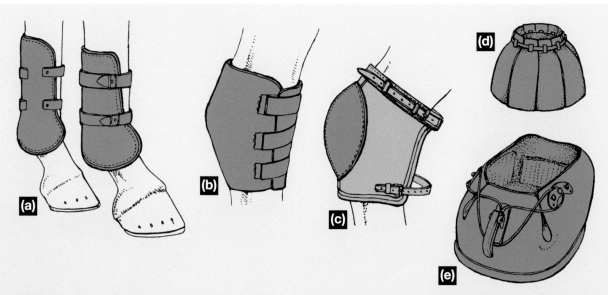

55 (a) Tendon boot; **(b)** Travel hock boot (Neoprene); **(c)** Hock boot (leather); **(d)** Petal overreach boot; **(e)** Equiboot; **(f)** Sport boot; **(g)** Knee boots (leather left, man-made right); **(h)** Overreach boot.

Select the correct boot from your set or pair and put it around the leg. Fasten the middle strap first. Work upwards and then downwards, making sure that the pressure is even all the way and no tighter than is necessary to prevent the boot slipping.

If boots are secured by straps, always use the keepers. They help to prevent the buckles coming undone if the straps work loose.

Boots fastened by metal clips can come undone if knocked.

When removing a boot, unfasten the middle strap last to prevent the boot from falling off if the horse moves.

Care of Boots

Boots must be thoroughly cleaned after use as any mud and muck left on them will harden and may cause sores later on. Depending on the material of which they are made, clean them as described for saddlery *(see page 289)*.

Try to keep straps and keepers as soft as possible. If they are stiff and hard, they will be difficult to fasten and unfasten, and they may crack and break.

Velcro fastenings must be kept free from dirt, etc., which clogs them up and makes them less secure.

10. Grooming

Grooming is daily attention necessary to the coat, skin, mane, tail and feet of the stabled horse. It is slightly different for grass-kept horses although the importance of a methodical approach remains the same. *(See pages 59 and 104 for notes on grooming a grass-kept horse.)*

An experienced groom will take between half and three-quarters of an hour to groom a horse, whereas a novice will probably need longer. Thoroughness brings its own reward, though, since few sights are more pleasing to the eye than a well-groomed, healthy horse.

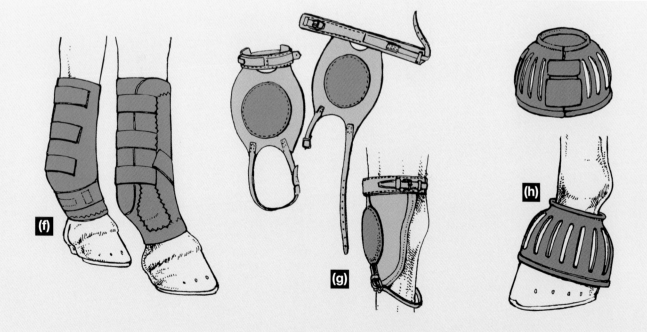

Hoof Pick
For picking out the feet.

Stable Sponges
For cleaning eyes, nose, muzzle and dock.

Plastic Curry Comb
For removing caked mud from a pony kept at grass.

Mane Comb
Normally used only for mane and tail pulling and when plaiting *(see page 108)*.

Dandy Brush
For removing heavy dirt, caked mud and dust. It is of special value for use on the grass-kept pony, but should not be used on a clipped or sensitive horse.

Mane Comb
For pulling.

Body Brush
For the removal of dust and scurf from the coat, mane and tail.

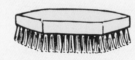

Water Brush
For use on the mane, tail and feet.

Metal Curry Comb
Made of metal for cleaning the body brush.

Cactus Cloth
For removing dried mud or sweat.

Rubber Curry Comb
Made of rubber for removing caked mud from a pony kept at grass.

Hoof Oil
For oiling the hooves.

Stable Rubber
For a final polish after grooming.

Sweat Scraper (not shown)
to remove surplus water when spongeing down the horse. (Not used for normal grooming.)

Wisp or Massage Pad (Not shown).
For promoting circulation, and for massage.

56 Grooming kit.

WHEN TO GROOM

Quartering

The objective is to remove stable stains and to make the horse look tidy before exercise. Give the horse a quick brush down using the body brush and curry comb. If the weather is cold and he is rugged up, fold the rugs halfway back in order to quarter the forehand, and then fold them forward to complete the task. Brush the mane and tail, sponge the eyes, nostrils and dock and pick out the feet.

Full Groom

This is usually carried out after exercise, and includes the entire grooming procedure. Grooming is most effective when the horse is warm, the pores are open and the scurf is on the surface of the coat.

Strapping

Strapping is a form of massage to develop and harden the muscles. (*See* Wisp or Massage Pad, *page 101.*)

Brush Over or Set Fair

In the evening the horse is given a light brush over when the rugs are straightened or changed, and the box is set fair— droppings removed and bedding tidied up.

HOW TO GROOM

- Collect the items of grooming kit. They are best kept together in a box, wire basket or bag.
- Put the headcollar on the horse and tie him up fairly short.
- It is more pleasant to work in a clean area, so before and during grooming, pick up any droppings (dung).
- Remove his rugs. If the weather is cold, leave a rug folded over his loins while grooming the forehand, and over his shoulder while grooming the quarters.

Hoof Pick

Always begin grooming by picking out the feet *(fig. 57)*. A dung-skip should be placed to catch the dirt, so that it does not drop on to the bed. Pick up each foot in turn. Remove whatever may be lodged in it with the point of the pick, working downwards from the heel towards the toe; this way there is no risk of the pick penetrating the soft parts of the frog. Clear the cleft of the frog and look for any signs of thrush. Tap the shoe to see that it is secure. Finally, run the tips of the fingers over the clenches to

57 Using a hoof pick.

see that they have not risen. *(To lift up the feet, see page 48 and fig. 30.)*

When picking out the feet it is permissible to lift the right feet from the left-hand side, a practice which a horse soon gets used to.

The feet should be picked out before the horse leaves his stable to prevent littering the yard.

Dandy Brush

On the grass-kept pony this is used all over the body. It can be held in either hand. Start at the poll on the left-hand side and work over the whole body and legs. When working on the hind limbs it may be helpful to grasp the tail with your free hand. Do not brush too hard over the sensitive parts of the body, but elsewhere you can use a to-and-fro movement to loosen stubborn dirt. On the stabled, clipped horse the dandy brush is used only on unclipped areas. Rubber or plastic curry combs are sometimes used as alternatives.

Cactus Cloth

On the stabled horse this can be used as an alternative to the dandy brush. The object is to loosen dirt, sweat and scurf. It is particularly useful in sensitive areas where some horses resent being brushed.

Body Brush and Curry Comb

The body brush is the main grooming brush, and the curry comb is designed to keep it clean *(fig. 58)*. The short, close-set hairs of the brush are designed to reach right through the coat to the skin beneath, lifting and removing the dirt.

Begin with the mane. First, throw the mane across to the far side of the neck and thoroughly brush the crest. Replace the mane and then start working on it, beginning at the head end. Insert a finger of your free hand into the mane to separate a few locks of hair. First brush the ends and

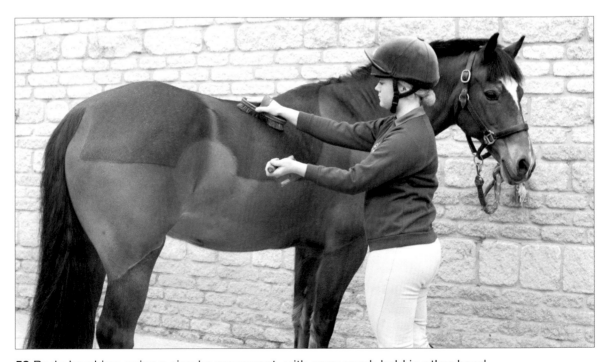

58 Body-brushing, using a circular movement, with curry comb held in other hand.

then the roots to remove tangles. Work slowly down the neck, dealing with only a few locks of hair at a time.

When grooming the body, begin at the poll region on the left side and gradually work back over the whole body, in the direction of the lay of the coat.

1 Take the body brush in your left hand and the curry comb in your right.

2 Work with a slightly bent arm and a supple wrist and lean the weight of your body behind the brush.

3 Work more gently on the sensitive areas.

4 Use short, circular strokes, finishing each stroke in the direction of the lay of the coat rather than to-and-fro.

5 After every four or five strokes, draw the brush smartly across the teeth of the curry comb to dislodge the dirt.

6 In turn, clean the curry comb by tapping it out—on the floor, and not against the wall or manger.

7 When the left side has been completed, pass to the right side and repeat the whole process. When working on the left side it is easier to have the body brush in your left hand and the curry comb in your right. When working on the right side it is easier to have the body brush in your right hand and the curry comb in your left. Exceptions to this are when you are grooming (a) those parts of the flank and under the belly where the coat lies in the opposite direction and (b) down the back of the hind quarters *(fig. 59)*.

Tail

Take only a few strands of hair at a time. Do this by holding the tail and shaking a few strands free, brushing the ends clean first. The use of the dandy brush on the mane or tail is generally wrong as it breaks the hairs, but on very thick manes and tails an old or soft dandy brush may be used. If loose hairs begin to appear on the brush, revert to the body brush before you ruin the tail!

Head

First untie the horse. Unfasten the headcollar and fasten the headstrap temporarily round the neck. Use your free hand to steady the head, and use the body brush with care. When you have finished, replace the headcollar and tie the horse up again.

Wisp or Massage Pad *(Fig. 60)*

Wisping is a form of massage to help develop and harden muscles of the stabled horse in full work. It stimulates the blood supply to the skin and brings a shine to the coat. Dampen the wisp slightly and

59 Holding the tail out of the way while body-brushing the hind quarters.

use it to massage the horse by slapping the muscles in a regular rhythm in the direction of the lay of the coat. The horse must only be wisped on the muscles of the neck, shoulders, quarters and thighs.

Sponge and Bucket of Water

Spongeing the eyes, nose and dock refreshes the horse and is appreciated perhaps more than any other part of the grooming routine. Keep two sponges of different colours, one of which is reserved for use in the dock region. Wring out the sponge so that it is soft, clean and damp. Start with the eyes. Sponge away from the corners and around the eyelids. Wring out sponge again and deal with the muzzle region, including the lips and inside and outside of the nostrils in that order. With the other sponge, if the horse is reliable, move behind him to attend to the dock. If he is a kicker or is not reliable, stand at one side to do this. Lift the tail as high as possible and gently sponge and clean the whole dock region, including the skin of the under-surface of the tail.

Water Brush

This is used to lay the mane and tail. Dip the bristle ends of the water brush into the bucket of water, shake off the surplus water and apply the brush flat to the mane. Brush the hairs from the roots downwards so that they are left slightly damp and in the required position. Lay the hairs at the top of the tail and either side of the dock in a similar manner. At this stage a tail bandage may be applied *(see page 93)*.

Hoof Oil

For special occasions, paint the walls of the hooves all over with a thin coating of oil to improve their appearance. Used too often, hoof oil may inhibit the absorption of moisture. If your horse has brittle feet, use a feed supplement and/or a hoof dressing, and consult your farrier.

Stable Rubber

This is a cloth which is used to remove the last traces of dust from the coat. Give the horse a final brisk polish, using the rubber in the direction of the lay of the hair.

60 How to make a wisp. Make a tightly woven rope about 1.8–2.5m (6–8ft) long by twisting up hay or straw. Soft hay is best and should first be dampened slightly. Make two loops at one end of the rope, one slightly longer than the other. Twist each loop in turn beneath the remainder of the rope until it is all used up. The far end of the rope should then be twisted through the end of each loop and finally tucked away securely under the last twist. The hay wisp should then be dampened and stamped on. A properly made wisp should be hard, firm, and small enough to be held easily in the hand. Alternatively, a leather-covered felt massage pad may be used.

WASHING

Washing The Tail

You will need a bucket of lukewarm water (at approximately 25°C (77°F)), a small amount of shampoo (not detergent) and a clean water brush and sponge.

Procedure:

First soak the tail to loosen the dirt. If the horse is quiet, most of the tail may, with advantage, be immersed in the bucket. Any remaining hair may be wetted with the water brush. Shampoo and rinse thoroughly, changing the water as necessary. Squeeze out the water with your hands, and swing the tail to dislodge any water remaining. Then, using a vertical movement, brush out the tail a few hairs at a time with a clean body brush. Finally, apply a tail bandage.

Washing the Mane

The mane should only be washed when the weather is warm and the neck and shoulders will dry without the horse becoming chilled.

You will need a bucket of lukewarm water, a small amount of shampoo and a sponge.

Procedure

Wet the mane with a large sponge from the withers to the forelock, bringing the forelock back behind the ears to join the mane. Rub the water well into the roots. Dilute the shampoo and, using the sponge, work forwards from the withers, taking particular care that no soap gets into the eyes or ears. Rinse well using the sponge, until all the soap has gone, working from the forelock to the withers. Water should not be allowed to run down the face. Use the sweat scraper to remove excess water from the neck and shoulders, and start the drying process with a towel.

Removing Stable Stains or Straw Marks

Stains and straw marks can be brushed out, and bent hair smoothed back into place, using lukewarm water with a water brush or sponge. Then dry off the areas with a stable rubber or towel. Stubborn stains can be washed out using mild soap.

Washing the Feet

After exercise, or on return from the field, it is sometimes necessary to wash mud off the feet. Use the water brush dipped in a bucket of water. Press the thumb of the hand which holds the horse's foot well into the hollow of the heel to prevent water being lodged there. Do not wash the feet too often. If you need to wash them in winter or wet weather, it is a good idea to smear some Vaseline into the heel area to lessen the risk of cracked heels or mud fever.

Spongeing Down

After working in hot weather, horses who are clipped or have fine coats can be made more comfortable by spongeing off the sweat where saddlery has been and under the elbows and hind legs. Do not allow them to become chilled. A horse returning from fast work should be walked around until his breathing has returned to normal, and may then be sponged down with lukewarm water. Remove surplus water with a sweat scraper, following the lay of the coat. Particular attention must be paid to the areas at the elbows and high up inside the hind legs and the dock region.

In this damp state a horse is susceptible to chill, so the appropriate rugs must be used, and the horse led round until relaxed and dry. If the weather is warm enough, rugs may not be necessary, but he must still be led round until he is dry and settled.

Washing the Whole Horse

This is not recommended either for horses or for ponies. British weather is unreliable and washing removes the oils in the coat and skin which provide natural protection against rain, wind and flies. Wetness caused by rain will not penetrate through to the skin on a horse's back, nor will it affect the coat under his belly. However, shampooing or prolonged washing will wet the horse through to the skin all over his body, leaving him cold at the time and vulnerable to outdoor conditions for days afterwards. It should be possible to keep your horse immaculate by grooming him thoroughly and regularly. If, however, for some exceptional reason there is no alternative to washing him all over, he must be dried off completely and not allowed to get cold in the process (so a horse with a winter coat must not be washed under any circumstances). For several days after being washed, the horse will need extra clothing. If he does not usually wear a rug he must be rugged-up for a week or so until the natural oils have returned.

GROOMING MACHINES

If used intelligently and according to the manufacturer's instructions, grooming machines are a boon in a large stable. Great care must be taken over their introduction and subsequent use. If a revolving brush is used, the whole tail must be bandaged up for safety. Remember that with this or any other similar electrical appliance it is essential to use a circuit breaker.

GROOMING PONIES WHO LIVE OUT

If a pony is living out at grass and without rugs, the skin should be in a thoroughly healthy condition and it is unnecessary to groom him unless he is being ridden.

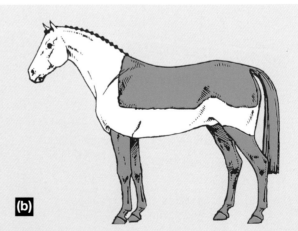

61 Types of clip: **(a)** Hunter; **(b)** Blanket; **(c)** Trace; **(d)** Belly and gullet. Blue = hair on, White = clipped areas.

Under these conditions grooming should be limited to:

- Picking out the feet and checking shoes.
- Brushing down with the dandy brush or rubber curry comb to remove mud and sweat marks.
- Using the body brush or an old or soft dandy brush to keep mane and tail tidy.
- Spongeing out the eyes, nose, muzzle and dock.

Too much grease should not be removed from the coats of horses and ponies living out of doors, as it helps to keep them warm and dry, so a body brush should not normally be used on their coats.

11. Clipping and Trimming

CLIPPING

Horses are clipped for the following reasons:

- To enable a horse to work in winter without undue distress.
- To maintain condition by avoiding heavy sweating.
- To permit a horse to work longer, faster and better.
- To facilitate quicker drying off on return from work.
- To save labour in grooming.
- To prevent disease.

Traditionally, hunters or horses who work hard in winter are clipped in late September and then every four to six weeks as necessary. Clipping after January may spoil the summer coat but cat hairs, the long untidy hairs which sometimes show at this time of year, can be lightly trimmed with the clippers.

Types of Clip *(Fig. 61)*
Full Clip
The whole of the coat is removed.
A horse with a full clip will need rugs.

Hunter Clip
As for the full clip, except that the hair is left on the legs as far as the elbows and thighs, and a saddle patch is left on the back. The coat left on the legs acts as a protection against cold, mud, cracked heels and injury from thorns, while the saddle patch helps to

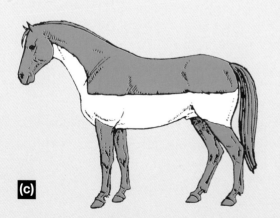

(c)

(d)

prevent saddle sores or scalded backs. Legs may be carefully trimmed *(see THE LEGS AND HEAD, page 107)*. Pay prticular attention to the position of the saddle patch. With the saddle correctly in place, the unclipped hair should show 2.5cm (1in) round the outside edge. Many hunters are clipped right out the first time, and given a hunter clip (with the legs and saddle patch left on) at the second clipping. On a common horse this has the advantage of making the legs appear less hairy than would otherwise be the case. Horses with a hunter clip will need rugs.

Blanket Clip

The hair is removed only from the head, neck and belly, a patch corresponding in size to that of a blanket being left on the body. This is a useful clip for horses with fine coats who might otherwise feel the cold. Rugs will be needed.

Trace Clip

This is a compromise between clipping fully or not at all, and is useful for horses and ponies kept out at grass all day. The hair is removed from the belly, shoulders and thighs up to the level at which the traces in driving harness would run, and is left on the legs as for the hunter clip. Usually the hair immediately under the neck is also removed. When out in cold, wet weather horses will need turnout rugs. In mild, dry weather, rugs may not be required on some ponies who do not feel the cold.

Belly and Gullet Clip

The hair is removed from under the belly upwards between the forelegs and up the lower line of the neck to the lower jaw. This clip is useful for native ponies who live out. Many ponies who have adequate shelter may not need a turnout rug, but some may feel the cold more than others.

Equipment

Standard clipping machines are operated either by electricity or on rechargeable batteries. There are also small, quiet clippers, useful for clipping around the head area.

Clipper blades come in different grades from very fine to the coarser leg blades. They must always be kept and sharpened in pairs. Before clipping, it is important to ensure that the machine is in good working condition and that the wiring is safe. A circuit breaker plugged directly into the wall socket must be used. This will cut off the electricity in an emergency. The machine should be lightly oiled and the tension of the blades adjusted according to the manufacturer's instructions.

Every half hour or so the head of the clipper should be stripped and thoroughly cleaned, oiled, and allowed to cool. With the type of clipper which has the motor enclosed in the body of the handle, the air filter must be kept clear, or the motor will overheat.

Have ready: clippers, spare blades, oil, a brush for the clippers, a twitch, appropriate clothing, tail bandage, dandy and body brush, and rug in case the horse gets cold while being clipped.

It is advisable to wear rubber-soled shoes, an overall or smock to which the horse's hair will not adhere, and a cap or headscarf.

A helper may be necessary, dressed in similar fashion but also wearing a riding hat and gloves.

How to Clip

A horse who has never been hurt or frightened by clipping should not be difficult.

It is therefore important to allow plenty of time, and to work patiently, stopping from time to time if the blades become hot or if they start pulling the hair. If you continue with hot or pulling blades your horse will soon become nervous and difficult.

Before you begin, the coat must be dry and as well-groomed as its length will permit; dirt will clog and overheat the clippers. To keep the tail out of the way, double it up and put on a tail bandage. As much of the horse as possible should be clipped without upsetting him or resorting to any means of restraint. The best place to start is at the side of the belly, but if the horse is nervous, begin at the shoulder region. It can be helpful to clip the head early on, before the horse becomes bored as the blades get blunter.

The clippers should be used against the lay of the coat, with an even pressure, the blades lying parallel to the coat without digging in to the skin. Apart from the head the most difficult parts to clip—both from the point of view of possible resistance of the animal and of achieving favourable results—are groin areas; inside the elbows; and up between the front legs, where it is particularly easy to nick the horse. These parts are best left until last, and when clipping them it is advisable to have an experienced helper at hand in case the horse requires soothing. The helper may be needed to hold up a foreleg so that you can clip smoothly and evenly around the elbow.

Care must be taken to clip neither the sides of the mane nor the root of the tail. The practice of removing a short portion of the mane at the wither region is not recommended. If a portion is removed to make space for the headpiece of the bridle, it should be only slightly broader than the headpiece.

On no account must hair be removed from the inside of the ears, since it provides natural protection.

As clipping proceeds, throw a folded rug over the loins; a cold horse soon becomes fidgety. While clipping his body and legs, allow the horse to feed from a hay net so that he will not get bored.

When a horse has been clipped out in late autumn or winter, his natural coat has thus been removed and it will not grow again until the following spring. It must be replaced by enough rugs and blankets to keep him warm. To leave him without covering would not only be cruel but would also cause him to lose condition. If he is to be turned out, even for a short time *(see A Programme of Stable Routine, page 57)*, a turnout rug will be necessary.

TRIMMING AND PLAITING

Trimming is the process of tidying up a horse and includes the pulling of the mane and tail.

The hairs of the mane and tail will pull out more easily when the pores of the skin are warm and open: that is, after exercise or on a warm day. To avoid soreness, pull the mane or tail gradually, achieving the required length or shape over several sessions. Some pony breeds are shown untrimmed with natural manes and tails.

The Legs and Head

The long hairs under the jaws, down the legs, and at the back of the fetlock joint provide protection from the elements. On the stabled horse these may be trimmed to improve his looks.

Unless the whole leg is being clipped, the use of clippers on the back of the tendons or fetlocks is not recommended, as the appearance of the legs will be spoiled for some weeks. When the hair does not pull easily, trimming scissors and a comb may be used instead. The comb is moved upwards, against the lay of the hair, lifting it so that it can be cut. The long hairs growing underneath the jaw are treated in the same way on an unclipped horse or pony. The whiskers around the eyes should not be cut. Some people clip the whiskers around the muzzle, but they act as protection from the flies and help with the horse's sensitive feeling around this area. If the animal is living out they should definitely not be removed.

The Ears

The sides of the ears should be gently squeezed together so that the outside edges meet. Then trim back any long hairs with blunt-ended scissors. Hair from the inside should not be removed.

The Tail

Plaiting a Tail

The unpulled hairs of the dock can be plaited to make them look neat and tidy for special occasions. This solves the problem of dealing with an unpulled tail when the mane is plaited. It is not always advisable to pull the tail; some horses resent it, and only tails with long hairs at the sides of the dock can be plaited successfully. The plaiting procedure *(fig. 62)* is as follows:

1 Dampen the hair, then from the top of the tail take three small bunches with the finger and thumb, one on one side and two on the other. If the hairs are sparse, or too short, knot them together with thread. The ends of the thread hang down the centre of the tail and they are used for plaiting small successive bunches (eight to ten hairs) from either side.

2 Alternatively, take a small number of

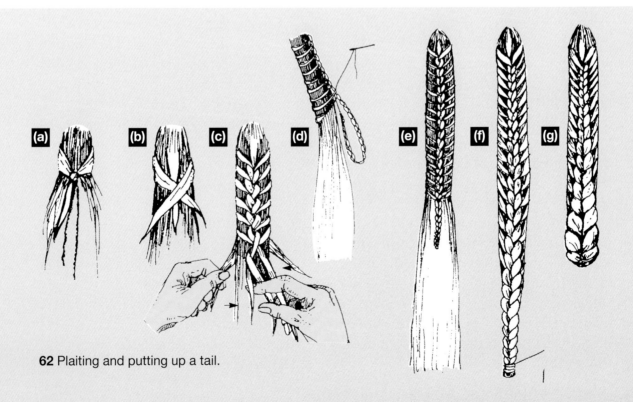

62 Plaiting and putting up a tail.

hairs from the middle of the dock and begin to plait successive bunches from either side in with them.

3 In both cases, continue plaiting this way down the centre, adding successive bunches from each side (that is, A to A and B to B). Work downwards for about three-quarters of the length of the dock. Thereafter, finish plaiting the hairs in your hand.

4 When you reach the end, secure it with thread and loop it back under itself, tucking it up beneath the plait. Then sew it firmly in this position.

5 The plait itself may lie on the outside or inside of the hairs, but the smartest effect is when it is on the outside (laced).

Putting Up a Tail

A tail is put up for activities which may cause it to get muddy and uncomfortable.

6 Begin plaiting as described above, but when you reach the end of the dock, divide the whole tail into three bunches, add them to the bunches in your hand, and plait to the end.

7 Roll up the plait neatly to the end of the dock and stitch it firmly on both sides so that it lies flat, directly below the last of the tail bones.

Pulling a Tail (Fig. 63)

A well-pulled and tidy tail adds greatly to the appearance of a stabled horse. A horse living at grass should not have his tail pulled, as this deprives him of natural protection when he turns his hind quarters towards the wind and rain. Clippers should never be used on a tail, except when banging, nor should a dandy brush be used. A mane comb can break and tear the hair and therefore should only be used when pulling a tail.

To pull a tail, you will need a body brush; a water brush; a mane comb and a tail bandage. The procedure continues as follows:

1 Groom the tail well to remove all tangles.

2 Begin pulling at the dock region by thinning the hair from underneath, and continue halfway down the dock.

3 Work sideways, removing the hair evenly on both sides of the tail. Take less hair from the central surface, so that it appears smooth and even. Remove only a few hairs at a time, either with your fingers or by winding the hairs around a comb and giving them a brisk pull. A little resin on the fingers will help.

4 After pulling, the tail may be bandaged (see page 94). The regular use of a tail bandage on the dock region greatly helps the preservation of the shape.

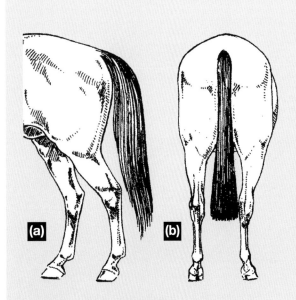

63 (a) An unpulled (full) tail;
(b) A pulled and banged tail.

A Bang Tail

A long tail collects mud, is likely to become straggly, and hides the hocks. To bang the tail, cut the end off square, approximately 10cm (4in) below the points of the hocks. You will need a helper to put his arm under the root of the tail while you cut it; the cut will then be square when the tail is carried naturally.

The Mane
Pulling a Mane

This is carried out to thin an over-thick mane; to reduce a long mane to the required length; to allow the mane to lie flat; or to make the mane easier to plait. The longest hairs from underneath should be dealt with first and should be removed a few at a time. Do this with your fingers or by winding a few hairs at a time around the mane comb and plucking them out briskly. Never pull the top hairs, or any hairs that may stand up after plaiting, because when they regrow they will form an upright fringe on the crest. You should not use scissors or clippers.

Hogging

This involves complete removal of the mane by means of clippers. It is sometimes done when a horse grows a ragged mane that spoils his appearance. Cobs and polo ponies often have hogged manes. Hogging should be repeated about every three weeks.

Once a mane has been hogged, regrowth can take at least two years to look neat, and even then the mane may not regain its former appearance. To hog the mane neatly, a helper is necessary. By taking hold of his ear, the helper can gently but firmly encourage the horse to lower his head (which will straighten the crest). Remove the whole mane, beginning at the withers and working forward towards the poll on both sides and up the centre. Take care not to leave an unsightly line where the mane meets the coat.

STEP 1

You will need: a water brush; a mane comb; a blunt-ended needle with a large eye; strong thread the colour of the mane; and a pair of scissors.

STEP 2

First damp down the mane with a wet brush and divide it into as many equal parts as required.

STEP 3

Now begin the plaiting of each lock of mane, starting behind the ears.

STEP 4

When a plait is completed, loop the ends of the thread around the plait and secure them. Push the needle through the plait from underneath and close to the crest, doubling up the plait. Fold the plait as many times as required to achieve the appropriate shape.

STEP 5

Finish by stitching through the underside of the plait to secure it.

64 Plaiting a mane using needle and thread.

Plaiting a Mane

This is done for neatness; to show off the neck and crest; and to train the mane to fall to the side preferred (normally the right, or off, side) of the neck. There should always be an uneven number of plaits along the neck, plus the forelock. There are several ways to plait a mane, but the method shown in *fig. 64* is one of the easiest.

Alternatively, use a rubber band instead of a needle and thread. Having finished a long plait, loop the band several times around the end; then bend under the end of the plait into the required position, folding it as many times as necessary, and loop the band around the whole plait until it is tight. Mane plaits should not be left in all night as they tend to pull, are uncomfortable, and spoil the mane.

12. The Foot and Shoeing

Every horseman should have some understanding of the care of a horse's feet and of shoes and shoeing. *'No foot—no horse'* is always pertinent. If your horse is lame and there is no obvious cause, the problem is usually to be found in the foot.

Your farrier should be employed regularly—every four to six weeks. He will maintain the principles of good farriery—encouraging the correct growth and balance of the feet—and will deal with short-term problems and/or those which need long-term remedial treatment.

In some situations it is easy to take the horse to the forge but often it is more convenient to employ a farrier who will travel to his clients.

Many have mobile gas-powered forges and will shoe hot. A mobile farrier will need the following if he is to work efficiently and in pleasant conditions:

- The horse—ready to be shod—with clean, dry legs and feet.
- A suitable sheltered place—with a flat, clean, non-slippery surface—where the horse will stand in a settled manner.
- If the horse is to be shod hot, a bucket of water in which to cool the shoes.

THE STRUCTURE OF THE FOOT

The Exterior of the Foot *(Fig. 65)*

This consists of three main structures: the wall, the sole and the frog. All three are horny structures and are insensitive, with neither nerve nor blood supply. This explains why shoeing-nails can be driven through the wall and why the frog and sole can be cut with a knife, without causing pain or bleeding.

The Wall

This is the part of the hoof visible when the foot is on the ground. It grows downwards from the coronary band, just like a fingernail. The wall encircles the foot, and at the heels is inclined inwards to form the bars.

The toe, the quarters and the heel all form part of the wall of the foot.

The Sole

This protects the foot from injury from underneath. It is rather thin for this purpose, and liberties cannot be taken with it. In its healthy state it is slightly concave, like a saucer turned upside down, which helps to provide a better foothold.

The Frog

The frog is nature's anti-slipping and anti-concussion device, and plays an important role in ensuring a good foothold. Its peculiar wedge shape, irregular surface and central cleft help its anti-slipping function. Its effectiveness as a shock absorber stems from its size, more flexible type of horn, upward flexibility, and the cushion within the foot upon which it rests. (It also acts as an arch support.) A healthy frog helps the foot to function more efficiently.

The Interior of the Foot

The inside of the hoof is a complex array of structures which all work together. There are bones, ligaments, tendons, nerves and a lot of blood vessels—and therefore a tremendous amount of structures that can be damaged.

SHOEING

The need for shoeing horses is a direct consequence of their domestication. Working a horse on hard roads or stony paths causes the wall to wear away more quickly than the rate at which it grows. Shoeing protects the wall from all wear, but since it continues to grow, the foot becomes unduly long. If it is neglected, lameness and loss of active life may result. The shod foot, therefore, calls for just as much attention as the unshod foot.

The tools used by the farrier for shoeing are shown opposite in *fig. 66*.

NOTE: Hoof cutters and pincers (shoe pullers) are similar to each other, but hoof cutters have either one or two sharp edges whereas pincers have blunt edges.

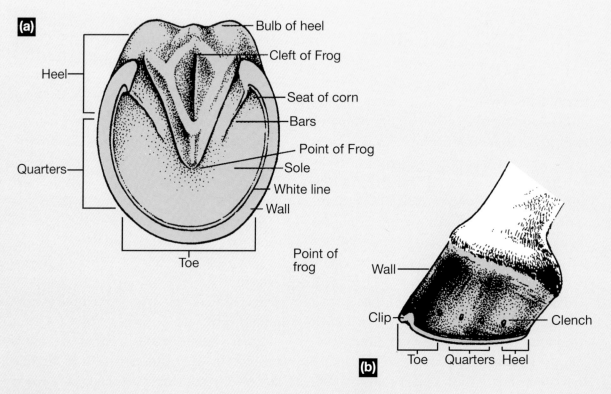

65 The exterior of the horse's foot: **(a)** from underneath; **(b)** from the side.

Re-Shoeing

As a general rule, a shod horse will need the farrier's attention every four to six weeks. Even when shoes are not badly worn, the horn will grow enough to need reducing. This is particularly true of the toe region; a horse with an over-long toe is likely to stumble.

The procedure by which a slightly worn shoe is taken off, the foot reduced in length and the same shoe replaced, is traditionally known as a remove but is sometimes described as a refit.

A horse subjected to heavy work on hard roads may wear his shoes through in less than a month, and will need new ones. The indications that he needs re-shoeing are:

- The clenches have risen and stand out from the wall.
- The foot is over-long and out of shape.
- Some part of the shoe has worn thin.
- The shoe is loose, and its heel may be pressing on the seat of corn (see CORNS, page 168).
- A shoe has been cast (has come off).

Systems of Shoeing

There are two systems: hot shoeing and cold shoeing. In hot shoeing the shoe is specially made to fit the foot. It is tried on hot, and adjustments are made before it is finally nailed on. In cold shoeing a shoe which has already been made is fitted. Minor adjustments to the shape are possible, in which case a forge is not required. Traditionally, hot shoeing is preferred.

Hot Shoeing

The procedure for re-shoeing a horse by this method falls into six stages: removal, preparation, forging, fitting, nailing on and finishing.

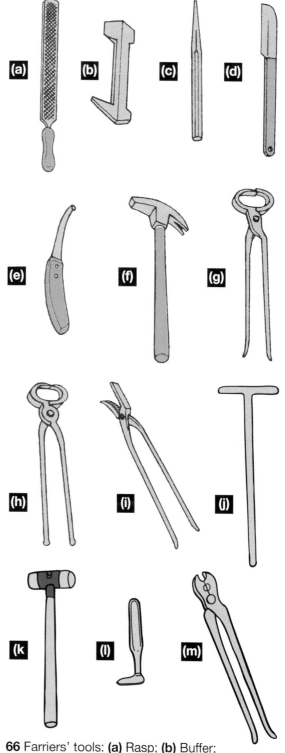

66 Farriers' tools: **(a)** Rasp; **(b)** Buffer; **(c)** Pritchel; **(d)** Toe knife; **(e)** Drawing knife; **(f)** Hammer; **(g)** Hoof cutter; **(h)** Pincers (shoe-pullers); **(i)** Nail clencher; **(j)** T square; **(k)** Plastic mallet; **(l)** Clench groover; **(m)** Nail pullers.

Removal: to remove an old shoe, the farrier first cuts all the clenches, using a buffer and driving hammer. He then levers the shoe off with pincers. If the clenches have been cleanly cut there should be no breaking or tearing away of the wall as the shoe is released.

Preparation: the farrier needs to see the horse walk to assess limb flight and foot fall so he can prepare the foot to the horse's individual requirements. He will clean the sole and frog, removing any excess, and will trim the hoof wall to the appropriate length, then balance and rasp it level.

Forging is the making of a new shoe. The weight and type of iron selected depends on the nature of the work that the horse is doing. After the iron has been shaped on the anvil, the nail holes are stamped and the clips are drawn. Most farriers use manufactured shoes which are made of fullered metal with nail holes already stamped. They come in a variety of sizes and weights and generally require some shape adjustments to provide a good fit.

Fitting: a shoe is then selected. It must be the correct size and selection of steel to suit both the horse and the type of work the horse is expected to do. It is fitted to the foot to check shape (which can be done hot or cold: if done correctly there should be no difference between the two).

Nailing on: the shoe is cooled by immersion in water and nailed on—the first nail usually being driven into the toe. Horseshoe nails are designed with a particular type of head which, correctly fitted, fills the nail hole however much the shoe wears away. Nails are made in various sizes and it is important to use the correct size. The head of a nail which is too large will project and wear away too soon. A head which is too small will not fill the nail hole. Both are equally bad faults which result in early loosening of the shoe.

The end of the nail, where it penetrates the wall, should be turned over and twisted off, leaving a small piece called a clench.

Clips *(fig. 65b)* help to keep the shoe in position and also ensure greater security.

Finishing: the clenches *(see fig. 65b)* are tidied up with the rasp, and a small indentation or bed is made for them in the wall beneath, after which they are embedded with the driving hammer. Finally, to reduce the risk of cracking, the rasp is run around the outer edge of the wall where horn and shoe meet.

The Newly-Shod Foot

When a well-shaped and balanced foot is newly-shod, check the following points:

- The shoe should give the horse a good platform for support and to move off.
- The type of shoe should be suitable for the work required of the horse.
- The weight of iron chosen should be in correct relation to the horse's size.
- The foot should have been suitably reduced in length at both toe and heel, and also on each side, to have a level bearing surface.
- The sole and frog should have been cleaned and trimmed as necessary.
- The size of the nails should be correct. They should fit and fill the nail holes.
- The nail heads should not protrude more than 1mm above the shoe.
- The clenches should be well-formed and well-seated. They should be in line and the right distance (approximately one third of the way) up the hoof wall.
- No daylight should show between the shoe and the foot—particularly at the heel region.
- The heels of the shoe should not be too short.

• The clips should fit smoothly to the hoof wall.

A farrier is a highly-trained craftsman, so if you wish to make any requests for adjustments, be tactful!

Remedial Shoeing

Remedial shoeing is a very specialised area which, if done well, can allow horses with conformational weaknesses to achieve a much higher athletic level and enjoy lengthened working lives.

Remedial shoes act to either improve support or stabilise the hoof capsule, but it must be remembered that before remedial shoeing takes place, conformation must be assessed and gait analysed.

TYPES OF SHOE *(Fig. 67)*

There are many types of shoe available, and they can be split into three main categories.

1 ***Shoes for fast-moving disciplines:*** these are fullered (have a groove in them) which gives a better grip on all surfaces.
2 ***Slow-moving disciplines:*** (for example, carriage driving, or for heavy horses.) They consist of an unmodified bar of iron, shaped, stamped with nail holes and provided with a toe-clip. They are only suitable for a horse doing slow work because they have no provision against slipping or interfering (knocking or brushing). (*See Self-Inflicted Wounds, page 159.*)
3 ***Remedial shoeing:*** there are many types of remedial shoes available covering a wide range of requirements, and shoes can often be designed for specific treatments. For example: ***broad web shoes*** are used mainly for horses whose legs suffer from the effects of concussion, have flat or brittle feet, or have suffered from laminitis. Wider than a standard hunter shoe (*see* fig. 68), they distribute the weight over a broader area and protect more of the solar surface. ***Bar shoes***—e.g. straight bar, egg bar, half bar, combination egg/heart bar and heart bar—*all* have an extra bar, which joins both heels of the shoe, or supports the frog to apply or relieve pressure where necessary. The straight bar *(fig. 67c)* prevents the heels moving against each other once the foot has been put into balance.

STUDS *(Fig. 68)*

Studs are regularly used for competition horses, but opinion is divided over whether one or two studs per shoe is best. Two studs give maximum grip and do not upset the balance too much, whereas a single stud allows the horse to twist and turn.

In polo, they are allowed only at the very heel on the outside of the hind shoes only, which allows for spinning on one leg without locking the foot to the ground.

Different shapes of stud can be used depending on the type of going. Pointed studs are designed for firm gorund, whereas square, blocky studs are for soft ground.

Metal studs can be fitted into the heel of a shoe to lessen the risk of slipping. Ideally they should be worn on the inside and outside of the hind shoes, thereby maintaining the balance of the foot. However, on the inside they increase the danger of treads. Studs worn on the front shoes can cause concussion and are not recommended, but in the case of a confirmed slipper, small studs or plugs are available.

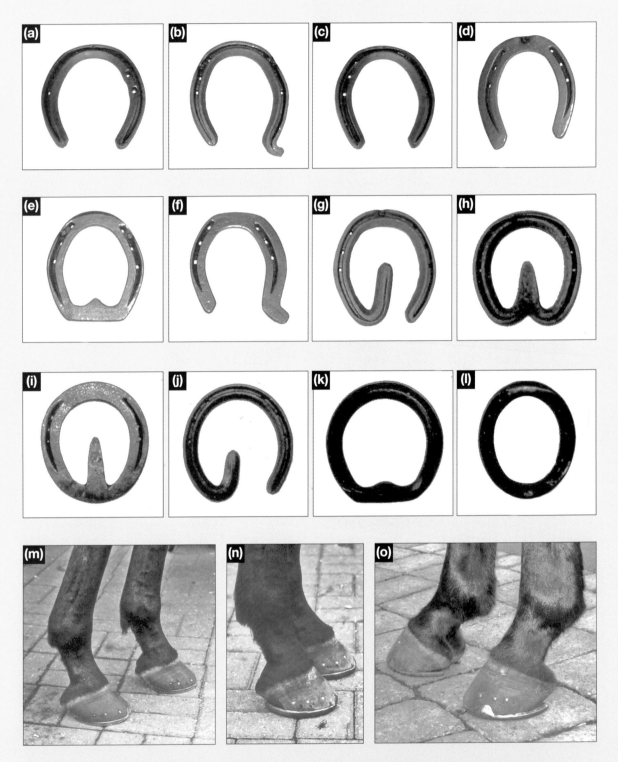

67   Types of hind shoes (a) lateral heel extension; **(b)** trailer shoe; **(c)** normal hind; **(d)** full lateral extension; **(e)** straight bar shoe; **(f)** lateral extension with trailer; **(g)** half bar shoe.

Types of front bar shoe: (h) heart bar; **(i)** egg bar with frog support; **(j)** half bar; **(k)** straight bar shoe; **(l)** egg bar shoe; **(m)** Poorly-shod front feet; **(n)** The same front feet [as (m)] shod correctly; **(o)** Well-shod hind feet.

Road Studs *(Fig. 68a)*

These have a hardened metal core which, being slower-wearing than the shoe itself, presents a rough surface to the ground. They are usually fitted when the horse is shod and remain permanently in the shoe. They do not protrude too much from the shoe, and the balance of the foot is hardly affected.

Competition Studs *(Fig. 68b)*

These can be obtained in various shapes and sizes to suit different conditions and needs. The farrier prepares a threaded hole, and the studs can be fitted or removed with a spanner. They are not designed for use on the roads and should be removed after use, as they distort the balance of the feet; they can also cause damage to the floors of horseboxes and other surfaces, such as tarmac. When the studs are out, oiled cotton wool inserted in the stud holes helps to prevent them from becoming clogged up; the cotton wool can easily be removed with a horseshoe nail. The nail can also be used to clean out the holes if they become caked with mud. A metal tap is used if the holes need rethreading. After use, the studs should be cleaned and stored in an oily cloth to prevent them from rusting.

CARE OF THE UNSHOD FOOT

Working Unshod

This is feasible, especially for native ponies, if work on hard, gritty roads or flinty tracks is avoided. It saves on shoeing costs, and an unshod pony has a more secure grip on every type of surface. Also, injury from a kick by an unshod pony is likely to be considerably less severe.

The feet of a pony working unshod must be checked regularly by the farrier, who will ensure that they present an even surface to the ground and that any splitting and cracking of the walls receive attention.

Unshod When At Grass

It is beneficial to remove the shoes from horses who are not in work if the rest period is to last for over a month. The hooves will grow without interference from nails. The farrier will be needed every four to six weeks to control the natural growth of the hooves and to encourage the correct shape and angle. Keeping the horse unshod will not be beneficial if the ground is hard or if the horse has flat soles. Hard ground may cause the hoof walls to break, and horses with flat soles tend to become footsore.

Youngstock

Feet of young horses must receive regular attention from a farrier because their feet may not grow evenly. Any defects must receive immediate remedial action to ensure that the feet are correctly shaped and balanced.

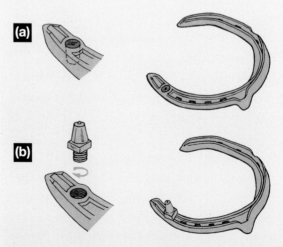

68 Two types of stud: **(a)** Road; **(b)** Competition.

13. Health, Condition and Exercise

HEALTH

The Signs of Good Health

It is important to recognise the signs of good health and to watch for any deviation from them. You will soon learn the characteristics of any horses or ponies in your care and will know if all is normal and well with them. The following are indications of good health:

- Standing and behaving normally; a confident and alert look.
- Coat sleek and lying flat.
- Skin loose and supple to the touch and easily moved over the underlying bones.
- At rest, no visible signs of sweating except in very hot weather.
- Eyes wide open and bright. When examined, the membranes under the eyelids and linings of the nostrils should be salmon pink in colour.
- Eating up well and chewing normally.
- Body well filled out (bone structure well covered) but not gross.
- Limbs free from swellings or heat (cool to the touch).
- Standing evenly on all four feet. Resting a hind leg (but not a foreleg) is quite normal.
- Sound in action; taking strides of equal length.
- Urine fairly thick and either colourless or pale yellow and passed several times a day.
- Droppings, which will vary in colour with the diet, passed approximately eight times daily, in the form of damp balls that break on hitting the ground. Their smell should be inoffensive. When the horse is at grass the droppings may be looser but should not be as sloppy as a cow's.
- Respiration (breathing rate)—when at rest 10 to 20 inhalations per minute.
- Temperature: 37.5–38.5°C (99.5–101.3°F).
- Pulse: 35 to 45 heartbeats per minute.

Maintaining Good Health

Your own perception and assessment of your horse's health and condition are vital to his welfare. On a day-to-day basis, any deviations from *The Signs of Good Health* from the horse's normal behaviour pattern should be noted and appropriate action taken when necessary.

In the stable, the horse should be checked first thing in the morning, so that any overnight problems (such as injuries) can be dealt with promptly. The horse at grass should be checked at least once a day even if he is living out on a large acreage in summer.

Whether the horse is living in or out, remember that the eye of the master is the most important single factor in making sure that the horse thrives.

- The horse must be watered and fed correctly.
- Work and exercise must be complementary. Be aware of the horse's condition and of how much work or exercise he is fit to carry out.
- 'No foot no horse'. Pick out his feet daily, even if he is out at grass. Check the condition of his feet and shoes. Look for any signs of thrush. Book the farrier in good time.
- Regularly assess the need for worming

against roundworm, tapeworm and bots. Your vet or SQP (suitably-qualified person) will advise you.

• The horse should be inoculated against tetanus and influenza. Your vet will advise you.

• Teeth should be checked twice a year by your vet or by a qualified horse dentist.

• If your horse is not thriving, seek expert advice, having first satisfied yourself that he is not overworked or under fed. Check that his respiration, temperature and pulse are normal. *(See also BAD [POOR] CONDITION, page 120.)*

NOTE: All the above are dealt with fully in the appropriate chapters or sections of this manual. Refer to the *Index* for exact page locations.

CONDITION

Good Condition

A horse is said to be in good condition when he is carrying the appropriate amount of weight for his stage of training or for the type of work required of him; and is also thriving, having an appearance of well-being, with bright eyes and a healthy coat and skin. A horse can be in good condition when he is in or between either of the following extremes.

Soft condition: the horse is well but not fit. His muscles are slack. He is fat but not necessarily unhealthy. He is incapable of sustained effort without sweating and distress. Unexercised horses at grass in summer are in soft condition.

69 A horse in hard condition.

Hard condition *(fig. 69):* the horse is fit and well. He is free of superfluous fat, both internally and externally. The muscles are hard and well-developed, and they ripple under the skin as the horse moves. The limbs are toned up to withstand sustained effort without injury or distress. A hunter in regular work in winter, or a horse properly prepared for horse trials is in hard condition.

Bad Condition

A horse is said to be in bad condition when he is not carrying the correct amount of weight for whatever he is expected to do and/or he is not thriving. He may be either:

- **Too thin:** there is no layer of fat under the skin and the muscle is underdeveloped. The neck, shoulders and quarters look thin and scrawny. The point of shoulder, withers, backbone, hips and ribs are prominent. The horse is hidebound, the coat and skin being tight, dry and starey. In this condition the horse will lack energy to work, and will be unable to fight infections or withstand the cold. An over-thin, thoroughbred-type horse may react by becoming hyperactive, due to anxiety. Such a horse will be more contented and settled if given an appropriate diet, with plenty of bulk feed. It is very difficult to build up a horse who starts the winter thin.
- **Too fat:** the horse has a gross appearance; pads of fat make the neck cresty, the shoulders stuffy and the quarters too round. The bone structure will be masked by layers of fat. The over-fat horse will find even moving round his field an effort. The excessive weight will impede his ability to move and perform

without strain. Serious problems, such as laminitis, may result. It is very difficult to reduce the weight of a horse at grass who is over-fat in early spring.

Other Terms for Bad Condition

Gross	Fat.
Light	Rather short of the ideal.
Poor	Ribs in evidence, quarters and neck short of muscle.
Debilitated	Very short of flesh. Coat dull and staring. The horse is altogether weak and incapable of work.
Emaciated	All skin and bone.

CAUSES OF BAD (POOR) CONDITION

Faulty Watering Arrangements
A constant supply of fresh, clean water is essential to maintain condition.

Faulty Feeding Arrangements
An ample supply of good quality hay or grass is essential as a basis of the diet.

Nutritional Deficiencies in the Diet
The horse may be lacking certain minerals, vitamins or fibre, most of which are contained in old pastures or good quality meadow hay. Indications of a craving for minerals are:
- Licking earth
- Gnawing wood or bark
- Eating dung (droppings)

Treatment
- Check the horse has access to a salt lick
- Feed plenty of fibre—meadow grass or meadow hay are best.

♦ Feed a proprietary brand of cubes or mix which contains a broad spectrum of vitamins and minerals.

Age

Unless they are fed carefully and are stabled overnight during the winter, **old horses** may deteriorate to poor condition. From about fifteen years of age they should be checked annually by a vet, both in their own interests and for the safety of their riders. Some horses—and especially ponies—continue to lead useful lives when they are twenty-five years old or more, as long as they are not suffering from physical disability or disease.

Young horses may be in poor condition because they are not receiving enough food for health and growth.

TEETH *(Fig.70)*

Defects in a horse's teeth can result in loss of condition, as well as pain. Among causes of discomfort in the mouth are sharp edges, teething and, occasionally wolf teeth.

Teething

During teething the mouth may be sore, so any work entailing the wearing of a bit should be curtailed. The problem normally resolves itself by the age of five, when teething is completed.

Wolf Teeth

These are small underdeveloped teeth just in front of the upper molars, which may or not be present. If the tooth is immediately in front of the first molar and is firmly embedded, and if the bit is correctly fitted,

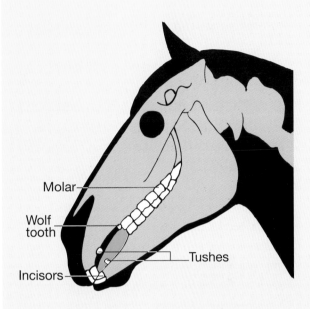

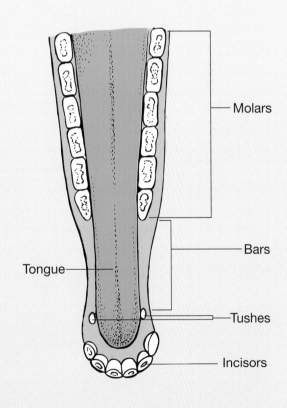

70 The shape of the jaw and mouth.

there is no reason why it should cause a problem. Wolf teeth are often blamed for an unsteady head carriage or reluctance to accept the bit, but this is rarely the case. If the tooth is mobile (or in other words, if it is not firmly embedded) or is sited further forward, it may be necessary to have the tooth removed.

Sharp Edges

Horses' teeth continue to grow after maturity. This balances the hard wear incurred when food, particularly hay and coarse grass, is masticated. Sometimes the wear is uneven. The grinding process carried out by the molar (back) teeth often causes sharp edges to develop. These occur on the outside edges of teeth of the upper jaw and the inside edges of those on the lower jaw. The inside of the cheeks and the tongue can become sore, even ulcerated; chewing becomes painful and ineffective; indigestion, reluctance to eat and loss of condition may then ensue.

Symptoms

* Quidding: partially-chewed food falling from the mouth while the horse is attempting to eat his concentrates or hay.
* Reluctance to be stroked down the sides of the head where the sharp edges lie under the skin.
* Discomfort and resistance when a noseband which presses against the sharp edges is fitted.
* Resistance to the bit. Any soreness in the mouth will cause this.
* Loss of condition.

Precautions and Treatment

(See CARE OF THE TEETH, *page 156.)*

Worms

Worms are one of the most common causes of poor condition. *(See* WORM CONTROL, *page 154.)*

CONDITION RELATED TO WORK

Fatness vs. Fitness

The fat, round, sleek appearance of a horse in soft condition at grass, though indicative of good health, is no indication of his physical fitness to undertake work. He will have excess weight to carry, which will cause additional strain.

The fit horse, in hard condition, is capable of physical exertion without detriment to his health. Such exertion may be in the form of concentrated bursts of energy, as in racing, horse trials and polo, or prolonged, sustained effort, as in hunting, long distance competitions and driving, or in steady exertion over long periods, as in trekking.

There are progressive stages of fitness in a horse, as in a human. The horse in light or medium work, such as hacking or short periods of flat work and jumping, will not require the same degree of heart and lung fitness as a cross-country horse or hunter. It is true to say, however, that the fitter the horse, the better he is able to perform.

Conditioning for Hard Work

Exercise and work must be sensibly coordinated to produce a fit, trained horse, but it is unwise to work the horse hard until he has reached a degree of fitness through regular, steady exercise. As the fitness programme progresses, so the feed must be adjusted to produce the muscle and energy required. *(See FEEDING, page 71.)*

The horse in work should have a day of rest per week when he is not ridden but, in the case of the stabled horse, is led out for a bite of grass and to stretch his legs.

During the first three or four weeks, short periods of hacking at the walk can gradually be increased to 1½ hours walking, with some trotting up the hills by the end of the month. The exercise will be most effective and need not be so long if the horse moves in a positive way, with a good, steady rhythm. The route taken should be varied, to maintain the interest of both horse and rider.

During the following three weeks, some schooling can be added. Thus the horse can begin to do some work. If he is worked correctly, into a supple, rounded outline, this should help to tone up the back and neck muscles and should result in the horse becoming a more balanced and pleasant ride.

If the horse is required for hard work, periods of slow canter should, after the first seven weeks or so, be increased in a systematic way, so that competitions and other activities for which he is required will be completed without undue fatigue.

The fitness programme will depend on individual circumstances, such as the time available, the type of horse, how long he has been at grass, etc. The permutations are countless, but the same principles always apply. Use your common sense—and if in doubt, take expert advice. Above all, make the process a gradual one in order to give the horse the best chance of standing up well to his work later on.

A PROGRAMME FOR GETTING THE HORSE FIT

The following programme is based on the assumption that the horse has been rested for three to four months and is in soft, but good, condition and will be needed for hard work, such as horse trials, twelve to fourteen weeks later.

Remember that no two animals are the same. If in doubt, take expert advice.

The whole process of adjusting the feed and increasing the exercise and work to bring the horse into really hard condition must be gradual. In the case of the hunter or eventer coming up from a complete rest at grass, this can hardly be accomplished in fewer than twelve weeks.

Preliminaries
* Check that your worming programme and your injections against influenza and tetanus are up to date.
* Have the teeth inspected and rasped if necessary.
* Have the horse shod.
* Trim and tidy up mane, tail and heels as necessary.

Stage 1: Walking Only
* Carry out daily walking work for at least three weeks.
* Start with roughly thirty minutes and build up to one to one and a half hours.
* If the horse has been rested for more than three months or has been rested due to a sprain, the walking stage should be extended to six weeks and built up to two hours per day.

After exercise, make sure that the horse is sponged clean of sweat marks and that there is no sign of galling under the saddle or girth. The saddle, numnah and girth must be kept clean and dry. Applying salt water or surgical spirit helps to harden the horse's skin.

Stage 2: Muscling-Up

- Combine walking with slow trotting for the same periods of time, the exercise extending for up to two hours. Active walking, particularly uphill, is a tremendous muscle builder and does not cause undue strain and jarring to the legs.
- Some steady trotting on a hard road helps to harden the legs, but if overdone, particularly with older horses, can cause jarring to the feet and legs.
- Schooling on the flat and some slow cantering can be included and, towards the end of the stage, some simple jumping.

Stage 3: Further Muscling-Up and Developing the Cardiovascular System

- After six weeks or so, your horse should be ready to do some cantering in a more open area. This will continue the muscling-up process and will help to clear his wind.
- A good hill to work on, at a slower pace, is helpful.
- Choose good going and do not canter too fast too far too soon so as to develop the efficiency of the heart and lungs. There is one respiratory cycle per canter stride which is the reason for increasing the canter speed and distance gradually.
- Start with about a quarter of a mile of cantering interspersed with trotting.
- Increase the distance gradually.
- Towards the end of the period the horse should be covering about a mile in a strong canter, but not a gallop, once or twice a week.
- On other days of the week he should be schooled, jumped or hacked out for exercise.

KEEPING THE HORSE FIT

Traditionally, a fit, stabled horse will be able to hunt or work hard for a maximum of three days during a fortnight, on a regular basis. Once the horse has reached a degree of fitness and is competing or hunting regularly he will not need as much exercise and work as in the interim periods. If he is stabled, he should still be ridden or led out every day.

A Horse on the Combined System

He will probably need to be ridden four or five times a week to get fit, and three or four times a week once he is fit. (The more often he is ridden, the fitter he will become.) The system is particularly convenient for those who wish to work the horse hard at weekends only. Remember to adjust the horse's diet so that condition is maintained as the work is increased.

Ponies at Grass

They are very adaptable and will maintain a good degree of fitness if they are ridden at weekends—and, possibly, once during the week—as long as they are kept at an appropriate weight.

For a Child Away at School

The pony will need some form of conditioning to prepare him for the holidays. If there is no-one light enough to ride him, he should be led from another horse *(see RIDE-AND-LEAD, page 49)* or as an occasional alternative, lunged *(see LUNGEING, page 126).*

ROUGHING OFF

This is the process whereby a fit horse is prepared for a rest at grass, day and night, for a prolonged period—for example, the summering of hunters, or wintering of polo ponies or competition horses. The process must be gradual and should take ten days to a fortnight.

- Gradually reduce the hard feed and the work. Increase the hay and/or periods of grazing, thus ensuring that the horse has enough to eat.
- Stop grooming, to allow the coat to form a natural oily protection.
- Remove rugs gradually. Having reduced the clothing to a single light rug, remove it during the day and, if the weather is cold, replace it at night.
- Remove shoes and trim feet.

Either increase time spent out at grass gradually, until his diet is based on grazing and his coat will give him sufficient protection to stay out all the time,

or if facilities are not available for turning the horse out for a period each day and he must be turned out away from your own premises, choose a settled period of good weather and a mild day.

HORSEWALKERS

These are circular pens with rotating partitions in which horses are exercised. Each horse has his own partition which rotates around the outer limits of the pen.

Horsewalkers come in various designs and sizes, usually accommodating a maximum of four or six horses. They may be erected under cover or out of doors and should be sited on flat, well-drained land. Expert advice should be taken to ensure that the footing is sound and suitable.

As labour-saving devices they are useful when short, light exercise is required. Once the horses are accustomed to the regime, one or more may be walked at a time, for any of the following reasons:

- To warm up a horse before strenuous exercise.
- To cool him down after strenuous exercise.
- To stretch his legs on his day off.
- To get him out of the stable while it is being mucked out.

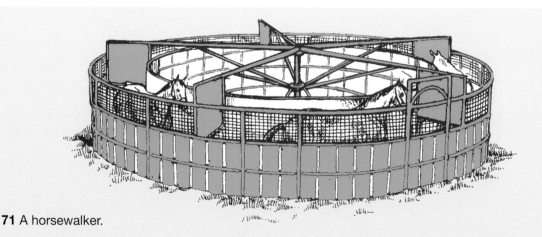

71 A horsewalker.

- To provide a change, particularly in yards which do not have facilities for turning the horses out.

Horsewalkers should be used to supplement normal exercise rather than as a substitute—horses can become very bored walking round in endless circles.

Accidents can and do happen—especially when experience and common sense are lacking—but as long as an experienced person keeps a vigilant eye, this method of exercise can be advantageous, particularly in large yards. *NEVER LEAVE HORSES UNATTENDED ON A HORSEWALKER.*

LUNGEING

Lungeing is a means of exercising a horse when, for any reason, he is not being ridden. The horse moves on a circle around the person lungeing him and is controlled by a long lungeing rein attached to a lungeing cavesson on the horse's head. *(See fig, 72).*

Teaching Yourself to Lunge the Horse

Control is achieved through the voice, the lungeing rein and the whip. If you have not lunged before, practise using all three aids with another person—instead of a horse—at the other end of the lungeing rein. Practise until you are able to control the rein and the lungeing whip. Also, practise the voice aids that you will use. Then, if possible, develop your lungeing skills using a sensible horse who is accustomed to this form of work. The technique of lungeing is covered in The Pony Club publication *Breeding, Backing and Bringing On Young Horses and Ponies*, and is not repeated here.

The Uses of Lungeing

Training Young Horses

Lungeing is used to train young horses, which is fully explained in The Pony Club publication *Breeding, Backing and Bringing On Young Horses and Ponies*.

Providing Exercise

Lungeing is also used to provide exercise, and is particularly useful in the following cases:

- When an exuberant horse needs to be settled before being ridden.
- When a horse has a sore or injured back.
- When a rider is for some reason unable to ride a particular horse, if he is sufficiently skilled he may exercise the horse on the lunge.

72 Lungeing.

• For the horse who has been rested for a length of time, as it will reaccustom him to the feel of the saddle.

NOTE: Lungeing is hard work, especially for the unfit horse. Do not continue for any longer than it takes to settle the horse enough for you to ride him.

Improving the Horse

The correct way of going and the basic paces are described in THE CORRECT WAY OF GOING, page 190, and THE BASIC PACES, page 193. The principles are the same when lungeing as they are when riding. The horse should move forward with confidence from the influence of the whip (leg) and seek the contact of the side reins.

To help to improve a stiff or spoiled horse, the use of ground poles is sometimes appropriate (see TROTTING POLES page 230). First lead the horse over the pole; then lunge him progressing from one pole to two or three placed individually on the circle. Side reins should not be attached. Unless you are very experienced, do not attempt to lunge over a series of poles.

14. Rallies and Competitions

This chapter covers taking your horse out for the day to a show, rally or other function. The requirements will vary, depending on whether the horse is stabled, kept on the combined system, or at grass. The day may be an easy one for the horse, or it may entail very hard work during a long-distance ride, at horse trials, or out hunting. If the horse returns tired after a long day he will need special care.

Travelling

All aspects of travelling, preparing the vehicle, preparing the horse (saddled or unsaddled) loading, unloading, etc., are covered in TRANSPORTING HORSES, page 135.

THE DAY BEFORE

Plan your exact route on a map and calculate the time at which you will be setting out next morning. If hacking on, aim to cover 10 kilometres (about 6 miles) per hour.

For a journey by horsebox or trailer down narrow lanes to local venues, allow for a speed of no more than about 40kph (25mph). If going to a meet, allow an extra 20 minutes for parking and unboxing at least a mile from the meet, and for hacking on from there.

Make a list of the equipment that you will need. Check that your saddlery is clean and that the stitching, especially on reins and stirrup leathers, is sound. Put out your clothes and personal items: clean shirt, tie, jodhpurs or breeches, gloves, hat, body protector, jacket, whip, etc. Clean your boots and your Pony Club badge!

Check and prepare the horsebox or trailer. If the vehicle is dry and secure against theft, pack as much as you can in advance—saddlery, rugs, boots, water bucket, feed, haynet, first aid kit, etc.

THE STABLED HORSE

Early Morning

Be up in good time and go to the stables.
• Look round the horse as usual. Water him and give him a small net of hay.

- Pick out his feet, muck out, rearrange the bedding and set fair, as there will be no time to do so later.
- Feed. Remove and refill the haynet so that it is ready on your return.
- Go for your breakfast.
- Quarter or groom as time permits.
- Plait the mane. This is usual for showing, dressage and hunting, but not required for rallies or cub-hunting.
- Put on a tail bandage. As many horses soil their tails while travelling, some people put the tail into a stocking and secure it at the dock with the tail bandage.
- If you are going by horsebox or trailer, prepare the horse for travelling. *(See* Transporting Horses: Preparing the Horse, *page 135.)* You may prefer to saddle up when you arrive, but if he is likely to be excited when you unbox him—especially if other horses are passing by on the road—this will not be easy. The bridle may be put on in the box, where he will be easier to control, but—depending on the circumstances—it may be sensible to travel him saddled-up.
- Load a container of fresh water, your personal equipment, and anything that you could not pack the night before, such as your grooming kit.
- If you are hacking, saddle up.
- In either case leave the horse tied up in his stable while you make final preparations.
- Put on your riding kit.
- Load up or mount.

Parking

At a competition or rally, unless specifically directed elsewhere, park in a convenient place, preferably in the shade, not too close to the next vehicle and not causing an obstruction to others.

At a meet, choose a safe place a mile or so from the meet itself. Avoid causing an obstruction on the road or in a gateway.

If you will be leaving the vehicle unattended, when you have unboxed and completed your saddling up, store all your equipment neatly and lock the vehicle. Put a headcollar and rope where you can easily reach them on your return. It is convenient to have a loop of string attached to your box or trailer to which you can tie up the horse while saddling up or preparing for the return journey. But you should not tie him up if he is excitable and there are other horses about.

Hacking to the Venue

Ride at a steady trot, interspersed with periods of walking. Having rechecked your girth when you mounted, check it after a few minutes. Your horse should be calm and not sweating when you arrive.

73 Arriving at a rally.

On Arrival

If you have hacked on, dismount, look round your horse, check shoes and make necessary adjustments to your saddlery. Keep well clear of other horses' heels. If the weather is cold, remount and walk your horse in order to keep him warm. If you have transported him by road, unbox in good time to be ready and warmed up when required. Remember to say, 'Good morning' to any officials at a show, and to the Master at a meet or mock hunt.

During the Day

If the preparatory work has been carried out efficiently, the horse should be equal to any demand required of him. Avoid expending his energy needlessly. At a show or event, never use him as a grandstand, but dismount at suitable intervals to give both of you a rest. Remember to offer him water and something to eat; but choose a time to do this when he is cool and calm, and will not be working for an hour or two.

Red and Green Ribbons

If you will be out hunting or riding in a group and your horse is liable to kick, you should put a red ribbon on his tail as a warning to others. This does not entitle you to ride through a crowd, particularly in a gateway, expecting other riders to keep out of your way. The responsibility for any damage by your horse—and kicks can be serious—is yours and yours alone.

If you are riding a young horse who is nervous and excitable, a green ribbon on his tail will indicate this. Other riders are usually helpful in keeping clear of you, but the responsibility for your horse's actions is still yours.

When on a long-distance ride or out hunting, choose good going whenever possible. At a check, if the horse is blowing hard, turn his head to the wind. Whenever you have the opportunity, dismount so as to ease the weight off his back for a moment. Sit well in balance with the horse at all paces and be quiet and correct with your aids.

Opening and Shutting Gates

If the horse has been trained at home and is obedient to the aids, this is comparatively simple. A young horse is often anxious about going close up to a gate, and finds it hard to stand still. A little time and patience are usually required.

Do not allow the horse to face the gate, as he may well try to jump it.

When opening a gate, make the horse stand still, parallel with and close to it, his head facing the latch. Use the hand nearest to the gate to unfasten the latch. Either pull or push the gate open *(fig. 74)*; then pass through.

74 Opening a gate.

To shut the gate, turn the horse round, transfer your reins and whip to the other hand, and either pull or push the gate shut. Again, make the horse stand still, parallel with and close to the gate, while you lean down to fix the latch with your hand.

If you cannot reach the latch with your hand, use your hunting whip. The hook of the whip can also be used to push the gate away or to pull it towards you. *(The hunting whip is shown on page 189 in fig. 89.)*

If you and your horse are not accustomed to opening and shutting gates, you will waste a lot of time while out riding or hunting, especially when hounds are running.

When passing through a swinging gate with a group of other riders, take care not to let the gate slam in front of the person following you. Push it well back so that he can catch it easily. If it is a self-shutting gate, hold it until he can reach it. If there is stock in the fields, it is vital to prevent them escaping, so the last person through the gate must make sure that it is shut. Never gallop off leaving someone else to shut the gate on their own.

At the End of the Day
After you have thanked the Master, organiser, or host, your prime consideration must be to get the horse home in a cool state as quickly as possible, without causing him extra fatigue.

Hacking Home
- Aim to cool the horse off, mentally and physically.
- Take the quickest and easiest route.
- Loosen the girth slightly and ride on a long rein, but do not dawdle.
- Your pace and route must be governed by the necessity of getting the horse into his stable cool and dry. It is the sweating, excitable horse who will cause most work when you get home.
- When the horse has cooled down, allow him to rinse his mouth and drink a few sips of water at a stream or cattle trough, if one is near at hand.
- After about ten minutes or so cooling off, trot slowly for a while and then walk again.
- If it is raining or getting dark, keep him walking, alternated with longer periods of slow trotting. When tired, a wet, cold horse takes longer to dry than a wet, warm one; but you should not ride home at a fast pace.
- Even if the horse seems quite cool, it is as well to walk him for the final mile or so in order to lessen the likelihood of his breaking out into a sweat once he is home.
- When you are about half a mile away, dismount, slacken the girth further, run your stirrup irons up, and lead him home. This will allow the circulation to return to his back.

If you finish the day at a distance from your box, use the same principles (described above) as if you were hacking home. Your aim is to return to the stable or box with a calm and cool horse.

Returning Home by Box or Trailer
The horse should be in a cool, calm state for loading. At a rally or gymkhana, if your horse is easy to handle you may prefer to take off his tack, prepare him for travel while he is tied to the side of the box, and load him from the headcollar.

After a long and tiring day it is better to travel him home with the saddle on, to prevent his back from becoming chilled.

In this case, before loading:

+ Put on a headcollar over the bridle.
+ If you have no helper to hold the horse, tie him up to the loop of string attached to the box or trailer.
+ Run up the stirrup irons and loosen the girth if you have not already done so.
+ If he arrived wearing a rug, put it on over the saddle, buckling it in front and securing it with crossed surcingles, or a roller or surcingle.
+ An unclipped horse who is still damp must not be chilled by draughts. He will therefore need a rug which wicks the sweat away from his body, or an anti-sweat covered by a light sheet. He will be better off too warm than too cold.
+ Prepare the horse for travelling and load him up.
+ Once he is safely in the box or trailer, remove the headcollar, take off the bridle, put on the headcollar again, and tie him up.

Put up a haynet for him to pick at on the way home. Before driving away make sure that the ramp is secure and the trailer legs are raised. Check that you have not left any of your saddlery, clothing, etc., lying around. Many a hunting whip, pair of gloves, or even a hat has been lost through being left on the mudguard of a trailer.

Back at the Stable

If the horse has had an easy day, has been groomed at the show, and is not dirty or covered with dried sweat, the principles described below should be followed, but the horse can be quickly groomed and set fair for the night.

Hunters or horses who are frequently returned to their stables tired and dirty, learn to expect a certain procedure. As they have carried their riders all day, every effort should be made to see that they settle down and that their tired systems return to normal as soon as possible. Adhering to a sensible, regular routine to suit the individual horse is the best way to help him to recover. The following is suggested.

On Return from a Hard Day

+ Check the horse over briefly, in a good light, for any obvious injuries, but do not let him get chilled while you do this.
+ Lead him into the box, remove the saddle and bridle and give his back a rub and a few sharp slaps to restore circulation.
+ Leave the horse, close the door, and give him a chance to roll and stale.
+ After a few minutes, return and put on a rug to wick away the sweat, or an anti-sweat rug under a light rug.
+ Next, give him up to half a bucket of water, with the chill taken off: that is, about 21°C (70°F). If he is very tired, one tablespoon of glucose—or some electrolytes administered according to the directions on the container—in half a bucket of water, will act as a pick-me-up.
+ Many horses, and particularly ponies, will not drink water with anything added, so it may be as well to offer a choice of plain water unless you are certain that he will take the pick-me-up readily. (See also WATERING AFTER HARD WORK, page 71.)
+ Allow half a bucket of water at a time, at intervals of 15 minutes or so, until he has quenched his thirst.
+ Put on a headcollar and tie the horse up within reach of his haynet, so that he can eat. This will help to settle him

down and get his digestion working before he has his feed.

- Your main concern is to keep the horse warm and, if he is tired, to do only enough to ensure that he is dry and comfortable. Rest and quiet will help him most.
- Pick out the feet and unplait the mane.
- Untie the horse. Sponge out his eyes and nostrils. Retie him and sponge out the dock.
- To check and groom him you will need to take off the rugs, but if it is cold, cover the parts of the body that you are not working on at the time.
- Check the horse carefully for injuries such as cuts, thorns and overreaches, and treat them as necessary.
- If he is dry, wipe off the sweat marks and remove the mud with a handful of dry straw or a cactus cloth. Pay special attention to the tender parts between the fore and hind legs. Feel carefully with your hands for cuts and thorns. Then groom him gently but quickly with a body brush.
- If he is almost dry, begin to work on the dry parts, as this will help him to settle.
- From time to time while you are working feel the ears, as they will indicate whether the horse is likely to break out (into a sweat) or not. If they are at all cold or clammy, and if the horse does not object, pull them by grasping them at the poll and allowing them to slip gently through your closed hands. Repeat this until they are warm and dry.
- Do not wash mud off the legs unless the hair is short and easily dried. The only circumstances in which mud must be washed off are when it has caused blistering to some part of the body. It may then be necessary to wash the relevant part. If so, do this gently; avoid scrubbing; and finish off by spongeing gently with a solution of one teaspoon of salt to one pint (0.65 litre) of lukewarm water.

- When you have done what is necessary to his body, rug up the horse, using an anti-sweat rug next to his skin. If you use straw bedding, you can thatch him with straw next to the skin, under the rug. This will help him to dry off, especially if he has a long coat.
- If the tail is wet and muddy, wash and rinse it in warm water and shake out surplus moisture.
- If the legs are wet and muddy, bandage them over a layer of hay, softened straw, or Gamgee, using comfortable stable bandages. Leave them to dry—if necessary until the following morning; this has the added advantage of keeping the extremities warm.
- Refill the water bucket. Wait until he has had time to drink and then give him a small feed. Then go off to have your own meal.

Later that Evening

- Return to the horse and feel his ears.
- If the ears are warm and dry, you have nothing further to worry about. If not, dry them off with a stable rubber and your hands, and look for further signs of breaking out over the loins and down the flanks. If these are very obvious, it may be necessary to lead the horse around or graze him in hand for a few minutes, to settle and dry him off; but in cold weather this can be risky. Normally it is sufficient to dry the ears off with a stable rubber and periodically replace any damp rugs with dry ones. Remember: a warm, slightly sweaty horse is better than a cold, dry one.

* If all is well, set him fair for the night. Check water, rugs, ventilation and hay. Then give him a final feed.
* If anything is amiss, keep going back until you are satisfied that the horse is comfortable.

NOTE: This routine is a guide only, for no two horses react in the same way, and individual conditions, stables, etc., vary enormously. In following these guidelines you should use your own good sense to achieve the desired result: a warm, contented, well-fed horse, settled comfortably for the night.

The Following Day

* Trot the horse up to see that no lameness has resulted from the previous day's activities.
* Run your hand over the saddle and girth regions to make sure that no saddle injuries are in evidence.
* Groom very thoroughly. Be especially on the lookout for girth galls, bumps, thorns and bruises.
* Be sure to check the feet and shoes.
* Avoid exercise, other than turning the horse out in the paddock for a while, or leading him out in hand. Both will help to take any minor filling and stiffness out of tired legs.
* Make sure that the horse has a good, deep bed, which will encourage him to lie down and rest.

THE HORSE KEPT ON THE COMBINED SYSTEM

The same principles apply as for the stabled horse, particularly in the winter when the horse is stabled overnight. In the summer, if the horse is normally out in the paddock at night it may be easier to bring him in

and remove any mud the night before.

On returning home, check him over and turn him out as soon as possible to resume his normal routine. If he wears a turnout rug, *see The Horse Living Out in a Turnout Rug, page 60.*

THE GRASS-KEPT PONY

Working a grass-kept horse hard in winter is not as a rule satisfactory. Native pony types, being more resilient, should be able to manage the winter activities, if they are properly fed and have access to shelter.

Make your preparations the night before. Follow all the principles described for the stabled horse in *The Stable Yard and Managing the Stabled Horse, page 50,* except where modified below.

The Previous Evening

It is impossible to dry the thick, greasy, natural coat by rubbing, and it is not satisfactory to saddle up when the pony is soaking wet. So if you have a stable and if the weather is likely to turn rainy, catch the pony the previous evening, pick out his feet and stable him in deep bedding to prevent draughts around his heels and legs.

If his coat is very wet, and if it is a cold night, put on a light rug with an absorbent lining, or with an anti-sweat rug or some straw underneath, so that he does not chill while drying off. Any rugs should be removed as soon as he is dry.

Give him a bucket of water and a haynet.

Leave the top half of the stable door, and any windows, open because he will be used to plenty of fresh air.

If the pony normally has a feed of concentrates, give this at the usual time.

Early Morning

If the pony has been brought in overnight, check him over, replenish his water supply, pick out his feet, and muck out.

- Brush out his mane and tail with a soft dandy or body brush and lay with a water brush. If the tail has been pulled (not recommended for an animal at grass) put on a tail bandage.
- Remove the mud and brush his body lightly with the dandy brush. The natural protection against wet and cold provided by the greasy substance in the coat should not be interfered with by too much grooming.
- Never wash a horse or pony who lives out at night, even in summer.
- Feed the pony if he normally receives a feed of concentrates, and then go for your breakfast.

If the pony has not been brought in the night before:

- Catch him and wipe any wet mud off his hooves with an old, dry cloth or towel. Then pick out his feet and check his shoes.
- Tie him up under cover and groom him as described earlier. If he is very wet and muddy, there will be little you can do. If he is only slightly damp and has dried by the time you return after breakfast, you will be able to groom him then.

Setting Out and On the Road

In winter the grass-kept pony, with his long coat, will be sure to sweat while hacking on to the destination, unless a quite impracticable slow pace is maintained. Progress will be slower than with a stabled horse, and 6 to 8kph (4 to 5mph) is a fair estimate. The girth will need adjusting two or three times in the first half-hour.

During the Day

The same principles apply as for the stabled horse. When on a long ride or out hunting remember that the unclipped, grass-fed animal is likely to tire more easily, and deserves even greater consideration from his rider. You should dismount frequently and, above all, decide in good time when to call it a day and start for home. A short day will leave the pony less tired and more likely to be in good heart for future activities.

Excessive sweating due to his long coat will cause the pony to lose weight, but nature's grease will protect him from the subsequent chilling, so there is no need to worry, if reasonable precautions are taken.

The Road Home

All that applies to the stabled horse applies here, but if the unclipped pony has sweated profusely, his long coat is unlikely to dry completely on the return journey. The aim is to arrive home with him reasonably cool under his damp coat. Dismount, loosen the girth, and lead him the last half-mile. If he is to come home by box or trailer, leave his saddle on to keep his back warm.

On Arrival Home

Remove the saddle and bridle and put on a headcollar. Examine his feet and body carefully. Check his coat to see if the hairs are dry close to the skin, which indicates that he is drying well. A draughty stable is highly unsatisfactory. It is best to give the pony a drink of water with the chill off and then to turn him straight out into the field, even if he is sweating. In this case he should be given his usual hay, and later, if required, a bran mash or small feed. However, if there are other horses in the field who are not being fed, you may have no alternative than to water him and give him a bran mash before turning him out. NOTE: it is a mistake to feed a tired horse or pony a large amount of concentrates as a pick-me-up. In these circumstances, the digestive system will be unable to cope, and colic may well result. A bran mash, perhaps with chaff and pony cubes—a handful of each—is the safest form of feed *(see BRAN MASH, page 75)*. A small pony will not need more than 0.5kg (l lb) of bran.

The Day After

Catch the pony and inspect him for cuts, thorns, bruises, faulty shoes, etc. Trot him up to check that he is sound. Remove the sweat marks from the areas under the saddle, girth and bridle.

15. Transporting Horses

Most horses travel satisfactorily as long as they have been sensibly and sympathetically introduced to the box or trailer and have not been frightened by inconsiderate driving.

Horses are sensitive to human moods, so allow plenty of time when loading and unloading and avoid showing signs of nervousness, haste or excitement.

THE VEHICLE

The height, width and length of the space allocated to the horse must be suitable for his size.

- Single axle trailers are not recommended.
- From time to time, check that the floorboards are not showing signs of rotting, that the tyres are in good condition and that the brakes are sound.
- Keep the metal fittings oiled and see that they are secure and easy to operate.
- Unless your box or trailer has floor matting, make sure that it is suitably bedded down with straw or shavings.
- Incorrect tyre pressures and faulty springs can cause towing problems as well as discomfort.
- The towing-hitch should be the correct height for the trailer.
- Before using the trailer, check the coupling, ramps, side doors, legs and lights (including indicators).
- Check that the horsebox or towing vehicle is taxed, insured and in a sound, roadworthy condition and that the brakes, lights, etc. are working properly. See that it has oil, water, and enough fuel for the journey. Horses travel more contentedly if they have something to eat. Unless you are travelling to a meet, rally, competition or other function where the horse must work hard within an hour or so of arrival, tie up a haynet ready for him when he is loaded.
- Remember to take the horse's passport whenever he travels. This is a legal requirement.

PREPARING THE HORSE

Never transport a horse in studs, other than road studs.

Rugs

The number of rugs needed, if any, will depend on the weather. Remember that a horse generates a good deal of heat in a confined space, and he may also sweat with excitement. Anti-sweat rugs or rugs which wick the sweat away from the skin are helpful in counteracting this. Designed for use under a rug or sheet, they allow the free flow of air while keeping the horse warm; used on their own they do not serve this purpose and can easily tear. The sweat rug should be secured at the front. The day rug or sheet can be folded back from the chest and secured with a roller. The horse should never be left to travel in a rug secured only at the chest, because it could slip round, down, and under his feet.

75 Horses ready for loading, wearing **(a)** full protection for a long journey and **(b)** a breathable rug and leg and tail protection with velcro fastenings, suitable for a shorter journey.

Protective Clothing

The following items will all help to prevent injury:

- Tail bandage and tail guard.
- Travelling bandages or travelling boots.
- Knee boots.
- Hock boots.
- Poll guard.

(For further information and for instructions on fitting, see BANDAGES, *page 92, and* BOOTS, *page 95.)*

Transporting a Horse Saddled-Up

On short journeys, a horse can travel partially or completely saddled up. If he is in a bridle, always put a leather headcollar over it, with the reins over his neck. If necessary, the slack should be taken up with a knot, or the reins should be twisted around each other under the throat, and secured by passing the throatlash through one of them. If they are very long you can loop them behind one or both stirrups.

NOTE: Nowadays, horses are often taken for short journeys in leg protectors with thick velcro straps, and breathable rugs. However, some horses will not tolerate the high hind leg protectors and will need correctly-fitted bandages instead. If you use a trailer with a partition and unload through the front ramp, the horse should not be saddled up, as the saddle might get caught as the horse is unloaded.

LONG JOURNEYS

Lengthy journeys by road should be broken every four or five hours. The horse should be checked and offered water and, unless it is very cold, the ramp or a door should be opened to admit fresh air. If the journey necessitates a period of eight hours or more continuously in a confined space, it is as well to feed a bran mash the night before to guard against constipation. Thereafter, feed as appropriate to the length of the journey and to the horse's condition, fitness and forthcoming work programme.

LOADING

- Never ride a horse into a trailer or horsebox.
- Always use a leather headcollar rather than a synthetic type as leather is more likely to break in an emergency. (This also applies when leaving a headcollar on a horse turned out to grass.)
- Always wear gloves and never wrap the headcollar rope round your hand.
- Lead the horse straight up the centre of the ramp.
- Look straight ahead yourself and do not look round at the horse.
- If the horse hangs back, do not pull at him, but position yourself by his shoulder and encourage him to walk up alongside you.
- When transporting a single horse in a double trailer without a partition, cross-tie him by securing him to both sides of the compartment. This will prevent him from trying to turn round.
- If there is a partition in the centre, put him on the right side of the trailer or box as he will travel more smoothly on the crown of the road.
- Do not tie the horse up until the bar, the breeching strap, or the ramp are in place—or, in the case of a box, until the partitions around the horse are secure.
- Tie him up quite short with a quick-release knot.
- Beware of any ramp which could accidentally fall on top of you. Always stand at the side to lift or lower a trailer ramp. If necessary, find someone to help you so that you can stand one each side rather than risk an accident.
- Box ramps usually have gates or doors, so they are less dangerous. To lift these ramps on your own you will need to be in the centre to cope with the weight and height. If for any reason this could put you in danger, find someone to help you and stand at the side.

With a helper: either come in on a circle from the side and lead the horse straight up the ramp. (This is usually the most effective method.)

OR position yourself and the horse not less than 4.5m (15ft) from the box or trailer and facing the ramp. Then lead the horse straight up it.

In both cases, the helper should then secure the bar or breeching strap, if fitted, and finally put up the ramp, standing to the side.

Without a helper: lead the horse up the ramp. If you are using a trailer, persuade him to go in ahead of you.

Secure the necessary partitions, breeching bar or strap, and put up the ramp. If the horse persists in running back before you can do this, you should find someone to help you.

Training Horses to Load Willingly

When introducing an inexperienced horse to a box or trailer, a vehicle with two ramps is preferable. Allow ample time for the horse's own senses to dispel any doubts that he may have. Do not fluster him.

Lower the front ramp of the vehicle and remove the partition. Let him take his own time to follow the person leading him up the back ramp and out via the front. This process can be repeated several times, rewarding him with a titbit while he stands inside.

To gain the horse's confidence, it is helpful if, for a few days, you load him and then feed him in the box or trailer without moving off.

Horses Reluctant to Be Loaded

There are many degrees of reluctance, but assuming that the horse has not previously had a fright, your success in coaxing him into a box or trailer depends largely on the confidence that he has in you and the discipline that you have instilled in him.

First decide why he is resisting, and adjust your methods accordingly. Is it fright? Is it unwillingness to leave stable companions? Is he just stubborn?

The following are some of the methods that may help, and you should select those most likely to overcome the resistance of the horse in question at the time. You will almost certainly need assistance.

- Either move the back of the partition to one side, thus making the entrance larger, or remove the partition altogether. Do what you can to make the interior appear light and spacious.
- Lower the front ramp of the vehicle, if it has one. A shy horse will sometimes enter if he can see the way out.
- Draw up alongside a wall, a hedge or another lorry, as this makes the box or trailer look less forbidding than if parked out in the open. It also provides a wing.
- If the ramp is too steep, lessen the angle by backing the box or trailer up against higher, level ground, and lower the ramp on to it. The end of the ramp must be firm and level.
- Load another horse first, to provide a lead.
- The helper should encourage the horse from behind, standing safely to one side. This may be sufficient by itself, but the helper should carry a whip, as a quick tap often makes up the horse's mind for him.
- Fit ropes or lungeing reins to the back of the box or trailer and have a helper on each side of the horse to hold them taut. This helps to keep a horse straight and often persuades him to go in. As the horse moves forward, the helpers should change sides, keeping the ropes taut but standing a safe distance from his heels. If necessary, apply pressure with both ropes above the hocks and around the lower part of the quarters.

If you are on your own, attach a lungeing rein or long rope to the right side of the vehicle. Pass it round his quarters above his hocks to the left side, keeping it taut in your right hand. Lead the horse forward in the normal way but with the headcollar rope in your left hand. If he hangs back, encourage him to move forward by increasing the pressure on the lunge line with your right hand. Always be firm, but avoid using force which, although sometimes effective, creates too much tension and seldom results in teaching the horse to load well. In the end it comes back to the confidence that the horse has in you, the way in which he has been transported previously, and your own feel and horse sense.

THE JOURNEY

Before driving away, recheck the trailer-coupling, ramps, side doors, legs and lights.

As a horse is unable to see out, he cannot anticipate the movements of the vehicle, and may lose his balance. As a general rule, drive at a steady pace—not more than 48 to 64kph (30 to 40 mph); less at roundabouts, and on winding or bumpy roads; and very slowly across fields and when reversing or turning. Proceed as smoothly as possible, avoiding jerks, violent braking and fast cornering.

Bad Travellers

Once a horse has been frightened, he will seldom regain his full confidence when travelling. Loss of confidence is usually the result of being loaded in a compartment that is too narrow, or of being taken too fast round corners, or of sudden braking by the driver. Careful driving promotes easy loading and confident travellers.

UNLOADING

Walking Forward Down a Ramp

- If you have a trailer, untie the horse or horses before lifting the front bars, in case they try to rush out. If more than one horse is travelling, first unload the one nearest to the ramp, keeping him near by while you move the front of the partition across to prevent the second horse scraping himself against it or getting stuck.
- When unloading from a horsebox, make sure that the horse will stand safely while any doors and partitions which might otherwise swing and hit him, are secured back. Unless you can do this single-handed, you will need help.

Always lead a horse straight and steadily down the centre of the ramp

Backing Out

With a helper, untie the horse before he/she lowers the ramp and removes the bars or straps. The helper should stand to the side and never directly behind the ramp or the horse, where he could get crushed. While you back the horse out, the helper should be ready to keep the horse straight by placing a hand on his quarters to prevent him stepping over the side of the ramp and scraping his hind legs.

If there are two horses, it is safest to have one person at each horse's head, and two helpers—one on each side of the ramp. Both bars or straps should be removed before the ramp is lowered, and the horses should be encouraged to back out independently, in a slow and careful manner.

If you only have one helper to unload two horses, park the trailer alongside a wall, hedge or substantial fence. Untie both horses, putting the rope over the neck of the horse who is on the side away from the wall. Your helper should then lower the ramp, unfasten both straps or bars, and stand at the side of the ramp away from the wall. You should follow the horse who is on the side of the wall, and your helper will be able to catch the other horse as he backs out.

NOTE: If a horse rushes back, on no account hang on to his head. All being well, a helper will be able to catch hold of the headcollar rope; but if not, it is far better for him to go loose than to damage himself by rearing and hitting his head, or going over backwards.

Without a helper, untie the horse before lowering the ramp and removing the bar or strap. If having untied the rope you leave it through the ring, many horses will think that they are still tied up, and will remain still. You can then either catch the horse as he comes back, or—if there is room—move up to his head and back him out. Alternatively, use a long rope or lungeing rein to retain some control of the horse. Try to get him to come back steadily and straight, but if he really rushes, do not hang on.

A single horse in a double compartment (with no partition) should be tied to both sides of the compartment (cross-tied) to stop him from trying to turn round during the journey. When he has been untied before unloading, he may well try to turn. Though there may be room for a pony to turn, there is seldom room for a horse, and you should try to prevent him from attempting it. Remove the rope from one side of the headcollar. Untie the other rope, leaving it through the ring. Lower the ramp, and quickly but calmly move up beside the horse before he begins to turn round. You can then back him out as described above.

AFTER A JOURNEY

Always muck out the box/trailer and ensure that you clear the drain holes. Push dry bedding up to the front to allow the floorboards to dry and reduce the risk of rotting.

AIR TRAVEL

Horses usually travel quite happily by air as long as they have a compartment wide enough to allow them to spread their legs and maintain their balance.

A capable attendant, able to deal with panic or fright, must accompany the horse. Before travelling, seek the advice of someone with knowledge and experience of air travel. They will guide you as to what clothing and protection the horse will need. *(For advice on feeding, see* LONG JOURNEYS, *page 136.)*

16. Safety and Insurance

SAFETY

The importance of safety is stressed throughout this book. All horsemen must be constantly aware of the hazards involved in riding and looking after horses.

RIDING ON THE ROAD

Riding on the road cannot be recommended, but if there is nowhere else to ride, or if it is the only way to reach safer riding areas, it may be a necessary evil. Some horses are more reliable than others, depending on their temperament and training.

Before riding or leading on the roads, children and adults should be aware of the dangers and should be conversant with the appropriate section of *The Highway Code*. Whenever possible, children should be accompanied by an adult.

The Pony Club prepares its members for the Road Rider Safety Test, which is taken at a variety of levels during their training, but although helpful, this is no guarantee of safety. (The Pony Club publication, *Junior Road Rider*, and *The Pony Club Road Rider* DVD, deal with this subject in greater detail.)

When planning to ride on the road, consider the following: firstly, the volume and speed of the traffic (rush hour traffic should be avoided); secondly, whether there is a suitable grass verge; and thirdly, whether you can be seen by other road users. It is always safer to wear reflective bands or jackets. Those printed with wording such as, 'Please pass wide and slow', or 'Young horse. Please slow down', help to make motorists aware of the need for caution when passing horses and ponies.

It is very important to thank considerate motorists—generally done by raising a hand—but if at the moment that the vehicle is passing it would for any reason be unwise to take a hand off the reins, look briefly at the driver, smile, nod your head and mime the words 'thank you'.

DRESSING SAFELY FOR RIDING

Riding Hats

For all Pony Club activities, Pony Club members must, when mounted, wear a hat which conforms to The Pony Club's current required standard. The hat must fit comfortably; the drawstring (if it has one) must be adjusted correctly; and the chinstrap must be fastened.

Hats are available in various shapes and sizes, so, when you buy a new one, make sure that as well as conforming to the required standard it is a suitable design for the size and shape of your head. The shop assistant should be qualified to give guidance as to which hat is suitable for your particular needs and to ensure that the fit and adjustment are satisfactory.

Footwear

Footwear must have smooth soles and heels of a sensible depth: jodhpur boots or riding boots are recommended, and are obligatory in Pony Club competitions. Trainers and other soft shoes—or those without heels—can slip through the stirrup and therefore cause serious accidents. Wellies and other boots with large treads are also dangerous because they can become wedged in the stirrup.

Jodhpurs and Breeches

These are designed specially for riding. You will ride better and feel more comfortable if you are wearing one or the other.

Body Protectors

These are recommended, especially for cross-country work. They are compulsory for the cross-country phases of Pony Club and other competitions. A list of approved patterns is available from The Pony Club's headquarters.

What to Wear When Handling Horses from the Ground

Shoes

Strong shoes or boots will protect your feet should the horse tread on you.

Gloves

When leading in hand it is advisable to wear gloves. They are essential for lungeing.

Riding Hat

A riding hat should be worn when leading or lungeing horses. It should be correctly fitted, with the harness secured (fig. 76).

76 The handler correctly dressed for lungeing.

FIRE PRECAUTIONS

+ You *must* have adequate fire extinguishers in the yard. (Contact your local Fire Brigade to get appropriate advice).
+ Devise a fire drill for your yard, and make a plan of how to evacuate the horses.
+ Make sure that everyone in the yard knows what to do in case of fire.
+ Never smoke anywhere in the stable yard, in barns, trailers or the back of horseboxes.
+ Remember that hay and straw are particularly inflammable.
+ Unplug all electrical appliances not in use, or before leaving the yard.
+ Make sure that bonfires or burning muck heaps are in a safe position. If there is any danger of fire spreading from them, they should be thoroughly dampened down.

In the Event of a Fire:
1 *Sound the alarm.*
2 *Evacuate the stables.*
3 *Call the Fire Brigade.*
4 *Fight the fire if you can do so without the risk of injury to yourself or others.*

Shout to attract attention if you do not have a fire alarm. Consider human safety first and make sure that everyone in the danger area has heard the alarm and can move to safety.

Evacuate horses according to your fire drill. If you have only one or two, and their headcollars and lead ropes are at hand, lead them to a field or other safe place, and turn them out. Otherwise:
1 Block access to any roads or other places of danger.
2 Open the stable doors to enable the horses to escape of their own free will. Direct them towards a field or other safe pace and shut them in.

3 If not done already, call the Fire Brigade and unblock the access to the road.

All animals are frightened by fire and horses are no exception. A terrified horse might refuse to be moved from his stable. In this case, put on his headcollar, take off your jacket and put it over his head with his ears in the sleeve holes; or cover his head with a wet cloth. Then lead him out of the stable. As he may try to return to his box, take him well away from the stable area.

Inhalation of smoke is dangerous to horses and humans, so if any horses or humans have done so, call for veterinary/medical help.

INSURANCE

A wide variety of policies are available, covering most of the risks involved in keeping and using horses, so seek expert advice before arranging a policy.

All members of The Pony Club are automatically covered for third party risks under the Club's third party insurance policy, but individual animals and saddlery must be insured independently.

The Pony Club and any person acting on its behalf are covered under the Club's central policy against legal liability for claims arising out of the usual activities of the Club within the United Kingdom. For further information, see the current edition of *The Pony Club Year Book*.

If you are involved in an accident:
+ *Do not admit liability by saying that the accident was your fault.*
+ *Obtain the name and address of any witness who might be able to help.*
+ *Write down what happened as soon as possible—preferably the same day..*

17. When to Call the Vet

ROUTINE VISITS

You and the veterinary surgeon form an important partnership which helps to ensure the health of your horse or pony. There are several situations in which a vet can help.

- *Prevention of diseases before they occur* by regular flu and tetanus vaccinations, worming and teeth rasping.
- *Diagnosis and treatment.* Your horse is ill, has developed a swelling or is lame. You need to make an appointment with your vet.
- *Assessment of a horse before purchase.* Your vet will examine the horse and, if appropriate, will issue a certificate to the effect that at the time of the examination he found no clinical signs of disease, injury or physical abnormality likely to affect the horse's usefulness for your purpose.

EMERGENCY VISITS

Make sure you have the number of your local equine vet stored in your phone as well as displayed clearly where your horse lives in case someone else finds your horse in distress.

Before calling an equine vet in an emergency you should be aware of what is covered by your insurance and also the excess level. You must be prepared to give your name, postcode, directions to find your horse and mobile phone number. Try to remain calm and describe exactly what is wrong. Prompt action can be the difference between life and death or the difference between a permanently lame horse and one that is able to return to full work.

RECOGNISING ABNORMAL BEHAVIOUR

It is important to recognise when something is wrong with your horse. In some cases this is easy but in others it is not so clear. You should know how to measure the temperature, heart rate (pulse) and breathing rate (respiration) of your horse—and know the normal values. There are three points to keep in mind:

- Make sure that you know your horse's normal habits.
- Learn to recognise the signs that your horse is not normal.
- Act quickly and calmly in an emergency.

Taking the Temperature

Some horses do not like having their temperature taken, so until you are sure that your horse does not mind, it is best only to attempt this with the guidance of an experienced person. Digital thermometers are a worthwhile investment as they are easier to read than mercury thermometers and are much less likely to snap. A mercury thermometer must read below 36°C (96.8°F) before you start. If it does not, shake the mercury column down.

Grease the bulb with petroleum jelly and gently insert the thermometer into the rectum. This is best done by standing to one side of the horse, using one hand to lift the tail and one hand to insert the thermometer, bulb-end first, to about two-thirds of its length. Grip it firmly and

The normal temperature is between 37.5°C (99.5°F) and 38.5°C (101.3°F). If the temperature is above 39°C (102.2°F), you MUST contact your vet.

leave it in place for two minutes, or until it bleeps if it is a digital model.

Withdraw the thermometer, release the tail and read the temperature. Wash the thermometer in cold water and replace it in its case.

Taking the pulse

Feel the pulse with your fingers. Do not use your thumb, as it has a pulse of its own which is usually faster than that of a horse. The two easiest places to feel the pulse are where the facial artery crosses the jaw bone, or just behind the eye in the groove which runs a short way towards the ear. To get a rate per minute, count the number of pulses in fifteen seconds and multiply this by four. Taking the pulse is not easy and it is worth practising rather than leaving it until you are worried.

The normal pulse rate ranges between 35 and 45 per minute, but the heart rate is very sensitive to stress and increases rapidly if your horse is excited. If your horse is quiet, with no distractions, and if the pulse rate is over 55, call your vet.

Taking the respiratory or breathing rate

Watch your horse's sides move in and out, or if the weather is cold watch the puffs of air from his nostrils.

The normal range is between 8 and 15 breaths per minute, but increases with excitement and exercise—especially if the weather is hot. Breathing should be regular, with little effort. A rate that is over 16 at rest requires veterinary attention.

Recognising Abnormal Behaviour

If you are familiar with your horse's normal habits and behaviour you will be able to recognise the warning signs when something is wrong. Does he usually eat up hungrily, stand with his companions in the field, and always drink the same amount of water?

* Common signs of illness include dullness or depression, separation from other horses with whom he is turned out; not eating or not finishing his food; weight loss; sweating; abnormal breathing; a running nose; and an increase in temperature.
* Signs of colic or stomach pain include sweating; not eating; box walking, with the horse looking at his sides; a tendency to lie down and get up repeatedly; and rolling. Reluctance to move may indicate laminitis or azoturia (tying-up).
* Swelling or heat in a leg may indicate infection in the foot, cellulitis, cracked heels or tendon or ligament injury. Nodding of the head at the trot indicates forelimb lameness. Dragging a hind toe may also indicate lameness.

WHAT IS AN EMERGENCY?

The following conditions all require veterinary attention as soon as possible.

* Colic *(see page 160).*
* Azoturia/tying-up *(see page 161).*
* Difficulty in breathing *(see page 161).*
* Choking for more than 20 minutes, unless caused by dry sugar beet *(see page 162).*
* Tetanus *(see page 162).*
* Severe lameness *(see page 162).*
* Severe wounds *(see page 156).*
* Severe blinking or discharge from an eye *(see page 163).*

Symptoms which might indicate the presence of these conditions include:

- Sweating; lying down, and getting up a lot; rolling.
- Reluctance to move.
- Severe stiffness.
- Lameness at the walk.
- Very swollen leg.
- Blood spurting from a wound that will not stop with direct pressure.
- Difficulty breathing.
- Food material or thick discharge from the nostrils.
- Severe blinking or discharge from the eye.

Symptoms Requiring Veterinary Attention Within the Day

The following symptoms *do* require veterinary attention, but are generally not emergencies.

- Nasal discharge (running nose).
- Discharge from an eye.
- Cough.
- Abnormal breathing pattern.
- Abnormal breathing noise during exercise.
- Depressed appetite.
- Difficulty in eating.
- Weight loss.
- Drinking a lot and urinating a lot.
- Soft faeces or diarrhoea.
- Rubbing the mane or tail.
- Patchy hair loss.
- Abnormally long hair coat.
- Skin lumps.
- Lameness.
- Poor exercise tolerance.
- Poor performance.
- Abnormal behaviour.

18. Veterinary Kit

It is useful to have around a box of basic veterinary equipment. It should include:

1 Blunt-ended scissors to trim hair from around a wound.
2 A thermometer (digital or mercury).
3 At least one roll of clean cotton wool, for cleaning wounds.
4 A commercial antiseptic solution for cleaning wounds. The best contains chlorhexidine and should be available from your vet as Hibiscrub. An alternative is povidone iodine (Pevidine scrub).
5 Non-adherent dressings (e.g. Melolin or Jelonet gauze) to apply to wounds.
6 Disposable nappy to use as an absorbent pad for wounds and poultices.
7 Gamgee, to wrap around a leg before bandaging, or clean Fibagee, or other soft conforming bandage, e.g. Soffban.
8 Clean, non-stick bandages, e.g. crêpe bandages or stable bandages.
9 Sticky bandage, e.g. Vetwrap, Elastoplast.
10 Roll of adhesive tape.
11 Animalintex poultice.
12 Epsom salts, for tubbing a foot.
13 A clean bucket.

It is unnecessary to have wound powders or creams, hydrogen peroxide, liniments or colic drench, as they are superfluous and potentially harmful.

Basic Equipment for Removing a Shoe

It is useful to have the following so that, in an emergency, you can remove a shoe *(see page 151 for more details)*:

- Rasp (or buffer and hammer—preferably rubber (which is kinder to a painful foot)).

- Pincers (shoe-pullers) or nail pliers, which are easier to use.
- Hoof testers, which can be useful to find the source of pain.

Travelling First Aid Box

It is convenient to have a basic veterinary kit to take to rallies and competitions. From the list on the previous page, it should include items 1 to 9 and item 12.

Keeping the Paperwork Up to Date and in a Safe Place

Keep your horse's vaccination certificate safe, because it shows when he was vaccinated against flu and tetanus. Write in a diary or on a calendar when booster vaccinations are needed. Also, keep a log of any problems which the horse develops, and record each time that he is wormed, foot-trimmed and shod, and when his teeth are rasped.

Read the terms of the policy carefully if the horse is insured for veterinary fees: it may be necessary to obtain the insurance company's permission before specialist veterinary help is obtained, or to inform them as soon as possible if it is an emergency.

19. General Nursing Care

STABLING

A horse with a small wound or mild lameness of known cause can sometimes be treated in a field, but it is usually better to confine a sick, lame or injured horse to a stable. Visit an unwell horse several times a day.

Bedding

The bedding in the stable should be clean, dry and thick. If the horse has a respiratory problem, paper bedding or shavings are better than straw.

Ventilation

Ventilation is important. There should be plenty of fresh air, but no draughts. If the weather is cold, it is far better to use extra lightweight blankets to keep the horse warm, rather than to shut the top door of the box.

Isolation

When a horse has a cough, a running nose, diarrhoea, ringworm or another possibly contagious disease, he should, if possible, be isolated, even before the vet has arrived. Isolation helps to prevent the spread of disease to other horses. If the vet thinks it unnecessary, the isolation can be stopped.

Move the infected horse to a box well away from the others. Have at hand: buckets, stable utensils, grooming kit, and tack, for use only on this sick horse. Ideally, the person looking after the sick horse should have no contact with other horses. If this is not possible, always deal with the infected horse last. Keep a pair of overalls and rubber boots for wearing only when dealing with the infected horse. It is also sensible to put outside the stable a tub with strong disinfectant in which to dip boots every time someone goes in or out. Frequent washing of hands will lessen the risk of infection of other horses or human beings. It is important to realise that some diseases in horses are also infectious to humans.

Contagion and Infection

A *contagious disease*, such as ringworm, is a condition which can be passed between horses or *between horses and people* by direct contact or by the handing of contaminated rugs, tack or grooming equipment.

An *infectious disease* such as influenza or strangles can be transmitted between horses. This type of disease is not necessarily transmitted by direct contact, since the micro-organisms (viruses or bacteria) which cause it can be dispersed in the air. Contagious diseases are infectious—but not all infectious diseases are contagious.

When stables and equipment have been used by an infected horse it is necessary to disinfect them thoroughly. Remove and burn all bedding, hay and salt licks. Before disinfecting, the stable must be thoroughly cleaned and pressure-hosed, as most disinfectants are inactivated by dirt. Disinfect all stable utensils, grooming kit and haynets. Follow the manufacturer's instructions which come with the disinfectants. After disinfection, buckets and mangers should be scrubbed out with a strong salt solution, made up with boiled water so that they do not taste or smell of disinfectant. Tack should also be cleaned with disinfectant. Most causes of disease in rugs and blankets will be killed by biological washing powder.

NURSING THE HORSE

Sick, lame or injured horses should be made as comfortable as circumstances permit. The horse is a creature of habit so familiarity will be a comfort when he is feeling low. If there is no risk of infecting others, it is better to leave him in his own stable.

Character

A horse feeling unwell or in pain can behave differently than he normally does. In these circumstances even a well-educated, friendly horse may suddenly kick or bite.

Boredom

This can be a problem when a horse is confined to his box because of an injury but is otherwise feeling fit and well. Boredom may lead to stable vices, so it is best to keep the horse occupied. This can be done in different ways:

- Feed small amounts of hay at regular intervals. Consider using a small mesh net.
- Lead the horse out in hand a few times a day for a pick of grass, as long as the vet approves and the horse is calm
- Otherwise, pick some grass by hand and feed it as a titbit.
- Do not neglect the horse because he is no longer in work. He will appreciate some extra attention or grooming.
- The horse may like a toy. There are several toys designed for horses, but a plastic bottle or ball can be sufficient.
- Recorded music may provide distraction.

Grooming

Even a horse who is not in work needs some grooming, and will often appreciate the attention.

Rugs

Sick horses must be kept warm. If necessary, put on an extra rug. If the horse is feverish and sweaty, an anti-sweat rug under the other clothing, next to the skin, will help the air to circulate. Specific rugs and hoods can be used to control sweet itch and give protection from flies.

Bandages and Dressings

If a horse is confined to his stable, the lack of movement may cause his legs to swell, especially if he is severely lame and tending to rest the injured leg. The application of stable bandages with plenty of cotton pads will help to control the swelling. Stable bandages on all four legs can help to keep a sick horse warm. *(See Applying a Stable Bandage, page 92.)* Dressings will protect wounds from becoming soiled. *(See VETERINARY BANDAGING, next page.)*

If the horse acquires the habit of tearing at bandages and dressings, try applying a commercial anti-chewing paste—or even mustard—to an old bandage over the outer dressing. This may help to deter him.

Exercise/Turning Out

When a horse is ill or lame, always follow your vet's advice about whether he can be exercised or turned out. Lameness is likely to become worse if the horse is allowed uncontrolled turn out. Horses do not protect themselves and will often continue to trot and canter in a field, despite lameness. If a horse has been confined to his box for some time and is resuming work, exercise must be built up gradually. At first, the horse may be very exuberant and difficult to control. A snaffle bridle, chifney, or lungeing cavesson with a lunge line attached to it, may be very helpful if the horse is being hand walked. Ridden exercise at the walk may be safer, and is not significantly more stressful to the horse.

When a horse is turned out in the field after a long period confined in a stable, he will probably immediately set off at full gallop. This can be dangerous, especially if he has been lame. It is advisable to turn him out after exercise, and when he is hungry and wants to eat grass. Put the horse in a small secluded area, possibly with a quiet companion who is well known to him. If in doubt as to how to turn the horse out, do seek professional advice. In some cases, it might be necessary for the vet to administer or prescribe a tranquillizer.

A horse might settle better if he is left out all the time instead of being brought in and out each day; but if the grass is young and rich, you should bring him in after an hour on the first day and gradually increase the time that he stays out.

FOOD, WATER AND MEDICATION FOR THE SICK HORSE

Food

A sick horse and/or a horse confined to his stable for a long period, should be fed enough roughage. Hay is perfectly adequate. If the horse has respiratory problems, it is best to soak the hay or give vacuum-packed semi-wilted grass. If the horse cannot be led out to graze, offer fresh grass in the stable. This should be cut as long as possible, and given in only small quantities. Grass will quickly overheat if left for some time. This could be dangerous and cause colic. Never give lawn mowings, as they could be poisonous because of herbicides. They also tend to overheat quickly.

A resting horse does not need much concentrate food. Overfeeding horses may induce more problems than under-feeding. Regular feeds, mainly of roughage, and access to fresh water, help to prevent constipation. If the horse is reluctant to eat, try feeding something different, or adding carrots or apples.

Never leave food that has not been eaten in the manger, as it will go stale. This turns the horse off his food completely. When in doubt about what to feed a horse, always ask the vet for advice.

Water

All horses, including those who are, sick, injured or lame need a plentiful supply of fresh water. Change the water at least once a day and make sure the buckets are clean.

Medication

Medicines can be given orally (i.e. by mouth) or parenterally (i.e. not by mouth but by injection. This should only be done by a qualified person).

Powders or syrups can be given in the food. With powders, it is best to moisten the food a little, so that the powder sticks to it, but some drugs become bitter when they are damp, so administer them in a small dry feed and disguise the taste with molasses, treacle, honey or sugar. Treacle should also help the powder to stick to the food.

If a horse refuses medicated food, it is better to make a paste of the powder with honey, or dissolve it in water and administer it on the tongue with a syringe. Syrup can also be given on the tongue with a syringe. Certain medications, such as wormer pastes, are given on the tongue. This is not as difficult as it seems and most horses accept it well. The following method is usually successful. Put a headcollar on the horse and stand next to

him on his left side. Hold his head with your right hand positioned over his nose, where the noseband goes. Then push the syringe gently into the corner of his mouth where the bit normally lies, and empty it on the back of the tongue, using your left hand. Then hold up his head until he swallows the medicine. Sometimes a horse is smart and will not swallow, dropping the paste on the ground the minute he can get his head down. Pushing on his tongue with a finger or with the syringe, while holding his head up, will make the horse move his tongue and eventually swallow.

• Tablets can be given in a piece of apple or carrot or a polo. They can also be crushed and mixed to make a paste, or dissolved in apple juice or water to be given with a syringe or mixed into food.
• Medicines should NOT be mixed with the drinking water, since it is difficult to check if the horse actually takes in the medicine and it is vital not to deter the horse from drinking.

If you have a problem in administering medications, ask your vet, as there are various ways of administering some medicines.

VETERINARY BANDAGING

A bandage may be applied to a leg to:
1 Reduce soft tissue swelling.
2 Protect a wound.
3 Help in the prevention of proud flesh (exuberant granulation tissue).
4 Prevent development of a filled leg.
5 Provide extra warmth.
6 Hold a poultice in place.
7 Hold a cold pack in place.

(The technique for applying a basic bandage is described on page 92.)

The keys to a successful bandage are snug fitting of the underlying padding, an adequate thickness of padding, and applying the bandage without excessive tension.

It is difficult to apply a bandage to a highly moveable area such as the knee or hock, since movement causes the bandage to move and potentially to rub, especially on protuberant points such as the accessory carpal bone (at the back of the knee). Figure-of-eight bandages used to be recommended, but they are not successful.

As long as sufficient firmly-conforming padding is in place, both the knee and hock can be bandaged normally, but this is really a job for an expert. Commercially produced, purpose-designed, strongly-conforming bandages (Pressage) are also available for the knee and hock.

A bandage on the foot may be kept in place by using silage tape or wide duct tape wound around the foot, an old sock, an adhesive bandage such as Elastoplast, or some sort of boot.

TREATMENT OF WOUNDS AND OTHER INJURIES

Poulticing

There are two types of poultice: hot and cold. A hot poultice is used to apply moist heat to an area, usually either to soften hard hoof horn or to draw infection from an area. A cold poultice is used on bruised areas to reduce swelling. Although kaolin and bran poultices were once commonly used they have been largely superseded by commercial poultices such as Animalintex, since these are quick and easy to use, are clean, do not ferment and do not stick to a wound. The poultice consists of impregnated cotton wool protected by gauze, and a thin piece of plastic which is placed over it in order to try and maintain either moisture and heat or the cooling effect of a cold poultice.

First, cut the poultice to the size that you need—it is usually better to cut it too big than too small. Follow the directions on the packet, then place the poultice in position and cover it with plastic. Around the plastic wrap a thick layer of cotton wool or gauze, and then bandage it, to retain the heat and to keep the poultice in place. Ideally it should be replaced every twelve hours.

When poulticing a foot it can be helpful to place the bandaged foot into the corner of a thick plastic bag and tape the bag on. Leg poultices are applied while the leg is bearing weight, but to poultice a foot it is obviously necessary to pick the foot up. To apply the poultice single-handed, have everything ready laid out on a tray or clean tea towel. Pick up the leg and hold it between your legs like a farrier, so that you have both hands free.

Tubbing

Tubbing involves placing the lower limb in a container of warm water plus a handful of Epsom salts, and leaving it in place for fifteen to twenty minutes. During this time you will need to add hot water from a kettle or flask, to maintain the warm temperature. Be careful not to scald yourself or the horse: the water must only be as hot as your hand can bear. The purpose of this is to soften the horn of the hoof, and to help draw infection. Ideally, it should be carried out at least twice daily. It requires a cooperative horse who does not mind standing with his foot in a bowl or bucket. A heavy plastic or rubber bowl or wide shallow bucket is ideal. Pick up the foot and scrub it with a coarse brush before immersing it in the water. After tubbing, dry the heel and pastern region, to prevent the risk of a cracked heel.

Hosing

Cold hosing can be used to clean a wound and to provide cold and massage therapy to reduce inflammation and soft tissue swelling, and to relieve pain. The area should be hosed for approximately 15 minutes and then allowed to reheat. The treatment can be repeated up to three times in a single session. Most horses tolerate this well, although some may be apprehensive to begin with. It is therefore preferable, at least at first, for the horse to be held, rather than tied up. Start by trickling water slowly over the foot and then gradually increase the water pressure to a steady flow, and move the jet up the leg to the damaged area. Afterwards, dry the back of the pastern carefully, to help prevent cracked heels.

Cold Compresses

Application of a cold compress is an alternative to hosing. A source of coldness (such as an ice pack or a commercial cooling pack), is held or bandaged on to the leg. Excessive use of cold can cause damage. Ice-cold applications should never be used for longer than 15 minutes.

Hot Fomentations

Hot fomentations are used for applying heat to an area inaccessible to poulticing, for example to an abscess on the neck or hind quarters. A piece of towelling or thick cloth is thoroughly immersed in hand-hot water, squeezed out and held over the area until the cloth starts to cool. The procedure is repeated. Heat should be applied for at least ten to fifteen minutes, and should be repeated two to three times daily. Keep the water hot by adding hot water from a kettle; but do not scald yourself or the horse.

Removal of a Shoe

It is extremely useful to know how to remove a shoe, especially if the horse has slightly displaced it and might be injured by either the shoe or by one of the nails. However, only attempt it if you have the experience and strength to carry it out successfully. All you need are a buffer, rubber hammer and pincers (shoe-pullers).

- Hold up the horse's leg between your legs.
- Raise the clenches by tapping the buffer up underneath them with the hammer.
- Using both hands, put the pincers under the back of either the inside or outside branch of the shoe.
- Lever forwards and downwards towards the toe to raise the heel of the shoe.
- Repeat the procedure on the other branch. This should help to raise the nail heads so that each nail can be levered out individually, using the pincers. If the nail heads are not clear of the shoe try banging the shoe down again. It may also be helpful to lever the shoe up again.
- When trying to remove a nail, place the pincers over the nail head and lever towards the centre of the foot. The shoe can usually be levered off by pulling it sideways towards the centre of the foot and slightly backwards.

COMPLEMENTARY THERAPY

Laser Therapy

A laser machine produces invisible radiation which may alter the metabolism of cells in superficial tissues. Applied correctly, lasering can reduce inflammation and may speed wound healing, but excessive use can result in substantial tissue damage.

Ultrasound Therapy

Therapeutic ultrasound, as opposed to diagnostic ultrasound, can be used to reduce inflammation in muscles and tendons. Carefully applied it may be of considerable benefit in relieving tenderness, muscle tension and swelling. However, it does not speed healing of tendon injuries. Even though ultrasound may reduce, or even eliminate, swelling associated with a tendon strain *(see page 170)*, the tendon remains damaged and will need considerable time to heal.

Stretching, Massage

Human athletes undertake bending and stretching exercises in their warm-up phase. Muscles with slight soreness or tension may be massaged. Athletes deliberately keep their tracksuits on to physically warm up the muscles. To an extent the same can be done in the horse by bending and stretching exercises: e.g. encouraging the horse to stretch his neck by enticing him with a carrot close to his front legs, or next to his left or right shoulder. Appropriate massage of the muscles can also be beneficial.

Physiotherapy, Osteopathy, Chiropractics

It is illegal for anyone other than a veterinary surgeon to diagnose and treat disease, which includes lameness, muscle and back injuries. Nonetheless, under the guidance of a veterinary surgeon, treatment may be given. There are distinct differences in what a physiotherapist, an osteopath or a chiropractor is attempting to achieve, but all can help to relieve muscle tension or spasm, and thereby relieve pain and help the horse. Muscle spasm often develops secondary to another problem—for example a poorly-fitting saddle, or a lameness. It is therefore vital that your veterinary surgeon assesses the problem first, and works together with, for example, a physiotherapist.

20. Disease Prevention

There are many steps that you can take to prevent your horse from becoming ill. These fall into two main categories:
- General measures that will help to keep your horse healthy
- Specific steps aimed at preventing certain diseases.

GENERAL MEASURES

Most of these should be part of a good management regime and are covered in other chapters, particularly HEALTH, CONDITION AND EXERCISE, *page 118*. Good management includes feeding fresh food which has been properly prepared, and avoiding rapid diet changes. These should help to prevent problems with the digestive system, especially colic *(see page 160)*.

- Train yourself to look at your horse, know what is normal, and to spot any changes. One of the most important factors in the prevention of disease is a well-informed, constantly observant owner.
- Soak sugar beet nuts or pulp sufficiently before feeding, to help to prevent either choke *(see page 162)* or colic.
- Prevent inadvertent access to the feed room so that a horse, and particularly a pony cannot gorge himself, which may predispose to choke, colic or laminitis *(see pages 162, 160 and 162, respectively)*.
- Control access to lush or rapidly growing grass, especially in the case of a pony who is prone to laminitis.
- If a horse has several days off, for whatever reason, reduce the concentrate intake to avoid predisposing to azoturia *(see page 161)*.
- Regular hoof care, including trimming at least every four to six weeks, helps prevent some lameness problems and diseases of the foot *(see The Foot and Shoeing, page 111)*.
- Appropriate conditioning *(see page 122)*, correct fitting of the saddle *(see page 247)* and keeping it and numnahs clean, should help to prevent girth galls, saddle sores and bit rubs.
- Regular grooming helps to prevent rain-scald *(see page 173)*, mud fever and cracked heels *(see page 174)*.

SPECIFIC MEASURES

Vaccination

Vaccines against tetanus, influenza and other diseases are available. If you are considering breeding from your horse, you should consult your vet about a suitable vaccination programme for pregnant mares.

It is possible to combine the influenza and tetanus vaccines.

Tetanus

All horses must be vaccinated against tetanus. Tetanus is a serious disease which usually results in death *(see page 162)*. The bacteria which cause the disease are present in the soil everywhere, whether or not horses have been there before. Vaccination against tetanus should prevent the disease. If the vaccination history of your horse is unknown, it must have an initial course of injections and then a booster every year. Always make sure that the injections are up to date.

Influenza (flu)

The influenza (flu) virus causes a similar disease to flu in humans *(see page 164)*. The clinical signs are most severe in horses who have not previously been vaccinated. The disease is transmitted from horse to horse via the air and is highly infectious. If you keep your horse with others, or if you ever go to places where there are other horses, e.g. Pony Club camp, pleasure rides or shows, you should vaccinate against influenza. Annual boosters are essential. Flu vaccinations may not totally protect a horse from contracting flu, but will make the clinical signs much milder.

It is wise to check with governing bodies responsible for horse sports if you wish to comply with the latest rules concerning equine influenze vaccination. At the date of publication of this manual, however, several such bodies agreed on the following:

- *Two injections for primary vaccination, not less than 21 days and not more than 92 days apart.*
- *A first booster injection not less than 150 days nor more than 215 days after the second primary injection.*
- *Subsequent booster injections given at intervals of not more than one year, commencing after the first booster injection.*
- *Any relevant injection must be given not less than seven days prior to the commencement of the competition.*

Try and arrange for booster vaccinations to be carried out when the horse is either not in maximum work, or can have a day or two off afterwards. Occasionally the horse may be slightly dull for twenty-four to forty-eight hours following the injection. *Do not work him until he is completely normal.*

WORM CONTROL

All ponies and horses can become infected with worms. In general, infestation is acquired by eating immature larvae from the pasture which develop in the intestine into adult worms. The adults then lay eggs which are passed in the droppings, and these in turn hatch to infect the pasture with immature larvae. This completes the life-cycle of the worm.

A low level of worm infection does not cause a problem and may even be beneficial, but excessive worm burdens can result in disease and even death, especially if the horse is very young, old or unwell.

There are a number of types of worm, all with different life cycles, that can cause problems in many ways, for example by migrating through the blood vessels of the intestines or damaging the lining of the gut. In general they all impair the horses' ability to absorb and process nutrients and result in disease. Typical signs of worm infection include weight loss, diarrhoea, colic and poor condition.

There are four main things to consider when controlling worms. They should be used in combination to work most effectively:

Pasture management is crucial to reduce the parasite challenge to the horse. Removing the droppings from the pasture significantly reduces the likelihood of horses accidentally eating worm larvae from the grass. In addition, resting the pasture for at least three months will help reduce the worm burden. Cross-grazing with sheep or cattle will also help as they can 'hoover' up the larvae but not be affected by them. It is also important to practise good stable hygiene, as not all worms require pasture to complete their life cycle.

Assessing the horse's worm burden: a faecal worm egg count (FWEC) measures the number of worm eggs in the horse's droppings. This gives an indication of the level of adult worms in the gut and allows you to decide whether the horse needs worming. For example a count of more than 200epg (eggs per gram) may indicate the need for a worming dose, both to protect the horse itself and to prevent further contamination of the pasture.

Assessing the risks to the horse: certain worms should be controlled at specific times of the year and some horses, such as youngsters, may need worming more frequently. You should consider all the factors when choosing a worming dose and talk to your vet or suitably-qualified person.

Worming dose: different wormers can treat different worms. Assessing the risks and the need for worming will mean you can choose the right worming drug for your horse at any given time. Ideally you should treat for roundworms over the grazing season as necessary, tapeworm in spring and/or autumn and 'encysted' small redworm and bots in late autumn/winter. New horses should be treated and kept separately for forty-eight hours to avoid bringing resistant worms or large numbers of worms onto the premises.

The worming drug can either be administered in the feed, in tablet form, or by using a paste delivered directly into the mouth *(see page 149).*

By reducing the need for worming doses and by using them at the correct time, we will help to prolong the efficacy of worming drugs and reduce the development of resistance in worms. Resistance, where the worms are no longer controlled by a wormer, is a real issue and inappropriate and overuse of wormers are the main contributing factors.

Types of Worm

Many types of worm can affect horses. The most common and the most important are:

Roundworms

- *Small Redworms (Cyathostomes)*
  The most common worm in most horses. The adults can cause ill-thrift and weight loss, but the larval stages can become 'encysted'—where they burrow into the gut wall and hibernate. Sudden mass emergence of these encysted larvae from the gut wall can cause severe diarrhoea and even death.
- *Large Redworms (Strongylus)*
  These are now less common but the adults can lead to ill-thrift and worm related disease. The larvae can cause life-threatening colic due to the damage caused by their migration through the blood vessels of the intestines.
- *Large Roundworms (Ascarids)*
  These are large, round, grey-coloured worms which can grow up to 40cm in length. They are a major concern in foals and youngstock as severe infestations can cause colic. Adult horses develop a level of protective immunity to large roundworms.
- *Pinworms (Oxyuris)*
  The adults live in the large intestine and lay their eggs around the anus causing irritation.

Tapeworm (Cestodes)

These have light-coloured ribbon-like bodies made up of segments. The end segments contain eggs and break off periodically, passing out in the droppings and releasing the eggs. The eggs are then eaten by the forage mite and the tapeworm larvae develop inside this intermediate host. When the mite is eaten by a horse during normal grazing, the horse becomes infected and the adult tapeworm develops. Tapeworm is a proven risk factor in certain types of colic.

Bots (Gasterophilus)

These are not worms, but the larvae of the bot fly, which looks rather like a bee and lays its eggs on the legs of the horse. The larvae are mildly irritating as they hatch, which may cause the horse to lick them. The larvae then migrate to the stomach of the horse where they attach to the lining, potentially causing issues with digestion and damage to the stomach lining. The larvae eventually pass out in the droppings and develop into the adult fly to complete the cycle. The eggs can be manually removed from the legs of horses to help control infection.

Lungworm (Dictyocaulus)

These are found in the airways of infected horses and can cause respiratory disease including coughing and breathing problems. Lungworm is uncommon in the horse and infection usually arises when horses are grazed alongside donkeys.

CARE OF THE TEETH

The horse has two main types of teeth. The incisors are at the front of the mouth. They are chopping teeth used for cutting grass stems. Molars are grinding teeth, used for chewing. They are much further back in the mouth and are difficult to see. Never put your hands in the mouth to try to feel the molars yourself, as even the most well-mannered horse may bite and crush your hand badly.

If the teeth on the upper and lower jaws do not meet perfectly, the continual wear of eating may cause sharp edges to form. Signs of teeth problems include food dropping from the mouth while eating (quidding), not finishing the food given, or not accepting the bit well. Your vet will be able to examine the teeth and, if necessary, will rasp them. This involves using a special rasp with a rough edge to grind off the sharp edges of the teeth. Some

horses never need to have their teeth rasped, while others need treatment regularly—at least twice a year. This is probably because of the way in which their teeth meet when the mouth is completely closed. If your horse has a wolf tooth, it may be necessary to remove it. *(See TEETH, page 121).* Even if you do not think that your horse has a problem it is probably worth getting the teeth checked regularly by your vet: for example, when the horse is vaccinated.

There are many horse dentists who are not vets but who are extremely competent at rasping teeth. It is illegal for anybody who is not a vet to remove teeth (including wolf teeth) or to diagnose or treat disease. Your vet is the ideal person to rasp the teeth, since during the same visit he can advise on the general health of your horse and assess any other minor problems; but in some circumstances you might use an equine dental technician recommended by your vet.

21. Wounds

WOUNDS WHICH NEED IMMEDIATE VETERINARY ATTENTION

There are many types of wound. Some are easily managed. Some need veterinary attention. A few are emergencies.

Blood Spurting in a Jet from the Wound
An artery has been damaged and the bleeding must be stopped.

Action: push a clean wad of cotton wool or Gamgee or disposable nappy into the wound. Hold or bandage it in place to slow the bleeding. Contact the vet.

Deep Wounds to the Foot

Puncture wounds, e.g. a nail. Deep wounds or penetrations may result in infection in the sensitive tissues and vital structures, such as the navicular bone. Infection deep in the foot is difficult to treat once established.

Action: if possible leave any foreign body (e.g. a nail) in the foot until the vet arrives, so that he can see exactly where the injury has occurred. Hold the foot up to avoid any further injury. If this is not possible, mark the puncture site with a circle of felt tip pen and if there is to be a delay before the vet arrives, tub the horse's foot. *(See TUBBING, page 150.)*

Wounds Over Joints, Tendon Sheaths and Tendons

Any wound close to a joint or tendon sheath can result in infection of these areas which unless treated immediately may cause severe lameness. The moving surfaces of joints and tendons are oiled by a fluid called synovial fluid which has a pale yellow colour. Leakage of clear yellow fluid from a wound indicates that a joint or tendon sheath may be involved, and infection may develop with disastrous consequences.

Action: A vet must be called immediately. Below the knee and hock, on the back of the leg (behind the cannon bone or pastern), the tendons are close to the skin surface, and any wound may have resulted in damage to a tendon or ligament. Emergency veterinary care is needed.

Wounds to the Eyeball

The eyeball is a delicate structure and any wound which damages it may be serious and may need surgery.

GENERAL WOUND MANAGEMENT

The size of cut does not necessarily reflect its severity. A small superficial graze can be managed by clipping the surrounding hair and then cleaning thoroughly. Any larger wound, a wound with severe bleeding, a deep puncture wound or any wound close to a joint, a tendon sheath or a tendon, or a wound on the back of the fetlock or pastern, should be examined by a vet, who will assess whether vital structures may have been damaged, and whether or not the wound needs stitching (suturing). If in any doubt call the vet.

Cleaning the Wound

Clip, or trim with scissors, the hair surrounding the wound, so that hairs do not lie in it. Wash the wound with clean water from a clean bucket, preferably using an appropriate antiseptic solution— chlorhexidine (Hibiscrub) or povidine iodine (Pevidine). Soak small wads of cotton wool in warm water. Squeeze the water out; water dripping down the horse's leg may frighten him. Pour some antiseptic solution on to the cotton wool and rub the wound. Repeat with multiple clean pieces of cotton wool, continuing for at least five minutes, or longer if the wound is not clean. If the wound is very dirty wash it from above with a hose first. Careful and thorough cleaning will help to prevent infection.

Do Not Apply Wound Ointments/Powders

They may make dirt stick and attract infection. Superficial small cuts will heal quickly if the wound edges are close together. If possible, apply a non-stick dressing and then bandage the wound.

Keep the Horse in a Stable if You Can

Wounds heal more quickly if the edges are not moving continuously and if it is easier to keep the wound clean. It may be necessary to use a fly repellant around (but not in) the wound if the horse is out at grass and it is not possible to keep the wound covered.

Check Vaccination Status

If the horse is fully vaccinated against tetanus, further treatment is not required, but if it is more than a year since the horse was vaccinated, or if the vaccination status is unknown, it is essential to call the vet, who will treat the horse with tetanus antitoxin and a booster vaccination. Tetanus is a potentially life-threatening complication of any wound *(see page 162)*.

Puncture Wounds

These can be dangerous because the surface cut may be small but it is difficult to assess their depth and bacteria are often pushed deep into the tissues. These wounds are therefore difficult to clean thoroughly.

If there is any chance that the wound is near a tendon or a joint, or on the back of the pastern, you must call a vet as an emergency. If the wound is not near any of these structures, a poultice *(see page 150)* is generally advisable and may help to clean it, but your vet may need to give antibiotics to control deep infection.

Large Cuts

These will probably heal quickest if the wound edges are brought together using stitches or staples. The final cosmetic result will also be much better: the amount of scarring will be reduced.

Bruised Areas

These may benefit from cold poulticing for twenty-four hours, to help to reduce painful swelling *(see POULTICING, page 150)*. After this period it is necessary to increase the circulation to the area to help to remove the inflammation. This is best achieved by gentle movement. The exception may be if there is a wound which has been sutured (stitched), since movement may disrupt wound healing. Your vet will be able to advise you about this.

SPECIFIC WOUNDS

Girth and Saddle Galls

The majority of galls are caused by poor management, due to either dirty or ill-fitting tack. A string girth may cause pinching and bruising, especially if the horse or pony is over weight. A girth gall is a painful swelling in the girth region. Sometimes there is hair loss and possibly an open sore. If the skin does become broken, wash it with a weak antiseptic solution. Application of surgical spirit may help to harden unbroken skin. The tack must be thoroughly cleaned and checked to ensure that it is correctly fitted. A tubular synthetic or a leather girth is less likely to cause a problem than a string or nylon one. Do not use the saddle again until the galls are completely healed.

Bit and Mouth Injuries

Bit and mouth injuries can be caused by a bit of the wrong size, a badly fitted or worn bit, a damaged bit, or by rough riding. Damage to the side of the mouth can occur if the teeth become overgrown. *(See CARE OF THE TEETH, page 156)*. Cracks in the corner of the mouth are most common and make the horse fussy in the mouth and reluctant to accept the bit. Application of a suitable cream allowed under competition rules will help. Check the bit itself for any rough edges or for a joint which may pinch the skin. Consider using a bit with a smooth synthetic mouthpiece, possibly with bit guards. In severe cases it may be necessary to avoid using a bit for several days. To bit your horse correctly, seek your instructor's advice so that you can control the horse without making his mouth sore.

Broken Knees

Broken knees is the term used to describe grazes on the front of the knees caused by the horse falling on them. This may result in wounds with jagged edges, filled with lots of dirt. With deep injuries there is a risk of penetration of the knee joint. If the grazes are any more than superficial, veterinary help should be sought. Treat a superficial graze as described in General Wound Management, *page 157*. Deeper wounds should be liberally hosed while awaiting the vet.

SELF-INFLICTED WOUNDS

These are grazes, cuts or bruising inflicted by the horse knocking himself when he moves.

- *Brushing* is when one foreleg or hind leg strikes the opposite foreleg or hind leg.
- *Overreaching* is when a back foot overreaches and treads on the bulb of the heel of a front foot.
- *Strikes* happen in a similar way to overreaches but higher up the leg. Sometimes the cut may even penetrate into the tendon.
- *Speedicuts* are injuries to the inside of the knee or hock caused by the inside of the toe of the opposite leg. Speedicuts are rare but serious. They may cause the horse to fall. A horse which repeatedly speedicuts is unsafe to ride.
- *Forging/pulling shoes off.* Forging is the term applied when a horse hits the toe of a front shoe with the toe of a hind shoe. It may occur because the horse is unbalanced or because his feet are inappropriately trimmed and shod.   Some horses may tend to pull front shoes off by treading on the heel of a shoe with a hind foot. Chunks of the hoof wall may thus be pulled away, which can cause problems in replacing the shoe. It can bring about an abrupt halting of the stride, possibly resulting in a tendon or ligament injury. If the shoe is pulled off a long way from home the foot may become bruised on the return journey. Seek advice from both your vet and your farrier as to how to resolve the problem.
- *Treads* are wounds to the coronet region caused by the horse being trodden on or treading on himself, usually while travelling.

Self-inflicted wounds sometimes happen purely by accident but some habitual occurrences may be the result of weakness caused by immaturity or poor condition, faulty action, poor conformation, and/or inappropriate shoeing.

When travelling, the horse can be protected from treads with padding over the coronet band secured by stable bandages. If he has a tendency to brush, overreach or strike into himself, brushing boots, overreach boots or tendon boots used appropriately, will help to protect his legs *(see Boots, page 95)* but note that rubber overreach boots tend to rub if they are worn for hours at a time. Treat self-inflicted wounds according to their severity. Ask your farrier if the way in which the horse's feet are trimmed and shod could help.

An overreach can result in a skin wound and bruising. The bruising may cause lameness for twenty-four to forty-eight hours, especially on hard ground. Some skin flaps will not heal and need to be cut off. Clean the wound thoroughly *(see page 157)*. If there is a big skin deficit, consider bandaging the heel; the bandage needs to extend beneath the branches of the shoe, otherwise it will ride up. If the laceration is deep and the edges are not jagged, it may heal best if it is stitched by your vet.

CELLULITIS

Cellulitis is low-grade infection of the tissues under the skin causing diffuse soft tissue swelling (a big leg), heat and stiffness. It is usually the result of tiny lacerations which were not previously identified and which allowed the introduction of infection. In severe cases the horse may be depressed and have a temperature. Call your vet, because a filled leg may be the result of a number of different conditions. Cellulitis is treated by identification of the primary wounds and thorough cleaning, antibiotic treatment and bandaging the leg.

LYMPHANGITIS

This usually occurs in a hind limb and results in considerable swelling often involving the entire leg up to the stifle, and severe stiffness. The cause is not entirely understood, but it is often a sequel to previous cuts on the leg. Circulation in the leg is impaired. Treatment using antibiotics, corticosteroids, massage and bandaging may control the condition, but recurrence is common.

22. Diseases Needing Immediate Veterinary Attention

Whenever you are unsure as to what is wrong with your horse you should ring your veterinary practice for advice. Every practice will be willing to help and would much rather that you rang too early than too late.

Colic

Colic means abdominal pain, usually from the intestines. You can help to prevent it by regular worming, frequent teeth checks, and avoiding rapid changes in diet. Colic has many different causes which may result in painful spasm of the gut wall, constipation causing blockage, distension of the gut with excess gas, or displacement or twisting of the gut, or a disease called grass sickness *(see page 166)*. It can be serious, occasionally needing surgery which is expensive and should be clarified with your insurer. Early treatment is essential.

Signs: the horse is uncomfortable, restless, looks at his flanks, kicks at his belly and gets up and down frequently. There may be patchy sweating. Heart rate, breathing rate and temperature may be increased.

Action: some horses with severe colic become distressed, violent and potentially dangerous; if this is the case do not go into the stable. If the horse is reasonably calm, remove any feed or hay from the box. Note if the horse has passed any droppings. Call the vet and follow his advice. It is not necessary to stop the horse lying down. The vet will assess the severity of the problem by measuring pulse and respiratory rates; listening to the gut sounds; looking at the colour of the gums; assessing hydration; passing a stomach tube via the nostril to see if the stomach is distended with fluid due to a blockage in the intestines; and feeling the intestines via the rectum to identify an impaction or gas-filled loops of bowel indicative of an obstruction. Severe pain which responds only transiently to painkilling drugs is an indication that surgery is necessary.

Azoturia (Tying-Up, Exertional Rhabdomyolosis)

Azoturia occurs in horses more often than in ponies and is sometimes difficult to distinguish from colic. The condition usually develops during or immediately after exercise, especially following a day off. The horse becomes reluctant to move.

The precise causes of azoturia are not known. Some horses seem particularly susceptible to it, and there may be a genetic predisposition. Maintaining a high carbohydrate level in the diet, particularly if the horse has several days off work, seems to be a triggering factor. Imbalances of electrolytes in the diet, such as sodium and potassium chloride, or of calcium salts, may predispose. Some horses require additional supplementation of these electrolytes to an already balanced diet.

Signs: the horse becomes stiff, may be distressed, and may not want to move. Patchy sweating may develop. Certain muscles usually become hard and painful, especially over the hind quarters. Breathing and pulse rates rise because of the pain. The urine may be discoloured red or brown.

Action: dismount immediately and loosen the girth. If possible try to cover the hind quarters to keep them warm. Do not try to move the horse, as this will cause further muscle damage. If possible offer the horse fresh water to drink and call the vet immediately. Some horses are more susceptible to azoturia than others. If your horse has had problems in the past it is more likely to happen again, so discuss with your vet any preventive measures that can be taken. These will include controlling the diet and developing a regular daily exercise programme with a slow warm-up phase. The horse should preferably be turned out for at least an hour daily.

Difficulty in Breathing

Any condition which causes a horse to have difficulty in breathing is an emergency. The most common cause of acute respiratory distress is a sudden attack of chronic obstructive pulmonary disease (COPD) in a horse which has an allergy to fungal spores or to pollens in hay and straw. *(See page 163).*

Signs: something triggers an acute attack. The horse stands with his neck outstretched and has difficulty in breathing. The flanks heave and the horse may cough.

Action: call the vet and describe exactly what you have seen. If the horse is indoors with hay and straw, take him outside into the fresh air. Your vet will give drugs that relieve airway spasm to help the horse to breathe more easily. It is important to try and identify the triggering factor to prevent it happening again.

Choke

Choke is a blockage of the oesophagus (the pipe which connects the mouth to the stomach), usually with food. The most common cause is eating dry sugar beet pulp or nuts or dry hay.

Signs: the horse is distressed and repeatedly attempts to swallow. Saliva drips from his mouth and food material may appear at his nostrils. Sometimes the food blockage can be felt halfway down his neck—but extreme care should be taken when trying to feel the neck, as the oesophagus is very delicate and easily damaged.

Action: Most chokes clear within twenty minutes: remove all food and water from the stable. If it has not cleared within this time or is due to dry sugar beet call the vet. This is an emergency because regurgitated food may pass into the trachea (windpipe) and predispose to the development of pneumonia. Your vet will sedate the horse, insert a stomach tube, and try to soften the blockage with water. Most cases of choke can be avoided by preventing access to the feed room, adequately soaking sugar beet, and by attention to the size of food being fed. Apples or carrots should be in long slices or whole, so that the horse has to chew them before swallowing them.

Tetanus

Tetanus is a disease caused by bacteria which live in the soil and can infect wounds. The bacteria produce a poison which stops the normal function of the nerves. Most horses affected by tetanus will die, so regular vaccination is essential. *(See page 153).* If, however, your horse has a wound and is not vaccinated against tetanus you must call the vet immediately to arrange treatment and vaccination.

Signs: the horse is stiff and reluctant to move. He may overreact to noises that would not usually bother him. His third eyelid may become more obvious, and his ears erect. The horse may stand with his nose and hind legs stuck out and may have difficulty eating.

Action: put the horse inside and close the top door of the stable. Try to keep the yard quiet. Call the vet immediately, though even with prompt and aggressive veterinary treatment it may be difficult to save the horse's life. Always make sure that the horse's vaccinations are up to date.

Severe Lameness

Most lamenesses do not need emergency attention *(see page 166)*, but if a horse will not put any weight on a leg, cannot move, or is in distress, you must call a vet. The horse may have a fracture, infection in a joint or tendon sheath, or severe infection in the foot. If possible, keep him in a stable. If this is not possible, the horse should be kept still until the vet arrives.

Laminitis *(See also page 167)*

Severe laminitis requires immediate attention. Small native ponies kept at grass are particularly susceptible.

Signs: the horse or pony is reluctant to move and may appear stiff. The feet are often hot. The pain caused by laminitis is principally in the front part of the foot, so the animal stands with his weight tipped onto the heels, to reduce the pain.

Action: *Do not* force him to walk.
Cold hose his feet.
Call the vet.

Trauma To The Eye / Excessive Blinking / Discharge From The Eye

Direct injury to the eye is an emergency; especially if the eye itself is cut, or if there is a penetrating foreign body. To save the eye, surgery will be necessary.

Excessive blinking, excessive tear formation or pus-like discharge from the eye may reflect damage to the covering membrane of the eye, the cornea (a corneal ulcer), inflammation of the conjunctiva (conjunctivitis) or inflammation of the iris (uveitis, moon-blindness, periodic ophthalmia). A corneal ulcer and inflammation of the iris are serious. Without prompt veterinary treatment, long-term damage may develop.

Action: seek urgent veterinary advice.

23. Diseases of the Respiratory System or Airways

Coughing, nasal discharge, an abnormal noise during breathing or poor exercise tolerance may reflect a problem involving the respiratory system.

Recurrent Airway Obstruction, Chronic Obstructive Pulmonary Disease (COPD) or Broken Wind

Chronic obstructive pulmonary disease is a common condition caused by an allergy to dust and fungal spores. The horse may cough, both in the stable and when being exercised. There may be a clear or white discharge from the nostrils, especially after work. The respiratory rate may be increased and breathing may be laboured. The temperature is usually normal.

Although the term broken wind implies a permanent condition, COPD can usually be controlled by appropriate management, including soaking the hay or feeding vacuum-packed, semi-wilted grass, changing the bedding from straw or sawdust to shavings or paper, and keeping the horse out as much as possible. To differentiate this condition from other common causes of either coughing or nasal discharge, such as a chronic bacterial infection, you need to call the vet. The vet may also treat the horse with drugs to relieve constriction of the small airways in the lungs and to help clearance of thick mucus from the lungs. Any horse who has had COPD is at risk of developing an acute, severe attack if exposed to potential allergens.

Pasture-Associated Allergic Respiratory Disease

Some horses develop an allergy to specific pollens in the pasture, which cause signs identical to chronic obstructive pulmonary disease. These horses usually need to be stabled temporarily in a dust-free environment: e.g. bedded on clean shavings or paper, and fed with soaked hay.

Lungworm

Lungworm causes a chronic cough, with or without nasal discharge, and poor exercise tolerance. It is only seen in horses which have previously grazed with donkeys. Lungworm is transmissible between donkeys, and from donkeys to horses, but not between horses. Your vet may need to collect a sample of fluid from the lungs in order to reach the diagnosis. Treatment is by specific worming drugs. Horses kept with donkeys must be wormed regularly with a drug effective against lungworm. Speak to your vet for advice. *(See* Worm Control, *page 154.)*

Upper Respiratory Tract Infections (Equine Influenza / Colds)

There are many viruses which can cause symptoms similar to a human cold. The horse may have a temperature for a few days, be off his food, and develop a nasal discharge or cough. Isolate the horse *(see page 146)*, keep him warm, do not work him and call your vet.

Vaccination against equine influenza protects against specific viruses, and reduces the severity of clinical signs *(see page 153)*. It is very important not to return the horse to work too quickly after apparent recovery from infection, because the airways remain hyper-sensitised for several weeks and the horse will be at risk of developing secondary problems.

Viral infections can spread from one horse to another, so any horses which have been in contact with an infected horse should be monitored carefully even if they are not showing obvious clinical signs. Monitor your horse's temperature twice daily and stop work if it increases.

There are also several bacteria which can cause similar symptoms. If your vet suspects a bacterial infection, a course of antibiotics will be administered.

Strangles

Strangles is an infectious disease caused by the bacterium Streptococcusequi. The main signs are a high temperature and a nasal discharge that looks like pus. The horse may be dull and off food, and often develops swellings around the top of the neck and under the jaw. You must isolate the horse *(see page 146)* and call your vet immediately. Infection is often introduced into a yard by a new horse. If possible, any new horse should be kept isolated for several days after arrival and blood-tested for this disease.

Travel Sickness

Travel sickness is generally induced by very long journeys and results in severe flu-like symptoms: high temperature, dullness, depressed appetite and increased breathing rate. It may be complicated by pneumonia or pleurisy. If your horse is off colour after a long journey and has a temperature, call your vet immediately, since early treatment is most likely to be successful. Keep the horse warm and do not exercise or stress him further.

Whistling and Roaring

Many horses make a noise when they breathe out or expire. This is normal, but a noise during inspiration (breathing in) may reflect partial obstruction of the airway and may compromise performance and cause the horse to tire easily and get out of breath. A whistle is a high-pitched noise during inspiration. A lower pitched noise is called roaring. Both of these noises can be caused by impaired movement of one of the vocal cords. This is far more common in horses than in ponies. If you think that your horse is affected, call your vet, who can use a flexible tube (an endoscope) to inspect the vocal cords. Unfit horses sometimes make a noise when breathing and are referred to as thick in the wind, but when they are fitter, the noise disappears and performance is not affected.

Partial or complete paralysis of the muscle controlling the movement of usually the left vocal cord can be treated surgically. This may be advised if the horse's performance is affected. The 'Hobday operation' involves removal of the lining of the sac adjacent to the vocal cord. The vocal cord needs to be held in a fixed position so that it will not vibrate or fall into the airway and cause restricted and turbulent airflow. This is achieved by the tie-back operation. These operations have varying degrees of success.

Bleeding from the Nose (Epistaxis)

Any bleeding from the nose is called epistaxis. Bleeding not associated with exercise is unusual but may be due to a serious problem in the airways of the head, especially either an abnormal growth (ethmoid haematoma) or a fungal infection (guttural pouch mycosis). The horse should be examined by a vet as soon as possible. By passing a flexible tube (an endoscope) via the nostrils, the airways can be inspected and the site of bleeding established. Surgical treatment may be necessary.

Bleeding from the nose after fast exercise usually originates from the lungs and is comparatively common. A large percentage of horses bleed slightly from the lungs after maximal galloping exercise. The blood is often swallowed, so it does does not appear at the nostrils. The diagnosis is confirmed by looking into the trachea (windpipe) within one hour after exercise: a trickle of blood from the lungs can often be seen.

Low-grade bleeding from the lungs is usually irrelevant to the horse and you will probably be unaware of it. Severe bleeding from the lungs may compromise performance and may reflect other underlying lung disease. If blood appears in the nostrils after work on more than one occasion, your vet should examine the horse.

24. Diseases of the Intestines and Liver

A horse with an intestinal problem may show signs of colic *(see page 160)*, develop diarrhoea, or progressively lose weight, often in spite of eating normally.

Colic

(See page 160.)

Diarrhoea

Very soft droppings or diarrhoea can have many causes including a sudden change in diet, stress, worms or a bacterial infection called salmonellosis. Salmonellosis is infectious to other horses and to people, so a horse with persistent diarrhoea must be isolated *(see page 146).*

Anyone handling the horse must wash their hands afterwards. Bandage up the tail to stop it becoming soiled. Rub petroleum jelly around the buttocks to prevent the skin from damage caused by being continually wet. Offer the horse plenty of fresh water. Call the vet..

Regular worming is essential to prevent diarrhoea associated with worms *(see page 154).*

Worm Control
(See page 154.)

Weight Loss
There are multiple causes of weight loss including:
- Inadequate feeding *(see FAULTY FEEDING ARRANGEMENTS page 120).*
- Difficulty in eating due to inadequate tooth care *(see page 156).*
- Worms *(see page 154).*
- Grass sickness *(see below).*
- Damage to the gut wall leading to loss of protein into the intestine.
- Failure to absorb nutrients properly.
- Infiltration of the gut wall with cancerous tissue.
- Liver disease: e.g. ragwort poisoning *(see below).*
- Kidney disease: you will need to call your vet to investigate the problem.

Grass Sickness
Grass sickness is a disease which only affects horses who spend some time at grass. It occurs most often in the spring and autumn, and is particularly prevalent in certain areas of the country. It either causes sudden onset and severe colic—mimicking a colic which requires surgical treatment *(see page 160)*—or more commonly it causes chronic low grade colic, occasionally with constipation, gradual loss of weight and muscle tremors. At present the cause is unknown. With long-term intensive care, some affected horses can be saved. As with any colic case, call the vet immediately.

Ragwort Poisoning
Ragwort poisoning results in liver disease. Clinical signs may include dullness, colic, loss of weight, and in severe cases standing with the head pressed up against the wall, repeated yawning and unawareness of the surroundings. Eating ragwort causes progressive damage to the liver, but since the liver has a large reserve capacity, clinical signs may not be evident until a large proportion of the liver has been irreversibly damaged. Treatment is therefore extremely difficult and the disease is often fatal. Prevention is essential. The living ragwort plants, with their characteristic yellow flowers are usually unpalatable, so a horse will not eat them unless there is nothing else available. Ragwort which has been pulled up or cut down, and has died, or is conserved in hay, is readily eaten and potentially dangerous. Therefore it is important that if living out, a horse always has enough to eat. Ragwort plants should be pulled up and removed from the field and preferably burnt. Try not to use hay which has been made from a field containing ragwort. *(See WEED CONTROL, page 64; PADDOCK MAINTENANCE PLAN, page 65; and fig. 39.)*

25. Lameness

Lameness may be sudden in onset and severe, or may be gradual in onset, intermittent, and mild to severe. If both front legs or both hind legs are affected, the horse may not have an obvious limp, but the stride lengths may be shortened or the horse may be reluctant to jump or go forward freely. Lameness is easiest to detect at a trot. If the horse has a forelimb lameness, the head and neck will drop when the sound forelimb is bearing weight—a head nod.

If the horse has a hind limb lameness, there is often a toe drag. There is more movement, up and down, of the hind quarter of the lame hind limb compared to the other. Most causes of lameness are made worse by work. If lameness is suspected, you should rest the horse, preferably restricting him to a stable or small paddock, and call the vet.

Some tendon and ligament injuries can occur producing swelling but initially no lameness. If swelling develops in the region of a tendon or ligament, rest the horse and call the vet, even if lameness is not apparent. It is therefore important to inspect the legs regularly in order to detect areas of heat, swelling or pain.

Foot Lameness

Pain in the foot is the most common reason for lameness, but there are a variety of causes. Bruising (corns), infections under the sole, and shoeing problems, occur most frequently. With any lameness it is important to call the vet, because early diagnosis and treatment is most likely to resolve the problem. Often there are no obvious swellings and areas of heat, so the vet may need to desensitize different parts of the leg (nerve blocks) in order to find out where the pain is. X-rays or ultrasound can then be used to obtain pictures of the area, in order to reach a diagnosis.

Laminitis

Laminitis is caused by inflammation of the sensitive lining of the hoof wall (the laminae) and is extremely painful. Ponies, especially small native breeds, are particularly susceptible. The hoof wall is usually hot and the pulse to the foot is increased. The horse or pony stands with his weight tipped back onto his heels, is unwilling to move, and may lie down. Do not force him to move. Call the vet.

Laminitis tends to result in abnormal hoof wall growth, with an increase at the heel but less at the toe. This produces abnormal horizontal rings on the hoof wall, which diverge at the heel. The rings are a definite sign that a horse or pony has had a previous attack of laminitis.

Laminitis is potentially very serious, as damage to the sensitive laminae of the foot can cause loss of support of the pedal bone, which may rotate and/or drop and ultimately penetrate the sole of the foot.

Laminitis has many causes but the most common in ponies is too much rich food, usually grass. Any pony which has had laminitis is susceptible to repeated attacks and must be strictly managed, by limiting access to grass and hard feed, and regular foot trimming. *(See fig. 77a.)*

Hoof Wall Cracks / Sandcracks

Some horses seem to be particularly prone to short hoof wall cracks which extend upwards from the solar surface (the outside edge of the sole) or downwards

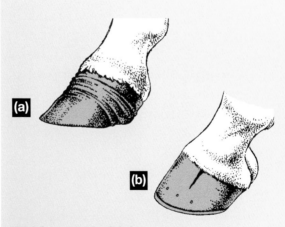

77 (a) Laminitis; **(b)** Sandcrack.

from the coronary band *(see fig. 77b)*. The causes are poorly understood, although inadequate trimming and shoeing may be a predisposing factor. They generally do not cause lameness, but may create problems keeping shoes on. If the horse is unshod, hoof wall cracks are more likely to become infected, resulting in a sub-solar abscess and lameness. Regular trimming and shoeing, supplementation of the diet with biotin and methionine, and the application of cornucrescine to the coronary band may help to prevent hoof wall cracks.

A single, vertical, full-thickness hoof wall crack (traditionally called a sandcrack) may result in instability of the wall, pinching of sensitive tissues, and lameness. This must be treated by immobilising the crack using a lacing technique and the application of an acrylic resin.

Subsolar Infection (Pus in the Foot)

Infection in the foot causes severe pain and lameness because it results in inflammation and swelling within the confines of the rigid hoof wall. Swelling may also develop in the pastern and cannon regions. The foot may be hot. If the infection has been established for several days a soft raised area may develop at the coronary band, and pus may burst out. Veterinary treatment is required in order to create a hole in the sole of the foot to allow pus to drain from the abscess. It may be necessary to poultice the foot *(see page 150)* for several days.

Corns

A corn is a bruise at the heel between the frog and the wall. It is often the result of an ill-fitting shoe, especially if the foot becomes overgrown. A corn

causes lameness which is most apparent on a turn on firm ground. Treatment is by removal of the shoe, paring away the overlying horn and poulticing for several days. To prevent corns, regular trimming and shoeing are essential. A good foot care regime will help to reduce the number of foot problems. The feet should be trimmed at least every four to six weeks whether the horse is shod or not. The feet must be picked out at least once, and preferably twice, daily and always after exercise.

Stone in the Foot—Stone Bruise

If a stone becomes lodged in the foot, sudden lameness will develop. Whenever sudden lameness occurs during a ride, always check the foot. In many cases, removal of the stone will relieve the lameness. Treading on a stone may result in bruising of the foot, or even penetration of the sole. The horse will need to be rested for several days and the foot poulticed *(see page 150)*.

Navicular Syndrome

Pain associated with the navicular bone in the back of the foot causes lameness which often affects both front feet resulting in a short, shuffling stride. It is relatively uncommon in ponies, and occurs more often in horses. Lameness may be mild or severe and is most obvious when the horse is turning. In the stable he may stand with bedding packed under his heels, or pointing his toe out in front.

Diagnosis of navicular syndrome is difficult and needs nerve blocks and X-rays. True navicular disease is incurable and causes permanent lameness. If the lameness is only mild, some improvement may be achieved by corrective farriery and regular exercise. Painkillers may help some horses following an in-depth diagnosis.

There are many other causes of pain in the back of the foot, and lameness associated with these is often helped by correct foot balance.

Inflammation of the Pedal (Coffin) Bone

If a horse has flat soles and does a lot of work on hard ground, he may be prone to inflammation of the pedal bone (so called pedal osteitis), pain and lameness. The condition is difficult to diagnose because

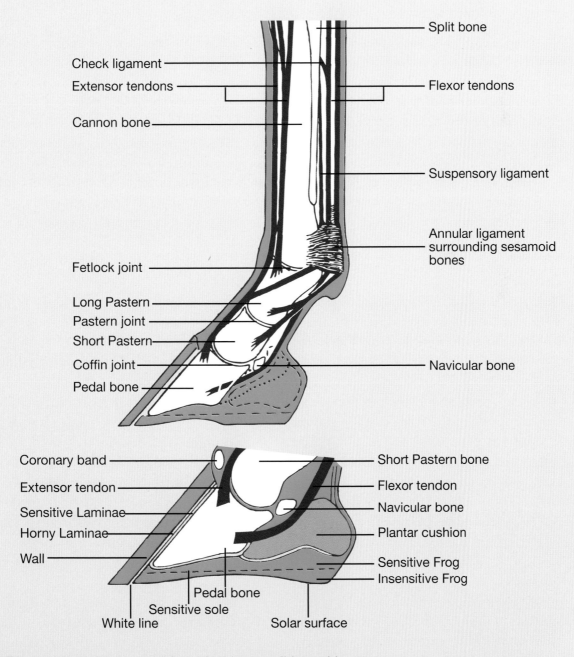

78 The structure of the leg and foot, showing possible trouble spots.

X-rays are not very sensitive and in normal cases there is considerable variation of the X-ray appearance of the pedal bone. The use of broad web shoes with a concave solar surface may help to manage the condition by providing added protection. *(See Types of Shoe, page 115.)*

Nail Bind

Nail bind is caused by a nail pressing on the sensitive laminae, causing inflammation and pain. It may be due to misplacement of the nail when the horse was shod. Lameness usually develops within twenty-four to forty-eight hours of shoeing. Alternatively, slight shifting of the shoe may have a similar effect. Lameness is usually worse as the horse turns. Prompt removal of the offending nail is important: the longer it remains the longer it will take for lameness to resolve.

Thrush

Thrush is a foul-smelling fungal infection of the foot usually in the frog region. There is black discharge from the frog. The horse may or may not be lame, depending on the depth of infection. Thrush is usually caused by poor stable management and poor trimming of the foot. The bed should be as dry as possible. The feet should be picked out carefully at least once a day, using a sharp-ended hoof pick and paying particular attention to the frog and its clefts. The frogs should be trimmed regularly by the farrier, and the toes kept short.

Sidebone

Sidebone refers to ossification of the lateral cartilages of the foot. The ossifications can be felt as firm protuberances above the coronary band on the inside and outside of the foot. Sidebone is common in heavier horses and ponies, and is rarely a cause of lameness.

Arthritis

Arthritis can occur in any age of horse. Also known as degenerative joint disease, it causes pain and lameness. Sometimes (but not always) the joint is swollen. Any joint can develop arthritis. Bone spavin (arthritis of the hock), high ringbone (arthritis of the pastern joint), and low ringbone (arthritis of the coffin joint) are terms commonly used. Diagnosis requires nerve blocks and X-rays. If a horse has arthritis, exercise must be controlled. Little and often is better than hard work followed by complete rest. Your vet may administer special drugs which help to control lameness and progression of the condition. *(See figs. 78 and 79.)*

Splints

A splint is a bony enlargement of the inside or outside splint bone. It can be caused by a blow to the bone, or can result from abnormal strains in a horse with poor conformation. When the splint develops, there is a warm, painful swelling and lameness. The lameness is worse on hard ground and deteriorates with work. The initial swelling is due to new bone formation and local inflammation. With time and rest the inflammation subsides, but some residual bony swelling persists. As not all splints cause lameness, you need your vet to examine the horse to determine the cause.

Tendon and Ligament Injury

The superficial and deep flexor tendons, the check ligament, and the suspensory ligament run down the back of the legs in the cannon region and take a lot of strain when the horse moves. Any damage to these structures is considered serious: therefore if there is any heat or swelling in this area, box rest the horse and call the vet, even if no lameness is detectable. This is one of the conditions in which early treatment and plenty of rest may possibly prevent more serious and possibly irreparable damage *(see figs. 78 and 80)*,

Sesamoiditis

This is a term used to describe inflammation of the sesamoid bones (on the back of the fetlock). It is a very rare cause of lameness and can only be diagnosed by using X-rays. Swelling in the region of a sesamoid bone is much more likely to be due to a suspensory ligament injury or due to local bruising or fibrosis following direct trauma.

Curb

Curb is a vague term describing swelling on the back of the hock which may be due to inflammation or fibrosis beneath the skin, or occasionally tendon strain, or sprain of the plantar ligament. Most commonly, a curb-like appearance is due to prominence of the top of the outside splint bone, which is of no clinical significance, and does not predispose to lameness.

Fractures

Fractures are relatively uncommon but must always be suspected if a horse has a sudden onset of severe lameness. The fracture may become much worse if the horse moves. If possible, keep him still and call the vet.

Joint Swelling

Swelling associated with a joint is usually due to an abnormal amount of joint fluid which is soft unless the fluid pressure is excessive, when it may be hard. The swelling may be associated with new bone formation, which is usually firm. An abnormal amount of fluid usually reflects inflammation due to:

* A sprain of the joint.
* Infection of the joint.
* Secondary to arthritis
* A chip fracture.
* A developmental abnormality of bone and cartilage called osteochondrosis.

Some horses, especially those with upright conformation *(see* Conformation, *page 21)*, may have enlargement of the fetlock joint

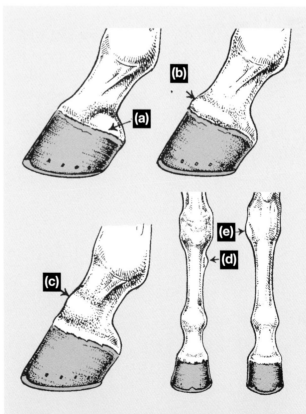

79 Bony enlargements: **(a)** Sidebone; **(b)** Low ringbone; **(c)** High ringbone; **(d)** Splint; **(e)** Bone spavin (hind leg).

capsules (so-called articular windgalls) without associated lameness. If a horse develops a new swelling, seek veterinary advice, even if no lameness is seen. If lameness is severe, urgent veterinary attention is required.

Bursal Enlargements

A bursa is an isolated fluid-filled sac. Some occur naturally at potential pressure points—e.g. the point of hock—whereas others are acquired due to repetitive low-grade trauma. Although unsightly, they are usually of no functional significance. They are difficult to prevent and tend to persist long term. Common examples include a capped hock and a capped elbow.

Enlargement of Tendon Sheaths

In some locations, tendons are surrounded by tendon sheaths which contain synovial fluid, similar to joint fluid. Enlargement of a tendon sheath may be seen incidentally, or occasionally associated with lameness. Enlargement of the digital flexor tendon sheath on the back of the fetlock—known as a non-articular windgall—is a common finding, especially in hind limbs, but is only sometimes associated with lameness.

Some joint swellings have traditionally been assigned a name, but these tend to be rather non-specific and tell you nothing about the underlying disease process. For example, *bog spavin* is a term describing distension of the tarsocrural (true hock) joint capsule which presents as a soft tissue swelling on the front and inside of the hock. It may reflect a joint sprain, a fracture, osteochondrosis or arthritis. Or it may be an incidental abnormality of no clinical significance.

A thoroughpin is a soft swelling above the hock, on the inside and outside, in front of the Achilles tendon region. It is an enlargement of the tarsal sheath and is only occasionally associated with lameness. If swelling of a tendon sheath develops suddenly, seek veterinary advice.

Miscellaneous Soft Tissue Swelling

Big Knee

Big knee is an imprecise term describing any soft tissue swelling on the front of the knee, most of which are due to trauma. The

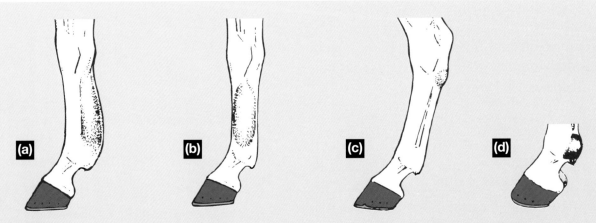

80 (a) Sprained tendons; **(b)** Sprained suspensory ligament; **(c)** Site of curb-like swellings; **(d)** Sesamoiditis.

swelling may be a haematoma (a blood-filled swelling), enlargement of one of the tendon sheaths, distension of one of the joint capsules of the knee, or cellulitis. Consult your vet.

Filled Leg

- Subsolar infection *(see page 168)*.
- Mud fever and cracked heels *(see page 174)*.
- Cellulitis *(see page 160)*.
- Sprain of a tendon or ligament *(see page 170)*.
- Lymphangitis *(see page 160)*.
- Direct trauma, resulting in bruising.

Confine the horse to a stable if possible, and consult your vet.

26. Skin Diseases

Most skin diseases are not serious and are easy to treat, but in some circumstances they cause pain which makes the horse difficult to handle. Some conditions such as lice, mange and ringworm, are infectious and can spread to other horses in close contact, and to people.

Ringworm

Ringworm is caused by a fungus that infects the roots of the hairs. The hairs fall out, generally in tufts, producing lots of small bare patches which are often circular. It is infectious both to other horses and to people. Isolate the horse *(see page 146)* and keep the tack and grooming kit separate. **Wash your hands after touching the horse.** Call your vet.

Lice

Lice are small insects which may live in the manes and tails of horses, or on their backs, and which cause itchiness. If you carefully part the mane it may be possible to see small pale bodies of the lice moving. The lice also lay eggs (nits). Lice are infective to other horses, but are not serious and are easily treated under veterinary supervision.

Rain Scald

Rain scald is a bacterial infection occurring along the back and hind quarters. Usually seen only in horses who live out, it results in multiple scabby skin lesions. It is generally controlled by keeping the horse clean and dry. The horse must be groomed regularly to remove caked mud and must be provided with enough shelter to dry off thoroughly if kept out all the time.

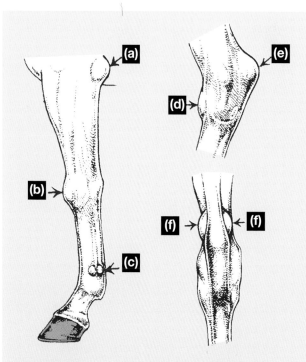

81 (a) Capped elbow; **(b)** Capped knee;
(c) Windgalls; **(d)** Bog spavin; **(e)** Capped hock;
(f) Thoroughpin.

Mud Fever and Cracked Heels

Mud fever and cracked heels are different names for the same condition. It is caused by a bacterial infection of the skin in the heel region. The skin becomes thickened and cracked, and may exude yellowish fluid. The legs may become swollen. The areas are very sore. Veterinary treatment is required. Mud fever can usually be prevented by removing all the mud and drying the heels thoroughly.

If the horse lives out, the feathers should be trimmed to help to prevent accumulation of mud; mud should be brushed off regularly.

If the horse is stabled, keep the feathers short. There is no problem in washing mud off after riding, provided the back of the pastern is dried afterwards.

Sweet Itch

Occurring more often in ponies than horses, sweet itch is a condition causing severe itchiness around the mane and tail. The pony rubs himself and may create open sores. Sweet itch stems from an allergy to the bites of midges. There is no cure, but with correct management most ponies can be made more comfortable. The midges generally bite at dawn and dusk during the summer so if the pony is kept in during the early morning and evening and fly repellent is applied, the number of bites will be reduced thus helping to prevent itchiness. Fly strips in the stable will also reduce the number of insects around the pony. Rubbing benzyl benzoate in the mane and tail twice a day will take away some of the irritation and make the pony more comfortable. Your vet can also inject drugs which help to relieve the irritation.

Urticaria

Urticaria is a general term used to describe multiple small skin lumps which appear suddenly all over the skin and usually disappear within twenty-four hours. They are generally painless and non-irritant and may arise through something the horse has eaten, a reaction to the bedding, nettle rash *(see opposite page)* or an allergic reaction to a drug. The lumps normally resolve spontaneously and only rarely is treatment required.

Warts (Papillomata)

Warts are small, pale, hairless nodules which may develop on the muzzle of young horses as a result of a viral infection. They are not painful and will usually disappear spontaneously over the next several months.

Sarcoids

Sarcoids are swellings of variable size and appearance in the skin. They develop particularly on the muzzle, lower abdomen, groin region and limbs. There is a genetic predisposition to sarcoids, and if a horse has one it may develop others. Sessile sarcoids are flat, hairless, slightly raised areas, which often do not spread. Large hairless swellings may ulcerate, especially if subjected to friction and can be a major problem if in an area likely to be contacted by tack. Consult your vet.

Melanoma

Most grey horses eventually develop skin tumours called melanomas—raised, firm areas, which are usually black and may be hairless. If large they may become ulcerated, especially in the anal region. Similar tumours may develop internally. Consult your vet.

Swellings in the Saddle Region

Firm nodular swellings, which may become hairless and which eventually ulcerate, often develop in the area under the saddle. The precise cause is unknown. They are generally of no consequence unless ulcerated. Some resolve spontaneously whereas others persist and occasionally multiply. Check the fitting of your saddle and numnah *(see pages 247 and 256)*. Saddle sores can result in local soft tissue swelling which usually resolves rapidly as long as due care is paid to the fitting of tack and progressive fittening of the horse.

Nettle Rash

If a horse is badly stung by nettles, multiple small skin bumps and severe lameness on the affected limb may occur. If several limbs are affected, a wobbly incoordinated gait may result. Although the clinical signs are dramatic, they usually resolve spontaneously within several hours.

Photosensitisation (Sunburn)

Sunburn, or photosensitisation, may occur on white-haired and pink areas of skin in horses who have eaten plants, such as St John's Wort, which contain certain chemicals. Though only depigmented areas are affected, crusty, sore skin lesions develop. The condition can be prevented by avoiding exposure to offending plants and to the sun, or applying high-factor sun screen.

Cushing's Syndrome (Pituitary Adenoma)

The pituitary gland lies at the base of the brain and secretes hormones which control many of the body's functions, including hair growth and sugar digestion.

In some old ponies this gland becomes over-active and stops the pony losing his winter coat. The pony becomes more susceptible to infections and laminitis *(see page 167)*. Call your vet. The condition can be diagnosed using a blood test.

27. Incoordination and Other Gait Abnormalities

Wobbler Syndrome

The coordination of limb movement is dependent on correct function of the nervous system. Damage to the spinal cord due either to a developmental abnormality or to trauma—e.g. a fall—can cause loss of coordination and weakness—the so called wobbler syndrome. Similar clinical signs may develop transiently after nettle stings. Seek immediate advice from your vet. Severe damage of the spinal cord is usually permanent, but sometimes, especially after a fall, the spinal cord may only be bruised and the horse will recover.

Shivering

Shivering is a condition which is poorly-understood and affects the nervous system, especially in draught breeds. Clinical signs are often only apparent when the horse moves backwards or makes an attempt to lift his hind legs. As an affected horse steps backwards, each hind limb may be lifted exaggeratedly, with elevation and quivering of the tail. It may be extremely difficult to pick up the hind limbs, making trimming and shoeing awkward.

Stringhalt

Stringhalt describes exaggerated flexion of one or both hind limbs. In some horses it is only apparent at walk, but in others it is also evident at trot and canter. The cause is unknown and there is no cure, although surgical treatment may help.

28. Abnormal Habits

There are a number of abnormal habits. Some of them, such as crib biting, wind sucking and weaving, have previously been known as vices, and they should be declared at the time of sale. These habits may arise through boredom. Wood chewing may be copied by other horses, but other abnormal habits will not.

Head Shaking

Head shaking is a problem which is usually sudden in onset during the summer. The head shakes up and down, usually only during exercise. The horse may try to rub his nose on his leg, or may strike out at his nose with a front leg. The problem may resolve spontaneously in the winter, or it may occasionally persist.

Crib Biting

The horse grasps any edge such as the top of a door or a manger, or a paddock rail. He may also chew the wood. The behaviour may be combined with windsucking. Crib biting may be prevented by putting metal strips over objects which might be grasped, or fixing a grille on the door. Painting the wood with creosote or another noxious substance might help—but some substances can be harmful, so make sure that the wood is dry before the horse has access to it.

Windsucking

The horse arches his neck and gulps in air. This results in chemicals (endorphins) being released in the brain which create a pleasant sensation. It is questionable whether it has any adverse effect on the horse. It can be helped by placing a cribbing strap around the throat, which may result in development of white hairs at the poll.

Weaving

The horse shifts his weight from one forelimb to the other, swinging his neck from side to side. Horses which do it over the door can be controlled using an anti-weaving grille, but some will continue to do it within the stable. It is rarely seen in horses turned out.

Box Walking

The horse walks round and round the box, especially if he is bored or stressed. Provision of toys, e.g. a plastic bottle hanging from the ceiling, may help to prevent it.

Self-Mutilation

Occasionally horses will bite themselves or tear their rugs. In some cases this may be caused by boredom.

PART TWO
The Rider and Riding

29. Mounting and Dismounting

MOUNTING

Before mounting, check that the girth is sufficiently tight to prevent the saddle from slipping; that the stirrup irons are down; that the stirrup leathers are approximately the correct length and that the saddle flaps are lying smoothly.

To mount from the left (near) side of the horse, stand with your left shoulder to the horse's left shoulder. Take the reins and the whip into the left hand, with the reins properly separated for riding and of suitable length to prevent the horse from moving. Keep the right rein slightly shorter than the left rein.

Place your left hand in front of the withers. With your right hand, turn the stirrup clockwise. Then put your left foot in the stirrup iron. Press your toe down so that it comes under the girth and does not dig into the horse's side. Pivot your body round to face the horse. Place your right hand either on the far side of the saddle at the waist or on the front arch, and spring lightly up, straightening both knees. Swing your right leg over—taking care that it does not brush the horse's quarters—and at the same time position your right hand on the front arch of the saddle. Let your seat sink gently, without a bump, into the lowest part of the saddle. Put your right foot quietly in the stirrup and take the reins into both hands. It is correct and useful to be able to mount and dismount from either side. Once you are mounted, it is sensible to recheck the girth after walking a short distance, as it may be necessary to tighten it *(see page 181)*.

DISMOUNTING

To dismount (from the left, or near, side), remove both feet from the stirrups. Put the reins and whip in the left hand. Put your left hand on the horse's neck, and lean forward. Put your right hand on the front arch of the saddle. Swing your right leg back and clear over the horse's back, allowing both feet to slip to the ground. You should land lightly, bending your knees and avoiding the horse's forelegs. Then with your right hand take hold of the reins a short distance from the bit.

To Dismount Using the Stirrup

Although this alternative method is given (it may be necessary in the case of a disability) it is not recommended for general use. *It is essential for the horse to be held by an assistant.*

Take the reins and whip in the left hand and rest them on the horse's neck in front of the withers. Put your right hand on the front arch of the saddle and at the same time slip your right foot out of the stirrup. Pass your right leg over the horse's back and put your right hand on the waist of the saddle. Remove your left foot from the stirrup and then let both feet slip to the ground.

THE STIRRUPS

The Correct Length of Stirrup

Before mounting, you can adjust your stirrups to approximately the correct length. Stand facing the saddle. Put the knuckles of your right hand on the stirrup bar of the saddle and adjust the leathers so that the stirrup iron reaches into your armpit. Then stand in front of the horse to check that the stirrups are level.

82 (a) Adjusting the stirrup length;
(b) and **(c)** Returning the buckle using the underpart of the leather;
(d) Alternative method of returning buckle by pulling top strap upwards and pushing down on stirrup-iron.

Once you are mounted and sitting centrally, allow your legs to hang down in a very relaxed way. You may then adjust the leathers so that the bars of the irons are on, or slightly above, the ankle bone.

If your leathers are too long, you will lose your balance and therefore your security. You may fall behind the movement in rising trot, lose your stirrups, or grip upwards, your heel coming above your toe. *If your leathers are too short,* you will appear to be sitting either on top of the saddle rather than into it, or too far back.

With a short stirrup you are less likely to be pulled forward or to lose your balance, as you will have the length of your thigh in front of you, but you will also have less use of your lower leg.

As your training advances, you will find it easier and more effective to ride with slightly longer leathers. The length will vary according to the standard of the rider and the type of work being carried out.

You should seek the advice of an instructor as to the length at which you should currently be riding.

Altering the Length of the Stirrup when Mounted

To alter the left stirrup, first take the reins in your right hand. With your left hand take hold of the spare end of the leather. Then, with your thumb on top of the buckle, steer the tongue of the buckle with the first finger, the other three fingers continuing to hold the spare end of the leather *(fig. 82a)*. Disengage the tongue and guide it into the required hole. Move the buckle up close to the bar of the saddle by pulling down on the inside of the leather, then replace the end *(see fig. 82b)*.

83 Tightening the girth when mounted.

- *Never remove your foot from the stirrup.*
- *Get into the habit of changing the length of your stirrups by feel, without looking down.*

TIGHTENING THE GIRTH WHEN MOUNTED

To tighten the girth on the left-hand side, take the reins and whip into your right hand. Keeping your foot in the stirrup, bring your left leg forward. Then, using your left hand under the saddle flap, tighten the girth as for the stirrup leathers. Ideally, the girth buckles should be at the same height on the girth straps on both sides of the saddle. When you have finished, make sure that the buckle guards are lying flat over the girth buckles *(fig. 83)*.

HELPING A RIDER TO MOUNT

Commonly termed giving a leg-up. First check that the girth is sufficiently tight to prevent the saddle from slipping, and that the stirrups are down.

The rider takes up the reins in his left hand and places it on the horse's withers, with the right hand on the right side of the skirt of the saddle.

A whip or stick, if carried, should be in the left hand.

The rider, standing close to the horse and squarely facing the saddle, lifts the left lower leg backwards from the knee.

The helper stands just to the left of the rider, turns to face him, and then places his left hand under the rider's left knee and his right hand around and under the rider's ankle.

On an agreed signal, the rider jumps upwards off his right foot, keeping back

straight and shoulders square to the horse's flank. At the same time, the helper raises the rider's left leg, from the knee, straight upwards, applying pressure mainly with his left hand and taking care to lift straight up rather than towards the horse.

At this stage the rider must keep his back straight and must not lean forward.

When the rider is able to pass his right leg clear over the horse's back, he turns his body to the front and lowers his seat lightly into the saddle. As the rider turns his body, the helper stops pushing upwards.

30. The Position of the Rider in the Saddle

It is important for the rider to sit in the correct position, as this will enable him to apply the correct aids, to remain in balance with the horse, and to ride with maximum ease and efficiency.

THE BASIC POSITION

Having mounted, you should sit in the lowest part of the saddle, your hips square with the horse's hips.

You should feel the weight of your body being carried equally on both seat bones.

You must be straight *(fig. 84b)*. You should look in the direction in which you are going.

Your body, while held upright, should be supple and without tension. It is particularly important for the seat, thighs and knees to lie relaxed on the saddle, as this allows the part of the leg just below the knee to rest against the horse's side.

A rider should at all times remain in balance with the movement of the horse. Suppleness at the hips, and flexibility of the spine and shoulders, will allow this.

The ball of the foot should rest on the bar of the stirrup iron, exerting just enough pressure to keep the iron in place. The foot should not tilt to one side or the other.

The line of the foot from heel to toe should point almost directly forwards. The ankle should remain supple, and the heel should be slightly lower than the toe *(fig. 84a)*.

Seen from the side a straight line would pass from the rider's bent elbow through to his hand and along the rein to the horse's mouth *(fig. 85)*.

The Contact

It is vitally important for you to be able to move your hands independently of your body. Your hands should move in harmony with the horse's mouth. When the horse moves his head and neck, your hands should follow that movement.

The hand movement is made possible by the suppleness and mobility of your shoulders and elbows. Wrists should remain supple, but they should not bend.

When you take up the reins, you should feel some weight in your hands. Ideally, you should have the same feel in your hands at all times and at all paces. This is known as the contact.

The horse should accept this contact happily and feel no pain or discomfort. He will do so only if the rider is able to go with all the movements of the horse's head and neck. This will be achieved when the rider attains an independent seat (i.e. does not rely on the reins to keep his balance).

The contact should be drawn forward by the horse from the rider so there is a comfortably secure and confident feeling between them, being neither too light nor too heavy. Some horses respond to a lighter contact than others so it is up to the rider to develop the 'feel' according to each individual horse and its stage of training.

The rider should also make alterations to the height of his hands as the horse moves

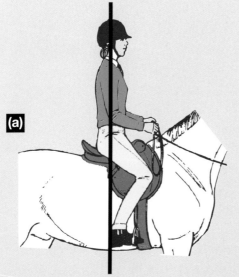
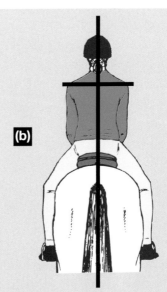

84 The correct position: **(a)** from the side; **(b)** from the rear.

his head up or down, thus maintaining the line—elbow, hand, horse's mouth.

Your hands should be carried with the thumbs uppermost and the backs of the hands facing outwards *(fig. 85)*. You should hold your wrists in a supple way so that there is a straight line down the forearm and back of the hand.

When holding the reins, the wrists, forearms and shoulders should be free from tension so the rider is able to maintain an elastic and therefore consistent rein contact with the horse's mouth. This will allow the horse to accept the contact offered without resistance.

THE REINS

Holding the Single Rein

The rein should pass directly from the bit, between the little and third fingers then across the palm and over the first (index) finger, with the thumb slightly arched on top. It is important that your

(a)

(b)

(c)

(d)

(e)

85 The line from rider's elbow to horse's mouth.

86 Holding the reins: **(a)** single rein; **(b)** single reins in one hand; **(c)** alternative to (b); **(d)** two (double) reins; **(e)** two (double) reins in one hand.

third finger holds the edges of the rein in the joints nearest the palm and that your fingers are closed securely but not tight and unyielding. Holding the rein this way prevents it from slipping through your hands *(fig. 86a)*.

Holding Both Single Reins in One Hand *(Figs. 86b and c)*

There are several ways of doing this. The usual way is to pass the right rein over to your left hand and hold it between your second and third fingers. Take the slack of both reins between your first (index) finger and thumb *(fig. 86b)*. Alternatively, pass the left rein outside your little finger and the right rein between your thumb and first finger. In this case, the right rein lies over the left as they cross the palm of the hand, the slack of the right lying between your palm and your little finger and the slack of the left between your first finger and thumb *(fig. 86c)*. Either hand may be used to hold the reins, but when schooling it should be the outside hand to the bend of the horse.

87 Rising trot, sitting on the right diagonal.

Holding Two Reins, for Double Bridle, etc.

Hold as for the single rein, except that the ring finger of each hand should divide the reins. The bridoon rein is usually held on the outside *(fig. 86d)* and the curb rein under the middle finger. This helps to keep the emphasis on the bridoon.

Holding All the Reins in One Hand *(Fig. 86e)*

Pass the reins from one hand into the other, so that the second finger divides the reins which you are passing. The slack ends pass over the index finger and are secured by the thumb.

THE POSITION OF THE RIDER IN MOTION

At Walk

The walk is a four-time pace *(see also page 193)*. The position of the body does not alter except that his legs will rest softly against the horse's ribcage and he will feel an alternate swing from side to side towards each leg as his hips and waist move in rhythm with the natural movement of the horse.

The rider's posture and supple contact will allow the horse to move fluently with correct use of his abdominal muscles, back and neck to maintain the qualities of the walk *(see also THE TRAINING SCALE, page 198)*.

At the Rising Trot

The trot is a two-time pace, the horse's legs moving in alternate diagonal pairs, with a moment of suspension in between *(see also page 193)*.

In rising trot the rider rises from the saddle on one beat and sits in the saddle on the alternate beat. This is also called posting *(fig. 87)*.

In rising trot your upper body should be inclined slightly forward from the hips so that you remain in balance with the horse's movements. While actually rising, your shoulders should lead the movement, but you must not tip forward.

Your body should feel as if it is being raised by the movement of the horse's swinging-back-and-forward energy, the seat returning quietly to the saddle without any loss of balance. Do not allow your weight to fall back onto the saddle; this would put you behind the movement of the horse.

Sit down with loose swinging hips and good core stability. Be careful not to collapse at the waist, causing a rounding of your back.

Hip and knee joints should remain supple and mobile while opening and closing, to accommodate the rising and lowering movements supported by the thighs.

The weight on the stirrup irons and the contact of the lower legs should not vary.

Elbow and shoulder joints should be supple and mobile, allowing the hands to maintain the same contact as you rise and return to the saddle. It is important for this consistent contact to be maintained at all times and that the reins are not used for support.

Diagonals

A rider is said to be riding on the left diagonal when his seat returns to the saddle as the left forefoot and right hind foot touch the ground. He is said to be riding on the right diagonal when his seat returns to the saddle as the right forefoot and left hind foot touch the ground. It is generally considered correct to ride on the left diagonal when proceeding to the right (on the right rein) and to ride on the right diagonal when proceeding to the left (on the left rein).

To change the diagonal, the rider sits down in the saddle for an extra beat, before rising again.

The rider should change the diagonal when changing direction, and also at intervals when out hacking, so that the horse makes equal use of the muscles on both sides of his body.

At the Sitting Trot

At sitting trot the rider sits for both beats of the trot. You should remain upright and your hips and back should be supple, absorbing the movement of the horse. Trying not to bounce causes stiffness and gripping so the rider should allow himself to bounce with the horse.

Sitting trot is used on the more trained horse to allow the rider to remain close to the saddle at all times. It should only be used when the horse's back is sufficiently muscled to carry a rider in this way. If sitting trot is used before the horse is ready, he will hollow his back and raise his head, thereby losing suppleness, relaxation and effective use of his hocks.

Sitting trot is sometimes a useful exercise to help to improve the rider's position.

The pace should not be affected as you change from sitting to rising or from rising to sitting trot.

At the Canter

The canter is a three-time pace *(see also page 194)*. It is normal and correct for the rider to ask the horse to lead with inside foreleg when cantering turns or circles.

At this pace suppleness of the hips is most important. Your upper body should move in rhythm with the three beats of the horse's stride. The seat should remain close to the saddle for all three beats, the back and hips allowing this through their suppleness. The suppleness and mobility of the rider's shoulder and elbow joints are also very important, as there is considerable movement of the horse's head, neck and back.

If the rider stiffens his back he will bump in the saddle, which is most uncomfortable for both horse and rider.

At the Gallop

The gallop is a four-time pace, and the fastest at which the horse moves *(see also page 195)*.

The weight of the rider's body should be taken forward on to the knees and stirrups *(fig. 88a)*. The reins will require shortening to allow the line, elbow-hand-horse's mouth to be maintained.

It is easier for the horse if this forward position is adopted, as your weight will be poised over the centre of gravity. To maintain a balanced position and not bump on the horse's back, you will need to be riding with a slightly shortened stirrup leather. You should not lose your balance and bump on the horse's back *(fig. 88b)*.

In Transitions (Changes of Pace or Speed)

During transitions it is important for your body to remain in balance with the horse's movement.

In transitions up and down the body must remain quiet and supple, neither anticipating nor being left behind the increasing or decreasing pace. You should resist the temptation to influence the horse by throwing your body about and by looking down or leaning in, as this will unbalance him. This particularly applies to transitions from trot to canter and is often the cause of the horse striking-off on the wrong leg.

In Circles and Changes of Direction

You should allow your weight to remain equally on both seat bones and to stay correctly in the centre of the saddle, sliding neither to the inside nor the outside.

Your hips should remain parallel to the

88 The gallop: **(a)** the correct position; **(b)** losing balance.

horse's hips and your shoulders parallel to the horse's shoulders. You should look in the direction in which you are going *(see fig. 84).*

Inside and Outside

The *inside* is the side of the horse that is on the inside of the movement: that is, when riding on a left circle, the inside is the left side of the horse.

The *outside* is the side of the horse that is on the outside of the movement: i.e. when riding on a left circle, the outside is the right side of the horse.

The Bend of the Horse

When moving on a curve, a circle or round a corner, the horse should appear to bend his body uniformly from poll to tail to comply with the curve on which he is travelling. This is termed the bend. *(See also fig. 91.)*

31. The Aids

Aids are the language used by the rider to communicate with the horse. The aim should be to give quick, clear aids at all times, and to receive immediate response from the horse. There are two types of aid:
- *Natural aids.* The influence of the rider's seat, legs and hands and the voice.
- *Artificial aids.* Whips and spurs.

NATURAL AIDS AND THEIR APPLICATION

These natural aids, logically applied, may be used without any alteration, for all paces and movements, at all standards of classical riding.

The Voice

In the early stages of training the voice can be used in conjunction with the other aids, clarifying them by saying, for example, 'walk on', 'trot', 'canter', 'steady' or 'halt'.

Rewarding the Horse

The voice is also used to praise or soothe the horse. It can be associated with a pat or stroke on the neck: a most useful method of communication to reward good work and as a way of saying 'thank you'.

Influence of the Seat (Whole Body)

It is important for young riders to learn how to sit naturally and softly on both seat bones, and to blend their body movements harmoniously with those of the horse. On more trained and muscled horses the seat aid involving the back, correctly used, can produce increased impulsion. It should be used with discretion. Strength and control of the core muscles of the rider are essential in order to retain a correct position, with minimum physical strength, and to be able to give clear, light aids to the horse which are easily understood. The rider must always remain in balance and be aware of the influence of his seat and weight.

The Legs

Relaxed thighs and supple hip and knee joints allow the legs just below the knee to rest in equal contact against the horse. The contact of the legs must be constant and should be sure, definite and unvarying, except when you are giving an aid.

The inside leg asks for impulsion with a quick, light inward nudge applied at any moment needed. A slightly increased pressure inwards encourages the horse to bend correctly.

The outside leg influences the quarters in two ways:

- It supports the inside leg when necessary in asking the horse to go forward.
- It controls and directs the hind quarters laterally by an increased contact of the lower leg behind the girth. The pressure of the leg continues until the correction or movement sideways has been completed.

The Hands

The hands, by means of the reins, should maintain a smooth and even contact with the horse's mouth at all times. Rein aids are given with the fingers closed around the reins like squeezing water from a sponge and from the turning of the wrists, both returning to their original position between aids. This is only made possible by the rider remaining in balance and keeping his shoulder and elbow joints relaxed, allowing an elastic contact to develop.

The outside hand (rein) controls the speed (tempo), flexion at the poll, bend of the neck and the outside shoulder of the horse. It asks for the downward transitions.

The inside hand (rein) keeps the mouth soft, asks for nemd and flexion to help suppleness and indicates turns.

The rider should avoid pulling backwards or across the line of the withers when giving rein aids but rather think of pushing the bit forwards without losing the contact with the mouth, so the horse is always encouraged to take the rein forwards while continuing to step under his body with the hind legs and therefore maintain his balance.

Hand and Leg Aids Summarised

To walk and trot: the rider asks for walk or trot by creating impulsion with the legs and by following the movement of the horse's head and neck with his hands. He controls the speed with the outside hand, while maintaining direction with the inside hand.

To canter: for true canter make sure the horse is in front of the rider's leg aids and that the reins are of a suitable length. Flex the horse to the inside at the poll while maintaining the tempo of the trot with the outside rein. The rider puts his outside leg, from the hip, a hand's breadth behind the girth which places his inside hip forward and indicates canter to the horse from the legs while following the movement in the lower back and hips and keeping the upper body and legs as quiet as possible. The rider should remain in contact with the saddle for all three beats of each canter stride to avoid the hips returning to the parallel 'trot' position which would allow the horse to break into trot.

To decrease speed or pace: the rider asks for decrease in speed and for a downward transition by using the outside rein in a 'take and give' action in conjunction with the seat, legs and upper body position which will stop following the movement for one stride before 'allowing' the horse to step forward in the new pace. The horse should remain lightly 'on the aids' even in halt. The voice is also recognised by the horse when used correctly and consistently in training.

Coordination of the Aids

The rider should aim towards giving aids that are invisible to the onlooker, though totally clear to the horse.

The desired pace is created and maintained by using coordinated leg and hand aids. The energy created by the horse's hind legs and quarters is received by the rider's hands without resistance. This should give the feeling that the horse is going forward in balance, between the rider's legs and hands, forming a harmonious partnership.

ARTIFICIAL AIDS AND THEIR APPLICATION

Whip

The whip is used to teach respect for the rider's leg aid. It may also be used to correct or discipline the horse; but a horse must never be hit in temper.

When a horse fails to react to the leg aid, the aid should be repeated and at the same moment the whip should be used just behind the leg which gave the aid: that is, behind the rider's inside leg for impulsion; behind the rider's outside leg for control of the quarters or canter strike-off.

In the manège, the whip should normally be carried in the inside hand, as the inside leg is the one most frequently disobeyed. You must therefore change the whip to the correct hand when you change the rein (that is, change direction). When the horse responds to the whip by moving forward, it is important that you allow the movement. In this way he will learn from the correction.

Standard Whip

Approximately 0.76m (2ft 6in) long. This is suitable for general use and for jumping. It should be held with the knob uppermost. The hand holding the whip must be removed from the rein when the whip is applied.

To change the whip from one hand to the other, take the reins and the whip into one hand. With your free hand, thumb uppermost, draw the whip through the retaining hand, and take up the reins again.

Long Whip

Approximately 0.9m (3ft) in length. This is used by experienced riders for training, often while keeping both hands on the reins. The whip is held close to the knob. It should not be carried when jumping.

To change a long whip from one hand to the other in the simplest, most efficient way: the whip should be passed over the horse's withers, the point making an arc directly above the rider's hands. For example, to change the whip from the right hand to the left, take both reins into your right hand. Pass your left hand over to grasp the whip, with the thumb and index finger below your right hand. Release the whip from your right hand; return your left hand to the normal position; and retake the left rein.

Cane

This is used principally for showing. It is held at the point of balance.

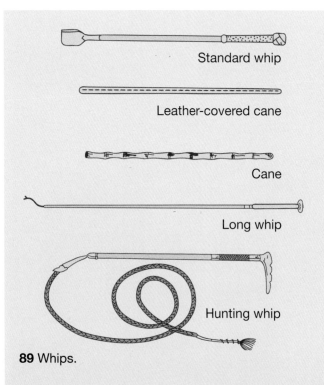

89 Whips.

Standard whip

Leather-covered cane

Cane

Long whip

Hunting whip

Hunting Whip

This whip should never be carried without its thong and lash. The thong is usually of plaited leather, and the lash a small piece of silk or whipcord attached at its end.

The hunting whip should be held at the point of balance, with the hook below the hand, the thong lying through the hand and hanging downwards.

The hunting whip has several uses:

- To reinforce the leg aids.
- To help the rider when opening, holding open, and shutting gates. *(See Opening and Shutting Gates, page 129.)*
- To crack, or to make tapping noises against the saddle when autumn hunting.
- To keep hounds off the heels of the horse.

Spurs

Only blunt spurs made of metal—without rowels or sharp edges—should be worn. If the spurs are curved, the curve should be downwards and the shank should point straight to the back and not exceed 3cm (1½in) in length.

Spurs are used by experienced riders to reinforce the leg aid. When required, the spur should be used without force so that the inside of the shank touches the horse's side.

Fitting Spurs *(Figs. 90a, b and c)*

Spurs are usually slightly curved and should always be worn pointing downwards, with the longer side on the outside of the boot. Several variations of shank length, shape, material and design are available, and when competing should be checked in conjunction with the relevant rule book. The spur straps should be long enough to allow the spur to lie along the seam (counter) of the boot and should be the same colour as the boot. The buckle of the spur strap should be fitted as close to the outside of the spur as possible.

32. The Correct Way of Going

When a horse is going correctly he should present a picture of perfect harmony and grace. He should never look unnatural, and will accomplish all that is asked of him without apparent effort. He should be a pleasure to ride.

Balance

A horse is said to be *in balance* when his own weight and that of the rider are distributed

90 Spurs: **(a)** correctly fitted; **(b)** too loose and too low; **(c)** upside down and too high.

in such a way as to allow him to use himself with maximum ease and efficiency.

A young horse when at liberty learns to balance himself. He must therefore learn to rebalance himself when he is carrying a rider. This is achieved by the progressive training of the horse, resulting in greater development of the correct muscles and increased use and engagement of his hind legs.

A horse with too much weight on his forehand is considered to be out of balance. By the suppleness and mobility of his back, allowing his hind legs to move under his body and without constraint (shortening) of his neck, which acts as a balancing pole, his weight is moved off his forehand.

- Untrained horses frequently lose balance when changing direction or pace.
- To improve a horse's balance, you must be ready to make alterations to the speed (within the pace) thus encouraging the horse to make his own adjustments to correct his own balance.
- An excellent method of helping a horse to develop balance is to ride him up and down hills. The horse should be allowed to find his own balance and the rider should in no way attempt to raise, lower, or position the horse's head with

the hands. The way a horse carries his head is merely an indication of the way he is using his body. When he carries himself correctly, the head and neck will automatically become part of the whole pleasing picture.

Rhythm

This is the regularity and evenness of the hoof beats. To be balanced the horse must maintain his rhythm and regularity of gait at all times. *(see THE BASIC PACES, page 193)*. This is achieved by the rider being aware of the slightest alteration to the speed of the horse's footfalls and almost instinctively making adjustments.

Tempo

This is the speed of the rhythm—the time it takes for a sequence of the footfalls to occur. The tempo of each pace should remain constant whatever the length of stride. The tempo is maintained when the horse stays in balance. This is achieved by the rider's careful adjustment of speed and energy whenever necessary.

Speed is the miles per hour at which the horse is travelling.

Suppleness

Suppleness is recognised by the whole horse appearing smoothly 'rounded' and supple from the poll to the tail.

- The neck arching gently from withers to poll.
- The back, loins and tail supple, relaxed and swinging.
- No resistance when the rider gives an aid.
- The jaw relaxed and quiet, without tension.
- The muscle underneath the neck soft and relaxed.

- The shoulders moving freely.
- The joints of the forelegs, elbows, knees and fetlocks moving with equal mobility and flexion.
- The joints of the hind legs (stifle, hocks and fetlocks) moving with equal mobility and flexion.
- The hind legs stepping well forward under the body and not left to dwell on the ground out behind him.

Contact

By accepting the bit the horse accepts the contact of the rider's hands through the reins, without resistance in the mouth. The horse responds to the rein aids willingly and without hesitation.

True contact can only be achieved when the horse accepts the driving and restraining aids from the rider's half-halts and learns to come through from behind over a loose, swinging back via a supple poll and relaxed jaw to the rider's hand. To do this the horse must use the muscles of his back and abdomen so he becomes connected from his hind- quarters right through to the bit. As a result he will gain the ability to go in self-carriage no longer relying on the reins for support.

Impulsion

This is balanced, contained energy—energy asked for by the rider and supplied by the horse. Impulsion can be produced only when the *rhythm, suppleness* and *contact* are present.

A horse is going with the correct amount of impulsion when he is willing to go forward actively and vigorously, his back is supple, his hocks are engaged and his steps show elasticity. He must be without negative tension, and both mentally and physically relaxed.

You must be careful not to confuse impulsion with speed. The rider increases impulsion with the legs. Speed is controlled mainly by your outside hand. The aids are fully explained on page 187.

Straightness

When moving directly forward, the horse should go as if on railway tracks—with the hind foot on one side directly following the line taken by the forefoot on the same side. He should be straight from the tip of his nose to his tail.

When moving on a curve he should bend uniformly from poll to tail. The footfall of the hind foot must follow the footfall of the forefoot on the same side *(see fig. 91b)*. The smaller the circle, the more acute the curve of the horse's body. *It is important that he does not bend his neck more than his body.*

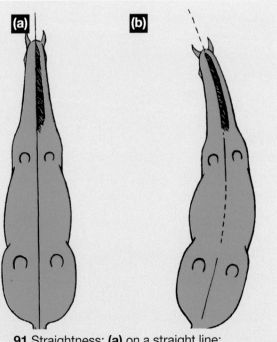

91 Straightness: **(a)** on a straight line; **(b)** on a left circle.

Straightness is maintained by the horse going forward in response to the rider's legs and accepting the rider's rein contact *(see The Contact, page 182).*

The Outline
The correct 'outline' or 'frame' is achieved when, in motion, the horse is accepting the bit and when his movements are rhythmic, balanced and straight. His way of going is correct because it follows the requirements laid down in *The Training Scale (page 198)* and as a result there is harmony, lightness and ease of movement between horse and rider.

33. The Basic Paces

At all paces the rider should be in balance and harmony with the horse and the horse should accept the contact of the rider's seat, legs and hands.

THE WALK (MEDIUM)
Medium walk is the pace between collected and extended walks.

The walk has four beats to a stride, so it is termed four-time. The steps should be even and regular so that the rider can count, 'one-two-three-four, one-two-three-four'. It is a serious fault if there are irregularities in the beat. The walk should be as purposeful and as regular as marching *(see fig. 92).*

The sequence of footfalls is:
(1) left hind, **(2)** left fore,
(3) right hind, **(4)** right fore.

The horse always has at least two feet on the ground at the same time. The walk should look and feel calm, active and purposeful. The horse's hind foot should pass over the print left by the forefoot on the same side. This is called over-tracking.

The considerable movement of the head and neck in time with the footfalls must not be restricted by the rider.

Walk on a Long/Loose Rein
Should you choose to offer the horse the relaxation of his head and neck by giving the rein away, the horse should stretch his head and neck forward and downward, as if seeking the contact. *(See fig. 97, page 203.)*

Free walk on a long rein is when the rider allows the horse to take the rein through the fingers, allowing him to relax and lengthen his stride, lowering his head and neck whilst maintaining a light contact throughout. The tempo of the walk must not change.

Walking on a loose rein is when the rider allows the rein to slide through the fingers until there is no contact with the horse's mouth.

92 Medium walk.

Aids to the Walk

From a halt, the rider asks for the walk by using both legs side by side on the girth telling him to move forward, and by following the movement of the horse's head and neck with his hands.

THE TROT (WORKING)

Working trot is the pace between collected and medium trot.

The trot is a diagonal two-time pace. There are two beats to a stride, which should be regular and even. The rider can count, 'one-two, one-two, one-two'. The trot should look and feel calm and rhythmic, but active.

The sequence of footfalls is: (**1**) left hind and right fore together, then (**2**) right hind and left fore together.

The horse springs from one diagonal pair of legs to the other, with a moment of suspension between each beat.

If the trot tempo is fast and hurried it is termed *running*. If the trot tempo is slow and the moment of suspension too long, it is termed 'passage-like' or 'elevated'. Both are incorrect.

Aids to the Trot

The previous pace must be of good quality. From halt or walk, the rider asks for the trot by giving a quick inwards nudge with the legs, the hands going with the movement of the head and in no way restricting the change of pace. The pace is maintained chiefly by the use of the rider's inside leg.

THE CANTER (WORKING)

The working canter is the pace between collected and medium canter.

The canter is a three-time pace with three beats to the stride. The rider can count, 'one-two-three, one-two-three, one-two-three', with a silent moment of suspension between strides. In canter the horse should look and feel light on his feet, balanced and rhythmic *(see fig. 93)*.

The sequence of footfalls when the left foreleg is leading is: (**1**) right hind, (**2**) left hind and right fore together, (**3**) left fore—the leading leg; followed by a moment of suspension when all four feet are briefly off the ground.

The sequence of footfalls when the right foreleg is leading is: (**1**) left hind, (**2**) right hind and left fore together, (**3**) right fore—the leading leg; followed by a moment of suspension.

Aids to the Canter

Before asking for canter, check that the preceding pace is of good quality.

The horse must be accepting the bit and going forward in balance and with impulsion. You should indicate the direction with your inside hand; sit for a few strides while maintaining the impulsion with your inside leg; position your outside leg just behind the girth. Ask for canter by giving a definite nudge to the horse's side with your inside leg on the girth. As the horse strikes off into canter you will feel the alteration of pace and you must be particularly careful to remain supple, relaxed and in balance.

Your hands must follow the considerable movement of the horse's head.

You should look up and forward. You will soon learn to feel which shoulder of the horse is slightly in advance of the other, and which hind leg comes to the ground first.

Terms Used When at Canter

A horse should always canter united. A horse is said to be cantering true, or united, when the leading foreleg and leading hind leg appear to be on the same side. He is said to be cantering disunited when the leading hind leg appears to be on the opposite side to the leading foreleg (which is most uncomfortable for the rider).

A horse is said to be cantering false or 'counter-lead' when he is cantering to the left with the right fore leading, or to the right with the left fore leading.

THE GALLOP

The gallop is a four-time movement, with four rapid beats to a stride. The rider can hear: 'one-two-three-four, one-two-three-four, one-two-three-four', with a silent moment between strides.

The sequence of footfalls with the left foreleg leading is: (**1**) right hind, (**2**) left hind, (**3**) right fore, (**4**) left fore—the leading leg; followed by a moment of suspension when all four feet are off the ground.

The sequence of footfalls with the right foreleg leading is: (**1**) left hind, (**2**) right hind, (**3**) left fore, (**4**) right fore—the leading leg; followed by a moment of suspension when all four feet are off the ground.

At the gallop, the horse's outline should lengthen considerably. As he increases speed, his stride may lengthen, or its tempo may be quickened, but always in rhythm. He should continue to accept the contact and remain in balance.

Aids to the Gallop

From the canter, the rider applies the aid for increased impulsion (a quick inwards nudge with the legs) until the desired speed is reached. The hands must allow the horse to lengthen his frame and must go with the movement of his head and neck.

You should take up the galloping position, maintaining a consistent shorter rein contact. To establish your balance and security you will need to shorten your stirrup leathers in order to close the joints of the hip, knee and ankle. This broadens your base of support, securing your lower leg and allowing your weight to stay off the horse's back.

93 Working canter.

TRANSITIONS

Transitions are changes from one gait or pace to another or within a pace such as from working trot to medium trot. They should be made with obedience and accuracy. They must be smooth and must flow one into the other without loss of rhythm, tempo or balance. The horse should not alter his outline other than to adapt to the new pace or speed required. He should go clearly into the new pace without any shuffling steps.

The quality of the preceding pace influences the transition.

The Half-Halt

'Half-halt' is the name given to the way in which you tell the horse to 'be prepared' as you are about to ask something of him.

- *Prepare* with a half-halt
- *Ask* by giving the aid then
- *Allow* him to do as you have asked.
- *Reward* his correct reaction with your voice or a pat in front of the withers.

When your horse understands and is able to react to the half-halt it can be used often, before any exercise or movement such as a transition, circle, corner, turn or lateral movement and also when riding a course of show jumps.

To ride a half-halt the rider needs to raise the upper body while feeling the weight onto his seat bones in the centre of the saddle, closing both legs round the horse, encouraging him to step under more with his hind legs and into the hand; which restrains for a moment (not more than three seconds), before relaxing (hand seat and legs) again. This may have to be repeated several times until the horse understands and is rebalanced enough for the rider to give the aid while maintaining suppleness and fluency.

The use of half-halts enables the rider to communicate his next move (command) more easily to the horse rather like using pedals, gears and brakes when riding a bicycle, so you maintain balance and control whatever the speed or terrain.

Aids for Upward Transitions

Improve the quality of the pace if necessary (as described previously in the *Walk*, *Trot* and *Canter* sections) and then give the aid.

Sit softly in the saddle, your body absorbing and feeling the movement of the horse and the alteration of the pace. Your hands should accompany the movements of the horse's head and neck throughout. This is of particular importance in all transitions, as any stiffening or fixing of the rider's hands will result in resistance and loss of rhythm as will any dropping of the contact which will lead to loss of balance and a poor transition.

Aids for Downward Transitions

Correct the quality of the pace if necessary, making sure that the horse is in balance, in front of your leg and going with impulsion. Throughout the transition you should sit softly and maintain core stability and the correct contact with the horse through your seat, legs and hands.

Ask with a quick take-and-give of your outside hand for the alteration to the pace—for example from canter to trot, or from trot to walk—while maintaining the direction with your inside hand.

As the horse responds and the change of pace is accomplished, you may have to make some adjustments to the speed or impulsion in order to correct the balance of the horse.

It is usual for an untrained horse to lose balance and go too fast in the first few strides after the decrease of pace. The solution lies in improving the quality of the preceding pace to allow the hind legs to step under for support.

Throughout the transition down, the horse must continue to accept the bit and maintain his outline and balance.

THE HALT

At the halt the horse must stand quite still and straight, his weight distributed correctly over all four legs. The forefeet should be in line with each other, as should the hind feet. This is called *standing square (fig. 94)*.

Throughout the halt the horse must remain in balance and continue to accept the bit, champing it quietly. Both horse and rider must remain attentive. The halt must not be abrupt. The steps preceding the halt should retain their correct rhythm and tempo.

Aids to the Halt

These are the same as for the aids to decrease pace. During the halt the rider should maintain the contact of hands and legs, with both rider and horse remaining attentive to each other. Less-established riders should avoid gripping up with their legs to keep their balance as this can confuse the aid to the horse.

How to Avoid Stepping Back

Stepping back usually occurs when the horse is allowed to drift into halt without maintaining his impulsion, or when the rein contact is too strong or fixed.

The horse should stand at attention and be ready to go forward when asked if the rider maintains the impulsion while riding forward into the halt and then pays particular attention to the contact of his legs and hands. The rein aids should be sympathetic and not forceful and if the rider breathes out it helps them both to settle.

THE REIN-BACK

The rein-back is usually carried out from the halt. It has two steps to each stride and is in two-time. *The sequence of steps is:* (**1**) left hind and right fore together, (**2**) right hind and left fore together. The steps should be active, and straight with the feet well raised and unhurried but of good length. The feet must be picked up and put down cleanly, with the horse maintaining his correct outline and remaining on the bit. He must not raise his head or hollow his back.

The rein-back should not be attempted until the horse is going correctly in his basic paces and is able to balance himself through transitions and in halt.

94 The halt.

Aids to the Rein-back

From an established halt, you should ease the weight from the horse's back (without collapsing the upper body forward): use both legs slightly behind the girth to ask for forward movement, but instead of allowing the horse to move forward, your hands should become slightly non-allowing. Your body should remain upright and your back and hips supple, thus allowing the increased rounding of the horse's back. Force must never be used. As the desired number of steps is completed, the horse must be asked to go forward immediately using both legs at the girth and offering an elastic rein contact. The last foot to step back should be the first to move forward.

CIRCLES AND TURNS

When moving on a curve, circle, or round a corner, the horse should bend his body uniformly from poll to tail to conform with the curve on which he is travelling *(see fig. 91b, page 192)*: that is, the smaller the circle, the more acute the curve.

When on a curve, the footprint of the outside hind foot should be on the same line as that of the outside front foot. The horse should be in balance and should not lose tempo or rhythm. His outline should not vary. The horse's head and neck should not be bent outwards, nor should they be bent inwards more than the rest of his body.

Aids to Circle and Turn

At all times you should keep your seat in the lowest part of the saddle, your hips parallel with the horse's hips, your shoulders parallel with the horse's shoulders, and your head looking in the direction in which you are going. The rider should be aware of how easily the seat can slip to the outside and check often that their seat remains central in the saddle.

Your inside hand indicates the direction.

Your outside hand controls the pace and allows the alteration in the bend of the horse's body. It also stops the horse's neck from bending too much to the inside, thus controlling the outside shoulder.

Your inside leg maintains the normal contact with the horse's side on the girth, while the outside leg maintains normal contact behind the girth. If more impulsion is required, ask for it by giving a quick nudge with your inside leg.

34. The Training Scale

The Training Scale— *rhythm, suppleness, contact, impulsion, straightening,* and eventually, *collection*—is a riding theory developed over centuries and refined by outstanding horsemen. It is horse-friendly and makes it possible for a horse, despite being ridden, to have a longer life expectancy than a horse spending its life freely at grass.

The Training Scale is learnt by all German riders in their early years and is what leading international dressage judges base their assessments on.

As a rule the Scale is approached in that order but there are times when one of its aims is skipped over to work on another. However until the horse works in *rhythm* it will be difficult to make him *supple* and until *supple, contact* will be spasmodic and until *contact* is true, *impulsion* will be elusive.

The Scale should improve and be of a higher standard as the training becomes more advanced. Therefore the *suppleness* accepted in a young novice horse as being good enough to start working more on the *contact* and *impulsion* is much less than expected in a horse that is advanced enough to learn flying changes.

Rhythm *(Takt)*

Rhythm should be both regular and a consistent tempo. The regularity should be correct for the pace.

* In the walk there should be four hoof beats—in a marching time.
* In the trot there should be two hoof beats—the legs move in diagonal pairs plus a moment of suspension when all legs are off the ground.
* In the canter three hoof beats—only one diagonal pair move together and there is a moment of suspension.

The tempo (speed of the rhythm) should have a pronounced beat to it and should not speed up or slow down whether the horse is going around a corner or on a straight line; whether he is lengthening his strides or shortening them.

Suppleness *(Losgelassenheit)*

The aim is that the horse's muscles have tone and are free from resistance, his joints are loose and he does not tighten against the rider's aids. The muscles and ligament that are really important are those over the top line from the hind legs over the quarters, loins, in front of the wither and up to the poll.

The test of whether a horse is supple and working *through* the back and neck is that when the contact is eased (as in a free walk) the horse wants to stretch forward and down and not try to hollow and lift his head.

Contact *(Anlehnung)*

The ideal contact is a light, even; elastic feel in both reins and this is achieved by aids from the legs and seat, not the hands. The legs are applied as a driving aid, the horse

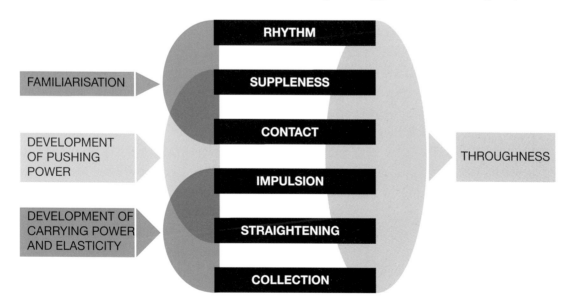

95 The Training Scale and the relationship of each component, which includes working through the back progressively through training, leading to throughness.

steps under more and works 'through' those muscles along his top line – over the back, neck and through the poll and the rider feels the energy thus created in the reins. When the contact is established in this way his outline and steps will be 'round' not hollow, and in the trot and canter springy and not flat. The horse's hindquarters and forehand are connected by that band of muscles and the ligament over the top line and the rider can feel this in his hands as there will be a lively forward tendency in the reins. The horse is then said to be 'connected'.

These first three training aims form the *familiarization* phase and are the basis of most Pony Club training.

Impulsion *(Schwung)*

This is the contained power of the horse. It is created in the hindquarters by getting him to take more energetic steps, to place his hind legs further under his body, and is contained by the rein contact that stops him from using up this extra energy simply to go faster. Any resistance, tightening of muscles, ligaments and joints, will block this energy getting through so he must be supple and connected to be able to build up real impulsion.

Riders aim to create enough impulsion to develop the horse's ability and show off his athleticism but not so much that cannot be controlled. The skill of the rider is to create as much energy as can be contained without the horse starting to pull and speed up.

Straightening *(Geraderichten)*

Horses, like humans, are born one sided and will tend to move forward with their bodies slightly curved. This crookedness can get worse if a rider sits to one side and/or keeps a stronger contact in one rein that the other.

When a horse is crooked it will be more difficult for him to stay balanced and develop impulsion.

The aim is that the hind legs step into the tracks of the forelegs both on a straight line and on a circle and that the rider has an even feel in his reins.

So these second, third, fourth and fifth aims enable the development of *propulsive force* or *thrust*.

Collection *(Versammlung)*

Dressage makes the horse a better ride, more manoeuvrable, more powerful and easier to control. To achieve this his balance has to be changed as he has to adjust to carry the weight of the rider in the most efficient way. When he is first ridden he will carry most of the rider's weight on his forehand. This will be cumbersome, he will tend to run faster when asked to lengthen his strides, he will find it difficult to stop quickly and will often lean on the rider's hands to keep his balance.

Through training the necessary muscles are built up and he is taught how to carry more and more weight on his hindquarters. This lightens his forehand, gives more freedom to move his shoulders and he will become an easier and more athletic ride.

Over time the horse is asked for more collection so his hind legs step further under his body and as he does this, the weight will be transferred backwards, he will be developing the carrying power of the hindquarters.

The fourth, fifth and sixth aims are involved in the *development of carrying power*.

In Grand Prix, this collection is such a high level that the horse can trot on the spot in piaffe or turn around practically on the spot in the canter pirouette. In most Pony Club and Novice tests no collection is asked for but there are movements that start to develop collection, including when a horse comes into a halt or changes from lengthened strides to a working trot. As he stops or shortens his steps he should step more under his body with his hind legs and transfer a little more weight onto his hindquarters, this is the beginning of collection.

Summary

The Training Scale can be used as a helpful check on the way of going for the rider when schooling the horse and for the judge when marking a movement. When there is rhythm, suppleness, contact, impulsion, straightness and in the more advanced tests collection, the horse is in self-carriage and the way of going is good. There is *throughness* or *durchlassigkeit*.

Fig. 96 presents the Training Scale in a slightly different way to demonstrate that, for example, a young horse will only be able to move forward regularly and rhythmically when it has been carefully and correctly suppled up and also that suppleness is only possible when the rider offers the horse a reliable and constant contact. Suppleness needs to be worked on every day and genuine collection cannot be achieved without the other aims in place.

The Pony Club introduces the Training Scale gradually through Pony Club Efficiency Tests, beginning with 'D' Test and introducing Rhythm at D+. As a result, members will understand the route along which to train their ponies and horses— whether they be happy hackers or keenly competitive jumping riders. After all *dressage* is just a French word for *schooling of the horse* and as a result they will be able to enjoy their horses for a long time.

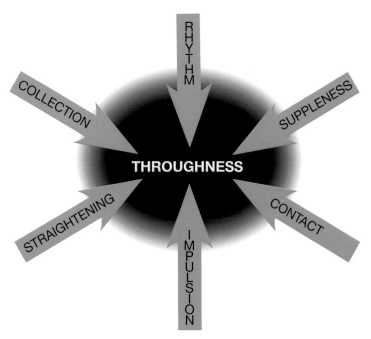

96 An alternative view of the Training Scale.

35. Beyond Basic Training— Advanced Paces

Advanced riding is merely an extension of correct basic riding. The training of the horse and rider must be progressive. All horses are individuals and take a different amount of time to reach the various stages of training. It is wise to remember the saying: '*Make haste slowly*'.

Only when a horse is going in the correct way in all his basic paces assessed by judging the quality of his rhythm, suppleness and contact can he be expected to proceed to more advanced work. This is the time to develop the impulsion and straightness towards a degree of collection (*see* The Training Scale, *page 199*).

To train the horse to a more advanced standard, the rider must have an established position and must be in balance and harmony with his horse (*fig. 101*).

Good riding requires a disciplined and thoughtful approach. The aids must be clear, precise and accurate. You must be aware of every aid you give, and of the effect that you have on your horse. Train yourself to think before you act. You must develop the ability to be aware and to recognise instantly when your horse is going correctly, balanced and in self-carriage. This is called *feel*.

It is easier for a rider to improve his riding on a trained horse which responds to correctly-given aids; it is easier for a horse to make progress when the rider is experienced. However, with good instruction it is possible for both horse and rider to make progress together.

If the horse has not responded satisfactorily, the rider should know whether it is because:
* The rider is at fault.
* The horse has not understood.
* The horse is unable to respond (physical weakness).
* The horse will not respond (disobedience).

Try to understand how the horse thinks and to be aware of his mental weaknesses and physical difficulties. Be quick to praise, know when to correct, always practise self-discipline, and never lose your temper.

Above all, learn to recognise the moment at which to stop each training session.

A precise definition of the recognised paces, as laid down by the International Equestrian Federation (F.E.I.) may be found in British Dressage's publication *Dressage Rules*. As small changes occur every year, it would be wise for those interested in further training to read a current copy with care.

The basic paces of walk, trot, canter and gallop are described in The Basic Paces, *page 193*. The more advanced paces are described below. Before attempting this more advanced level, the horse must be working calmly in his basic paces:
* With rhythm, suppleness and contact.
* Accepting the rider's aids in transitions and movements.
* Going forward in balance with confidence and purpose.

THE WALK

Medium Walk and Free Walk
These are described in The Basic Paces, *page 193*.

Before, during and after periods of work you should allow the horse a few minutes of relaxation at the free walk (*fig. 97*) to allow the musculoskeletal system, to warm up and warm down gradually so as to aid circulation and prevent damage or injury.

Collected Walk

The rhythm and tempo (speed of the rhythm) are the same as in medium walk, but this walk shows greater activity. The steps are higher and travel further through the air consequently covering less ground.

- The joints of the hind legs and forelegs are more flexible and mobile.
- The hind feet may not overtrack the prints left by the forefeet.
- The forehand becomes lighter and the head and neck are raised as the head approaches the vertical position.

This walk is difficult to ride correctly and should not be attempted too soon or for too long. The natural regularity of the pace is easily spoiled by over-restriction.

The Aids

The rider asks for collected walk by increasing the engagement of the hindquarters while maintaining the rhythm and tempo with the sensitive influence of the legs and hands.

Common Faults

The rhythm may become irregular (lateral or broken). The horse may attempt to slow the tempo instead of bending and flexing the joints of the hind limbs through the air to produce shorter more elevated steps.

Extended Walk

The rhythm and tempo are the same as in medium walk, but the horse covers as much ground as possible, without hurrying and without losing the regularity of the steps. As the steps are longer the horse moves from point to point in less time.

- The hind feet should clearly overtrack the prints left by the forefeet.
- The frame of the horse should appear to lengthen, with the head and neck stretching forward.
- More impulsion is required for extended walk than for medium walk.
- The horse must continue to accept the contact.

The Aids

Before asking for extension, the rider should first check the quality of the previous pace, and then ask for extended walk by creating more impulsion, his seat remaining in harmony with the movements of the horse. The hands maintain the contact and move with the stretching of the horse's head and neck.

Common Faults

The horse may lose balance and suppleness, and his steps may become irregular. He may attempt to quicken the tempo of the walk instead of lengthening his strides.

97 Free walk (on a long rein).

THE TROT

Working Trot
(See THE BASIC PACES, page 193.)

Shortened and Lengthened Strides
Once the working trot is established, the rider may ask for shortened and lengthened strides. During these slight adjustments, the rhythm and tempo of the trot should not alter. The horse will cover less or more ground *(figs. 98 and 99)*.

The Aids
To shorten the steps while maintaining the rhythm and suppleness the rider asks for more engagement with the seat and legs whilst maintaining the contact. Having achieved a few shorter but active steps, the rider rides the horse forward to the contact allowing the frame to open while maintaining the same rhythm and impulsion. As a result, the horse will lengthen his steps. At first you should aim to achieve only a slight difference; if you ask for too much, the movement may well be spoiled. The steps must be shortened

before any lengthening can be shown. If the rider asks the horse to lengthen without first establishing enough impulsion, he will lose balance on to his forehand. (This work is preparatory to collection and extension.)

Common Faults
- The horse may become tense and stiff in his back—losing suppleness and regularity.
- He may lack impulsion, lose balance, quicken the tempo and run.
- He may misunderstand and break into canter.

Collected Trot
The rhythm and tempo are the same as in working trot, but the horse covers less ground. The steps are shorter, higher and lighter. The speed (mph) is thereby decreased.
- The joints are more flexible and mobile.
- The increased action of the joints of the hind legs makes the hind quarters appear lower, while the weight on the forehand is lightened. The head and neck are raised, and the head approaches the vertical position.

98 Trot, showing shortened strides.

99 Trot, showing lengthened strides.

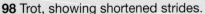

- The horse may not track up—that is, the hind feet might not stretch as far forward as the prints left by the forefeet.
- The horse remains supple and flexible, with a swinging back.
- He must continue to accept the contact.

The Aids

The rider asks for the collected trot by increasing engagement while maintaining the rhythm, suppleness and contact.

Common Faults

- The horse may become tense and stiff in his back, thereby losing suppleness and activity.
- His steps may become irregular.
- He may attempt to slow the tempo of the trot instead of heightening and shortening his steps.

Medium Trot

This is the pace between working and extended trot. The rhythm and tempo remain the same, but the horse covers more ground than in the working trot. The steps are longer. The speed (mph) is therefore increased.

- There is more impulsion—the horse going forward with rounded and moderately extended steps.
- The frame of the horse lengthens with the head and neck stretching forward, and with greater engagement of the hocks.
- The horse must remain in balance.

The Aids

From working trot, slightly more collection must first be achieved. The rider then asks for the medium trot by creating more impulsion and then allowing the horse to lengthen his outline and increase the length of his steps by following the movement of the head and neck with his hands.

As the desired length of steps is reached, the rider maintains the pace. The rein contact must remain constant while following the stretching of the horse's head and neck.

Common Faults

- The horse's steps may become irregular.
- He may attempt to quicken the tempo of the trot instead of lengthening his strides; this is known as running.
- He may lose his balance and fall on to his forehand.
- He may break into canter.

Extended Trot

The rhythm and tempo remain the same, but the horse covers as much ground as possible with every step, thereby increasing the speed over the ground *(fig. 100)*.

- The extended trot requires more impulsion than the medium trot.
- The hind quarters must be particularly well-engaged and active to enable the horse to maintain the correct balance.

100 Extended trot.

- The feet should come to the ground in a continuous forward movement and not stretch forward and then draw back.
- The frame of the horse should lengthen with a corresponding stretching forward of the head and neck.
- The horse must continue to accept the contact.

The Aids

From the collected trot, the rider asks for the extended trot by creating impulsion and, while maintaining the contact, by allowing the horse to lengthen his outline.

The balance of the horse is maintained by the rider controlling the rhythm, tempo and speed of the pace. It is important that the rider's body is inclined slightly forwards so the thrust of the hind legs is not disturbed by the rider leaning back out of balance.

With all lengthening of strides the rider must create more impulsion in preparation for the increase of ground cover speed. The horse will lose balance if the rider attempts to lengthen the strides when insufficient engagement from both hind legs is available to step underneath his centre of gravity.

Common Faults

The same as for medium trot, plus:
- While looking spectacular viewed from the front, from the side or behind they either don't cover enough ground forwards with the hind legs or move wide behind.
- If the horse doesn't stretch forward to the contact the neck will be short and the back will be unable to swing as it should to achieve the longer steps..

THE CANTER

Working Canter

(See THE BASIC PACES, page 193.)

Collected Canter

The rhythm and tempo are the same as in working canter, but the horse covers less ground. The strides are shorter *(fig. 101)*.
- The hind quarters are more engaged and active, lightening the forehand and giving the shoulders greater freedom. The head and neck are raised and the head approaches the vertical position.
- The horse shows increased suppleness over the back.
- The horse must continue to accept the bit.

The Aids

From the working canter, the rider asks for the collected canter by increasing engagement and maintaining the rhythm and impulsion.

Common Faults

The horse may become tense and stiff in

101 Riding in balance and harmony at the collected canter.

his back and hind legs, thereby losing his suppleness and activity.

- He may lose the rhythm and tempo.
- He may lose the correct sequences of footfalls.
- He may swing his hind quarters, thereby becoming crooked.

Medium Canter

This is the pace between working canter and extended canter. The horse covers more ground than in working canter, the strides being rounder and longer. The speed (mph) is thereby increased, but the rhythm and tempo remain the same.

- There is more impulsion, with greater engagement of the hind quarters.
- The frame of the horse lengthens with a slight stretching out of the head and neck.
- The horse must continue to accept the contact and remain 'on the aids'.
- He must remain in (balance) self-carriage, maintaining the rhythm and tempo.

The Aids

From working canter slightly more collection must first be achieved. The rider asks for medium canter by creating more impulsion and then allowing the horse to lengthen his outline and increase the length of the stride. As the horse stretches his head and neck, the rider's hands must follow the movement of the canter, so that the contact is retained but does not restrict the strides. The rider maintains the pace when the desired amount of lengthening is reached.

Common Faults

The horse may lose his balance and fall on to his forehand. He may quicken the tempo due to lack of impulsion/engagement.

Extended Canter

The rhythm and tempo remain the same, but the horse covers as much ground as possible. Without losing calmness and lightness the speed is increased.

- There is considerable impulsion emanating from the hind quarters and carrying the horse forward over the ground.
- The outline of the horse should lengthen with a corresponding lengthening of the head and neck.
- The horse should continue to accept the contact.
- He should remain in balance and maintain the rhythm and tempo of the pace.

The Aids

From the collected canter, the rider asks for the extended canter by creating more impulsion and, while maintaining the contact, allows the horse to lengthen his outline and his strides. As with the extended trot, the horse will lose balance if the rider attempts to lengthen the strides before sufficient impulsion is created.

Common Faults

These are the same as for medium canter. *Remember compression is needed, like a coiled spring, for collection and extension. There can be no extension without collection.*

THE COUNTER CANTER

This exercise is used to increase the balance, straightness, suppleness and obedience of the horse once he has reached the stage when he can carry himself and begin to shorten and collect his canter. A bird's-eye view is shown in *fig. 102*.

- Counter canter is when the horse is asked to lead with the outside foreleg instead of the inside foreleg: for example, cantering on a right curve, the horse leads with the left foreleg.
- The horse is ready to begin this exercise when: his canter is balanced; he can canter on a named leg; and he can shorten and lengthen his stride within the pace with ease.
- Introduce the exercise by riding long, shallow loops and progressing gradually

to deeper ones. In advanced training the horse will eventually be able to complete a full circle in counter canter.
- The horse maintains the bend towards the leading leg.

The Aids

The rider should check that the canter is balanced and that there is a degree of collection (see COLLECTED CANTER, page 206).

The rider maintains the correct bend towards the leading leg. For example, when riding counter canter to the right (left leg leading) the rider maintains the bend towards the leading leg and the impulsion by keeping his legs in contact to help maintain and develop the straightness of the horse.

The right (outside) rein controls the pace and limits the degree of bend, the left (inside) rein maintains the flexion. The rider should sit centrally allowing the movement to draw his inside seat bone forward.

When riding this movement, the inside is the side of the leading leg and direction of the bend even though the horse is travelling in the opposite direction.

Common Faults

The horse fails to maintain his balance and rhythm.

- The horse becomes crooked: that is, his hind feet do not follow in the track of the forefeet.
- The movement becomes stilted or stiff.
- The horse loses the bend towards the leading leg.
- The correct sequence of canter is lost.
- The horse breaks into trot.

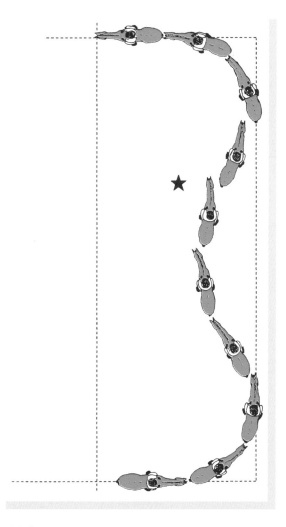

102 Counter canter. A good way to teach this movement: in the starred position the horse canters left while moving to the right.

TRANSITIONS

In more advanced riding, transitions may be directly from any one pace to any other, in which case there would be no transition through an intermediate pace. For example, transitions can be from canter to walk, or from halt to trot or vice versa or even from canter to halt. Direct transitions upwards are easier for the horse than direct downwards which require the ability to increase engagement by lowering the croup and taking weight onto the hind legs.

36. Lateral Work

Lateral means sideways. In lateral work the horse moves forwards and sideways, with fore and hind legs moving on different tracks *(fig. 103)*.

Most lateral work may be performed at the walk, trot or canter.

Turn on the forehand and leg-yielding can be used as training exercises before the horse has achieved collected paces; but before attempting shoulder-in, half-pass or half-pirouette, a degree of collection is necessary.

Throughout all lateral work the horse must remain on the aids and continue to accept the bit. He should work in a correct outline, in balance and going forward without resistance, maintaining the rhythm, tempo and impulsion of the pace. Above all he must be relaxed; a tense horse cannot develop the suppleness that lateral work encourages and requires. The quality of the pace should not suffer.

MOVING OVER

This is the horse's first exercise in lateral movement. He is taught how to move away from the leg.

As a preliminary, the horse can be taught to move over in the stable if you hold his head and lightly push him just behind the girth, while saying: 'move over'. Later, try the same exercise outside when he is saddled up. It is then logical for him to move away from the leg when the rider exerts some pressure either on or behind the girth, depending on the movement required.

TURN ON THE FOREHAND

This may be taught as soon as the horse understands the preceding exercise. While turns on the forehand, carried out equally on both reins, are a good way of teaching the first lessons in moving away from the leg, they should not be attempted too often as they

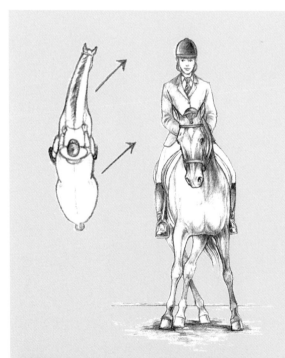

103 An example of lateral work: half-pass.

do not encourage good forward movement and are inclined to lighten the hind quarters rather than encourage their engagement.

This exercise is a test of a horse's obedience to the rider's legs and is useful training for when you open and shut gates. It is also a valuable exercise for the rider, as it develops your ability to use one leg independently of the other *(fig. 104)*.

The easiest way to prepare the horse for a turn on the forehand is by collecting the walk slightly and, if in a manège, by riding in from the track at least 1.5m (5ft). If working in a field, walk parallel with the hedge or fence, about 1.5m away.

Halt the horse squarely. Then turn him, head towards the track or hedge. His hind legs should cross over, step-by-step, making a half-circle round the inside

104 Turn on the forehand to the right.

foreleg on the side to which he is turning. The turn will be 180°. The hedge or side of the manège will help, because it will prevent the horse from walking forward.

Smaller turns (of less than 180°) can be performed by halting the horse at right-angles to the track or hedge.

The turns described above will be complete when the horse is alongside the hedge or track. He must then go forward at once into walk, trot or canter.

The correct four-beat sequence of walk steps must be maintained throughout. The horse should be flexed slightly in the direction in which he is turning. He should not step backwards, nor hurry. There should be no resistance in the mouth or dropping of the bit. The horse must continue to accept the contact.

The Aids
The rider asks for a turn on the forehand by halting squarely and immediately indicating the direction of the turn with the inside rein, *while maintaining the contact of the outside rein* to prevent the horse offering too much neck bend or gaining ground. The inside leg, just behind the girth, nudges the quarters over, step-by-step. The outside leg behind the girth receives and regulates each step in a passive way so as not to contradict the aid from the inside leg.

Summary
To turn on the forehand to the right: proceed on the left rein. Come in from the track as described. Halt. Indicate the direction of the turn with your right hand. Maintain the contact with your left rein. Nudge the quarters over with your right leg. Regulate and receive the steps with your left leg.

Common Faults

- Resistance due to the horse not accepting the bit.
- The horse may show too much bend in his neck in the direction in which he is going. This is corrected by maintaining the outside rein contact.
- The horse may step backwards. This can be avoided if the rider maintains the activity and keeps both legs in contact.
- He may walk a small circle. This is due to lack of coordination of the aids. To correct the fault, establish a square halt. Then, at first, ask for only one step. Reward the horse when he responds.
- He may lose the correct sequence of footfalls (usually through lack of fluency).

LEG-YIELDING

This is carried out at the walk or trot and is used to teach young horses early lateral work and an understanding of lateral aids. Collection is not required. It is a useful suppling exercise.

In leg-yielding, the horse moves on two tracks: that is, both forwards and sideways. His body is straight except for a very slight flexion at the poll, away from the direction in which he is going *(see fig. 105)*.

The Aids

A good way to perform leg-yielding is from an inner track, along a diagonal line to the side of the manège, as illustrated in *fig. 105*.

When leg-yielding to the right, the rider's inside leg (left) either on, or slightly behind of the girth, moves the horse forward and over; the outside leg (right) also ensures forward movement and helps to maintain the straightness. The inside

hand (left) indicates the flexion at the poll, and the outside hand (right) controls the straightness of the neck and shoulder and the speed of the forward movement.

Common Faults

- The horse may lose impulsion and rhythm, and fail to go forward.
- His quarters may either trail or lead, instead of remaining straight in line withe the forehand.
- ***He may bend his neck too much and put too much weight on his outside shoulder.***
- He may fail to cross his legs sufficiently. The rider can correct this by increasing impulsion and thereby the activity of the hind legs.

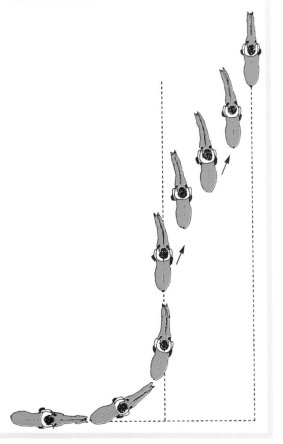

105 Leg-yielding, performed towards the side of a manège or field fence.

SHOULDER-IN

This is an important training exercise for horses already able to show some collection in trot, and it is often included in dressage tests. It is of great value when carried out correctly. It helps the rider to control the horse's shoulders, and is an excellent suppling exercise which will increase collection when performed well and is useful in developing straightness.

The horse is ready to begin the exercise when he is able to increase engagement while maintaining rhythm, suppleness, contact, impulsion and relaxation. The quality of the shoulder-in will depend

106 Shoulder-in, performed along the side of a manège or field fence.

on the quality of the collection in the preceding pace.

Shoulder-in is a lateral movement in which the horse is bent slightly but uniformly from head to tail around the inside leg of the rider. The shoulders and forelegs are brought off the straight line, the inside foreleg passing in front of the outside foreleg. The hind legs remain on the track, and continue to proceed straight forward. Thus the horse's body forms an angle to the straight line and he travels partially sideways *(fig. 106)*.

The angle to the straight should not normally exceed 30°; the usual angle is such that the horse moves on three tracks, with the inside hind foot stepping in the track of the outside forefoot. The angle may be increased until the horse is travelling on four tracks, with each foot making its own track: however, this needs a very supple horse to be performed correctly. Shoulder-in may be practised down the long side, down the centre line, or off a circle. The shoulders are always brought to the inside, off the track (right rein, right shoulder-in).

On completion of the shoulder-in, the rider may either ride forward on a curve across the school or straighten the horse by bringing the shoulders back on to the straight line. The former is less demanding and also more encouraging and rewarding to a young horse, the latter is used in competitions and is a greater test of obedience and balance.

The Aids

The rider asks for shoulder-in by further engaging the hind legs *(see SHORTENED AND LENGTHENED STRIDES, page 204)* and possibly making a 10-metre circle in the corner at the beginning of the long side to develop the balance and correct bend. He then proceeds down the long side, bringing the forehand just off the track as if he were beginning a second circle. At the moment when the shoulders and forelegs leave the track, the rider's outside hand prevents the horse from gaining ground, and controls the degree of bend to the inside, while the inside leg, on the girth, maintains the impulsion and encourages the forward and sideways movement. The outside leg is a little behind the girth and prevents the quarters escaping outwards which if allowed would produce a leg-yield movement.

The rider sits centrally in the saddle and looks up the track in the direction of the movement. His shoulders are kept in line with the horse's shoulders and his hips in line with the horse's hips.

Common Faults

- The horse may lose impulsion and thus will not continue to accept the bit because the connection from behind over the back will be lost.
- The angle of the shoulder-in may vary. The variation should be corrected by the rider making his aids consistent and finding a balance between leg and hand. This problem sometimes starts when a rider asks for too great an angle at the beginning of the movement or takes their eyes off the line.
- The horse may bend his neck too much, putting excessive weight on his outside shoulder. This is usually caused by insufficient outside rein contact or too much rein contact due to loss of activity from the inside hind leg or too much

influence from the inside rein contact.

- The horse's quarters sometimes go out instead of the shoulders coming in. You must pay particular attention to bringing the shoulders in at the beginning of the movement and controlling the position of the quarters with your outside leg to prevent them swinging outwards.
- Varying rhythm and differing angles on left and right reins are problems which you must be quick to feel and correct. The value of the exercise is lost if the horse becomes tense and is no longer working through his body in a relaxed way.

TRAVERS

Travers is a good preparation exercise before half-pass. It asks for the horse to move along the track with the quarters in while the bend is maintained to the inside in the direction of the movement. The hind legs cross and it can be ridden in all three paces. The shoulders and front legs should stay straight on the track while the quarters are asked to step inwards off the track making an angle of 30° on four tracks, so it is more than that of shoulder in. If too much angle is asked for then the shoulders will not stay square to the track and the regularity, fluency and balance will be lost.

The Aids

This exercise is best explained to the horse in walk and as with shoulder-in can be prepared on a 10-metre circle at the beginning of a long side. Just before the circle is completed ask the horse to continue down the track maintaining the aids and bend from the circle. Build up the angle gradually as his suppleness and understanding develops.

The forward movement is often lost but this can be regained, in training, by changing the flexion at the poll so the movement becomes a leg-yield until the impulsion is regained. The bend towards the direction of the movement can then be re-established. Other common faults are as for half-pass.

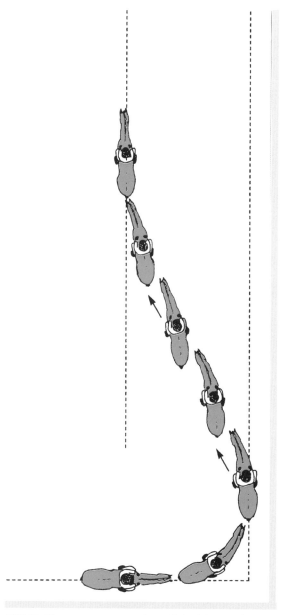

107 Half-pass: one way in which this can be performed in a manège or field.

HALF-PASS

In half-pass the horse bends uniformly throughout his body in the direction in which he is going. He moves on two tracks with his shoulders slightly in advance of his hind quarters. The outside legs cross in front of the inside legs.

Half-pass is usually carried out either from the centre line to the long side, or from the long side to the centre line.

It is important for the horse to continue to move fluently forward as well as sideways. He must maintain good rhythm and impulsion.

Half-pass is carried out from collected paces and should not be attempted until these have been achieved. It may be performed either in trot or in canter, and can be easier to ride in canter as there is more time in the air during the moment of suspension for the sideways movement. *(See figs. 103 and 107).*

The Aids

The rider asks for half-pass from a collected trot or canter, either by turning down the centre or by moving off the long side. You always begin the half-pass in the same direction as the rein you are on. For example, after a right turn down the centre, half-pass to the right.

Bring the horse's shoulders off the track as for shoulder-in, indicating bend and direction with your inside hand, and the inside leg on the girth maintains the impulsion. Your outside hand prevents the horse making too much ground forward, and controls the extent of the bend.

The outside leg behind the girth moves the hind quarters over and the horse sideways.

Both the horse and rider must look in the direction in which they are travelling.

Common Faults

+ The horse may show the wrong bend and put too much weight on to the shoulder that is leading the movement. This then becomes leg-yielding
+ The horse may lack engagement/collection, which may cause his hind quarters to lead or trail. You must be aware of the correct angle and try to maintain it by judicious use of the correct aids and vision.
+ Insufficient forward movement may cause loss of rhythm and varying impulsion.
+ Too much bend can produce loss of freedom of the inside shoulder (cramped).
+ Insufficient crossing of the legs indicates lack of suppleness and lack of engagement of the hind legs.

PIROUETTE

In a full pirouette the horse completes a turn of 360°, with the forehand making a circle around the inside hind leg. The sequence of steps remains regular and active. It may be performed at walk or canter. At canter it is a most advanced and difficult movement.

Half-Pirouette (Demi-Pirouette) in Walk

This is a turn through 180° *(fig. 108)*. Lesser turns should be performed while you are teaching the horse.

During the entire movement the horse should remain on the bit and there should be no backward steps. The outline should be maintained with no resistance in the mouth or loss of suppleness in the body. Throughout there must be a feeling of forward movement, and the sequence (regularity) of the walk steps must be retained.

The Aids

The rider prepares for a half-pirouette (demi-pirouette) from a collected walk, or at least by increasing the activity from medium walk.

The rider should sit centrally, with his head and shoulders turning slightly in the direction of the pirouette. The outside hand controls the speed and limits the bend; the inside leg at the girth maintains the impulsion and makes sure that the rhythm of the pace is maintained. The outside hand then prevents the forward movement and guides the shoulder at the same moment the inside hand gives the direction. The outside leg, behind the girth, holds the quarters in position preventing any stepping back or to the side. On completing the turn, resume the forward steps, which should appear unhurried, regular and clearly-defined.

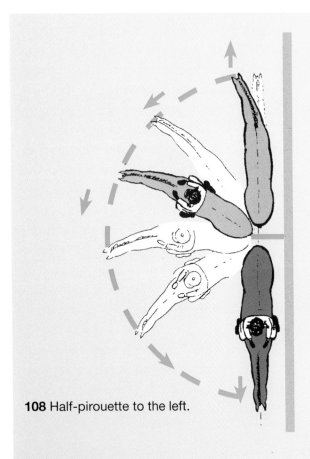

108 Half-pirouette to the left.

The horse should be flexed at the poll in the direction in which he is going.

Common Faults

- The horse may lose the sequence of footfalls as a result of lack of activity or from tension.
- The hind foot may stick and not continue to march. This is usually due to lack of impulsion.
- Stepping back may be the result of too strong an outside rein.
- Turning on the centre—i.e. not around the inside hind leg and can be due to insufficient outside leg aid and/or too much inside rein.

GIVE AND RETAKE (UBERSTREICHEN)

This movement is often asked for in dressage tests from novice level upwards and is rarely performed correctly. The rider is expected to push one or both hands forward, as stated on the test sheet, in a continuous movement to release the contact for two or three strides before retaking it. Its purpose is to show that the horse remains in self-carriage, balanced, keeping the same rhythm, tempo, suppleness of the back and level of engagement, and accepts the retaking of the contact without any loss of submission.

It is essential that the reins are released so that they hang in loops. It is not enough to put your hands forward and keep the contact. Neither should you lean forwards as this will unbalance the horse just when you are showing how well balanced he is without any rein support.

This *give and retake* exercise is a test of all the training you have put in to your horse as it demonstrates the *correct way of going* with the horse truly in *self-carriage*.

37. Analysis of the Jump

PHASES OF THE JUMP: THE HORSE

It is important to understand exactly how a horse jumps. For this reason the jump is here divided into five phases: the approach; the take-off; the moment of suspension; the landing; and the getaway (or recovery).

Phase 1: The Approach

The horse must be going forward in balance, with impulsion and rhythm. The quality of the jump is closely related to the quality of the pace during the approach. The jump itself depends largely on a correct approach.

Phase 2: The Take-Off

Before the moment of take-off, the horse lowers his head and stretches his neck, measuring up the fence and preparing for the spring.

109 The five phases of the jump

At the moment of take-off he shortens his neck slightly, raises his head and lifts his forehand off the ground, immediately bending his knees and folding up his forelegs. He then brings his hocks underneath him and, as his hind feet touch the ground, he stretches his head and neck and uses the power of his hind quarters to spring forward and upward.

Phase 3: The Moment of Suspension

While in the air, the horse stretches his head and neck forward and downward to their fullest extent. He rounds his back. The forelegs are tucked up. The hind legs, having left the ground, follow the parabola of the body.

If the horse fails to lower his head and neck and hollows or flattens his back, the jump will be inefficient and he will need to make more effort to clear the fence.

Phase 4: The Landing

The horse straightens his forelegs and prepares to meet the ground. He momentarily raises his head to balance himself. His forelegs touch down one after the other, followed by the hind legs.

His back should remain supple so that his hind legs can move well under him before they touch the ground.

Phase 5: The Getaway (or Recovery)

The getaway stride should be fluent, with the horse's hocks coming well underneath him, so that the balance, rhythm and impulsion of the pace are re-established as soon as possible. This is important because the approach to the next fence may have already begun.

PHASES OF THE JUMP: THE RIDER

Throughout the phases the rider should be able to maintain a balanced, established position so that he can be in harmony with the horse.

Phase 1: The Approach

The rider sits in a balanced position, maintaining a trot or canter which is rhythmical, balanced and has the correct impulsion and speed for the type of obstacle. The lower leg rests against the horse's side to give the horse confidence and to make a quick correction if necessary. The hands keep a steady, light contact, which must be constant throughout, especially during the last few strides of the approach when the horse's concentration must not be disturbed.

The Beginner's Approach

For a beginner to gain confidence and remain in balance, it is necessary to ride the approach with the upper body slightly further forward in anticipation of the horse's spring. A neck strap should always be used for novice riders or when teaching young horses to jump. (See NECK STRAP, page 281.) The rider tucks the first two fingers of one or both hands round the neck strap during the approach.

Phases 2 and 3: Take-Off and Moment of Suspension

Seat: the rider's body folds forward from the hip joints, going with the movement of the horse. His back should be flat but with no stiffness. He should look in the direction in which he is going. His weight should be evenly distributed (not leaning to one side).

His legs should rest lightly against the horse's sides, with relaxed knees and ankles.

The rider's body should remain folding forward until the horse's hind legs have passed the highest part of the jump.

Hands: while maintaining an even contact, hands and arms must follow the full head and neck movements of the horse and should allow him as much rein as he requires. He will not take the rein unless he is totally confident that he will not be pulled or caught in the mouth at this time.

Slipping the reins: in the event of an error by horse or rider, the latter should be ready to open his fingers instantly to allow the horse to take the reins through his hands, re-establishing the contact as soon as possible on landing.

Phases 4 and 5: Landing and Getaway

The rider's upper body remains in balance, becoming slightly more upright again. As the horse lands, the rider absorbs most of the shock through his knees and ankles. His lower leg remains lightly in contact with the horse's sides, ready to help the horse to pick up the stride for the getaway.

The rider must not collapse with a thud on to the saddle when landing. This would act as a punishment to the horse for jumping, and the bad memory could influence a future jump. A well-ridden getaway helps the horse quickly to re-establish a balanced and rhythmical pace and can save vital seconds when time is important, such as during a timed jump-off, or on the cross-country phase of tetrathlon or horse trials.

38. The Rider's Position for Jumping

The basic balanced position *(see THE POSITION OF THE RIDER IN THE SADDLE, page 181)* should be maintained when jumping. Depending on the length of stirrup leather that you use, it may be advisable to shorten them. This will close the angles at your knees and ankles (make them more acute), which will help you to maintain a balanced and secure position throughout all the phases of the jump.

The horse will only be able to perform to the best of his ability if the rider's weight is balanced over his centre of gravity.

Adjusting the Stirrup Length for Jumping *(Fig. 110)*

As a practical test, remove your feet from the stirrups and let your legs hang long. Now try folding forward from your hips (from the top of your legs, not from your waist). You will find it very hard to balance. Your lower leg will slide back and you may have to lean on your hands to catch your weight.

Shorten your imaginary stirrups—as short as those of a jockey. Fold forward. Now you will find that balance comes easily, because you will have a broad base of support; but you will not be able to use your legs effectively. You should find a length which is short enough to enable you to fold forward in comfortable balance, but long enough for you to be able to use your legs effectively. Adjust the leathers accordingly. Stirrup length is entirely a matter for the individual rider, the criterion being a balanced, independent position.

Your hips, knees and ankles must remain as flexible as well-oiled hinges. These joints act as shock absorbers. Any stiffness makes it difficult to absorb the impact of the movement, especially on landing.

The lower leg lies in contact with the horse's sides. The ball of the foot is placed in the stirrup, with your weight evenly distributed across the bar—not pressing down on one side or the other.

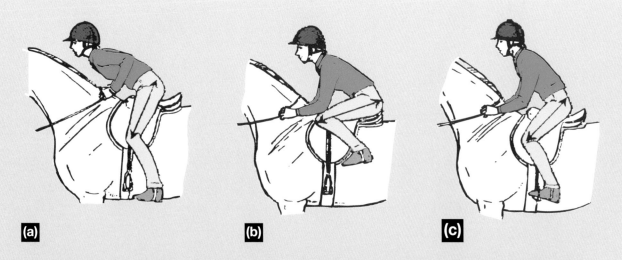

(a)   **(b)**   **(c)**

110 Stirrup lengths: **(a)** Too long. Difficult to balance; **(b**) Too short. Legs ineffective; **(c)** Balanced.

Swinging Forward as the Horse Jumps

You can now practise folding your upper body forward—the movement that you will make to go with the horse as he takes off. First practise this at the halt. Fold forward from your hip joints (the top of your legs) with a flat back and with your spine in line with the horse's spine, not tipping to one side or the other. Look straight between the horse's ears and keep your head up. Check that your hips, knees and ankles remain supple and that your lower legs are in the correct position, neither too far forward nor too far back *(fig. 111)*.

In folding forward, feel as if you are putting your stomach towards the horse's withers with your shoulders following. This will ensure that you keep your back flat (not rounded) and that you fold forward from your hip joints, not from your waist.

This swinging forward from your hips can now be perfected at the walk, trot and canter. Practise with shortened reins, resting your hands on either side of the horse's neck or withers.

Gradually take your hands away from their resting place. Make sure that, while forward, you stay in balance. Until you can do this and return to your basic jumping position at the trot and canter without resting on your hands, you have not yet established a balanced, independent position. Without this you cannot allow with your hands and follow the movements of the horse's head and neck *(see PHASES OF THE JUMP: THE HORSE, page 216)*.

Hands

When the reins are shortened, the hands will be further forward towards the bit, but the same contact from the elbow, through the hands, down the reins to the horse's mouth will be maintained.

COMMON FAULTS *(Fig. 112)*

Many faults are interrelated, and one may lead to another. Stiffness and tension are the most common causes of faults in both horse and rider. They are sometimes brought about by apprehension and fear.

111 (a) Sitting in balance; **(b)** Beginning the movement that you will make as the horse jumps. (You can actually fold further forward than the rider iillustrated here).

112 Some common rider faults while jumping: **(a)** Left behind; **(b)** Legs back, hands up; **(c)** Losing contact and unbalancing the horse; **(d)** Fixed hands, stiff rider; **(e)** Hands raised, ankles stiff; **(f)** Raising an elbow; **(g)** Overchecking; **(h)** Losing position.

RIDER FAULTS IN THE APPROACH

Lack of Planning

A poorly planned approach does not encourage good jumping. The track should be planned in advance. The pace should be balanced, with rhythm and impulsion. (See PLANNING YOUR ROUTE, page 228.)

Lack of Determination

Perhaps through apprehension or uncertainty, the rider fails to use effective leg aids and the horse senses this indecision.

Losing Position

The horse becomes anxious and rushes towards the fence. The rider is left behind and tense, causing the horse to be even more anxious. The rider must go with the horse.

Or the horse suddenly slows down during the last few strides. This shifts the insecure rider forward. The horse may then refuse, run out, or jump badly and there will be little that the rider can do. The rider should stay in balance as the horse slows down, so that he can use his legs effectively.

Suddenly Losing Contact

The rider drops the reins and often holds the horse's neck in anticipation of the spring, one or two strides before take-off. This unbalances the horse and often causes him to run out or refuse.

Looking Down

The rider leans forward, rounds his back and looks down into the bottom of the fence or ditch. This unbalances the horse. The horse will jump much better if the rider looks and rides forward to where he is going.

Over-checking

By trying to alter the horse's strides in the approach, the rider constantly checks the horse until speed, balance and impulsion have been almost lost. It is then very difficult for the horse to jump.

Interfering

The rider continually fiddles with his hands. This constant change of rein contact causes the horse to lose confidence in the rider and upsets his concentration during the approach.

Over-riding

The rider hurries the horse, driving him on to his forehand by going too fast for too long. The horse must then steady himself to restore balance before he can jump.

RIDER FAULTS DURING THE JUMP

Weight Too Far Forward

The rider tips forward abruptly and too early for the take-off. This unbalances the horse on to his forehand, often causing him to put in an extra rebalancing stride before taking off. The rider is then unbalanced during the jump.

Getting Left Behind

The horse takes off before the rider is ready. The rider then gets left behind and, unless he slips the reins, catches the horse in the mouth.

Hand Faults

* Fixing the hands.
* Raising the elbows.
* Raising the hands as the horse takes off.

♦ Straight arms, stiff shoulders and elbows. You should aim to follow the movement of the horse's head and neck during the take-off and throughout the whole of the jump, so that the horse will be able to use himself to the best of his ability.

Incorrect Leg Positions

If the rider stands up in the stirrups as the horse jumps, or tips on to his knees, with his lower legs swinging back and up, the horse will be unbalanced during the jump. Unnecessary movements as the horse takes off, or during the jump, do not help the horse to jump higher.

Swinging the Body to One Side

This also unbalances the horse and can cause him to jump in a crooked way.

RIDER FAULTS ON LANDING

Upper Body Collapsing Forward

The rider tips forward on to his fork with his lower legs too far back, sometimes almost falling off over the horse's shoulder.

Landing Heavily on Back of the Saddle

The rider is behind the movement of the horse and collapses onto the back of the saddle. This causes the horse to hollow his back, which spoils the landing and causes the getaway stride to be tense and awkward. You should absorb most of the shock of landing through your knees and ankles and not through your seat. This will allow the horse to round his back and bring his hind legs further under him, resulting in a quick and easy getaway.

HORSE FAULTS

Refusing and Running Out

The main reasons for this are:

♦ *Inexperienced or bad riding.*
♦ *Pain*—caused by:
  • Lameness.
  • Discomfort in the mouth due to bad riding, over-bitting or sharp teeth.
  • Problems in the back.
  (For each of the above causes of pain, veterinary attention may be needed.)
♦ *Fear*—caused by:
  • Lack of confidence in the rider: in particular, fear that the rider's weight will move about on the horse's back if he jumps.
  • Loss of nerve, often due to an unpleasant memory at a previous fence.
  • Over-facing the horse by asking him to jump a fence beyond his ability or stage of training.
  • Lack of confidence when asked to jump from a slippery surface.
♦ *Disobedience*—caused by:
  • Lack of correct training. The basic paces from which the horse will jump lack the necessary balance and impulsion; and/or the horse has not been taught to respond to the rider's aids.
  • Inexperienced or bad riding. The horse has discovered that the rider cannot control him or make him jump.
♦ *Fatigue*—caused by:
  • Lack of fitness or condition.
  • Lack of consideration by the rider, who continues to jump for too long. The horse will eventually become bored or tired.

Rushing

The main causes of this are:

* *Inexperienced or bad riding.*
* *Incorrect training:* the horse has never been taught to approach the fence in a relaxed and rhythmical way.
* *Fear or pain:* either of these will cause a tense, or even frantic, approach.

Propping

This is a sudden slowing down in front of the fence, and is caused by:

* *Lack of confidence.*
* *The rider not ensuring that the horse goes forward with rhythm and impulsion.*
* *The horse's laziness.*

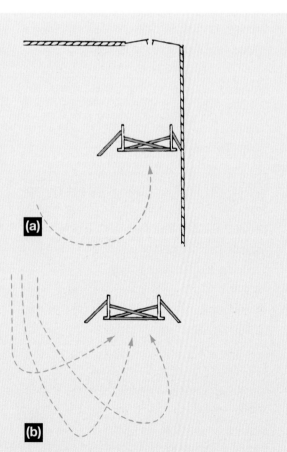

113 (a) A well-planned approach;
(b) Three difficult approaches for the horse.

* *Going too fast too early in the approach.* This causes the horse to steady himself just before the fence, in order to balance.
* *The rider dropping the contact at the last moment before take-off.*
* *Soreness or pain, usually in the feet.*

Jumping with a Flat or Hollow Back

In this case the horse does not extend his head and neck or round his back, and therefore does not jump to the best of his ability.

The main causes of this are:

* *Incorrect training.* The horse's basic paces have not been established and he may approach the fence with his head too high and his back hollow.
* *The rider has not allowed the horse to jump with freedom to use his head, neck and back correctly.*
* *The rider unbalances the horse with his weight.*
* *The horse has a stiff or an injured back.*
* *Some horses have a natural tendency to jump with a flat or hollow back.* They can be helped to overcome this by correct progressive training.

39. Training Exercises for Jumping

Training young horses to jump is fully covered in The Pony Club publication *Breeding, Backing and Bringing On Young Horses and Ponies.*

When you are jumping your horse, it is sensible to have someone with you. If problems arise, you may need expert help. It may be necessary to reaffirm early lessons. The following ideas may be useful:

- In the schooling area, a small inviting obstacle with a wing can be used to restore confidence. Place it beside the wall or fence and towards the exit as this will help to keep the horse straight and encourage him to go forward towards the jump *(fig. 113a)*.

- Plan the approach on a wide, flowing arc *(fig. 113a)*. Avoid sharp turns as they will unbalance the horse *(fig. 113b)*. If your horse is inclined to jump awkwardly, or if you sometimes lose your position while jumping, you should use a neckstrap. Fit a narrow stirrup leather so that it rests snugly one third of the way up the horse's neck ready for you to hold in an emergency.

- The quality and success of the jump depends on the quality of the approach, so before jumping, work the horse on the flat to encourage good quality, balanced and rhythmical paces.

- It is important for your horse to be willing to approach a fence from the trot. A few canter strides before and after the jump are permissible.

- An experienced companion to instil confidence and give a lead can be helpful for a young horse, or if problems arise; but soon the horse must learn to jump without a lead.

- When jumping more than one obstacle, try to maintain a balanced, rhythmical pace between the fences.

- Aim to train the horse to jump in an unhurried, confident and efficient way.

114 Trotting confidently over a pole.

SIX STAGES OF TRAINING FOR JUMPING

The following stages suggested for a young horse (*fig. 115*) are also useful as training exercises to correct faults and to re-establish confidence and discipline. *Fig. 115* shows a horse working at stage 1. A young horse may take several weeks to reach stage 6. An older horse may work on more than one stage in a day. The stages should always be used progressively and the horse must be performing one stage calmly, confidently and consistently before progressing to the next.

Stage 1

- Begin by walking the horse over a single pole placed on the ground between two wings and against the side—not in the middle—of the school or field.
- Break into a trot. The approach at this stage should be on a large, even arc.

Stage 2

Build a small fence of single crossed poles directly behind the pole on the ground. Crossed poles help a young horse to jump straight, guiding him towards the middle of the fence. Approach at the trot because:

- You will have more control.
- It is easier for the horse to arrive at the right place for the take-off, because a trot stride is less than half the length of a canter stride.
- Unhurried and in balance, the horse will have more time to see the fence.

Stage 3

When the small fence can be jumped with ease on either rein, add a single pole behind the crossed poles. This small spread should be about 30 to 60cm (1 to 2ft) high and 30 to 60cm (1 to 2ft) apart. It should be no wider than it is high. This fence will encourage the horse to jump fluently.

Still in trot, practise jumping on either rein, gradually widening and raising the fence as the horse gains confidence. You will need to adjust the fence before jumping it in the opposite direction. Keep your fences small. Never over-face the horse. The approach should still be in trot and from a wide arc.

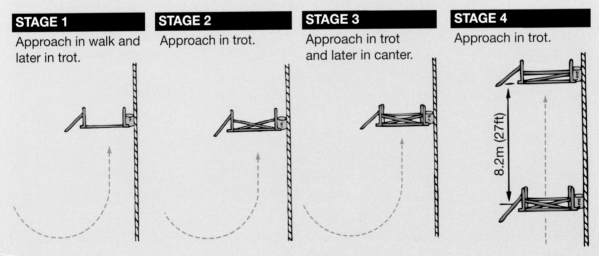

115 Six stages of training for jumping.

Gradually, as the horse gains confidence, he can be allowed to break into a canter in the last few strides. Should he rush or jump in a tense, flat way, return to the approach in trot until the fault has been eliminated. He must remain calm and relaxed, as any tension causes bad jumping.

Stage 4*

The horse should now be ready to jump a small double. Young horses should be introduced to doubles as early as possible. As long as the fences are small and well built and the distances correct, they will encourage good jumping, help to train the horse's eye and teach him to think and to concentrate. Check that the distance is not too long, as over-long distances tend to make a horse hurry the canter strides in the double and jump with a flat back.

Start with a two non-jumping stride double, with the previous fence as the first element and a simple upright pole with a ground line and dropper roughly 8.2m (27ft) away as the second element. Approach in trot for this distance.

Stage 5*

- Widen the double to approximately 8.8m (29ft) and jump from the canter, only breaking into canter in the last few strides.
- When the horse is completely confident over the two non-jumping stride double, close up the double for one non-jumping stride. The distance will depend on the size of the horse or pony and on the pace of the approach. As a guide it will be approximately 5.8m (19ft) at the trot; and 6.4m (21ft) at the canter.

The distances given in Stages 4 and 5 for fences of roughly 60cm (2ft) are suggested for horses. For ponies jumping doubles with two non-jumping strides, the distance should be shortened by approximately 90cm (3ft); and for doubles with one non-jumping stride, by 50cm (1ft 9in). The exact distance will always depend on the length of stride of the individual horse or pony.

Stage 6

Small fences of differing types can now be placed away from the side of the school or field, some on the diagonal—always with a true ground line and of solid appearance. (See SCHOOLING FENCES, page 237.)

Building up Confidence

If correctly trained from the start, a horse should never know how to refuse. By only asking him to jump when his pace is relaxed and rhythmical, and never over-facing him, refusals will probably be avoided. However, if problems arise and the horse refuses, the fence must be lowered at once, and be kept very small until confidence, calmness and obedience return.

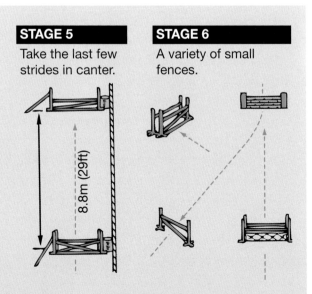

STAGE 5
Take the last few strides in canter.

8.8m (29ft)

STAGE 6
A variety of small fences.

PLANNING YOUR ROUTE

When schooling over a series of fences or during a showjumping or cross-country round, the rider must plan the line, or route, to be followed. It should be planned with care, so that the jumps on the course are met and negotiated by the horse with maximum ease. Turns should be flowing, with no sharp corners. Thoughtless riding, resulting in pointed, abrupt turns will unbalance the horse.

The Centre Line

When riding a course, on the turns and during the approach to the fence the rider must be aware in his mind's eye of the centre line. This is an imaginary line running along the ground straight through the centre of the fence or combination of fences. You should ensure a good approach to each fence, by making an even, rounded turn on to this line *(fig. 116a)*. Overshooting it and having to make an S-turn back, will unbalance the horse and cause him to lose impulsion and rhythm in the approach *(fig. 116b)*. This will result in a poor jump.

Approaches which take a short-cut on to the centre line (causing the horse to meet the fence at an angle) should not be attempted by novice horses or riders because the horse could easily run out *(fig. 116b)*.

When approaching doubles or combinations, sight the fences down the centre line, so that they are straight in the horse's line of vision, one behind the other. Otherwise he will see a way out and may well take it.

Plan your line between the fences with care, and aim towards unhurried, confident jumping.

Once the horse is jumping small fences of all types, and is going forward between leg and hand in an established, balanced outline, you can begin more advanced training.

If take-off problems arise, a placing pole can be introduced from approximately stage three onwards.

PLACING POLES

Experience has shown that placing poles should not be used in the earliest stages of training. They tend to muddle and confuse a very young horse. However, once the horse has mastered small fences and is going forward between the rider's leg and hand in an established, balanced outline, placing poles can be used if take-off problems should arise. They must be treated with caution, as incorrect distances can be dangerous. Regular use can cause the horse to become too dependent on them.

A placing pole is a pole not less than 10cm (4in) in diameter and the same length as the poles forming the fence. It is set on the ground approximately 2.7m (9ft) from the base of the fence on its take-off side. Its purpose is to help a horse to arrive in the right place for take-off, to encourage

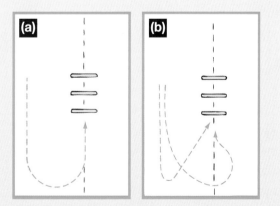

116 (a) The correct approach on to the centre line; **(b)** Two incorrect approaches on to the centre line.

him to lower his head and neck, and to make a smooth, comfortable jump.

The following distances are for horses. Generally speaking ponies are better balanced and they seldom benefit from the use of placing poles. For approaches in trot, the pole should be 2.7m (9ft) from the fence *(fig. 117a)*. For approaches in canter, the placing pole should be 5.2–5.8m (17–19ft) from the fence, depending on the length of the horse's stride *(fig. 117b)*.

DITCHES AND WATER

Horses and riders are usually wary of ditches and water. To overcome this problem, careful and progressive training, using a confident lead, is necessary. Start with tiny, shallow ditches, preferably in a natural fence line, and work up to larger, deeper ones.

Difficulties arise from:

* Approaching too fast from too far out, thus startling the horse. Always give him time to look—especially in the case of strange or starey obstacles.
* Over-facing him without having built up his confidence by starting with very small ditches.

If you look down into the bottom of a ditch it will make you and the horse apprehensive. Always look ahead and onwards.

40. Towards More Advanced Jumping

THE HORSE

The advanced horse must be trained to:

* Respond confidently to the aids and go forward from the leg immediately when asked.
* Shorten and lengthen his stride.
* Remain in balance through turns and corners without losing impulsion or rhythm.
* Change direction in balance without becoming disunited—a very common fault in novice jumpers.

All the above must be taught on the flat. The importance of ground work cannot be too strongly emphasised. Success in jumping depends largely on the correct approach.

Before starting jumping practice, at least twenty minutes should be spent working on the flat, in order to ensure that the horse is settled in his paces, supple, obedient, in tune with his rider, and well warmed-up.

THE RIDER

When riding cross-country and showjumping courses it is important for the approach to be made in a balanced and rhythmical pace,

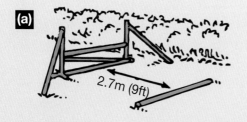
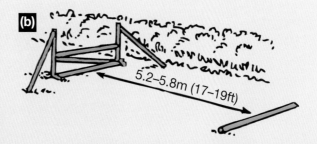

117 Placing poles: **(a)** With the approach in trot; **(b)** With the approach in canter.

with sufficient impulsion and at the correct speed for the size and type of obstacle. Impulsion must not be confused with speed. It is a common fault to approach a fence at too great a speed, from too far away, thus losing rhythm and balance. Such over-riding (or lack of speed control on a cross-country course) gives the horse no time to assess the fence and to jump correctly.

During the last few strides, the rider, while maintaining impulsion and rhythm, should not disturb the horse in any way. At this time the horse must be allowed to concentrate on the jump and be given a chance to make his own adjustments if necessary.

Some riders have a good, natural eye and with experience can help the horse to arrive at the correct place for the take off, while maintaining the quality of the pace in the approach. Unless the rider is certain that he can be accurate, it is better to keep the horse going forward calmly in balance, with impulsion and rhythm, maintaining

contact with legs, seat and hands, and leaving the horse to make his own final stride adjustments.

If a horse is continually interfered with during the approach, or habitually brought to the fence on a poor stride to jump (put wrong) he will soon learn to mistrust his rider—which will result in apprehension, rushing, propping, or refusing. Rider and horse must work together to achieve confident and efficient jumping.

TROTTING POLES (GROUND POLES)

Trotting poles are heavy poles not less than 10cm (4in) in diameter, and roughly 3m (10ft) long. For trotting pole exercises, they should never be more than 15cm (6in) high; setting them higher than this causes tension and loss of rhythm, and will encourage hopping.

The poles should not be easily moved by the horse. Two useful ways *(fig. 119)* to prevent them from rolling, and to give a little height when necessary are:

* To set each end in a scalloped log or wooden block, approximately 30–60cm (1–2ft) long.
* In an arena, to heap sand on either side at each end, you can use squared-off poles which will not roll when kicked.

NOTE. Traditional cavalletti—poles with a wooden 'X' bolted at either end—have proved to be dangerous because they can roll. The alternative forms of trotting pole, described above, are preferable. Cavalletti should never be piled together to form a jump. Such jumps have caused serious falls and are considered to be dangerous.

118 Trotting over poles rhythmically and with confidence.

Value to the Horse

Trotting poles:

* Develop balance and rhythm.
* Teach obedience.
* Teach mental and physical coordination, calmness and concentration. They help to develop the horse's natural eye.
* Develop the correct muscles and help to supple the horse by stretching the neck and lowering the head, rounding the back, engaging the hocks.
* Help to regulate and establish the stride.
* Teach the horse to approach any obstacle correctly and confidently and without tension.

Value to the Rider

Trotting poles teach and develop:

* Balance.
* Rhythm.
* Feel and coordination of aids.
* The rider's eye for distances.
* A knowledge of how to use the arena, leading to a sensible line of approach (see PLANNING YOUR ROUTE, page 228).

Trotting Poles in Rising Trot

Trotting poles should be ridden in rising trot, firstly to encourage the horse to relax and swing his back; secondly to develop rhythm in both horse and rider. Sitting trot should not be used until the horse and rider have reached an advanced stage of training. The horse will otherwise become tense and hollow in his back.

Approximate Trotting Pole Distances

Pony: 1–1.35m (3ft 3in–4ft 6in) apart, depending on size and type.
Horse: 1.3–1.5m (4ft 3in–5ft) apart.

When a distance of 2.7m (9ft) between poles is used (see stage two on the next page) this is suitable for both horses and ponies.

Trotting poles should be set just off the track so that they can be approached on either rein, or bypassed. The turn into them must not be sharp—an arc of at least 15m (50ft).

Never use only a pair of poles at a distance of one trotting stride (approx. 1.3m or 4ft 3in apart) as this may encourage the horse to jump both of them instead of trotting over them one at a time.

PROCEDURE FOR USING TROTTING POLES

Stage 1 *(Fig. 120a)*
Place single poles far apart, at random around the arena.

Method: walk over the random poles, planning your route with purpose so that the horse becomes completely relaxed and at ease, eventually walking on a loose rein.

Pick up the contact quietly, trot on, and trot over the poles. Change the rein at intervals, avoiding any sharp turns. Make sure that the quality of the trot remains the same *(see WORKING TROT, page 204)* and that the horse does not try to hurry. If problems arise, return to walk.

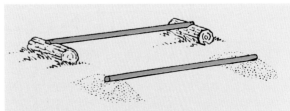

119 Types of trotting (ground) poles.

Stage 2 *(Fig. 120b)*

Lay the trotting poles out as shown.
Method: Start by walking over the three poles set 2.7m (9ft) apart. Never walk over poles 1.35m (4ft 6in) apart; this is the wrong distance for the walk stride and will only upset and confuse a young horse. Use poles 1.35m apart for trotting exercises only.

Stage 3

When the horse is completely calm and relaxed at the walk over the 2.7m (9ft) poles, establish the rising trot. Check the quality of the trot and proceed over the 2.7m (9ft) poles, coming in on an even, well-rounded arc to ensure balance and rhythm. Change the rein and repeat.

Stage 4

Dispense with the 2.7m (9ft) poles. Using a full circuit of the arena to re-establish the trot, proceed over the 1.35m (4ft 6in) poles. Repeat on either rein. Do not hurry;

concentrate on rhythm *(fig. 118)*.

Remember that the distances between the poles are approximate and will vary according to the length of steps of the individual horse.

Checking Distances, Balance and Rhythm

The instructor should check that the trotting poles are set at the right distance so as to ensure that the hind foot falls midway between the poles *(see fig. 121)*.

To check that balance and rhythm are firmly established, one more pole can be added to the 1.35 (4ft 6in) line, at a distance of 2.7m (9ft). Ride on either rein, starting with the 2.7m (9ft) space at the far end. Check that the horse maintains his rhythm, even with the 2.7m (9ft) space, where there is no pole on the ground to guide him.

Balance

Ride in a settled, relaxed way when working over trotting poles, looking forward and

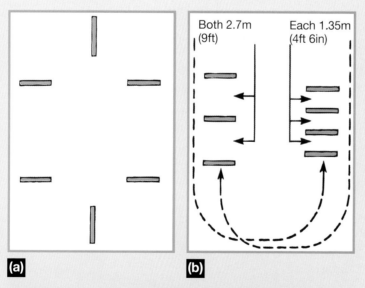

120 Suggested layouts for trotting poles: **(a)** Stage 1; **(b)** Stages 2,3,4. Poles are set at distances for walking and trotting on the left and for trotting only on the right.

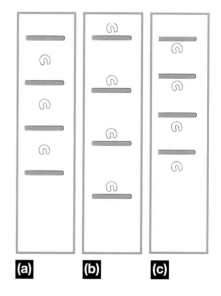

121 Position of trotting poles: **(a)** Correct; **(b)** and **(c)** Incorrect.

onward. Getting tense, looking down, dropping your head, or tipping forward tend to unbalance the horse and destroy his natural rhythm, which invites him to rush or jump over the poles.

Rhythm

Some riders find it difficult to acquire a sense of rhythm. If so, it is helpful to repeat out loud a jingle such as, 'Monday, Tues-day, Wednes-day', or 'one-two, one-two, one-two', during the approach and over the trotting poles. *Rhythm is essential for all successful riding.*

ALTERNATIVE EXERCISES

Trotting poles can be laid out on the diagonal line for a change. The value of this is to teach the rider to maintain impulsion and rhythm through the corners (while riding a correct line) and to become aware of and practise the use of the centre line *(see PLANNING YOUR ROUTE, page 226)*. The track should flow like a river *(fig. 123a)*, with no pointed, sharp or square turns *(fig. 123b)*. *Smooth, well-rounded turns promote balance.*

Solving Problems

The horse must be working correctly in a confident and relaxed way before moving from one stage to the next. If he becomes tense, return to the previous stage or, if necessary, to the beginning. Incorrect, hurried, trotting pole work has no value.

If the horse rushes or jumps the poles, you must first check that his basic pace is correct. Do not proceed over the poles until his rhythm is steady and he is working in a relaxed and settled way. Then:

- Trot in a circle in front of a single pole.
- When the pace is rhythmical and relaxed, come off the circle at a tangent and trot over the pole without changing balance or rhythm *(fig. 122)*.

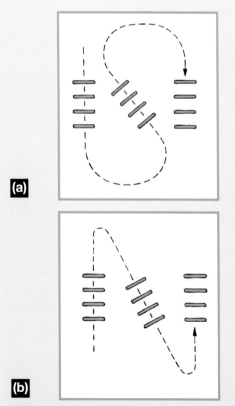

123 Alternative layouts for trotting poles:
(a) A well-planned route;
(b) A badly-planned route.

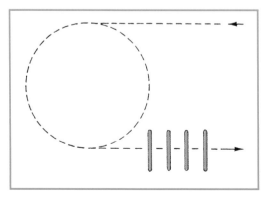

122 Circling in front of trotting poles.

- When the horse remains settled, more poles may be added at correct distances behind the first.
- Occasionally circle at the side of or in front of the poles before proceeding down the line.
- Always circle in front of the poles if the horse starts to rush.

GYMNASTIC JUMPING

Relaxation

If carried out correctly, gymnastic exercises will promote relaxation and the horse will have no reason to feel fear or apprehension.

Trotting Poles Leading to Gymnastic Jumping

Do not attempt to start gymnastic jumping with trotting poles until your horse is proficient in all his trotting pole work and has mastered small fences, including doubles.

For more advanced work and, if space (the width of the arena) permits, set trotting poles and fences down the centre of the arena, which allows for the approach to be on either rein. The turn into the fences should be smooth and as wide as space allows. A tight, sharp turn will unbalance the horse and cause him to lose rhythm.

Jumps preceded by trotting poles down the side of the school or against a hedge will help the horse to keep straight, but he will be able to come in on one rein only.

PROCEDURE FOR GYMNASTIC JUMPING *(Fig. 124)*

Stage 1

Trotting poles should be used on their own until the horse is familiar with them.

Use three or four trotting poles placed 1.35m (4ft 6in) apart, followed by a small spread fence 2.7m (9ft) away. For this, use crossed poles with a ground line pole in front and a single pole behind. At first, build it about 60cm (2ft) high and 60cm wide.

Proceed in rising trot, coming in on an even, well-rounded arc, having already established the trot down the long side. Trot over the poles, and jump the fence. Keep straight on after landing. Repeat this once or twice. If the horse is settled and relaxed, proceed to stage two.

Stage 2

Add another similar fence at a distance of 5.5m (18ft) from the first. Measure from the back of the first fence to the face of the second fence. A distance of 5.5m (18ft) between fences should ride correctly for one non-jumping canter stride between the two elements, as long as the approach is in a settled, rhythmical trot via the trotting poles.

Proceed as for stage 1. The first element should remain a simple, inviting and fairly low staircase fence. As training progresses—and once you are certain that the distance is correct—the second element can be widened, raised, and

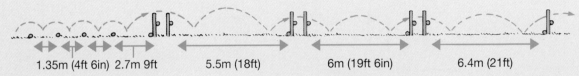

1.35m (4ft 6in) 2.7m 9ft   5.5m (18ft)   6m (19ft 6in)   6.4m (21ft)

124 Four stages of gymnastic jumping. *This page:* Stage 4 from the side. *Opposite:* From above.

eventually become a parallel. When the horse is performing in a relaxed, confident way, proceed to stage three.

Stage 3

Add a third fence approximately 6m (19ft 6in) from the second fence. Start by using another simple spread fence. As training proceeds, vary the type of fence. Ride as for stages 1 and 2, making an even, rounded turn and then trotting over the poles and jumping down the line with one non-jumping canter stride between each element. Remember: always keep straight on after landing.

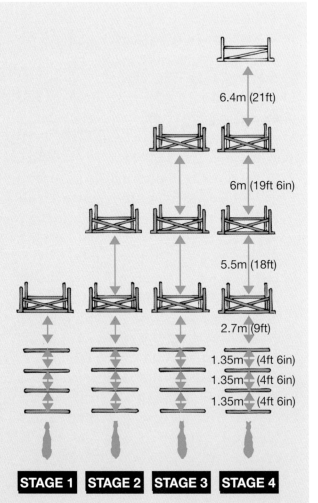

6.4m (21ft)

6m (19ft 6in)

5.5m (18ft)

2.7m (9ft)

1.35m (4ft 6in)
1.35m (4ft 6in)
1.35m (4ft 6in)

STAGE 1   **STAGE 2**   **STAGE 3**   **STAGE 4**

Stage 4

Add a fourth fence—a simple upright—consisting of one pole with a dropper approximately 6.4m (21ft) from the third fence. Use the upright (rather than a spread) until confidence has been completely established over all four elements. A faulty attempt at an upright fence will cause less grief.

For ponies and short-striding horses, a distance of 6.4m (21ft) between the last two elements may be too long. They may not be able to reach the distance in a single non-jumping stride without an effort, and may be tempted to fit in a quick extra stride or to jump with a flat back. On the other hand, for a free-striding horse it may be too short.

Check the distance between all the fences at each stage. If you increase the size of the fences, you may need to increase slightly the distance between them.

The distances between all trotting poles and combinations of fences must be adjusted to suit the individual pony or horse.

Heights and Spreads

- Never over-face the horse: use small fences for schooling until he is confident and happy.
- The four obstacles described in stages one to four can remain the same size or become gradually and progressively larger.
- In combinations, never have one element lower than the previous one (which would cause the horse to drop on to his forehand).
- Small ponies and very novice riders should not attempt gymnastic jumping with spreads. They should use only upright fences.
- Spreads in combinations can cause difficulties.

Alternative Gymnastic Exercises

Once the horse has mastered simple gymnastic jumping (in stages 1 to 4), the exercises may be varied using a bounce and one or two non-jumping canter strides between the elements *(see below)*. The types of fence may also be altered.

From now onwards, trotting poles should not be necessary as an introduction to the obstacles. When the approach is made in canter or if the fences have been enlarged, the distances must be wider than those given in *fig. 124*. Make sure that they are correct before progressing with the exercise. The outline distances given should be used as a guide, but may need modifying depending on:

+ The length and quality of the horse's strides.
+ The pace of the approach.
+ The types and sizes of fences used.
+ The condition of the surface.

Bounce Fences

A bounce—that is two fences with no stride between them—may be introduced later on in training. The distance for a bounce is crucial. If it is too long for the horse, he will try to put in an extra stride. If it is too short, he will try to jump both elements at once. The distance must be correct.

Approaching in trot, bounce fences for horses should be about 3m (10ft) apart, and in canter about 3.7m (12ft) depending on how much ground the horse covers. The distances will be a little less for ponies.

Bounce distances may be incorporated into gymnastic jumping, preferably as the first and second elements.

Unless the horse is thoroughly experienced and obedient, do not attempt a bounce at the end or middle of a gymnastic jumping line, where the preceding distances have been for one or two non-jumping strides. (The horse will try to jump the bounce.)

Warnings

+ Gymnastic exercises should not be attempted unless the rider has sufficient knowledge and experience, without which the result will be a disaster, especially if distances are wrong.
+ Training must be progressive.
+ Each day, decide what you would like to accomplish. Carry out as much of your programme as you can, always bearing in mind that you must end at a time when the horse is not too tired and is going well.
+ Beware of short cuts. Never plunge in halfway through the stages. Start each exercise from the beginning (stage 1) until training has become advanced and all the exercises are fully established, without any mistakes being made.
+ When in trouble seek expert advice/help.
+ When training is interrupted, or if things go seriously wrong, it is essential to return to the early stages. Reintroduce the trotting poles. Reduce and simplify the fences.
+ Using correct distances will teach a horse to jump well (achieving the required height and spread with the minimum of effort) as long as the approach is made in a rhythmical, unhurried pace.
+ As the horse progresses and is able to shorten and lengthen his stride on the flat, he may be taught to shorten and lengthen his stride between closely related fences and the elements of a double. He must be taught to shorten before he is asked to lengthen.

41. Schooling Fences

When gymnastic jumping exercises have been mastered, you can introduce the horse to all the different types of obstacle, including combinations (doubles and trebles) and a variety of cross-country fences, working first in trot and then in canter.

Maintain the impulsion but do not hurry the horse. Give him ample time to jump and to remain in balance, especially over uprights and parallels. Never use incorrect (impossible or trick) distances between doubles and other closely related fences. *Fig. 125* shows a horse jumping an easy schooling (ascending oxer) fence.

THE GROUND LINE

A horse is inclined to look at an obstacle from the base upwards, and he assesses his point of take-off from the bottom of the fence—the most solid part, nearest to the ground. This is known as the ground line.

True Ground Lines *(Fig. 126a)*

A clearly defined ground line will help the horse's judgement. A pole on the ground pulled out in front of a vertical will prevent him from taking off too close to the fence. It will become his ground line—his guide—and he will take off from it, standing off at the correct distance to jump the fence. For this reason, a horse finds it far easier to jump an ascending oxer, or any fence that slopes away from him. He will take off from the bottom—the ground line—and his natural jump will follow the shape of the obstacle.

False Ground Lines *(Fig. 126b)*

A false ground line is one in which the base of the fence is set back behind the vertical. False ground lines should generally be avoided, and in showjumping they are against the rules. The following obstacles all have false ground lines: a gate leaning towards you; upright rails with the bottom pole, or a ground pole, pushed back behind the line of the vertical face; and a triple bar set the wrong way—with the highest pole nearest to you.

125 Schooling over a 'spread' fence with a ground line.

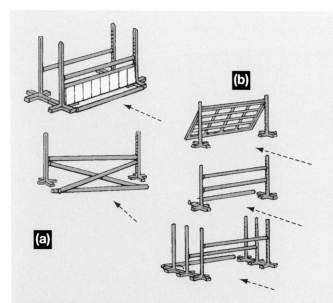

126 (a) True ground lines:
(b) False ground line (to be avoided).

A false ground line will confuse a horse and cause him to get too close for take-off. He will assume that the top of the fence is directly above the ground line, and will judge his point of take-off accordingly. Often he will hit the fence by taking off far too close to it, which could result in a bad fall.

THE TAKE-OFF ZONE *(Fig. 127)*

Broadly speaking, depending on the height and type of fence and the slope of the ground, the horse should take off in an area between the height of the fence and 1.8m (6ft) from its base. For example, the take-off zone for a 1.2m (4ft) gate should be between 1.2 and 1.8m (4–6ft) from the bottom of the gate. This would not apply to a wide triple bar, some types of spread fence, or to water, where the take-off would be much closer to the first element of the fence.

As fences become larger, more accuracy is essential and the point of take-off must be more precisely judged to bring the horse into his take-off zone with rhythm, balance, impulsion and sufficient speed to clear the fence.

TYPES OF FENCE *(Fig. 128)*

There are four basic types of fence, excluding ditches and water. They are (in ascending order of difficulty:

* *Staircase or Ascending Oxer.* Triple bars, or a pair of ascending bars, etc.
* *Pyramid.* Tiger trap, hog's back, etc.
* *Upright or Vertical.* Gate, post and rails, etc.
* *True Parallel or Square Oxer* (the most difficult to jump). Parallel bars, planks with a parallel pole behind, etc.

All four types may be included in schooling courses. However, a Hog's Back should not be included in combination fences (doubles, trebles and quadruples) as it could cause problems if a horse lost fluency and failed to negotiate the last pole.

Buildint Schooling Fences

In schooling, much depends on the correct construction of the fences. They should be inviting, of solid appearance, and with a good ground line. Poles must be thick and strong— minimum 9cm (3½ins) in diameter—and not easily dislodged. Flimsy poles and airy fences do not command respect, and they

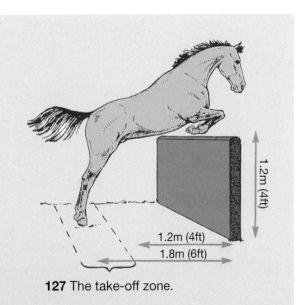

127 The take-off zone.

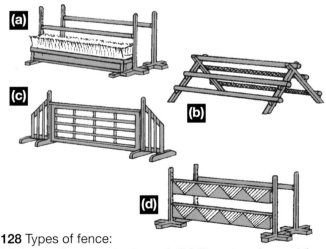

128 Types of fence:
(a) Ascending oxer (staircase); **(b)** Tiger trap (pyramid); **(c)** Gate (upright); **(d)** Planks and rail (parallel).

encourage careless jumping. However, very small ponies respect poles with a smaller diameter. Over thicker poles they may jump too high for their small riders.

Construction of an Ideal Basic Schooling Fence *(Fig.129)*

The staircase type is the most simple and inviting fence to jump. Its advantages are:

- The front pole forms a solid ground line.
- Crossed poles help to give a more solid appearance. They draw the horse's eye to the centre of the fence and help to keep him straight. He will aim for the lowest part.
- The back pole gives height and calls for more spring and effort than is needed for jumping single crossed poles

Equipment Required: 4 stands
                                  4 poles
                                  4 cups or pegs

Method

1 Set one pole on the ground to show the position of the stands and the distance between them.
2 Place the stands in pairs, toe-to-toe, approximately 60cm (2ft) apart, at either end of pole 1.
3 Put two crossed poles on the first pair of stands, arranged so that the centre is approximately 40cm (16in) high.
4 Add one pole straight across on the second (back) pair of stands, approximately 60cm (2ft) high.
5 Place a pole on the ground directly in front of the crossed poles (use pole 1).

Variations

The basic schooling fence can easily be changed into any of the following five:

- Ordinary crossed poles.
- Ascending oxer (staircase).
- Parallel bar with dropper.
- Upright with variations.
- Aachener.

To build an Aachener, add one more pair of stands and crossed poles on the far side of the fence. Adjust heights so that both sets of cups for the crossed poles are two holes higher than those of the middle straight-across bar. This is a useful pyramid schooling fence. You can jump it from either direction, and it helps to promote correct jumping style, making the horse round his back. A disadvantage is that the extra pair of crossed poles on the far side of the fence can cause falls. The Aachener is therefore not included for general use in showjumping or cross-country courses.

Droppers

A dropper is an under-pole set diagonally, with one end on the ground and the other supported in a wing-cup. It helps to fill up the fence, and the lower end can be pulled forward on the floor side to form a helpful ground line.

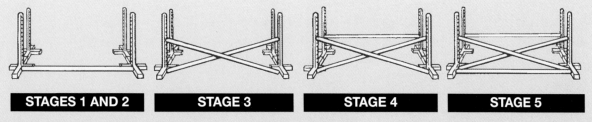

| STAGES 1 AND 2 | STAGE 3 | STAGE 4 | STAGE 5 |

129 Stages of construction of an ideal basic schooling fence.

SUMMARY OF JUMPING DISTANCES

The measurement of distances between doubles and combinations is taken from the back of one obstacle to the face of the next.

Reasons for Adjusting the Distances

The distance between fences depends on:

- The pace of approach.
- The length of the horse's stride.
- The height and type of fence.

(a) With the approach in TROT and fences approximately 60cm high	Pony (according to size)	Horse
Between elements 1 and 2 For one non-jumping stride: For two non-jumping strides: *(see figs. 131a and 131b)*	4.9–5.5m (16–18ft) 7.3–8.2m (24–27ft)	5.5–6.1m (18–20ft) 8.2–9.1m (27–30ft)
Between elements 2 and 3 For one non-jumping stride:	5.5–6m (18–19½ft)	6–6.4m (19½–21ft)
Between elements 3 and 4 For one non-jumping stride:	6–6.4m (19½–21ft)	6.4–7m (21–23ft)
A BOUNCE, no non-jumping stride: *(see fig. 131c)*	2.7–3m (9–10ft)	3–3.3m (10–11ft)
(b) With the approach in CANTER and fences approximately 1m high	Pony (according to size)	Horse
One non-jumping stride between elements (See fig. 132a)	6.1–7.3m (20–24ft)	7.0–7.8m (23–25½ft)
Two non-jumping strides: *(see fig. 132b)*	9.4–10.4m (31–34ft)	10.4–11m (34–36ft)
A BOUNCE, no non-jumping stride: *(see fig. 132c)* Fences approximately 75cm high	3–3.6m (10–12ft)	3.3–4.3m (11–14ft)

130 (a) Distances for gymnastic jumping; **(b)** Distances for combination fences.

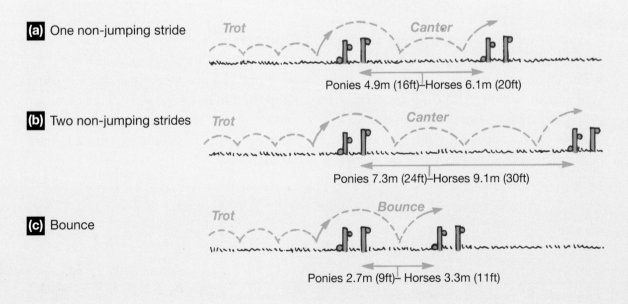

(a) One non-jumping stride

Trot   *Canter*

Ponies 4.9m (16ft)–Horses 6.1m (20ft)

(b) Two non-jumping strides

Trot   *Canter*

Ponies 7.3m (24ft)–Horses 9.1m (30ft)

(c) Bounce

Trot   *Bounce*

Ponies 2.7m (9ft)– Horses 3.3m (11ft)

131 Gymnastic distances for approaching in TROT.

- The condition of the surface in the schooling area.
- The slope—up or down hill.

Cross-Country Combination Distances

Across country, when galloping on, distances can be longer than those given for approach in trot and canter, and they must be ridden accordingly.

Distances for Gymnastic Jumping

When the approach is in TROT, the distances will be considerably shorter than when in CANTER and will vary between the different elements (fig. 130a).

Distances for Combination Fences

The distances given in the table overleaf are approximate and your choice will depend on the condition of the ground, the ability of the horse, and the type and size of fence (fig. 130b).

SAFETY HINTS FOR BUILDING FENCES

- A staircase fence as the first element of a combination encourages novice horses to jump. It is more inviting than an upright.
- Spreads should *NOT* be used as a second element for very novice horses or ponies, or for those with little scope, especially out of a one non-jumping stride double.
- Use a two non-jumping stride double for very novice horses and small ponies: if necessary, they can put in three strides.
- Never leave empty cups on wings. Spare cups with no poles in them are dangerous.
- Use only one pole on the far side of a parallel or near-parallel. Never have a plank on the far side of this type of fence.
- Use flat cups for planks and gates.
- When making a fence higher, to avoid leaving airy gaps, raise all the poles, or put in an extra one.

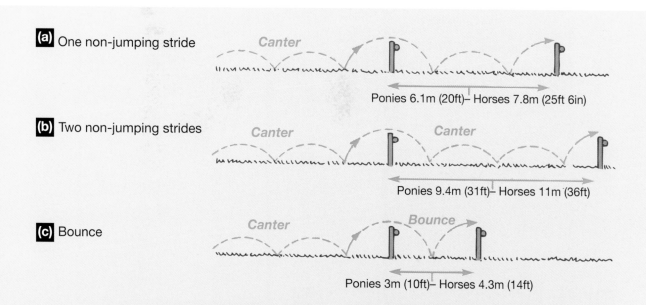

(a) One non-jumping stride   Canter   Ponies 6.1m (20ft)– Horses 7.8m (25ft 6in)

(b) Two non-jumping strides   Canter   Canter   Ponies 9.4m (31ft)– Horses 11m (36ft)

(c) Bounce   Canter   Bounce   Ponies 3m (10ft)– Horses 4.3m (14ft)

132 Distance for combination fences, with approach in CANTER.

HINTS TO ENCOURAGE GOOD JUMPING

- In the early stages of schooling, approach in trot.
- Keep fences small until style and complete confidence become established.
- Build inviting fences that look solid and have a true ground line.
- Obstacles built alongside a school wall or a fence will help novice jumpers— both horse and rider.
- Distances between combinations and in gymnastic jumping must be correct.
- The use of parallel bars encourages horses to be supple and to round their backs.
- Relaxation is vital. Tension ruins style and ability. When building showjumping courses, distances between individual fences are usually measured in multiples of the length of a horse's stride. Outdoors in good conditions this might be 3.7m (12ft). *For example:* 14.6m (48ft), 18.3m (60ft), 22m (72ft).
- Unless you are experienced, when setting up or designing a course, first use a simple figure-of-eight track. Later you can vary it *(fig. 134)*.

	Pony	Horse
Walk stride	0.8m (2ft 9in)	0.9m (3ft)
Trot stride (Trotting pole distances)	1.9–1.4m (3ft3in–4ft 9ins)	1.3–1.5m (4ft 3in–5ft)
Canter stride	Depends on size and type of pony	3.3–4.3m (11–14ft)

133 Approximate lengths, depending on the size and type of horse. For correct schooling, it is helpful to know the length of your horse's stride.

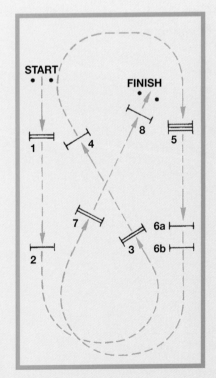

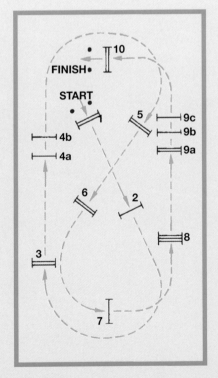

134 Sample showjumping courses: **(a)** A simple figure-of-eight; **(b)** Variations on a figure-of-eight.

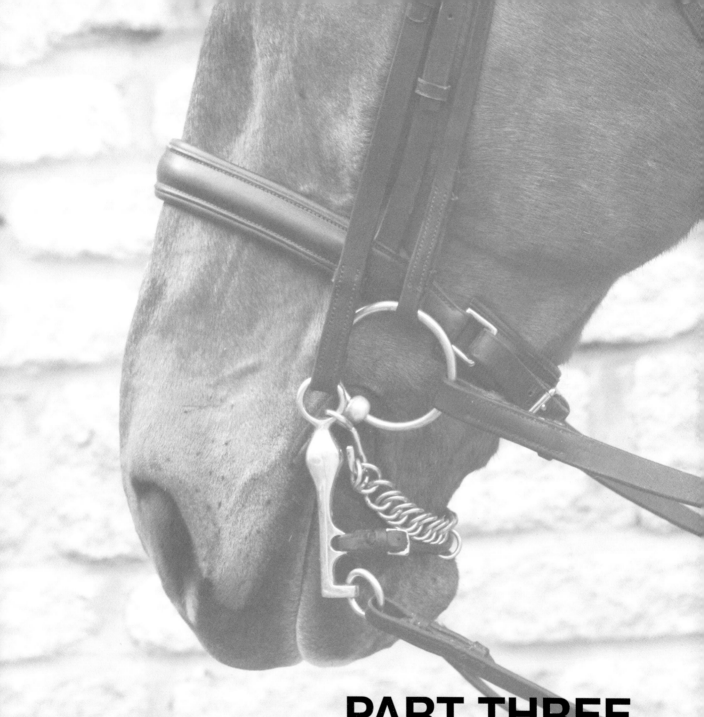

PART THREE
Saddlery and Lorinery

42. Choosing Saddlery and Fitting the Saddle

MAKING YOUR CHOICE

Saddlery—often referred to as tack—is a necessary and frequently expensive investment. The basic requirement is a saddle with its fittings—girth, stirrup leathers and stirrup irons, plus usually a numnah or saddlecloth—and a bridle with its bit.

An enormous variety of saddlery and additional items is available to suit different horses and different types of riding, but here we will deal mainly with what you need for general purpose riding and schooling. Always check your Pony Club rule book if you are unsure whether or not an item is permitted.

The Essentials of Good Saddlery

Well-cleaned and well-fitted saddlery contributes greatly to the comfort and appearance of both horse and rider.

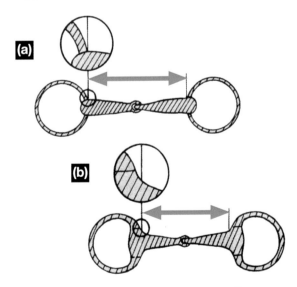

135 Measuring a bit: **(a)** Loose-ring snaffle (pelhams are also measured in this way); **(b)** Eggbutt snaffle.

A good saddle:
- Will fit the horse and rider.
- Will be of the correct type for its purpose.
- Will be well cared for, clean and supple.

Badly-fitting saddlery and hard, dry, cracked leather:
- Are dangerous for both horse and rider.
- Cause pain and injury to the horse.
- Devalue an expensive investment.

BUYING SADDLERY

Seek expert advice when buying saddlery. A good place to start is with someone who is registered with the Society of Master Saddlers and/or holds its saddle-fitting qualification. It is not recommended that you make important purchases via the internet; it does not always work out cheaper and you cannot put a price on being able to examine tack and benefit from knowledgeable advice. Checking the fit and suitability, particularly of the saddle and the bit, requires knowledge and experience. (These topics are covered in detail later.)

Leatherwork

Leather is the best material for long life and comfort. Good saddlery is made of the best leather and is therefore expensive. You can buy it secondhand, but if you do, check that the stitching and leather are in good condition, and ensure that the saddle tree is not broken. *(See page 252.)*

There are many kinds of inferior saddlery on the market and some may even be dangerous. Some synthetic saddlery has improved enormously in quality, design and appearance, but is unlikely to last as long as well cared-for leather tack. Brightly coloured tack is not recommended for general use.

Metalwork

Bits and stirrup irons should be of best quality metal. Stainless steel is the safest and most satisfactory. Plated metal chips and flakes off. Nickel is dangerous because it is soft and can bend or break.

Bits are available in measurements varying from traditional inches and half-inches to a range of approximate metric equivalents. As a rough guide, find a bit which fits the horse and measure the width of the mouthpiece *(fig. 135)*. For the type and size of bit that your horse needS, *see Bits and Bitting, page 263*. (Stirrup irons, stirrup leathers and girths are covered in *Saddle Fittings, page 254*).

Bridles

Bridles and their component parts are made in standard sizes—usually, pony, cob and full—but the size of the horse does not always relate to the size of his head. In some cases, you may need to mix and match parts to achieve a good fit; for instance, you may need to use a full-size headpiece with cob-size cheekpieces. When a bridle is fitted correctly on a horse, the buckles should be on or near the centre holes—so that, if necessary, minor adjustments can be made up or down. For the parts of the bridle and how to assemble it, *see page 262*. There are many enticingly fashionable bits and gadgets on the market. Most of them are for the use of the specialist, and their merits are not discussed in this book. In certain circumstances they may be helpful, but they should not be bought or used without expert advice.

THE SADDLE

A good saddle is an investment to be proud of and, if treated with care, it will last a lifetime. Before making this important choice it is helpful to understand the functions of the saddle and to have a basic knowledge of how it is constructed. The saddle should be comfortable for both horse and rider. Its purpose is to distribute the weight of the rider as comfortably as possible over the horse's back, and to help the rider to adopt a correct position.

From time to time The Pony Club approves certain saddles which, in the correct size, should fit and be comfortable for most horses and riders.

THE STRUCTURE OF THE SADDLE

The Tree *(Fig. 136)*

Most saddles are built on a tree, a framework which can be made from and incorporate a variety of materials including laminated wood, flexible steel, carbon and plastics. The size, width and profile of the tree determines the size and width of the saddle and whether or not it will suit the shape of your horse's back.

Most trees have some flexibility, though you may find older saddles which are built on rigid trees. Buying from a knowledgeable, reputable saddler will help ensure that you buy a saddle built on a tree which meets relevant specifications, is undamaged and is suitable for you and your horse.

You may also see saddles which are built on partial trees, or are treeless. Not every design is suitable for all horses and a treeless or part-treed saddle must be fitted and balanced with as much care as is given to any other type.

The Seat

The seat is built on a base formed of strips of webbing which are stretched along and across the tree. These strips must be of exactly the correct tension if the seat of the saddle is to have the right dip, with its deepest part in the centre. The seat is padded over the webbing and covered by leather.

Girth Straps

Girth straps are attached to the webbing strips which are stretched crosswise over the tree. There should be three straps: the first attached to one web over the tree, and the second and third to another web. For safety, the girth should always be buckled to the first strap and either the second or the third.

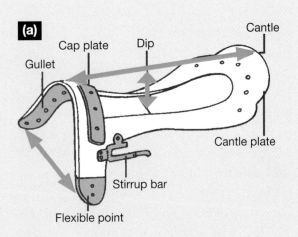

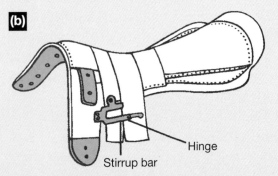

136 Structure of the saddle: **(a)** The tree; **(b)** Tree with webbing stretched along and across.

Stirrup Bars

These are attached to the tree, and are traditionally open-ended to allow the stirrup leathers (which are looped over them) to slip off, thus preventing a rider being dragged after a fall if a foot is caught in the stirrup iron. On most stirrup bars there is a hinge that allows the point to be turned up so that the leathers will not slip off when a saddled horse is being led without a rider. The points should never be up when the horse is being ridden.

Bars which are not open-ended, or are in the form of a D, are unsafe unless safety stirrups are used.

The Panel

The panel is the underside of the saddle, acting as a cushion for the horse. It is padded and shaped to ensure that the rider's weight is evenly distributed over the back muscles, and that the horse's spine is completely protected—untouched by the saddle. Therefore panels should be soft, wide and flat with a wide gullet running between them.

There are various designs of panel, with many incorporating knee rolls at the front which help the rider to maintain a correct leg position. Some also have thigh rolls behind the rider's legs.

Continental and French Panels

The two designs are made in a slightly different way, but for the rider the only variation is that the French panel has a single thickness of leather under his thigh, whereas the Continental design has a double thickness. In both cases the panel reaches almost to the bottom of the saddle flap. The panels shown in *fig. 137* could be either Continental or French.

Full and Half Panels

A full panel reaches almost to the bottom of the saddle flap and is sometimes quilted. A half panel provides only the cushioning of the rider's weight for the horse. It reaches halfway down the saddle flap and has a large sweat flap on which the girth buckles lie.

Stuffings

All panels are stuffed with wool or wool mix (pure wool is superior); synthetic foam, or felt, or they are air-filled. The panel must never feel lumpy, especially on the weight-bearing areas. A new saddle should have symmetrically-stuffed panels, but there may be occasions when a saddler will alter the distribution of the stuffing to take into account a horse's asymmetry. However, a saddler may prefer to suggest the use of a numnah incorporating removable pads to achieve the same effect. (*The reason for a horse's asymmetry should be investigated, which inevitably demands input from a vet.*)

Linings

Leather linings are easy to clean and last a long time if well looked after and if the saddle is used frequently. Clean other materials according to the manufacturer's instructions.

Buckle Guards

All types of saddles should have buckle guards to prevent the saddle flap from being damaged by the girth buckles. Some are detachable; others are attached under the saddle flap.

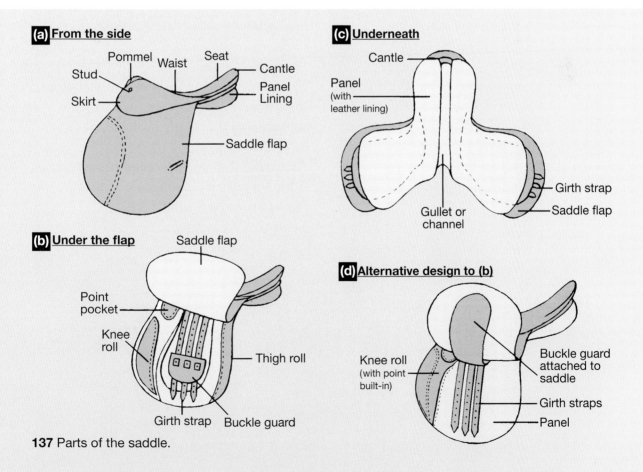

137 Parts of the saddle.

TYPES, SIZES AND WIDTHS OF SADDLES

Types *(Fig. 138)*

A saddle must fit the horse and rider. It must also be suitable for purpose. You do not need a specialist design until you reach a good level in a specific discipline; a well-designed general purpose saddle will suffice. The most common types of saddle in use by English-style riders are:

General Purpose Saddle

As its name implies, this saddle is designed for general riding. It is a suitable type for most Pony Club activities. The cut of the saddle flaps and the length of the seat are midway between those of the dressage and showjumping saddles. The panel is usually Continental or French.

Dressage Saddle

This has a straight-cut flap and is designed to accommodate a longer, straighter leg position than those adopted for hacking or jumping. It is fitted with long girth straps and a short girth to prevent the girth buckles lying under the rider's thigh. Most, but not all, dressage saddles have a deeper rather than a flatter seat, but, as always, must be built on a tree which suits the profile of the horse's back.

Showjumping Saddle

This type of saddle usually has a flatter seat than the dressage type. Designed for riding with shorter stirrup leathers, it has a forward-cut saddle flap. Some saddles are designed specifically for cross-country. They have flat seats to allow maximum adjustment of the rider's position and will accommodate a shorter stirrup length than that used for showjumping.

Synthetic Saddles

These types of saddle are being produced in ever-increasing quantity and quality. In some cases they may prove to be a cheaper but satisfactory substitute for leather.

Showing Saddle

Modern designs have a straighter cut flap than general purpose saddles, but are not as straight cut as dressage models, and have flat seats. Care must be taken that the saddle does not make it difficult for the rider—especially in the case of a child—to maintain balance and stability.

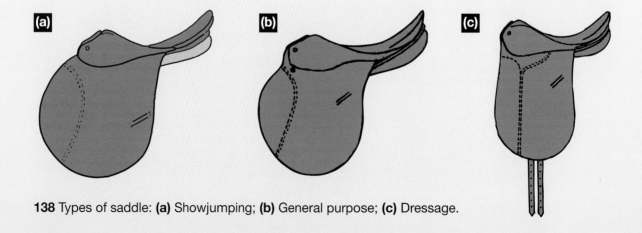

138 Types of saddle: **(a)** Showjumping; **(b)** General purpose; **(c)** Dressage.

A working hunter saddle or one marketed as a VSD model (usually translated as 'very slightly dressage') usually falls halfway between a general purpose and a dressage model.

Designs For Small Children

Pad saddles made from felt were traditionally used for very small children. They have either no tree, or just a tree forepart. These are still available and if used, should have a tree forepart or front arch to help the child sit correctly.

Some pad saddles are fitted with D-rings instead of standard stirrup bars. In these cases the stirrup leathers are attached firmly to the saddle, so to prevent the possibility of a rider being dragged after a fall, safety stirrups must be used. Get expert advice on whether the girth straps, attachments and the girth itself are safe before using a traditional pad.

Some modern, synthetic designs are more comfortable and give greater support. When small children are learning to ride, a saddle must give enough security to help them find balance and confidence.

Sizes

Saddle seat sizes are measured from the metal stud at the side of the pommel to the cantle *(see fig. 139)*. Standard sizes are from 38–45.7cm (15–18in). The saddle should be the correct size for the shape and size of the rider.

Widths

Many types and sizes of saddle are made in three widths—narrow, medium and wide (see The Tree, page 245). Some saddles are also produced in extra-wide versions. The width of the saddle must be correct for the width of the horse. When choosing a new saddle, decide with your saddler's help on one which fits your horse and suits the length and profile of his back and is of the type and size appropriate to your own needs. If your horse has muscle wastage or asymmetrical muscle structure, the use of remedial pads may be necessary.

MEASURING THE WIDTH OF A HORSE FOR A SADDLE

If you are buying a new saddle, or having an old one restuffed, it is important for the saddler to know the width and profile of your horse's back. The saddler should measure the horse and fit the saddle for you. The usual method of taking a wither profile, which will be used to help decide on the correct width, is to use a malleable ruler, usually called a Flexi-Curve or something similar.

This is moulded over the withers, about 5cm (2in) back from the point of the shoulder (scapula) where the front arch of the saddle should rest. Lift it off and pencil the shape (inside) on a piece of stiff paper or cardboard.

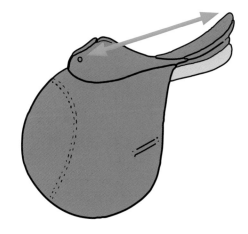

139 Measuring a saddle from stud to centre of cantle.

FITTING THE SADDLE TO THE HORSE

Fitting saddles is a specialist job, but riders need to be aware of fitting criteria so they know when to call in a saddler to check and adjust a saddle if necessary. The guidelines below apply whether you are buying a new or second-hand saddle.

If your horse has any exaggerated conformation points, such as very prominent withers, or if the balance of the saddle needs to be adjusted so it sits correctly on the horse's back without tipping you forward or back, your saddler must fit the saddle to the horse and make any necessary adjustments. The saddle will be fitted without a numnah but the saddler will, if necessary, make any adjustments to take into account any numnahs or pads which need to go underneath it.

- The saddle tree must be the correct width for the horse (fig. 140). If it is too wide the arch will be too low over the withers (fig. 141a). If it is too narrow, the panel on each side of the channel will pinch the spine, and there will be too much pressure underneath the points of the tree *(fig. 141b)*.
- You should be able to see a clear passage all the way through the channel over the horse's spine, but the saddle should not perch too high on the horse's back. Saddles with cut-back heads are particularly suitable for horses with high withers; the pommel being cut-back avoids the necessity of having a very high arch.
- There must be no weight on the loins. This may happen if the saddle is too long.
- The saddle should lie flat on the horse's back and the centre of the seat should be the lowest point.
- Check that the panel stuffing is appropriate for the horse's musculature.

Having decided that the saddle fits the horse you should saddle up and ride on it.

If it is new and you have arranged to try it, put a thin cotton saddlecloth, or any other that the saddler recommends, underneath it so that you can keep it clean. Check that you are comfortable and can ride in balance in all paces and, if necessary, over jumps. Check that the fit of the saddle is still good for the horse when you first sit on it. After you have ridden on it for fifteen to twenty minutes make sure that it is still clear at the withers and at the back. To do this, carry out the following procedure (which is also useful when you are checking the fit of your usual saddle if your horse has lost or gained weight, or to see if the panel needs re-stuffing):

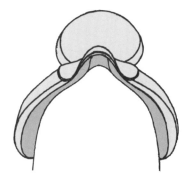 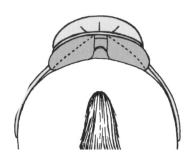

140 A saddle which fits correctly, seen from front and back.

- Ask someone to look at the back of the saddle while you are sitting square. Pressure on the horse's spine often goes unnoticed here because riders cannot see for themselves.
- Check that the saddle is clear of the horse's withers by standing in the stirrups, leaning forward and placing your fingers between the saddle and the top of the withers. If your fingers are pinched, the saddle does not fit the horse. If you are checking your own saddle and if the problem is minor and you have no alternative, use a wither pad—a fabric or sheepskin pad—placed between the pommel of the saddle and the horse's withers. This should only be a temporary measure. Have the saddle checked and restuffed as necessary as soon as possible. If you suspect a broken tree, do not use the saddle until your saddler has checked it.
- The saddle must not hamper the movement of the horse's shoulders. This may happen if the panel is too forward-cut, or if the saddle is fitted too close to the back of the scapula/shoulder.
- The panel must be correctly stuffed to avoid causing the rider to lose contact with the horse, and should be regulated so as to give some support for the knee. It should have sufficient stuffing at the back to ensure that the seat does not slope, causing the rider to slide backwards.
- The saddle must not slip forward. If it does so on a fat horse, or on one with flat withers, ask your saddler to advise you on ways to prevent this movement while allowing freedom of the shoulders. On ponies it may be necessary to fit a crupper *(see page 256)*.

NOTE: When a horse is fat, perhaps after a summer's rest, the saddle which fits him when he is in hard condition may perch too high on his back. In this case it is better to begin riding him in a wider saddle than to risk spreading the tree of your best saddle, which he will use later. This should be fitted with as much care.

THE EFFECT OF THE SADDLE ON THE RIDER

The saddle must be the correct size for the rider. One which is too small will not be comfortable and the rider's knees will overlap

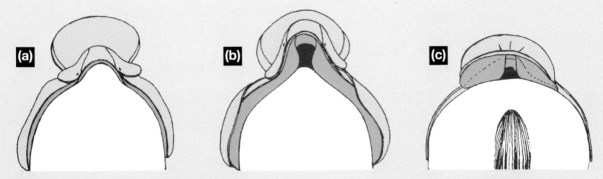

141 Saddles which do not fit correctly: **(a)** Too wide—pressing on withers and spine. Also, crooked; **(b)** Too narrow—pinching the withers and spine; **(c)** Sloping down on one side (in need of stuffing).

the saddle flap. One which is too large may affect the rider's security and balance.

The saddle must allow the rider to sit in the centre of balance without tension *(fig. 142)*. The seat must not slope down towards the back. If it does, the rider will sit on the back of the saddle with the lower leg stuck forward. If the saddle slopes up too much at the back it will pitch the rider forward. If the saddle slopes down on one side (which can be due to unlevel stuffing OR because the rider puts more weight on one stirrup than the other) it will sit crookedly.

A saddle which puts the rider out of balance may do so because:

- The design is faulty.
- It does not fit the horse.
- It does not fit the rider.
- It needs re-stuffing to put it into balance. If you buy a new saddle, your saddler should check it after it has had time to settle. He or she will tell you when this will need to be done.

142 The saddle must allow the rider to sit in a balanced position without tension.

TESTING FOR A SUSPECTED BROKEN TREE

It is useful to know how to do this, especially when buying a second-hand saddle; but if in any doubt always seek expert advice, as a saddle with a broken tree should not be used.

The Front Arch

If the front arch is broken, the saddle will tend to fit too low and will probably touch the top of the withers.

To check for a break, apply strong hand pressure to the points (on each side of the saddle), pressing them towards, and then away from, each other. There should be no movement or noise (click or squeak).

Do not confuse the movement of the flexible ends of the points with that of a broken tree. If the tree is broken, the movement will come either from underneath the arch, which is the most usual place, or from the area of the metal stirrup bars upwards to the arch of the saddle.

The Cantle

Check that the cantle is rigid. If you can twist it, the tree has broken. A rider who mounts from the ground and pulls on the cantle not only causes discomfort to the horse, but may distort the saddle tree. For these reasons, use a mounting block when possible.

The Waist

Hold the saddle in front of you with one hand under the cantle and the other under the pommel. Lift one of your knees above the saddle, press down on the waist, and carefully try to bend it in the middle. Or press the cantle in towards your ribs and try to bend the waist by pulling the pommel in towards you.

A spring tree saddle when tested in this way should flex across the centre of the waist and seat. It should feel as if it is about to spring back firmly into place. If the spring tree is weakened or broken, you will feel a softness and lack of spring. A spring tree is liable to break on one side, so you may well feel more give on that side only.

Be careful not to confuse a broken tree with a well-used spring tree, which although it may have become very soft, still retains its springiness. A broken spring tree is almost impossible to repair, as reinforcement would completely eliminate the spring effect of the tree.

Wrinkled leather across the seat is often a sign of a broken tree.

A Twisted Tree

This would injure a horse's back, so it must be recognised. From the cantle, look towards the pommel to check that the cantle and pommel are symmetrical in relation to each other.

A rider pulling on the cantle whilst mounting from the ground can cause the tree to twist. Again, whenever possible, use a mounting block.

SADDLE FITTINGS

Girths *(Fig. 143)*

A girth keeps the saddle secure on your horse's back, so is vital for your safety and his comfort and efficiency.

The stitching should be checked regularly. Girth sizes are determined by their measurement from end to end, including the buckles.

The materials most commonly used for girths are leather or soft but strong synthetic materials, sometimes incorporating cotton. A girth's design and the material from which it is made should help to ensure that it does not pinch the horse behind the elbow.

Leather Girths

These are very satisfactory and wear well, but you should pay particular attention to the stitching—for your own safety—and to the softness and cleanliness, for the comfort and efficiency of the horse.

The traditional Atherstone girth is shaped for the comfort of the horse. You will also see curved designs said to add to saddle security and increase the comfort and even the stride length of the horse. These are often referred to in general as anatomical girths.

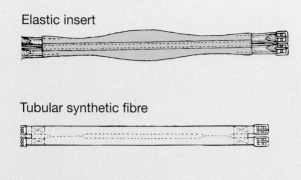

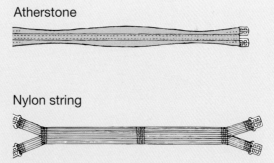

Elastic insert

Atherstone

Tubular synthetic fibre

Nylon string

143 A selection of girths.

Elasticated Girths

Leather or synthetic girths may have an elastic insert at one or both ends, between the main girth and the buckles or at the centre. This allows greater freedom of movement, and eases the horse's breathing, especially across country. Girths with elastic inserts at both ends, or in the centre, are preferable as those with elastic at one end only are more likely to distribute pressure unevenly. If you do use a girth with elastic at one end, the elasticated end should be fitted on the off side to avoid inadvertent over-tightening of the girth.

NOTE: A girth which is too tight can cause a haematoma (swelling).

Tubular Synthetic Fabric

These have a soft filling and are comfortable and strong (but check after cleaning. *(See page 294.)* Some are shaped like the Atherstone (see above) and have similar advantages.

Nylon String Girths

This is a traditional design that has come back into use. It consists of tubular nylon strands, joined at intervals with woven string and with two buckles at each end. These are good general purpose girths which let the air through between the strands and offer security, particularly on an unclipped horse.

Surcingle (Over-girth)

Usually made of webbing with an elastic insert, a surcingle is used principally for cross-country work to act as a safeguard to secure the saddle should the girth break. It is fitted around the horse, lying over the girth and passing across the top of the saddle. It is fastened to itself like a belt, with the buckle lying directly over the centre of the girth. The surcingle must pass through the loop of the breastplate or martingale to prevent it slipping back off the girth.

You cannot tighten a surcingle while you are mounted, so you will need a helper to

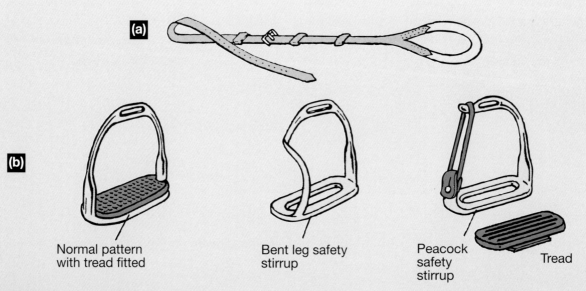

Normal pattern with tread fitted

Bent leg safety stirrup

Peacock safety stirrup

Tread

144 (a) A crupper; **(b)** stirrup-irons.

check, and if necessary tighten your girth and surcingle when you would normally tighten the girth yourself.

Surcingles are also used to prevent the saddle flaps slapping against the panel, or blowing upwards, when a horse is being lunged in a saddle but without a rider.

Stirrup Irons

Irons should, in general, be made from stainless steel. They must be large enough to allow about 7mm (¼in) at each side of the rider's foot *(fig. 145)*. The measurement should be taken at the widest part of the boot or shoe, which must have a low heel to avoid the risk of the rider's foot slipping through and becoming jammed.

It is particularly dangerous for small children to use stirrup irons designed for adults which allow their whole foot to slip through.

Rubber treads are fitted to the irons to help prevent the rider's foot from slipping and to add comfort.

You may see specialist designs, including lightweight carbon irons, used by some jockeys and event riders. Some riders, particularly those involved in endurance riding, prefer irons with extra broad treads for support.

Safety Stirrup Irons

These are designed to prevent the rider's foot from becoming wedged in the stirrup. They are recommended for all riders but particularly for children. The two most popular designs are the Peacock and the Bent-Leg (Australian) irons.

Peacock

Peacock safety irons have a thick, rolled ring of rubber replacing the metal on one side. This ring should be on the outside. This design's disadvantages are:

- They do not hang straight, as they are weighted more on one side than the other.
- The inconvenience caused when a rubber ring comes off or breaks. The chances of losing the ring are lessened if it is attached to the stirrup at one end by a small, tight-fitting loop, which will retain it if the other end comes off.
- They have been known to bend or break under heavy pressure and are not suitable for riders other than lightweight children.

Bent-Leg (Australian)

The bent-leg should be on the outside and should protrude forwards. These irons hang straighter than the Peacock type and are usually satisfactory once you have become familiar with the feel of them. Until then they will feel strange and your feet may tend to slip out too easily.

Safety irons are always recommended and are essential if the saddle is not fitted with safety stirrup bars. Depending on the construction quality and condition of the saddle, a stirrup leather may not release quickly even when safety stirrup bars are fitted and the end left down—something that should be checked.

Stirrup Leathers

Many leather stirrup leathers stretch when new, so it is as well to wear them in at exercise rather than at a competition, and to keep a check that, after stretching, the holes are still level with each other. It is a good idea to switch over the left- and right-hand leathers on your saddle from time to time; the one on the left tends to stretch more, due to the rider mounting on that side. Some stirrup leathers are made with a central synthetic core to prevent stretching.

Choose stirrup leathers of an appropriate type for the rider and the use to which they are put—a knowledgeable saddler will advise you. To avoid stirrup leathers wearing in the same place all the time, every now and then you should shorten them at the buckle end.

Dressage riders often prefer leathers which adjust near the top of the stirrup irons rather than at the stirrup bars, as this minimises bulk under the rider's thigh. These are not recommended for jumping as the adjustment fittings may not be as safe.

Stirrup leathers are traditionally made from three different types of leather:

* *Ordinary leather (stirrup butt leather):* can break under extreme pressure, but top quality leather is the smartest and most comfortable for normal riding.

Bonded stirrup butt leather over a nylon core is very strong.

* *Rawhide:* virtually unbreakable and a traditional favourite for cross-country riding. Some types are rather thick and clumsy. Those made for racing are finer.
* *Buffalo hide:* also virtually unbreakable, but being reddish in colour, the least attractive, especially as it will never tone down to match the saddle. It often stretches more than other types.

ADDITIONAL FITTINGS

Cruppers

A crupper is used to stop a saddle or roller from slipping forward (fig. 144a). It consists of an adjustable leather strap with a loop on one end, which fits under the tail. The other end of the strap passes through a metal D which has been attached to the back of the cantle of the saddle, or to the roller. The tail loop must be made and maintained to avoid rubbing the pony's dock. *(See PUTTING ON A CRUPPER, see page 283.)*

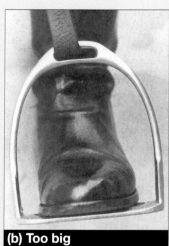

(a) Too small **(b) Too big** **(c) Correct for size of boot**

145 Stirrup sizes.

Numnahs and Saddlecloths

A numnah is a pad cut in the shape of a saddle; a saddlecloth is square-shaped. Worn under the saddle, they have the following purposes:

- To protect a sensitive back.
- When fitted with removable pads, they can be used by a saddler or by a rider who understands saddle fitting to help adjust the balance of saddle. Although it is recommended that every horse has its own saddle, balance pads may mean that a saddle can be used on more than one horse as long as the profile and width is correct for both.
- Cushioning between rider and horse can be advantageous as long as the saddle is wide enough to accommodate it.
- Many numnahs and saddlecloths absorb sweat. This, of course, means that they must be kept clean.

Materials And Design

Numnahs are usually made from:

- *Cotton:* inexpensive, warmer to a horse's back than leather, and helps to keep the saddle clean.
- *Sheepskin (sometimes sheared):* Being a natural fibre it absorbs sweat.
- *Synthetic sheepskin:* varies in price and quality. The type that absorbs sweat is satisfactory.
- *Cotton-covered foam:* semi-absorbent.
- *Other synthetic materials:* a wide variety is available. Some are non- or semi-absorbent and can cause skin problems by 'drawing' a horse's back or by generating friction. Others, made of top-quality materials, are expensive but are absorbent, easy to wash, and minimise pressure and concussion for the horse. Before buying numnahs made from synthetic materials, seek expert advice.

Numnahs and saddlecloths should be designed to fit into the saddle gullet, not slip down and cause pressure on the withers or back. Check that straps which attach to the girth straps, or through which the girth passes, are correctly placed.

Fitting a Numnah or Saddlecloth

A numnah should be slightly larger than the saddle, so that when in place it is visible for not more than 7.8cm (3in) all round. The same guidelines apply to a saddlecloth, though its shape obviously makes it more visible. On each side of the numnah there is usually a loop attached to the front, and another sewn across the bottom edge. One of the girth straps is slotted through the front loop. The girth is passed through the bottom loop and then buckled. These hold the numnah in place (fig. 146).

Before saddling the horse, fit the numnah to the saddle. Push it well up into the front arch and along the length of the channel. Check this again when saddling the horse, and see that the numnah is lying flat on both sides. It must not lie wrinkled or folded up under the saddle.

146 The numnah correctly attached to the saddle.

43. The Bridle, Bitting and Additional Saddlery

THE BRIDLE

Snaffle bridle is the name given to a bridle which takes one bit, although that bit does not have to be a snaffle bit but can be from one of the other families of bits.

A *double bridle* is one which can, with an additional headpiece, called a sliphead, hold two bits, the bradoon and curb.

THE PARTS OF THE SNAFFLE BRIDLE

Headpiece

The headpiece, in conjunction with the cheekpieces, supports the bit in the horse's mouth and is made from the same piece of leather as the throatlatch.

Throatlatch

The throatlatch *(pronounced throatlash)* is designed to help keep the bridle in place, but when it is correctly fitted (not too tightly) it will not prevent the bridle from being pushed forward over the horse's ears (particularly if the rider falls off over the horse's head). It is made from the same piece of leather as the headpiece.

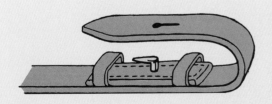

147 A hooked billet with a sturdy leather platform.

Browband

The browband stops the headpiece from slipping backwards.

Cheekpieces

The cheekpieces are attached at one end to the bit and at the other end, to the headpiece.

Bit

Various bits may be used with the snaffle bridle: the most commonly used are snaffles and pelhams *(see BITS AND BITTING, page 263)*.

The cheekpieces and the reins are attached to the bit by one of the following methods:
- *Stitching* is safest but often impractical, as the bit cannot be removed.
- *Hooked billets (fig. 147)* are practical because the reins and cheekpieces can be easily detached for cleaning. They are also convenient as they enable you to use different bits on the same bridle.
- *Buckles* are also serviceable (but look rather clumsy). However, buckled reins are safer than billeted ones.

NOTE: Hooked billets must be held firmly in place by leather platforms as thick and of the same quality as the leather on which they are mounted; otherwise, with wear, they will become loose and therefore dangerous.

Reins

Reins should have a centre buckle. They are made in varying widths and should suit the size of the rider's hand: too wide and they will be uncomfortable to hold, but too narrow and they will slip through the fingers too easily. Bright colours should be avoided except in endurance riding or when using a high-vis bridle on the roads; black or brown are the most commonly used.

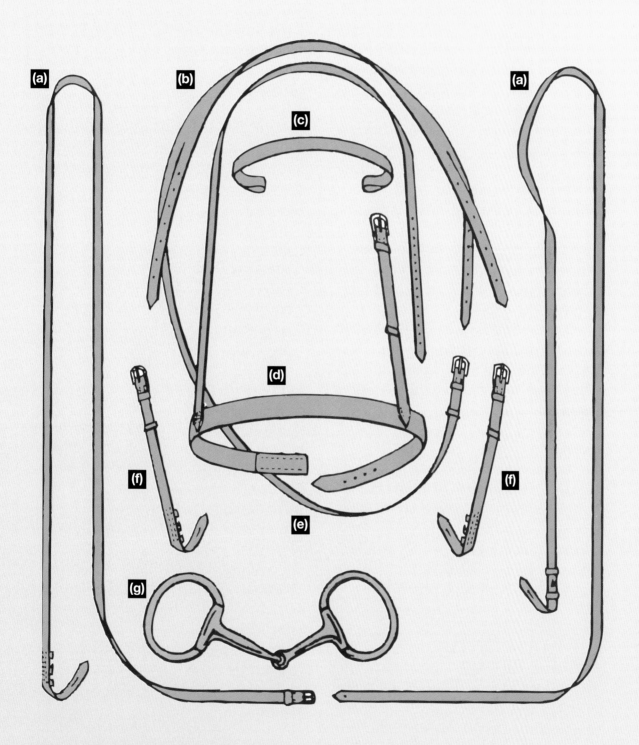

148 The parts of the snaffle bridle:
(a) Reins; **(b)** Headpiece; **(c)** Browband;
(d) Cavesson noseband; **(e)** Throatlatch;
(f) Cheekpieces; **(g)** Snaffle bit.

Reins are made of the following materials:
- *Plain leather* gives a good feel: but they can become slippery in the rain or on a sweaty horse. Wearing suitable gloves can overcome this problem.
- *Laced or plaited leather.* Less slippery, but more difficult to clean. They are often used on the bradoon of a double bridle or as the top rein of a pelham when two reins are used.
- *Rubber grip over leather* gives the best grip in rain or on a pulling or sweaty horse. Strong but soft rubber grip reins, sometimes nicknamed 'jelly rubber' reins, are less bulky and more comfortable to hold.
- *Web, with leather bars.* ('Continental' reins). Give a good grip and the bars prevent the reins from slipping through the fingers; but this can result in a rather fixed length of rein.

Noseband

The cavesson is the standard, simple noseband. It fits around the nose above the bit. Apart from the cavesson portion of the Flash noseband, it is the only one to which a standing martingale can be attached. Other types of noseband, used for specific purposes, are described on page 278.

THE PARTS OF THE DOUBLE BRIDLE

The headpiece and throatlatch, the browband and the cheekpieces are the same as those for the snaffle bridle, but the cheekpieces hold the curb bit. The bradoon (snaffle) is secured by a separate sliphead which is buckled on the right (off) side.

Bits

These are shown in fig. 149. (*See also* THE DOUBLE BRIDLE, *page 274.*)

Lip Strap

A lip strap has two parts: a short buckled end attached to the D on the left lower cheek of the curb bit; and a strap end threaded through the D on the right lower cheek. Its job is to:
- Hold the curb chain if it becomes unhooked.
- Prevent a horse catching hold of the cheeks of the bit.
- Prevent the cheeks of a Banbury-action bit (which—as they are not fixed—can revolve around the mouthpiece) from revolving forward and up.

Curb Chain

This is attached to the hooks on the rings of the upper cheeks of the bit. It has a special fly link in the middle through which the lip strap is threaded. For very sensitive horses curb chains made from special strong elastic may be fitted, or you can use a rubber or leather cover.

Cavesson Noseband

This is the only noseband which should be used with a double bridle. Some riders use a doubleback noseband which has a cinch action, but this is designed to be fastened very tightly and is not recommended.

Reins

These are attached to the rings of the bradoon and to the rings at the bottom of the lower cheeks of the curb bit. The bradoon rein is slightly wider, and may be longer, than the curb (bit) rein.

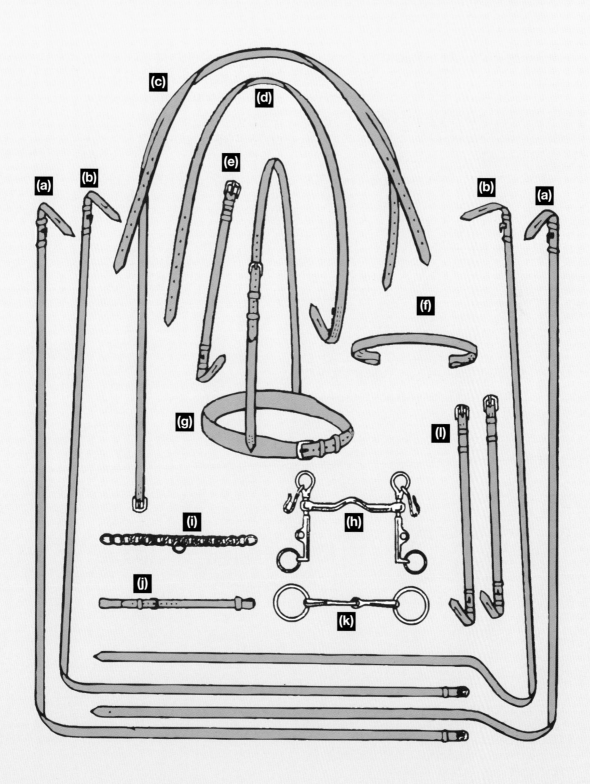

149 The parts of the double bridle:
(a) Bradoon rein; **(b)** Curb / Bit rein; **(c)** Headpiece; **(d)** Headpiece for bradoon (sliphead);
(e) Cheekpiece for bradoon; **(f)** Browband; **(g)** Cavesson noseband; **(h)** Bit; **(i)** Curb chain;
(j) Lip strap; **(k)** Bradoon; **(l)** Cheekpieces.

Assembling a Snaffle Bridle

See fig. 150.

Assembling a Double Bridle

Follow the instructions for a snaffle bridle but with the curb bit on the main cheekpieces. Thread the bradoon headpiece (sliphead) between the headpiece and the noseband's headpiece to buckle up on the right-hand (off) side. This will avoid having three buckles on the left-hand (near) side. The bradoon should lie above the curb bit.

Attach the curb chain and the long part of the lip strap on the right-hand (off) side of the curb bit. The buckled end of the lip strap is attached to the left-hand (near) side. Put up the double bridle as shown in *fig. 151.*

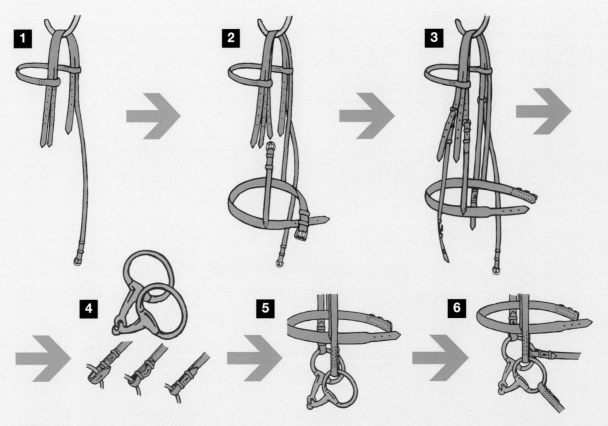

150 Assembling a snaffle bridle.

STEP 1: Thread the headpiece up through the right-hand side of the browband and down through the left hand side. Hang it on the hook with the throatlatch to the right.

STEP 2: Thread the headpiece of the noseband through the browband as in (a), so that it lies under the main headpiece, and buckle it up.

STEP 3: Buckle on both cheekpieces.

STEP 4: The bit is shaped to fit over the horse's tongue. Be sure that it is the right way round. To fasten it (with the hook stud billets) first pass the leather end through both keepers, press the centre down over the billet, and slide it back to lock it in place.

STEP 5: Fasten the other cheekpiece to the bit-ring.

STEP 6: Attach the reins to the bit-rings in the same way. Put up the snaffle bridle. *(See fig 151.)*

BITS AND BITTING

What is Lorinery?

We all use the term *saddlery* but *lorinery* is less well known. It refers to all the metal used upon the horse, including bits, stirrups, spurs, saddle-trees, horse brasses, and all saddlery furniture (such as buckles and clips). A loriner makes and sells these items. The word *lorinery* is derived from the Latin *lorum*, which translated means a thong or rein used as the earliest form of horse control/bridle.

Why Do We Bit Horses?

Horses are bitted to help control their speed and direction and to aid performance.

The Rider's Goal When Bitting

To bit the horse for maximum comfort and performance free from the pain or fear of the bit, working in union with the rider. Bits and bridles are communication tools. As with all good communication success will rely upon the rider listening as well as asking.

Keeping Bitting Simple

Bitting is a huge subject with a diverse range of opinions and techniques, so it is usually best to first learn the basics, and to build on that knowledge later. This makes the process of choosing the appropriate bit for each individual horse much less confusing.

Riders must understand not only the *individual action* of a bit upon the horse but also the horse's *consequent reaction* to it. Thus, bits can be selected logically. It is also important to take the conformation (shape) of the horse's mouth into consideration, because the more comfortably a horse is

bitted the more likely he is to accept the bit and work happily in it.

Above all, riders have to remember that regardless of the bit's design, any bit will only be as mild or strong, successful or ineffective, as the rider using the reins. Their balance, skill and understanding as riders, not simply the selected tack and bit, will create the desired results. Correct bitting, training and riding is demonstrated by the horse's acceptance of the bit *(see* THE CONTACT, *page 182)*. The rider should try and think of the bit as being placed in their hands rather than the mouth of the pony.

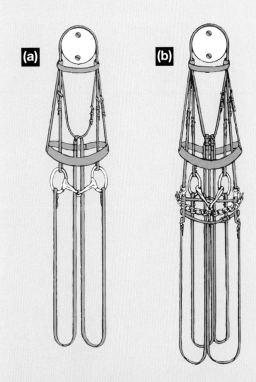

151 How to put up bridles. Hang the snaffle bridle **(a)** or double bridle **(b)** on a suitable bracket, to keep the headpiece in its correct shape. Thread the throatlatch through the reins and buckle it up. Put the noseband around the cheekpieces, with the end pushed through the keepers only. For (b) hook up the curb chain as shown.

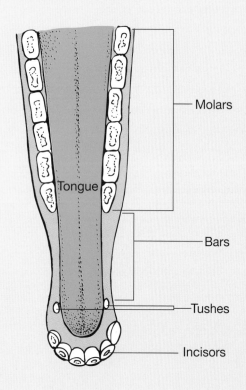

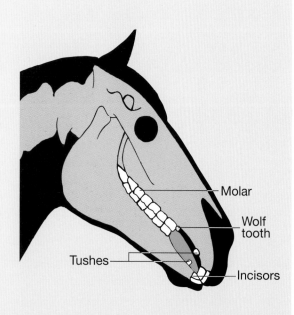

152 The shape of the jaw and mouth.

PRE-BITTING CONSIDERATIONS

The Equine Dental Arcade *(Fig 152)*

It is important to know what a horse's mouth looks like if you wish to understand both how a bit fits and how it works.

The Horse's Mouth Conformation

Spend time studying an individual horse's conformation. Observe (with adult supervision if necessary) the details of the horse's head and mouth as well as his overall conformation. Knowing how the horse is put together will help you to understand the influence that this will have on the successful selection of his bit.

It will also help you fit a bit correctly. For instance, if he has very fleshy lips, they will wrinkle at the corners when the bit is in place but if he has fine lips, a correctly adjusted bit will fit snugly into the corners without obvious wrinkles.

* Does he have a long fine mouth and jaw or a short 'full' mouth with thick lips and a full (big) tongue? Will he be happier in a thick (fat) or fine (thin) bit?
* Where is his chin groove in relation to the corner of his lips? Will a curb chain fit on him so that it acts in the correct position?
* Is the roof of his mouth high or low? Select a bit that will best suit this.
* Does he have tushes, the canine teeth found behind the incisors (front teeth), normally absent in mares? Make sure that the bit will not interfere with these.
* Does he have wolf teeth? Also known as *Premolar 1*, these are small under-developed teeth just in front of the upper molars. Seek professional advice. Look at as many horses as you can to

compare the different mouth conformation. This will help your knowledge to grow.

Care of the Horse's Mouth

Regular professional examinations of the horse's mouth and teeth (at least every twelve months), will help to avoid problems and stop any that do exist from developing into bigger ones. No horse will be happily bitted if he has discomfort in his mouth. (To understand how to recognise the signs of a horse that is in discomfort, *see* Resistance to The Bit *page 274.*)

Stable Management and Contributing Factors

When selecting a bit, first ask yourself the following questions and consider how they may influence the correct selection of the bit and bridle:

- What work has the horse been doing in the past and how does that compare to what is he doing now?
- What level of schooling has he achieved? Are you asking too much of him too soon?
- What are the abilities of the rider?
- What is his day-to-day stable routine (e.g. amount of field turnout, diet and fitness etc.)? This can affect the horse's behaviour.

If a horse is being difficult, ask yourself why this is. Try to find the reason *before* deciding to use additional tack or a stronger bit.

Materials Used for Making Bits

Bits are made from a choice of several different metals, alloys and synthetic materials, and all of them have advantages and disadvantages. When selecting the bit's material it is important is to understand what is being used and why.

- *Stainless steel* is strong, bright, rustless and easy to clean. (Good quality '18/8' stainless steel is best.)
- *High copper-content* bits encourage salivation and help the horse to have a moist mouth, which in turn helps him to accept the bit. Many high copper-content bits are now nickel-free, which is thought to be preferable for sensitive horses that may be allergic to nickel. Never use an old bit made solely from nickel, as it is too soft and will bend easily or break.
- *Copper and stainless steel:* some bits have alternate sections of both these metals, giving a combination which creates a reaction that also encourages the horse to have a wet mouth. Copper, when used alone and not as part of an alloy, is soft and wears faster than stainless steel. Check these bits regularly—even better, replace them with bits made from alternative materials.
- *Sweet iron* or *pig iron* oxidises (rusts) to form a sweet taste that some horses prefer, and this also helps them accept the bit.
- *Synthetic mouthpieces* are softer than metal ones. The main materials are special plastic, hardened rubber and nylon. All should have a solid or wire centre for additional strength and cannot be expected to withstand wear in the same way as metal bits.

FITTING THE BIT

All horses' mouths and their tongues vary in size and shape. The bit must be the correct size and type for the horse. Before fitting the bit you will need to put on the bridle *(see* Putting On a Bridle, *page 284),* but leave the noseband unfastened.

A bit which is too narrow for the horse will pinch the corners of his mouth, while one which protrudes too much can move excessively from side to side and cause soreness. In the case of a jointed snaffle a mouthpiece which is too wide will lie with the joint too low in the mouth, which often encourages the horse to put his tongue over the bit. This leads to discomfort and problems, as the cushioning effect of the tongue is lost.

A traditional single-jointed snaffle has a stronger squeezing action than one with a central lozenge or a correctly shaped French link and a single joint applies concentrated pressure to the centre of the tongue. Some designs minimise this via curved arms and specially designed joints which may or may not be covered with a sleeve or barrel.

- It is easier for the horse to accept the bit when there is not too much pressure on his tongue. A bit should be chosen which allows the tongue to lie comfortably below the mouthpiece.
- The mouthpiece should be the correct thickness for the size of the mouth. If it is too thin, it may be too severe, as all the pressure will be exerted on only a small area of the bars of the mouth. A thick mouthpiece, has a greater bearing surface, but if it is too thick, the horse will have difficulty accommodating it in his mouth.

Fitting the Jointed Snaffle

Measure the width by holding the bit with a hand on either side so that the joint is straight in the horse's mouth. The width is correct when the mouthpiece protrudes about 5mm (¼in) on each side (or sometimes a little more, if the bit has cheekpieces).

To check the height of the bit in the mouth, put a finger lightly on each side and press down gently to check that the horse is not holding the bit in place himself. Then, if necessary, adjust the bridle cheekpieces so that the bit is at the correct height. Look in the horse's mouth to check that it lies on the bars of the mouth without touching the teeth, dragging the corners of the mouth too high or dropping down too low on the tongue. When the rider is mounted and has taken

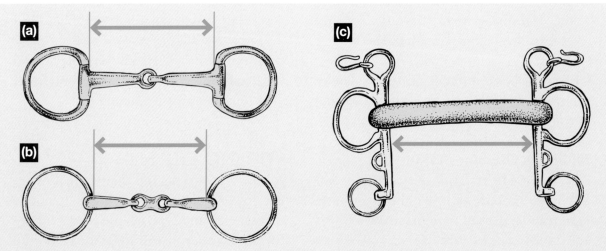

153 Measuring bits: **(a)** Eggbutt jointed snaffle; **(b)** Loose ring double-jointed snaffle; **(c)** Pelham. All measurements must be made with the bit laid flat.

a contact with the reins, the cheekpieces should not sag outwards but should lie against the horse's face.

Fitting the Mullen Mouth, Straight-Bar Snaffle and Pelham

The principles are the same as for the jointed snaffle. The mouthpiece should protrude about 0.5cm (¼in) on each side, and the height is correct when the mouthpiece lies against the corners of the mouth without causing wrinkles.

No matter how well the bit fits, the horse will not be comfortable if there is any soreness in his mouth. *(See Bit and Mouth Injuries, page 158, and Teeth, page 121).* If in doubt, seek expert advice.

MEASURING

There is no advantage in having the correct type of bit if it is the wrong size or wrongly fitted. Get experienced help if you are unsure about the fitting of a bit.

Bit Length

A bit that it too narrow for your pony will pinch at the corners of the mouth, whereas one too wide can move from side to side in the pony's mouth and cause soreness.

If the bit is jointed, and too wide, the joint will be too low in the pony's mouth. He may get his tongue over the bit, or it might hit the roof of his mouth.

Mouthpiece Fitting

The mouthpiece needs to be the correct thickness for your pony's mouth. A thin bit can be really severe, as all the pressure will be in a smaller area. However, it may work well for a pony with a 'full' mouth. A thicker mouthpiece has a greater bearing surface but if it is too thick it will not fit comfortably in your pony's mouth.

The Role of the Rider

A rider's position and aids are the most important ways they can control their horse effectively. An out-of-balance rider, half-way up their horse's neck and shouting 'Whoa!' at him yet inadvertently giving a clear driving aid will confuse the horse and cause problems.

NOTE: It is important to remember that harsh, unyielding hands and poor riding will cause damage to a horse's mouth and make him frightened and/or resistant.

BITTING BASICS

It is now accepted that there are six bitting pressure points. It was once considered acceptable to put pressure on the roof of the mouth, but modern riders and trainers agree this is not the case. Three points are inside the horse's mouth, and act through direct but gentle pressure caused by the bit on the lips, tongue and bars. The other three are situated on the horse's head and act through indirect pressure from the bit through the straps of the bridle or curb chain on the poll, the nose, and the chin groove.

Reaction to the Six Bitting Pressure Points *(Fig. 154)*

Not all bits use all six pressure points. The mechanics of each bit will define which of the seven 'bitting families' a bit belongs to. A rider who understands this will be clear about the bit's action upon the horse when combined with other appropriate aids and consequently the horse's likely reaction. This is therefore a factor in the logical selection of bits.

• Pressure on the poll encourages a horse to lower his head.

• Pressure on the nose encourages the head down and inwards.

• Pressure on the chin groove acts to bring the head down and inwards (also known as 'flexion of the head and neck') as the upper section of the curb bit tilts forward with rein contact on its shanks (using the bit's mouthpiece as a fulcrum). Pressure is thus applied to the chin groove through the curb chain.

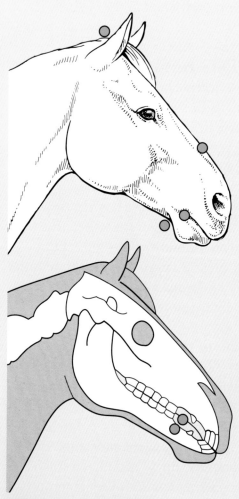

154 Bitting pressure points.

• The roof of the mouth is not used in English-style riding today. A curb bit with a high port (central arch) places additional pressure on the roof of the mouth as the bit tilts forward with rein contact on its shanks (using the bit's mouthpiece as a fulcrum). Some bits have a very shallow port to allow more room for the horse's tongue: this is more comfortable. Study each bit to see how high or low the port is and how it will fit and act in the horse's mouth.

Every kind of bit places pressure on the lips, tongue and bars, but the degree varies according to the bit's design.

FAMILIES OF BITTING

• **Snaffles** have no curb chain and do not apply any leverage.

• **Pelhams** are fitted with a curb chain and attachments for two pairs of reins/a pair of roundings.

• **Curbs** include the double bridle. A true curb should not be used in English-style riding unless as part of a double bridle.

• On **gags**, the bridle's cheekpieces run through the bit's rings.

• **Bitless bridles** obviously do not have a bit in the horse's mouth.

• The leverage action of **lever snaffles** applies pressure on the poll, but lever snaffles do not have a curb chain. Examples include two- and three-ring snaffles (also known as Dutch or Belgian snaffles) and those with long shanks but no curb chain. The rein is attached below the direct line of rein action to the bit, and consequently the leverage action places downwards pressure on the horse's poll and mouth. It is often possible to use two pairs of reins with these bits. Wilkie, bevel and similar designs of snaffles are not lever snaffles, as their designs limit their action. Hanging cheek snaffles apply poll pressure but again, are not lever snaffles.

- Combination bits have built-in nosebands and act on the nose as well as the mouth.

THE SNAFFLE *(Fig. 155)*

A Selection of Snaffles

Jointed Loose-Ring Snaffle
Made of metal, rubber or synthetic material, with a single joint in the middle, its action is principally on the lips and corners of the mouth, the bars of the mouth and the tongue.

Eggbutt Snaffle
This has the same action as the ring snaffle, but the smooth side joints prevent possible pinching. Eggbutt (side rings) may also be used with most of the other varieties of snaffle described below.

Snaffle with Cheeks
This can help to gently reinforce steering. It will not pull through from one side to the other or pinch the horse's mouth. When keepers are used to attach the cheeks of the bit to the cheekpieces of the bridle, there is minimal movement of the bit in the mouth.

Double-Jointed Snaffle
There are four different types, available with a variety of rings or cheekpieces:
- The first type has a central lozenge, so the bit follows the internal contours of the horse's mouth and does not have a concentrated pressure point on the centre of the tongue. It avoids the nutcracker action of the traditional single-jointed snaffle.
- The second type is the *French link*. The central plate is rounded and lies flat across the tongue. The action of the bit is on the lips and corners of the mouth, the bars of the mouth and the tongue; again, the nutcracker action of the single-jointed snaffle is avoided. This sometimes makes it a satisfactory bit on a horse with a large tongue or a narrow lower jaw.
- The third design has a single ring in the centre and is known as the *Dick Christian snaffle* after its inventor. It is now rarely seen.
- The fourth type is called the *Dr. Bristol*. Its central plate is rectangular, with squared sides, and is set at an angle, so that it presses onto the tongue. The action on the tongue and corners of the mouth can be quite severe. It is important to fit it angled upwards towards the back of the tongue, otherwise it is much too severe as it would press into the tongue.

These four types must not be confused, as the Dr. Bristol is not permitted in dressage competitions. Always check your rule book, as there is a wide range of permitted snaffles and many which are prohibited.

Mullen Mouth (Half-Moon) and Straight-Bar Snaffle
The action of these bits, made of metal, vulcanite, synthetic material or rubber, is primarily on the lips and corners of the mouth and the tongue. A mullen mouthpiece has a slight arch to allow room for the tongue, so is more comfortable for the horse. Straight

bar bits are used mainly when leading, such as when showing in-hand, or when driving—though straight bar bits made from flexible materials act more like a mullen mouth design. Some horses go well in unjointed mouthpieces, but others learn to hold the mouthpiece away from the bars by pushing up with the tongue. This can also indicate a sore mouth or that the horse is or has been ridden by an insensitive rider.

Hanging Cheek Snaffle

Suspended, rather than resting, in the mouth, this snaffle is suitable for a horse who dislikes too much weight on his tongue. The action is on the lips and bars of the mouth, and to a lesser degree on the tongue.

Twisted Snaffle

This is severe and is not recommended.

Gag Snaffle

The action is on the lips and corners of the mouth, the tongue and the poll. It can be very severe. It may be used with one or two pairs of reins. For maximum effectiveness it should be used with two pairs of reins, one direct to the snafle ring and the other attached to the cheekpiece which runs through the bit rings, to offer the choice of an ordinary or gag snaffle action. Some riders and trainers prefer to use a single gag rein when jumping, especially cross-country.

Other Types

There are many other bits on the market, but some are very severe. Before making any changes, discuss with your instructor whether it is advisable and if so, which type to use.

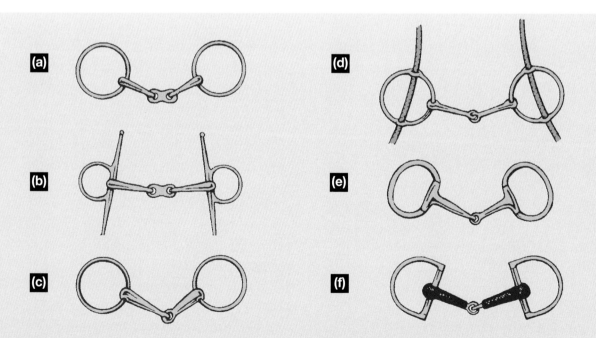

155 Snaffles. **(a)** French link snaffle; **(b)** Full cheek French link; **(c)** Fulmer loose ring single-jointed.; **(d)** Gag; **(e)** Eggbutt; **(f)** D Ring; **(g)** Straight bar; **(h)** Dr. Bristol; **(i)** Single-jointed with cheeks; **(j)** Hanging-cheek. The inset (right) shows a hanging snaffle and Flash noseband.

THE DOUBLE BRIDLE *(Fig. 156)*

A double bridle has two bits: a bradoon and a curb. Together, they may be referred to as a Weymouth set.

Bradoon

This is a form of snaffle (usually loose-ring or eggbutt) and acts in the same way, but has a thinner mouthpiece. It usually has small rings, but some riders prefer to use bradoons with larger rings because they feel these give more direction.

Curb Bit

This is used with a curb chain and lip strap. It acts on the bars of the mouth, the tongue, the poll, and—via the curb chain—on the curb groove. The cheeks of the bit act as a lever to increase the action. The curb chain is the fulcrum. The longer the upper and lower cheeks (the lever arms), the more potentially severe is the bit. A curb is sometimes referred to as a Weymouth bit, but strictly speaking, this is a particular design, not a general term.

Cheeks

They may be fixed or of the type which allows the mouthpiece to slide slightly up and down. The fixed type gives a more precise action. It is suitable for a horse who needs to be encouraged to hold the bit quietly in his mouth. The action of the sliding-cheek type is fractionally delayed, and therefore less precise. The slight movement of the mouthpiece encourages a horse to mouth the bit and may help encourage him to relax his jaw.

Mouthpiece

This generally has a tongue groove or a port, which can be of variable height. A tongue groove is a small hollow in the centre of

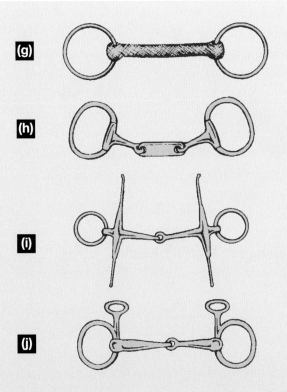

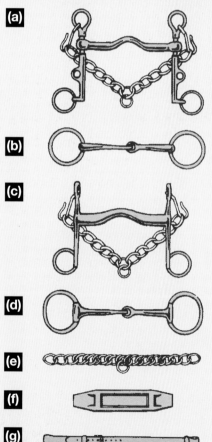

156 Bits used with the double bridle. **(a)** Curb bit with sliding mouthpiece; **(b)** Loose-ring bradoon; **(c)** Curb bit with fixed mouthpiece; **(d)** Eggbutt bradoon; **(e)** Curb chain; **(f)** Rubber cover; **(g)** Lip strap. The inset shows a fixed-cheek Weymouth with loose-ring bradoon.

the mouthpiece and a port is a raised arch of varying height, again in the centre of the mouthpiece. It is more common to find a port, but both are designed to allow a degree of room for the tongue. Both the curb bits in *fig. 156* have small ports. The length and angle of a port also affects its action. For instance, horses with thick tongues and low palates may be comfortable when the port is angled forward.

Fitting a Double Bridle
Pages 284 to 287 contain instructions for putting on a bridle and the curb chain. The inset photograph *(fig. 156)* shows a fixed-cheek Weymouth with loose-ring bradoon.

The bits are the correct size for the horse when the mouth pieces protrude about 5mm (½in) on each side. *(See Fitting the Bit, page 265.)* The bradoon should be fitted above and not in front of the curb bit, which should lie immediately below it. The curb chain should lie snugly and flat in the chin groove and be adjusted to come into play when the cheekpieces of the bit are drawn back to an angle of 45° with the horse's mouth. If the curb chain is too loose, it is inclined to ride up above the chin groove when the curb rein is used, thereby losing the correct effect and possibly creating soreness. If it is too tight, the action will be too severe and might damage, or even deaden, the bars of the mouth.

Using the Double Bridle
A double bridle should only be used when the horse has been trained in a snaffle bridle to accept the bit cnfidently and happily.

While the bradoon acts in the same way as a jointed snaffle, the curb acts to give a more refined aid that helps to maintain a supple poll and a relaxed jaw.

The curb (or bit) rein should be applied only when required and should not be used continuously. Use it tactfully and *never ride in a curb without a bradoon*, as its continuous action would deaden a horse's mouth.

THE PELHAM *(Fig. 157)*

This bit is a combination of the curb and bradoon on one mouthpiece. The bradoon and curb reins are attached to separate rings, thus attempting to make the one bit perform the duties of two. In principle, this is not a sound policy, but experience has shown that some horses will go better in a pelham than they will in anything else. The top (bradoon) rein causes the bit to act on the corners of the mouth (the lips), and on the tongue. The lower (curb) rein causes the bit to act on the bars, the chin groove and the poll.

The pelham can have a variety of mouthpieces, but the most commonly used and usually the most effective is the mullen mouthpiece. The mouthpiece can be made from various materials.

(For putting on the bridle and hooking up the curb chain, *see pages 284 to 287.*)

Sometimes a single rein is used with a pelham, attached to leather roundings which are themselves attached to the bradoon and curb rings on the cheeks of the bit *(fig. 161a)*. This is not recommended for use by those who wish to take advantage of the correct action of either part, but it can prove advantageous in some cases.

Ideally, a cavesson noseband should be used with a pelham to ensure that the action of the curb chain is not compromised

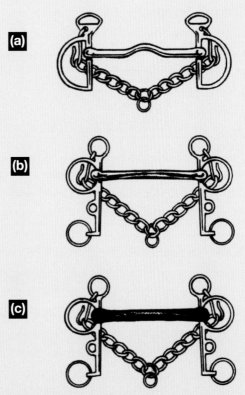

157 Pelhams. **(a)** Kimblewick; **(b)** Half-Moon pelham; **(c)** Vulcanite pelham. The inset shows a vulcanite pelham correctly-fitted.

by a strap fastening below the bit. However, some riders use a Flash or Grakle because they feel this gives extra control when jumping. Get expert advice if you feel this is necessary.

The Kimblewick

This looks like and acts in a simlar way to the top part of a pelham. Like the pelham, it can have a variety of mouthpieces. Strong ponies sometimes respond well to its fairly mild action. (For putting on the bridle and hooking up the curb chain, *see pages 284 to 287.*)

RESISTANCE TO THE BIT

A horse may resist the bit for any of the following reasons:
  • Lack of balance and training.
  • Condition of the teeth.
  • Pain and fear of the bit.
  • Insensitive (damaged) mouth.
  • Conformation.
  • Poorly-fitting tack (bit, bridle or saddle).

Lack of Balance and Training

Before his muscles are developed and he has accustomed himself to the weight of the rider, a horse will often—through lack of balance and through no fault of his own—experience difficulty in answering the rider's aids. He will respond in a slow, and often clumsy, way. It should be realised that at this stage the horse's mouth is still unmade: so unless the rider uses tact and sympathy, much harm will result. The mouth may seem insensitive because the horse is unable, and in any case has not yet learned, to respond quickly. If the rider uses force, the situation will worsen.

Condition of the Teeth

A sore mouth, although sometimes caused by bad riding, may also be due to the condition of the horse's teeth or through a condition such as an ulcer or injury. *(see* TEETH*, page 121).*

Pain and Fear of the Bit

Any bit which does not lie comfortably in the horse's mouth will cause resistance. *(See* FITTING THE BIT*, page 265.)* A sore mouth or an ill-fitting bit will often cause a horse to pull, in order to escape from the resulting pain. His natural instinct is to flee.

A tongue over the bit, a dry mouth, or an excessively frothy mouth may all be evasions of pain which have been caused by incorrect bitting and/or bad training. The bars of the mouth are easily injured, and the underpart of the tongue may also be damaged if the tongue is over the bit.

Insensitive (Damaged) Mouth

The bit lies across the tongue and on the bars of the mouth, which are extremely sensitive, as they are thinly covered with skin containing a mass of nerves. These nerves easily become numbed; then the feeling in the mouth is lost. Finally, the bars may develop splint-like bony lumps. When this happens, the horse may resist permanently. He may be referred to as hard-mouthed and veterinary advice, together with a careful choice of bit or the use of a bitless bridle, is needed .

It is a mistake to put a more severe bit on a pulling horse. The secret of a good mouth lies in the training or retraining of the horse in a suitable bit, and in the horse's increased attentiveness and obedience to the rider.

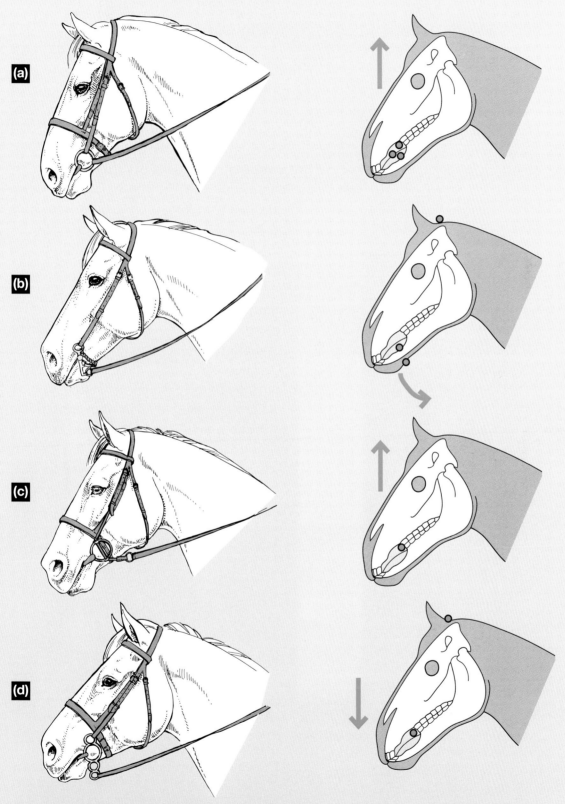

158 The effects of **(a)** Snaffle; **(b)** Curb*; **(c)** Gag; **(d)** Leverage bits on the head of the horse, also showing areas affected. *The curb must never be used on its own.

1	Memorise the seven families of bits, their action on the horse and the horse's probable reaction to them.
2	The bit you choose must be the correct size and fitted correctly.
3	Be aware of the effect of additional tack upon the bit. Do not over-tighten nosebands or martingales.
4	Know the different materials used in bit manufacture and understand their effects on the horse.
5	Consider the individual shape of the horse's mouth when selecting his bit.
6	Choose the bit according to the horse's age and level of schooling and also the rider's ability.
7	Adopt a correct position in the saddle with a seat independent of the reins.
8	Develop a seat independent of the reins and use the reins sympathetically.
9	Remember that the bit is only as severe as the rider holding the reins.
10	Never be rough. Always have giving, rewarding hands.
11	Wash the bit after every ride (to avoid soreness and infection.)
12	Have your horse's mouth and teeth routinely maintained by a vet or equine dental technician at least once a year. Check the horse's mouth regularly for bruising.

159 The twelve rules of good bitting.

Conformation

The conformation of a horse's head, neck and jaw is important in bitting. If the head and neck are too closely coupled (thick through the jowl) the horse may have difficulty in flexing correctly. If the jaw is too narrow or the tongue too thick there will be less room for the bit to lie comfortably in the mouth. If you think that these faults are the reason why your horse is resisting, seek the assistance of an expert to help you to choose and to fit a suitable bit.

Temperament

Horses who are calm and cooperative by nature are easier to manage—but, regardless of temperament, some horses (particularly young ones) will often become strong when excited. Ideally they should be ridden in a snaffle and care should be taken not to damage their mouths. If a mouth becomes sore, it must be allowed to heal before the horse is ridden again. A spoiled horse who is unwilling, resentful or nappy will often display his characteristics by a refusal to accept the bit correctly.

Opposite page:
160 The characteristics, action and probable reaction of the main bitting families.
Whenever a rider picks up a bit, they should ask themselves which of the six bitting pressure points it will act upon, even if they are unaware of the name of the bit. By looking at a bit in this way, it is possible to work out which bitting family it belongs to.

BITTING FAMILY	CHARACTERISTICS	ACTION	REACTION
SNAFFLE	No leverage to its action, no curb chain and no pulley system.	Acts upon the lips, tongue and bars.	The general action is an upwards one.
DOUBLE BRIDLE (CURB)	Two bits on one bridle and two pairs of reins.	Bradoon (snaffle) acts on the above plus the poll and chin groove. Weymouth (curb) gives additional pressure on the mouth, poll and chin groove.	The combination of these two bits gives a higher level of communication if both horse and rider are sufficiently trained to use them. The curb bit encourages the horse to lower and flex whilst the bradoon controls the paces and direction.
PELHAM	Fitted with a curb chain and with attachments for two pairs of reins/contact.	A combination of a curb and snaffle bit on one mouthpiece. The two points of attachment for the reins and two sets of reins are used to allow definition between the action of the upper and lower rein.	Snaffle action on the top rein and a curb action on the bottom rein. If pelham roundings and one rein are fitted to this bit, it is reduced to a combined action of the two. If you are unsure whether a bit is a pelham or a curb (Weymouth), does it have one or two points of attachment for reins each side? If two, then it is a pelham.
GAG *	Looks like a snaffle but with additional holes top and bottom of the bit's rings each side (through which the bridles cheekpieces run).	The bridle's running cheeks through the bit gives a gag a very strong upwards action on the corners of the horse's mouth.	Although some pressure is placed upon the horse's poll, the clear action of a gag is one of lifting the horse's head and neck upwards (due to the strong action on the corners of the mouth).
LEVER BIT **	The rein contact is attached below the direct line of rein action to the bit, and this creates a leverage action putting downwards pressure on the horse's poll and mouth. Many of them look like a pelham but without a curb chain attachment. e.g. multi-ring bits, and all those with long shanks but no curb chain. As with pelhams, it is often possible to use two pairs of reins with lever bits.	Work with a leverage action which places pressure on the poll.	Acts to lower the horse's head.
BITLESS BRIDLES ***	Easy to identify because they have no bit in the horse's mouth.	Act by placing pressure on the face, jaw and poll.	Pressure on nose encourages flexion, bringing the head inwards. Pressure on the poll encourages the head to lower. Some designs cross under the horse's jaw to spread pressure.
COMBINATION BIT	Incorporates a specially designed noseband and usually has a strap which fits round the back of the jaw.	Acts on the nose as well as on the bitting pressure points.	Asks the horse to bring in his nose and respond to the bit.

To be a defined as a gag, a bit must have the bridle's cheekpieces running through the bit's side rings.

**Confusingly these bits are often referred to as 'gags', but they are not and produce the opposite reaction.*

*** Types include those which act on the nose alone, those which cross under the jaw and those which have metal shanks on each side to which the reins attach. Those with short shanks are commonly known as English hackamores and those with long shanks, as German hackamores. Both have straps or covered chains which run across the back of the jaw.*

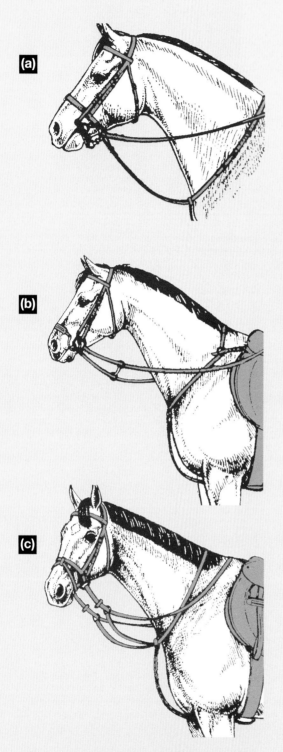

161 Additional saddlery: **(a)** Pelham with roundings, cavesson noseband and standing martingale; **(b)** Kineton noseband, Irish martingale and breastplate; **(c)** Flash noseband and running martingale.

ADDITIONAL SADDLERY

Nosebands

Cavesson Noseband

This is the standard type of noseband. It fits around the nose, above the bit. It is the only noseband which should be used with a double bridle and, ideally, with a pelham. *(To fit, see ONCE THE BRIDLE IS ON, page 285)*

The following types of noseband have been designed to help overcome specific resistances in the horse's mouth. The drop noseband should be used only in conjunction with a snaffle. It is important that the pressure does not come too low down on to the weak part of the nose bone.

Get expert advice before using a particular type of noseband on a horse who habitually puts his tongue over the bit, or lets his tongue hang out of his mouth.

Drop Noseband

This noseband must be very carefully fitted to avoid interfering with the horse's breathing. It is fastened below the bit, which must be some form of snaffle.

The front should be four fingers' width above the nostrils, and the back should rest in the chin groove.

The front must remain high; this is achieved either by the front strap being fitted on to a spike on the ring to which it is sewn, or by a short piece of leather sewn in to join the front strap to the cheekpiece.

The front strap must be short enough to allow the cheekpieces to be well in front of the line of the horse's lips, so that the noseband will not pinch or rub the corners of the mouth.

The noseband should be fitted loosely

enough for the horse to be able to relax his jaw, but snugly enough for him to feel the pressure on his nose when he tries to open his mouth too wide, to cross his jaw, or to draw his tongue back.

Grakle (or Crossed) Noseband

This is used for the same purpose as the drop, but has an additional strap above the bit. It acts over a wider area and is thus more effective in preventing the horse from crossing his jaw. It is made up of two leather straps which cross over on the bridge of the nose with a pad beneath the join. The straps pass around the horse's face and are buckled above and below the bit.

There are two types of Grakle. The high-ring or Mexican Grakle fastens higher on the horse's face than the traditional Grakle and so avoids pressure on the cheek teeth. The Grakle is fitted higher up on the nose than a drop noseband and acts over a wider area, which makes it a useful design for cross-country use. The principle of fitting is the same as that for the drop noseband.

Flash Noseband

This is a cavesson noseband, fitted as such but with an additional lower strap which is attached to the front of the noseband. This strap should pass well above the nostrils at the front of the nose, and should be fastened below the bit like a drop noseband. Ideally, the cavesson should be padded for extra comfort. A standing martingale can be used by attaching it to the back of the cavesson.

Kineton Noseband

Unlike the nosebands described above, this has no back strap to prevent excessive movement of the horse's jaw, but when it is correctly adjusted the effect is that the pressure through the reins, instead of being only on to the bit, is partially or wholly transferred to the front of the nose. Some horses respond well to its action.

The noseband has an adjustable leather front strap fitted to a metal loop on each side. The loops are hooked round the mouthpiece of the bit, between the bit ring and the horse's mouth. The front should be at least four fingers' width above the nostrils. It is designed to be used with a mullen-mouthed bit to avoid pinching of the lips, as can happen when it is used with a jointed bit.

MARTINGALES

Standing Martingale

This is fitted from the girth at one end to a cavesson noseband (or to the cavesson part of a Flash noseband) at the other. It passes between the forelegs and through a loop on the neckstrap which supports it. A thick rubber ring holds the two together.

Its purpose is to prevent the horse raising his head beyond the angle of control. It also helps to prevent the horse hitting you in the face with his head. It should not be fitted any tighter than is necessary and should not be used to hold the horse's head down.

Fitting a Standing Martingale

Check the correct length after the martingale has been attached to the girth and noseband. When the horse is standing with his head in the correct position, put your hand under the martingale and lift it up. As a rough guide it should just reach as far as the throat.

The buckle of the neck strap should be on the left side of the horse's neck. It should fit so that it will admit the width of a hand at the withers.

To keep the girth loop neat and safe, one runner should be positioned immediately behind the buckle and the other next to the girth.

Running Martingale

This is attached to the girth, and passes between the forelegs. It then divides into two, each of the two ends being fitted with a ring through which the reins are passed. Like the standing martingale, it is supported by a neck strap.

A running martingale provides a regulating influence on a horse which carries its head too high. It must be correctly fitted, so that it only takes effect when the horse raises his head beyond the angle of control. If it is fitted too short, its effect is to bring constant pressure on the bars of the mouth, which can only result in their becoming bruised or dead.

Fitting a Running Martingale

As a rough guide, when the martingale is attached to the girth and both rings are taken to one side, the martingale should be long enough to reach to the horse's withers.

If used with a double bridle, the rings should be on the curb (bit) rein.

The reins should be threaded through the rings, so that the rings can run freely up and down the reins, as shown in *fig. 161c.* The reins should be fitted with stops between the rings and the bit, to prevent the rings getting caught over the hook billets of the rein, or any part of the bit.

The neck strap should be fitted as for the standing martingale.

Irish Martingale

This consists of two rings connected by a strap approximately 10cm (4in) long and the purpose is to keep the reins in place and prevent them from going over the horse's head.

Fitting an Irish Martingale

The snaffle reins should be passed through the rings underneath the horse's neck.

Bib Martingale

This is a combination of running and Irish martingales. A triangular leather bib fills the space where the running martingale becomes divided into two straps. Its fitting is the same as for the running martingale, and the action is the same except that the rings hold the reins slightly closer together. It is safer to use than a running martingale on a horse who grabs hold of the rings.

Breastplate and Breast Girth

A *breastplate* is a leather neck strap attached to the Ds at the front of the saddle by a strap at each side of the horse's neck and to the girth by a broader strap passing between the forelegs. Its purpose is to prevent the saddle from slipping back, but it cannot turn a poorly fitting saddle into one which fits correctly. This happens more often if the horse is fit and not carrying any excess weight, or if he is naturally herring-gutted; but a breastplate is a sensible addition to your security during cross-country work, or when riding in hilly country. Specially-made standing, running or bib martingale attachments may be fitted to the breastplate if required.

Fit the breastplate so that there is room to slide the width of your hand under the neck strap. The straps to the D-rings should lie flat and quite loose when the horse is standing normally. Remember that his shoulders and neck will need freedom to extend when he is galloping.

A **breast girth** is a strap of web or elastic fitted across the horse's breast and attached to the girth straps on both sides. A leather strap attached to it passes over the neck in front of the withers to hold it in position. Its purpose is the same as that of the breastplate, but as it is light and easily fitted it is especially useful on a young horse, who may buck and move his saddle out of position. The breast girth should be fitted loose enough to allow the full width of your hand between it and the horse's breast. It must not lie so high that it restricts the movement of the neck or the functioning of the windpipe.

It is important to note that neither a breastplate nor a breast girth can turn a poorly fitting saddle into one which fits correctly.

Neck Strap

This is a simple leather strap that passes around the horse's neck. The neck strap of a martingale or breastplate is the neatest, but a stirrup leather will do equally well.

Its object is, in an emergency, to provide the rider with something to hang on to other than the reins and thus to lessen the risk of his pulling on the horse's mouth. It is a great help, especially to young riders in rough, hilly country, and particularly when riding a horse with a hogged mane.

It is essential when riding a young horse or teaching a rider or horse to jump.

To prevent it from slipping forward when the horse lowers his head, it can be attached by straps to the front Ds of the saddle.

For jumping it should be fitted one third of the way up the horse's neck.

Lungeing Cavesson and Lungeing Rein

The lungeing cavesson is fully described in The Pony Club publication *Breeding, Backing and Bringing On Young Horses and Ponies*. It is designed to be used with a lungeing rein for lungeing, and as a training aid to control young or exuberant horses without risking damage to their mouths by leading them from a bridle. The horse in *fig. 76* on page 141 is being led by means of a cavesson and lungeing rein.

The noseband should be well-padded and fitted snugly. The jowl strap must be buckled firmly around the cheekbones, so that the cheekpieces cannot pull forward and touch an eye. For normal exercise on the lunge, and for leading, the lungeing rein should be attached to the centre ring of the cavesson.

The lungeing rein should be at least 7m (23ft) long and is usually made of cotton webbing or lampwick. Those made of nylon can cause friction burns and should not be used.

A lungeing rein is used as described above. It is also useful as a means of persuading a reluctant horse to load into a horse box or trailer *(see* HORSES RELUCTANT TO BE LOADED, *page 138)*.

A horse who is being led on the road should wear a bridle and bit.

Hackamore

The hackamore is a bitless bridle. It has no mouthpiece but acts by leverage on the nose, poll and chin groove. Although the mouth area is not affected by the hackamore, it should be realised that the nose, poll and chin groove are all delicate, highly sensitive areas, and are just as easily damaged. Severe injuries on these areas, which are sometimes permanent, can frequently be observed after the prolonged use of this bridle. In the hands of an expert it is sometimes effective on a horse with a spoiled, damaged or otherwise difficult mouth. If you think you need to use a hackamore, or any type of bitless or combination bridle, get expert advice on its use and fitting.

44. Saddling-Up and Unsaddling

PREPARING TO SADDLE UP

First, tie up the horse—whether in or out of the stable—and keep him tied up, until you are ready to mount. This will help to keep him under control. It will prevent him from damaging his saddlery by rolling or treading on the reins.

Groom him as necessary. Be sure to remove any dry mud or old sweat, particularly where the saddle or girth will lie.

If he is rugged, unfasten the crossed surcingles, undo them and knot them up so that they cannot swing against the horse's legs. Then quarter the horse as described on page 99, and leave him with his rug on, but unfastened at the chest. This way, if the rug slips it will fall clear instead of being hung up around the horse's neck, which could frighten him and damage the rug.

Collecting Your Saddlery

Collect together the tack you are going to use, with your whip, hat, gloves, etc.

The Saddle

* Check that the stirrup irons and leathers are on the saddle and neatly run up.
* Check that the buckle guards are on.
* Attach the girth on the right side, leaving at least four holes above the buckles.
* Fold the girth back over the seat of the saddle.
* If you are using a numnah, place it on the saddle horse and put the saddle on top, pulling the numnah well up into the front arch *(see page 257)*.

The Bridle

Checks and adjustments are best carried out away from the horse, preferably in the tack room.

* Unfasten the throatlatch and the noseband. If a double bridle or pelham is being used, unfasten the curb chain and lip strap from the left side.
* If a martingale is used, release the reins from the rings and place the centre rein buckle on top of the headpiece.
* If it is not the horse's usual bridle, leave the cheekpieces buckled, but not in their keepers or runners. (You will need to measure the bridle against the horse's head, and adjust it so that it will be a generous size for him when you put it on. You can then readjust it to fit correctly.)

Additional Saddlery

If you use them, collect the breastplate or martingale, and also any leg coverings, such as brushing boots.

Carry your saddle and bridle as described on page 291. When you get to the horse, hang up the bridle nearby. Put the saddle over a fence or door, or on the ground, also described on page 291. Do not leave it where the horse can reach it with his feet or teeth.

If the horse usually wears brushing boots or other protective leg coverings for the type of work that you will be doing, put them on following the instructions given on page 96.

SADDLING-UP

Putting On the Saddle

Talk to the horse as you approach. If he is strange to you, saddle up from the left side; otherwise, make a habit of saddling up from either side. Proceed as follows:

- If you use a neck strap, breastplate or martingale, untie the horse and put it on. (The buckle of the neck strap should be on the left side.) Tie him up again.
- If the horse is rugged, fold the rug back behind where the saddle will lie.
- Smooth down the hair with your hands where the saddle and girth will lie, making sure that there is no mud or old sweat to cause a sore or gall.
- Pick up the saddle with the front arch in your left hand and with the cantle in your right.
- Place it lightly, but firmly, well forward on the withers.
- Slide it back into position, checking that you will not be sitting too far forward or too far back—either on the horse's shoulder or on his loins.
- Never slide the saddle forward against the lay of the coat.
- See that the sweat flap and buckle guards are lying flat and that all is smooth under the saddle flap.
- If you are using a numnah, see that it is lying flat and is pulled well up into the front arch and gullet of the saddle.
- Go quickly but quietly under the horse's neck to the right side, lift the girth and bring it down gently. See that all is smooth and flat under the saddle and the flap. (Go round the horse to do this, as you cannot check properly by leaning over the saddle.)
- Return to the left side—keeping your shoulder close to the horse's shoulder— bend down and take hold of the girth. Put it through the loop of the martingale or breastplate (if used) and buckle it up just tightly enough to keep the saddle from slipping. (You should then attach the straps of the breastplate.)

The girth buckles should be on approximately the same height of holes on both sides of the saddle. From time to time, tighten the girth on alternate sides. You should always have a few holes to spare. Run your fingers down between the girth (where it meets the panel of the saddle) and the horse's skin, to make sure that the skin is lying smoothly.

If the horse is rugged, leave the rug on over the saddle with the front buckle undone.

Before you mount, make sure that your girth is tight enough; then check it periodically while you are riding— especially if your horse is inclined to deliberately blow himself out.

Putting On a Crupper

The crupper is described on page 256. If used, it should be put on after the saddle is girthed up. Again, a crupper should not be used to try and compensate for a badly fitting saddle.

- Standing close to the left hind leg, gather up the tail in the right hand and pass it through the crupper.

- Take care that the crupper lies well to the top of the dock and that all the tail hairs are through it, and lying flat.
- Pass the strap through the D on the back of the saddle and adjust the length so that it steadies the saddle, but is not so short that it pulls up the tail.

Fitting an Exercise Rug Under the Saddle

Traditionally, an exercise rug is useful for exercising clipped horses in bad weather. A lightweight, waterproof design which will not cause over-heating can be used when you need to keep a horse dry, perhaps because you are rugging and turning him out immediately afterwards. Some riders like to use a high-vis exercise rug as part of their visibility equipment when riding on the road.

Specially designed exercise sheets which fit round rather than under the saddle are the most popular, but you can also use one with a square front (a quarter sheet) or even an ordinary day rug made from lightweight wool mix, fleece or thermal fabric fitted under the saddle. Any rug must be securely fitted to prevent it from slipping back while the horse is being ridden *(see* page 89 *and* fig. 49*)*. The rug should have a fillet string to prevent it from flapping up. With a rug which fits under the saddle:

- Place the rug on the horse, and then put on the saddle.
- Push the rug well up into the gullet of the saddle so that there can be no pressure on the withers and backbone.
- Secure the rug either by running the girth through the loop fittings on each side, or by folding the front corners back between the saddle panel and the girth straps before fastening the girth.

If a day rug is used, make sure that the chest buckle and strap are not beneath the saddle flap or the rider's legs.

Putting On a Bridle

Two different methods of putting on a bridle are shown in fig. 162. The first steps are the same for both method, but the second method gives you more control, as you are closer to the horse and have your right hand to steady his head and stop him moving about. It is also safer when introducing the bridle to young horses.

First Steps for Both Methods

- Take the bridle and hang it over your left arm with the browband nearest to your elbow and the buckles of the rein over the headpiece. This will leave both your hands free.
- Untie the horse's lead rope.
- Place the reins over the horse's head and neck. If necessary, you can hold him with the reins around his neck when you remove the headcollar.
- Remove the headcollar and hang it up. Do not just drop it where you and the horse can tread on it.
- If the horse is in a box or stable, turn him to face the light, and proceed in one of the two methods described below.

Method 1 (Fig. 162a)

- Standing close to the horse's shoulder on his left side, take hold of the headpiece of the bridle with your right hand.
- With your left hand under the horse's muzzle, allow the mouthpiece of the bit to rest on your first finger and thumb.
- If the horse doesn't open his mouth to take the bit, press your thumb gently between

the horse's lips on the left side where there is a gap between the teeth. This will encourage him to open his mouth

• Keeping your right hand close to his forehead, draw up the bridle, using your left hand to guide the bit gently into the horse's mouth.

• Your left hand can now help the right hand to pass the headpiece over each ear in turn.

Method 2 (Fig. 162b)

• Put your right hand under the horse's jaw and up round the other side to the centre of his face, just above the nostrils.

• Take both cheekpieces in this hand, keeping it close to the horse's face.

• With your left thumb, open his mouth and guide the bit in as in *Method 1*, while your right hand eases the bridle up.

• Using both hands, place the headpiece over the horse's ears.

Once the Bridle is On

• Arrange the mane and forelock so that they are not caught up under the leather.

• Check that the bit is level and that the browband and noseband are straight.

• Fasten the various buckles. Be sure to put the end of each strap neatly through its keeper and runner. The bridle should fit as described below.

Throatlatch

This should be fastened first. It must never be fastened so tightly as to interfere with the horse's breathing or flexing. Allow the full width of your hand between it and the side of the jawbone.

Browband

The browband should not be so long as to sag in the centre of the forehead, but long enough not to interfere with the hang of the bridle or to rub the horse's ears. It should lie just below, but not touching, the ears.

Noseband

This should be adjusted to allow two fingers' width between it and the front of the horse's face, thus allowing the horse to open his mouth slightly and relax his jaw. Adjust the height of the noseband so that

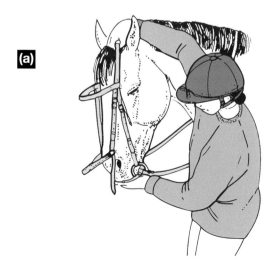

162 Putting on a bridle: **(a)** Method 1; **(b)** Method 2

it lies at the correct height for its design, without rubbing on the facial bones. If necessary, straighten it by easing up its headpiece just below the browband on one side and manoeuvring it down on the other. Do not try to pull it through both loops of the browband at the same time, as this will almost certainly pull the whole bridle crooked. Check that it is fitted so that its side-pieces will not touch the horse's eyes.

A martingale or breastplate should be fitted as described on page 280.

Bit

The level of the bit should, if necessary, be adjusted through the buckles of the cheekpieces. Adjust the bit as explained earlier. Count the holes on each side of the headpiece to make sure that they are as level as possible. Fine tune the adjustment, if necessary, by adjusting the bridle a hole higher on one side than on the other

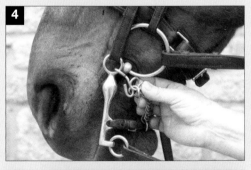

163 Fastening a curb-chain.

STEP 1: Hook one of the end links of the chain to the right-hand hook. This first link should be hooked so that, when twisted flat in a clockwise direction, the fly link (the loose link in the middle of the chain) falls from the lower edge of the chain.

STEP 2: From the left side, twist the curb chain in a clockwise direction until the links are lying flat.

STEP 3: Giving it an extra half twist, hook the end link on to the left-hand hook.

STEPS 4 and 5: If necessary, shorten the curb chain evenly on both sides by selecting a shorter link and hooking it over the end link so that the spare links lie flat. If you use a pelham, fit the curb chain from hook to hook, either directly or via the bradoon rings. For a double bridle, fit the curb chain under the bradoon..

then gently adjust the bit so it is level in the mouth. (For further information, *see* FITTING THE BIT, *page 265.*)

Bradoon

The bradoon of a double bridle should be adjusted using the sliphead buckle on the right side. Ease it up or down as necessary in the same way as described for the noseband. (For fitting the bits of the double bridle, *see* FITTING A DOUBLE BRIDLE, *page 274.*)

Fitting the Curb Chain and Lip Strap

If a double bridle, pelham or kimblewick is used, fit the curb chain as shown in fig. 163. The curb chain should come into action when the cheeks of the bit are drawn back to an angle of approximately 45° to the line of the mouth. Fit the spare end of the lip strap through the fly link and buckle up on the left side.

If You Leave the Horse Saddled and Bridled in the Stable

Make sure that the headcollar is on over the bridle and that the horse is properly tied up. Otherwise he may roll and damage the saddle, or shake the reins over his head, tread on them and break them. If the reins are very long, loop them under the stirrups, or, as an added precaution, twist the reins round each other under the throat and pass the throatlatch through one of them. This is a good way to foil a horse who habitually chews the reins. It should be done before putting on the headcollar. If the horse is rugged, fasten the front buckle, lengthen the surcingles and fasten it over the saddle and the rug.

If the horse is to be left where there are two stout pillars or posts—for example in the passageway of indoor stables—he may be cross-tied (*see page 48*).

When you are ready to leave the stable, pick out the horse's feet into a skip. Complete your own preparations—hat, stick, gloves, etc.—and finally, untie the horse and remove the headcollar.

Take the reins over the horse's head and make sure that the stirrup irons are run up to avoid them getting caught on any projections, particularly in the doorway. Hang the headcollar on a hook or on the latch of the door, so that it is handy when you return.

Before mounting, look around once more to be sure that your saddlery is correctly fitted. Tighten your girth and adjust the buckle guards. It is a sensible precaution, but not essential, to lift each foreleg in turn and pull it forward, thus smoothing out any wrinkles that there may be in the skin under the girth. Pull both stirrup irons down. You are then ready to mount and move off (*fig. 164*).

164 Ready to go.

UNSADDLING

It is usual to unsaddle from the near side in this order: (1) saddle; (2) bridle; (3) martingale. The method varies, so the following is a guide:

To Take Off a Saddle

- When you dismount, run up your irons. Take the reins over the horse's head and loop them over the arm nearest to the horse's head.
- Raise the saddle flap and unfasten the girth.
- If a martingale is worn, slip its loop off the girth.
- Release the girth carefully so that it does not swing down and hit the horse on his legs.
- With one hand under the front arch and the other holding the cantle, slide the saddle off towards you and on to your forearm, with the front arch in the crook of your elbow.
- Take hold of the girth with the other hand as it comes over the back, placing its underside on the seat of the saddle. (Grease washes off, but mud scratches.)
- Put the saddle on the stable door or on a fence, or lay it carefully on the ground— not too close to the horse's feet.

NOTE: If there is a crupper, it must be taken off first. Tie the horse up, using a headcollar, or ask a helper to hold him while you unfasten the crupper, and slide it off down the tail.

To Take Off a Bridle

- Take the headcollar over your arm or shoulder.
- Put the reins over the horse's neck.
- If you are using a curb bit, unhook the curb chain on the left side, leaving the lip strap fastened.
- Unfasten the noseband and slip off the loop of the standing martingale (if used). If a running martingale is used, unbuckle the reins, remove the martingale rings and re-buckle the reins.
- Unfasten the throatlatch.
- You are now ready to remove the bridle.
- Put your left hand on the horse's face, well above his nostrils.
- With your right hand, slip the headpiece over the ears and lower it slowly, allowing the horse to ease the bit out of his mouth. If it is dropped out quickly, he may throw up his head and frighten himself by catching it on his teeth. For this reason, never remove a bridle with the curb chain or noseband fastened.
- Slip off the martingale neck strap and place it, together with the headpiece, on your left shoulder, leaving the reins around the horse's neck to give you some control over him while you put on the headcollar.
- Take the reins over the horse's head on to your left shoulder and tie him up. Keeping the bridle and martingale over your left shoulder, pick up the saddle, girth and whip, and carry them correctly *(see next page)* to a safe place. In this way you will leave nothing behind and will avoid trailing the girth or reins on the ground.
- Put the saddle on a peg or saddle horse, and the bridle (and martingale) on the cleaning bracket or other hook. It is a good idea to wash the bit with a sponge and water soon after removing it, and before any dirt on it hardens.
- Return to your horse and run your hands over his back and girth groove, to

feel for lumps or soreness. Pat the back briskly, but not heavily, to restore the circulation and help it to dry. Remember to deal with both sides.

* Groom as necessary *(see Grooming, page 97).*
* Rug up if appropriate *(see Putting on a Rug, page 90).*
* Check the corners and bars of the mouth and the chin groove for any signs of rubbing. Any sore places should be treated with petroleum jelly, and whatever has caused the rubbing should be avoided in the future.
* Check that nothing is lying about in the stable that might get lost or damaged.

45. Cleaning and Care of Saddlery

Saddlery is an expensive investment which if properly cared for will last a lifetime. If it is left lying around, it can easily be damaged. Unless it is cleaned and maintained correctly it will not last very long. The message is clear: *take care of your saddlery.*

PROTECTING SADDLERY

Saddlery should be kept in a place set aside for it which must be secure, clean, dry, and free from vermin. *(See also The Saddle Room, page 51.)*

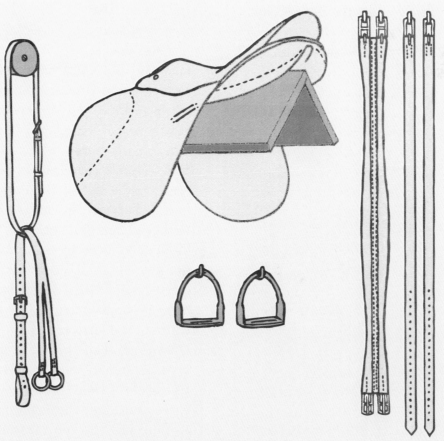

165 Saddlery put up.

Putting Up a Saddle

A saddle may be kept on a peg or bracket made for the purpose, about 46cm (18in) long, attached to the wall of the saddle room at a convenient height, or on a purpose-built stand called a saddle horse. Put the saddle on the peg with the front arch to the wall. It is better for the girth and stirrup leathers to be put up hanging straight, so fix two hooks under the peg from which to hang the stirrup irons and four more on the wall beside the saddle, for the girth, stirrup leathers and martingale. Alternatively, put up the saddle, with its fittings, on the saddle horse *(figs. 165 and 168)*.

Carrying Your Saddle and Bridle

To prevent the cantle being scraped and knocked against walls and doorways, and to leave one hand free for opening doors, gates, etc., use one of the methods shown in *fig. 167*.

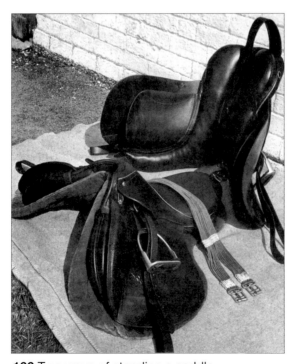

166 Two ways of standing a saddle.

Standing a Saddle

A saddle can easily be damaged between taking it from the saddle room and placing it on the horse's back. Allowing it to fall to the ground can scratch the leather, or even break the tree. Always place it where it cannot fall or be scratched or trampled on. A saddle left on the ground is always at risk, but if there is no alternative, put it on a rug or a clean, soft surface, either: pommel down and cantle against a wall or fence, with the girth folded under the front arch and up over the cantle to protect it; or: flat upon the ground as if it were on the horse's back *(fig. 166)*.

INSPECTION, PRESERVATION AND REPAIR

Saddlery should be inspected frequently, and minor defects attended to immediately. Remember that your safety depends upon it—a broken rein, girth or stirrup leather could result in a bad fall. All safety checks apply to synthetic tack as well as to leather saddlery.

- *Check stitching,* which deteriorates more quickly than leather, especially on reins, girths and stirrup leathers. At the first sign of wear, or if in doubt, take these to the saddler for restitching. Tug hard at vulnerable areas to check stitching; do not rely on visual inspection.
- Check any areas where metal rests on leather: in particular, reins, stirrup leathers and girth straps.
- *Check bits.* Look for signs of roughness or wear, and replace if necessary.
- *Check the saddle.* Look for wear on the girth straps and check the panel. If the stuffing has become uneven, lumpy or flattened with wear, ask your saddler

to check it and if necessary, make adjustments before it is used again. Also, the horse might gain or lose weight. This means that his shape will change and the saddle may no longer fit him correctly. Always make sure that a saddle is adjusted when necessary *(fig. 141)*.

- *Examine the tree* after a fall or if you have reason to suspect that it might be broken. (To test the tree, *see page 252*.) If there is any doubt about its condition, ask your saddler—sometimes, it is necessary to strip down a saddle so that the tree itself can be inspected for damage.

- *Check the leather*, because it becomes dry; unless it is kept pliable with suitable cleaning and leather food preparations, it cracks. Ask your saddler's advice about suitable products and do not over-use them, particularly those which are oil-based. Over-oiling causes the fibres in leather to stretch and lose strength. Mineral oils, such as those used for cars and bicycles, and linseed oil, should not be used on saddlery.

When in regular use, saddlery should need only saddle soap and the occasional application of leather food to keep it soft and pliable.

When stored for any length of time, it should be kept in a suitable environment and farther protected against damp or dryness with the use of a suitable product to preserve suppleness and minimise the risk of mould.

Daily Care
Clean and saddle soap all saddlery after use.

Weekly Care
Completely dismantle it. Clean and saddle soap it thoroughly, particularly where metal rests on leather. Check stitching, fastenings, stirrup leathers, etc. When necessary, apply leather food, though you should not need to do this every week.

Yearly Care
At least once a year the saddler should check your saddle and attend to the tree, the stuffing and the stitching, where applicable.

167 Two ways to carry a saddle and bridle, with one hand free for opening doors, etc:

(a) Carry the saddle with the front arch in the crook of your elbow. This allows the bridle to be carried on the same shoulder. Alternatively, carry the bridle in your hand, holding it around the cheekpieces to prevent it from dragging on the ground.

(b) Carry the saddle against your side, with the hand in the front arch.

If at any time you find or suspect a problem, or your horse changes shape, ask your saddler to check your saddle—do not wait until the time for a routine check comes round.

Storing

Completely dismantle the saddlery, dress it with a suitable leather food, and wrap it in newspaper or breathable fabric—which, unlike plastic, allows the necessary circulation of air. The leather food may need to be renewed periodically, especially if the atmosphere is dry.

CLEANING SADDLERY

Equipment Needed
- An apron or overall to protect your clothes.
- A piece of rough cloth (towelling) or a sponge for washing.
- A chamois leather or a dry cloth for drying.
- A small sponge or piece of foam rubber for applying saddle soap.
- Saddle soap.
- Leather food if needed.
- Appropriate metal polish if needed.
- A lint-free cloth such as a stable rubber for polishing metalwork if necessary.
- A sharpened matchstick or its equivalent to clean out any remains of saddle soap from buckle holes in the leatherwork.
- A rubber or plastic bucket filled with cold or lukewarm water.
- A saddle horse, and hooks and brackets on which to hang bridle, girth, leather etc. *(fig. 168)*.

Cleaning A Leather Saddle

Place the saddle on the saddle horse. Do not try to clean or store a saddle on the back of a chair or any angular object which allows it to rock or to rest on the gullet.

Strip the saddle. Remove the girth and

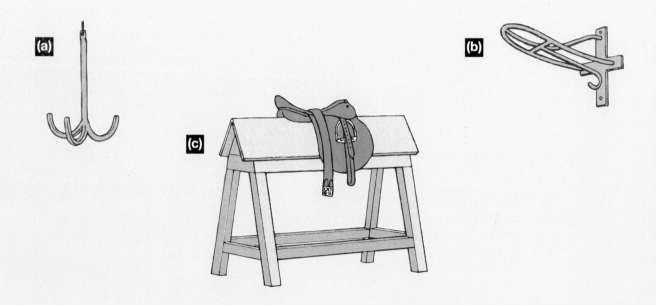

168 (a) Cleaning hooks; **(b)** Saddle bracket; **(c)** Saddle-horse with saddle cleaned and ready for use.

buckle guards (if detachable), stirrup leathers and irons. Certain parts of modern saddles should not be soaped; your saddler will advise you. If you buy a new saddle, always ask the saddler's advice before cleaning it in case there are any special recommendations.*(fig. 168).*

If leather tack becomes very wet in use, blot dry and leave it dry at room temperature, away from a source of direct heat, before cleaning and apply leather food if necessary. If it is muddy, clean off the mud with a wet sponge, blot dry and then clean and apply any leather food needed as above.

Take the saddle and hold it, pommel down. Clean the leather of the panel and the underside of the saddle as follows:

- Use a towelling cloth dampened with lukewarm water to remove all the dirt and grease. Wring out the cloth firmly, as the stuffing will suffer if you allow water to get into the panel.
- From time to time rinse the cloth in the bucket and wring it out firmly.
- If the accumulations of black grease and dirt (known as jockeys) are difficult to remove, carefully use your fingernail or try the traditional method of using a bundle of hairs previously pulled from your horse's mane or tail. Never use a sharp instrument.
- Dry the panel with a chamois leather or with a cloth.
- Clean the upper side of the saddle in the same way, again being careful not to wet the leather too much.
- Apply saddle soap to the rough (flesh) side of the leather, using a sponge kept for the purpose and used as dry as possible. Apply a minimal amount

to the smooth (grain) side only when necessary and if the saddler or manufacturer recommends it, then polish with a clean cloth when dry. Do not use anything that will make the seat or flaps slippery.

- If using bar-type soap, dip the end of the bar into the water and rub it on to the sponge—or, if you are using a tin of soap, put the damp (almost dry) sponge into the tin. If using saddle soap in its own dispenser, follow the instructions for use.
- Work using a circular movement. If the soap lathers, the sponge is too wet and the leather will dry hard and dull.
- Leather must never be washed with household soap, detergent or very hot water. Neither should it be placed near a fire or hot radiator, or in a warm airing cupboard, as it will dry it out too quickly and lose suppleness.
- *Never use soap on top of dirt.*

Synthetic Saddlery

The materials used in synthetic saddles should never be oiled or soaped. Instead, sponge the saddle clean with water, or use a shampoo recommended by the manufacturer. Always follow the manufacturer's recommendations.

Using Leather Food

Care for new leather saddlery as your saddler or the manufacturer recommends. With most saddlery, you need to apply suitable leather food from time to time. Apply leather food to the (rough) underside of the leather, which is more absorbent.

Leather food should not be applied too liberally or too often because the leather will become saturated and will weaken.

Cleaning Metalwork

All metalwork—bits, stirrup irons, buckles, rings, etc.—should be cleaned regularly with water. (The mouthpiece of the bit should be washed immediately after use). Metalwork may occasionally be cleaned with an appropriate product and polished with a duster. Do not put metal polish on the mouthpiece of the bit and be careful not to leave traces of it on the leather.

Stirrup irons should be removed from the leathers. Wash and dry them, removing and washing the treads separately if necessary. Occasionally polish the irons as described above.

Cleaning Stirrup Leathers and Leather Girths

Detailed advice on the cleaning of leather is given on page 292. To clean stirrup leathers and leather girths, hang each one on a cleaning hook and hold it near the bottom. Then wrap your cloth or sponge around it and rub firmly up and down, first to remove the dirt and later, when dry, to apply the soap.

Cleaning Tubular Synthetic Fibre and Nylon String Girths

These can be washed in an ordinary domestic washing machine. They must be put into a firmly tied linen bag or pillow case to prevent the buckles from damaging the machine.

NOTE: When the girth is dry, check that it is still sound and safe to use, as it may deteriorate after frequent washing over several years. Feel the internal strip of tubular synthetic fibre girths (which you will not be able to see) to check that it

feels strong and safe to use.

Finally, put up the saddle as described on page 290 and shown in figs. 165 and 168.

Anti-chafe Synthetic Girths

These should be cleaned according to the manufacturer's instructions. They can often be wiped over and scrubbed when necessary.

Cleaning Numnahs, Wither Pads and Protective Sleeves

There are many different types *(see page 257)*. They should all be kept clean, supple and well aired. Wash, brush, or follow the maker's instructions.

- *Sheepskin* is sometimes used for numnahs or protective sleeves for girths, breast girths, etc. It should be brushed as clean as possible with a dandy brush, to remove loose hairs and any caked sweat. Follow the manufacturer's instructions on washing.
- *Synthetic fur*, used instead of sheepskin for the above purposes, should be similarly brushed as clean as possible and then washed as the manufacturer directs. *Take care that the sheepskin or synthetic fur fabrics do not form hard knots or lumps which will cause pressure points.*

Cleaning a Pad (Felt) Saddle

- Brush to remove dirt and if necessary, wash by hand with pure soap in cool water. Dry thoroughly before use.
- Keep free of hard knots of felt.
- Protect from moth damage.
- Check for worn stitching, and repair as necessary.
- Clean the metal and leatherwork as for other items of saddlery.

Cleaning the Bridle

(1) Without Taking the Bridle to Pieces

- Hang the bridle up on a cleaning bracket or hook.
- See that both the throatlatch and noseband are unbuckled.
- Let out the cheekpieces to the lowest hole on each side, noting the holes that you have been using
- Take the bridle off the hook.
- Wash the bit with a sponge or piece of towelling in a bucket of water, taking care not to get the leather parts wet.
- Remove dirt from the headpiece and the noseband's headpiece by folding a damp sponge or towelling cloth around each in turn, and wiping thoroughly. Replace the bridle on the bracket or hook.
- Clean the rest of the bridle in the same way, keeping it taut with one hand and rubbing it up and down with the other.
- When dealing with the reins, step backwards and away from the hook and wipe down towards the buckle. Then hang them over another hook to keep them from trailing on the floor.
- Wipe the noseband clean.
- Dry off the surplus moisture with a chamois leather or a dry cloth, or allow the leatherwork to dry naturally.
- Dry the bit and check it for roughness.
- Soap all the leatherwork thoroughly by wrapping the sponge around each strap and rubbing it up and down. Put as much soap on the underside as on the top.

(2) When Completely Dismantled

This should be done at least once a week.

- Unfasten all buckles and mounts.
- If the mounts are hooked billets, unfasten them by pushing with the pad at the base of your thumb. Once off the billet, the strap is easily pulled out of the keepers. Always push any difficult buckle-fastening back through the buckle from above. It is easier to do this than to pull the end.
- Hang up the various parts.
- Clean and soap each part separately, taking special care to soap thoroughly the insides of the bends and folds.
- When soaping, you may prefer to lay each part on a flat surface and rub the soap in on one side at a time.
- Use leather food when needed and in the same manner as for saddles.
- Polish the bit and buckles as described for METALWORK on page 294.
- Reassemble the bridle as described on page 262 and put it up as shown in *fig. 151.*

Cleaning Leather Accessories

Martingales, neck straps, breast girths, breastplates, cruppers, etc., should all be cleaned as described for CLEANING STIRRUP LEATHERS AND LEATHER GIRTHS, *page 293.*

The webbing on breast girths should be brushed after use, and occasionally washed with soap and rinsed thoroughly. Take care not to get the leather part too wet. Polish all buckles and rings when necessary as described for METALWORK, page 294.

Remember that well-mainitained tack ensures a lifetime of safe and reliable performance.

Glossary

Above the bit Head position avoiding acceptance of the contact by putting the head forward and upward.

Action The way in which a horse moves.

Activity Energy, vigour and liveliness in the hind legs.

Against the bit Horse pushes mouth against the bit with rigid neck/poll/jaw.

Bail A plank of wood. Swinging bails hung from the wall and ceiling are used in temporary stalls to divide one horse from another.

Banbury action Action of a curb bit in which the cheeks move independently of each other. *See also* WEYMOUTH ACTION.

Basics The correct foundation of progressive training of the horse: all the criteria of the training scale.

Behind the bit/aids/leg An evasion in which the horse retracts from the bit/contact; avoids working forwards from behind into an accepting rein contact; refusing to move willingly forwards from the seat and leg aids.

Behind the vertical The head position in which the nose line comes behind the vertical.

Bone A term used in conformation referring to the circumference of the bone below the knee. If the measurement is generous, the horse is said to have good bone or plenty of bone; if it is not generous, the horse is short of bone.

Bottom Low-growing vegetation.

Bounce When landing over an obstacle the horse immediately jumps the next one without taking a stride.

Breaking out Starting to sweat again after exercise, having previously cooled off.

Bringing up Bringing a horse to live in a stable when he has previously been living in a field.

Broken neckline Excessive longitudinal flexion one third of the way down the neck so the poll is no longer the highest point.

Calkin A raised and squared thickening of the metal of the hind shoe at the outer edge of the heel, which increases grip. A similar effect is produced on the inside heel by thickening the metal into a wedge shape (wedge heel) which is less likely to cause brushing than a calkin.

Cast, to (a shoe) A horse is said to have cast a shoe when the shoe comes off by accident: i.e. is not removed deliberately.

Cast (in box or stable) A horse lying down and unable to get up: usually as a result of rolling over too close to the wall, or getting his feet caught under the manger.

Check, to To steady the horse. Also used in hunting when hounds lose the scent, thus allowing a short respite for the field (mounted followers).

Cheek (on a bit) The straight side-part of some bits.

Chifney A bit used for leading horses who are difficult to control.

Circuit breaker A safety device fitted in a wall socket. When electric clippers, for example, are plugged into it, the power will instantly be cut off if there is a fault in the machine or its cable—thus preventing an electric shock.

Clench The part of the nail which during shoeing is left projecting from the wall of the hoof after the end of the nail has been twisted off. The metal is then bent over and hammered in to secure the shoe to the foot.

Cold hosing The use of a gentle stream of cold water to reduce inflammation.

Concussion The jar caused to the feet and legs of a horse when working on hard ground. Also, a brain injury.

Contact Works from behind through a supple swinging back into a consistent and elastic contact.

Disobedience Wilful determination to avoid doing what is asked.

Double bridle A bridle with two bits and two sets of reins.

Dumped toe This occurs when the wall of the hoof is rasped and rounded at the toe so that it fits the shoe.

Falling in This occurs when, in order to compensate for stiffness or loss of balance, a horse turning on a circle or around a corner moves his shoulder in and comes off the true circle.

Flexion Lateral/Longitudinal flexion at the poll.

Gait/Regularity The sequence of footfalls in a pace.

Gamgee Cotton wool encased in gauze.

Going, the The condition of the ground.

Hacking Exercising (i.e. going for a ride), as opposed to working.

Hacking on Riding to or from a venue without making excessive demands on the horse's energy.

Half-Halt A momentary increase of collection, or an effect of the aids which increases the attention of the horse and improves its balance.

Hollow back Horse comes above the bit dropping the back away from the weight of the rider to give a 'hollow outline'.

Hot up, to A horse who becomes unduly excited, particularly when ridden, is said to hot up.

Impulsion Increased energy from hindquarters. Forward thrust, pushing power. Hind legs swing forward with supple swinging back.

Irregular Unlevel or uneven which may or may not be due to unsoundness (not unsteady tempo).

Keep Meadow forage for grazing.

Keepers Fixed loops which keep the ends of bridle straps, etc., in place. *See also* RUNNERS.

Lateral To the side as in flexion, bend, suppleness or direction of a movement. Incorrect walk sequence.

Leg blade The lower of the two blades on a clipping machine. It is coarser than normal and is sometimes used on the horse's legs, to avoid cutting the hair too close to the skin.

Longitudinal Lengthwise dimension front to back or back to front.

Long and short sides Terms used to differentiate between the sides of a rectangular arena, manège, or school.

Manège An enclosed arena or school, usually rectangular, used for training.

Nappy A nappy horse is one who is stubborn, wilful, obstinate, and unwilling to go in the required direction.

Near and off sides The near is the left side of a horse, the off is the right side.

Off side *See above.*

On the aids Willing, confident and immediate reaction to the rider's aids.

On the bit Supple, quiet acceptance of the contact with lateral and longitudinal flexion.

On the forehand Longitudinally poor balance, too much weight on the forelegs for the task.

Over bent Behind the vertical with too much longitudinal flexion in the poll or upper joints of neck.

Over-face, to To ask a horse to jump an obstacle which is beyond his capability or stage of training.

Over track The hind foot is placed in front of the print of the forefoot.

Pacing A gait where the lateral pairs of legs move at the same time.

Pointing A horse standing with one foreleg stuck out markedly in front of the other. This usually indicates discomfort in a foot. The same action with a hind leg is normal and is referred to as resting a hind.

Puller A horse who pulls on the reins and is difficult to stop.

Pulling (mane or tail) Removing hairs from the underside of the mane and sides of the tail to improve their appearance.

Quartering A quick grooming, to tidy up a horse before exercise.

Resistance Physical opposition by the horse against the rider.

Rhythm The evenness of the footfall and regularity of the beat.

Rocking in canter The neck goes up and down too much due to stiffness in the back and lack of engagement.

Roundness The convexity of the profile of the horse's topline.

Runners Leather loops which slide up and down and are used to keep the straps of a bridle, etc., in place. *See also Keeper.*

Run up a stirrup iron Slide the iron to the top of the leather.

Safed-off shoe A hind shoe on which the outer ground edge is rounded and the shoe then set back under the foot to minimise the risk of damage to a foreleg: i.e. through overreaching.

Scalded back Inflammation, or in severe cases blistering, of the back under the saddle, caused by heat and sweat.

Scope Athletic ability.

Scouring Suffering from diarrhoea.

Self carriage The horse carries itself in a balanced and unconstrained manner without taking support or balancing on the rider's hand.

Set fair, to To give the horse a light brush over, remove droppings, and tidy up bedding.

Short side (of manège) *See Long and Short Sides.*

Skip, *also* **skep** A strong basket used for removing droppings.

Stale, to To urinate.

Staring coat A coat standing up and looking dull instead of lying flat and looking glossy. It is usually a sign that the horse is cold or unwell, or both.

Stiffness Inability to flex the joints or stretch the muscles to the required degree for the task.

Straightness Forehand is in line with hindquarters on curves and straight lines. Horse is able to bend equally on both reins.

Strike-off The first step of the canter.

Suppleness Ability to adjust the carriage (longitudinally) and the position or bend (laterally) without loss of balance and fluency.

Suppleness Relaxed mentally and physically. Horse works over the back and through the neck with elasticity.

Tempo The speed of the rhythm.

Top line The horse's outline from the ears along top of neck and back to its tail.

Tracking up The hind feet step into the tracks of the forefeet.

Trailing In Lateral movements to describe not being parallel or when the hind legs are too far behind the horse.

Turn out, to To put a horse out in a field (out to grass).

Turnout The general appearance of horse and rider—grooming, trimming, saddlery, dress, etc.

Twitch A thick stick with a loop of cord at one end. It should be used only by experts, to restrain an impetuous horse during clipping, etc.

Uneven Unequal in length of steps.

Unlevel Unequal in height of steps or unequal bearing of weight on both sides.

Unmade mouth A mouth that does not respond to the bit aids because of lack of training.

Uphill The horse's longitudinal balance; higher forehand relative to the croup.

Weymouth action Action of a curb bit in which the cheeks move at the same time, whether pressure is exerted on one or both reins. *See also Banbury action.*

Wide behind Hind feet travel further apart than forefeet (an evasion of engagement when lengthening trot or in halt.

Wind A horse's breathing or respiration when working.

Wings Extensions to the sides of a fence which are generally higher than the obstacle itself. They are used to discourage a horse from running out. In showjumping they also provide support for the fence.

Differences in Terminology Between the UK and USA

UK	USA
Brushing	Interfering
Anti-sweat rug	Sweat sheet
Bad doer	Unthrifty horse
Bandage	Leg wrap
Beetroot	Beets
Corn feed	Grain
Cubes	Nuts or pellets
Dishing	Paddling
Equiboot	Easyboot
Fetlock	Ankle or joint
Gamgee	Cotton encased in gauze
Going	Footing
Good doer	Easy keeper
Hogging	Roaching
Horsebox	Van
Lead rope	Lead shank
Numnah	Saddle pad
Overreach boot	Bell boot
Plait	Braid
Rasping	Floating
Roughing off	Letting down
Rug	Blanket
Running up in hand	Jogging up in hand
Shelter shed	Run-in shed
Spanner	Wrench
Stable	Stall
Stables/stable yard	Barn
Surcingle	Over girth
Swede	Rutabaga
Whorl	Cowlicke

List of Illustrations

Picture Credits

ILLUSTRATIONS AND DIAGRAMS

Maggie Raynor Figs. 2, 7, 8, 9, 10, 11, 12, 13, 15, 16, 19, 24, 26, 28, 29, 31, 33, 35, 42, 45, 49, 50, 51, 52, 53, 54, 55, 61, 62, 63, 64, 65, 66 (j–m), 70, 71, 72, 75, 77, 79, 80, 81, 84, 85, 86, 87, 88, 91, 92, 93, 94, 97, 98, 99, 100, 101, 103, 109, 110, 111, 112, 127, 140, 141, 142, 152, 153, 154, 156, 156, 161, 162

Anne Woodrow Figs. 102, 104, 105, 106, 107, 108

Carole Vincer Figs. 14, 17, 18, 21, 22, 23, 25, 27, 32, 34, 37, 39, 40, 41, 43, 46, 56, 60, 66(a–i), 68, 78, 89, 113, 115, 116, 117, 119, 120, 121, 122, 123, 124, 126, 128, 129, 131, 132, 134, 135, 136, 137, 138, 139, 143, 144, 147, 148, 149, 150, 151, 155, 158, 159, 165, 168

PHOTOGRAPHS

Hugh Pinney Figs. 90, 146

Iian Shaw Figs. 30, 48, 73, 74, 76, 118, 167

Jane Berridge Figs. 1, 4, 5, 57, 58, 59, 82, 83, 114, 125, 147, 163, 155 (inset), 158 (inset), 159 (inset)

Martin Deacon Fig. 67

Nikki Herbert Figs. 6, 164

Outhill Photography Fig. 166

Index